accounting

7e

Charles T. Horngren Series in Accounting

Auditing and Assurance Services: An Integrated Approach, 11th ed.
Arens/Elder/Beasley

Governmental and Nonprofit Accounting: Theory and Practice, 8th ed.
Freeman/Shoulders

Financial Accounting, 6th ed.
Harrison/Horngren

Cases in Financial Reporting, 5th ed.
Hirst/McAnally

Cost Accounting: A Managerial Emphasis, 12th ed.
Horngren/Datar/Foster

Accounting, 7th ed.
Horngren/Harrison

Introduction to Financial Accounting, 9th ed.
Horngren/Sundem/Elliott

Introduction to Management Accounting, 13th ed.
Horngren/Sundem/Stratton

study guide for accounting

7e

Helen Brubeck
San Jose State University

Florence McGovern
Bergen Community College

PEARSON

Prentice
Hall

Upper Saddle River, New Jersey 07458

Library of Congress Cataloging-in-Publication Data
Horngren, Charles T.
     Accounting / Charles T. Horngren, Walter T. Harrison, Jr. — 7th ed.
       p. cm.
     Includes bibliographical references and index.
     ISBN 0-13-243960-3 (hardback : alk. paper)
     1. Accounting.   I. Harrison, Walter T.   II. Title
HF5635.H8   2007
657—dc22   2006029536

Executive Editor: Jodi McPherson
VP/Editorial Director: Jeff Shelstad
Developmental Editors: Claire Hunter, Ralph Moore
Executive Marketing Manager: Sharon Koch
Marketing Assistant: Patrick Barbera
Associate Director, Production Editorial: Judy Leale
Production Editor: Michael Reynolds
Permissions Supervisor: Charles Morris
Manufacturing Manager: Arnold Vila
Creative Director: Maria Lange
Cover Design: Solid State Graphics
Director, Image Resource Center: Melinda Patelli
Manager, Rights and Permissions: Zina Arabia
Manager, Visual Research: Beth Brenzel
Manager, Cover Visual Research & Permissions: Karen Sanatar
Image Permission Coordinator: Nancy Seise
Photo Researcher: Diane Austin
Manager, Print Production: Christy Mahon
Composition/Full-Service Project Management: BookMasters, Inc.
Printer/Binder: RR Donnelley–Willard
Typeface: 10/12 Sabon

Credits and acknowledgments borrowed from other sources and reproduced, with permission, in this textbook appear on the appropriate page within text.

Pearson Education LTD.
Pearson·Education Singapore, Pte. Ltd
Pearson Education, Canada, Ltd
Pearson Education–Japan

Pearson Education Australia PTY, Limited
Pearson Education North Asia Ltd
Pearson Educación de Mexico, S.A. de C.V.
Pearson Education Malaysia, Pte. Ltd

10 9 8 7 6 5 4 3 2
ISBN 0-13-223461-0

Brief Contents

Contents

3 The Adjusting Process   124

To Billie Harrison, who taught me excellence

The *Accounting, 7e,* Demo Doc System: For professors whose greatest joy is hearing students say "I get it!"

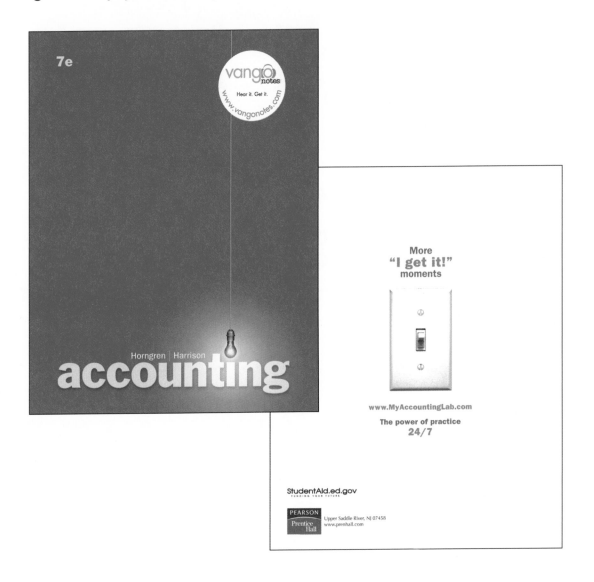

Help your students achieve "I get it!" moments when you're with them AND when you're NOT.

When you're there showing how to solve a problem in class, students "get it." When you're not there, they get stuck—it's only natural.

Our system is designed to help you deliver the best "I get it!" moments. (Instructor's Edition, Instructor Demo Docs)

But it's the really tricky situations that no one else has zeroed in on— the 2 A.M. outside-of-class moments, when you're not there—that present the greatest challenge.

That's where we come in, at these "they have the book, but they don't have you" moments. *Accounting 7e*'s Demo Doc System will help in those critical times. That's what makes this package different from all other textbooks.

The *Accounting 7e,* Demo Doc System provides the vehicle for you and your students to have more "I get it!" moments inside and outside of class.

Duplicate the classroom experience anytime, anywhere with Horngren & Harrison's *Accounting, Seventh Edition*

How The System Works

- The Demo Docs are entire problems worked through step-by-step, from start to finish, with the kind of comments around them that YOU would say in class. They exist in the first four chapters of this text to support the critical accounting cycle chapters, in the Study Guide both in print and in FLASH versions, and as a part of the instructor package for instructors to use in class.

- The authors have created a "no clutter" layout so that critical content is clear and easily referenced.

- Consistency is stressed across all mediums: text, student, and instructor supplements.

- MyAccountingLab is an online homework system that combines "I get it!" moments with the power of practice.

The System's Backbone

Demo Docs in the Text, the Study Guide, and MyAccountingLab.

▶ *NEW* **DEMO DOCS** – Introductory accounting students consistently tell us, "When doing homework, I get stuck trying to solve problems the way they were demonstrated in class." Instructors consistently tell us, "I have so much to cover in so little time; I can't afford to go backward and review homework in class." Those challenges inspired us to develop Demo Docs. Demo Docs are comprehensive worked-through problems, available for nearly every chapter of our introductory accounting text, to help students when they are trying to solve exercises and problems on their own. The idea is to help students duplicate the classroom experience outside of class. Entire problems that mirror end-of-chapter material are shown solved and annotated with explanations written in a conversational style, essentially imitating what an instructor might say if standing over a student's shoulder. All Demo Docs will be available online in Flash and in print so students can easily refer to them when and where they need them.

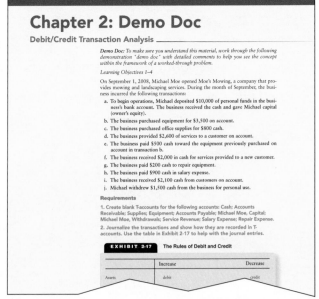

MyAccountingLab – This online homework and assessment tool supports the same theme as the text and resources by providing "I get it!" moments inside and outside of class. It is in MyAccountingLab where "I get it!" moments meet the power of practice. MyAccountingLab is about helping students at their teachable moment, whether that is 1 P.M. or 1 A.M. MyAccountingLab is packed with algorithmic problems because practice makes perfect. It is also packed with the exact same end-of-chapter material in the text that you are used to assigning for homework. MyAccountingLab features the same look and feel for exercises and problems in journal entries and financial statements so that students are familiar and comfortable working in it. Because it includes a Demo Doc for each of the end-of-chapter exercises and problems that students can refer to as they work through the question, it extends The System just one step further by providing students with the help they need to succeed when you are not with them.

The System's Details

CHAPTERS 1–4 We know it's critical that students have a solid understanding of the fundamentals and language surrounding the accounting cycle before they can move to practice. To that end, we're spending extra time developing the accounting cycle chapters (Chs 1–4) to make sure they will help students succeed. We're adding extra visuals, additional comprehensive problems, and a Demo Doc per chapter to give students additional support to move on through the material successfully. You'll be able to stay on schedule in the syllabus because students understand the accounting cycle.

CONSISTENCY – The entire package matters. Consistency in terminology and problem set-ups from one medium to another—test bank to study guide to MyAccountingLab—is critical to your success in the classroom. So when students ask "Where do the numbers come from?," they can go to our text **or** go online and see what to do. If it's worded one way in the text, you can count on it being worded the same way in the supplements.

CLUTTER-FREE – This edition is built on the premise of "Less is More." Extraneous boxes and features, non-essential bells and whistles—they are all gone. The authors know that excess crowds out what really matters—the concepts, the problems, and the learning objectives. Instructors asked for fewer "features" in favor of less clutter and better cross-referencing, and Horngren/Harrison, *Accounting, 7e,* is delivering on that wish. And we've redone all of the end-of-chapter exercises and problems with a renewed focus on the critical core concepts.

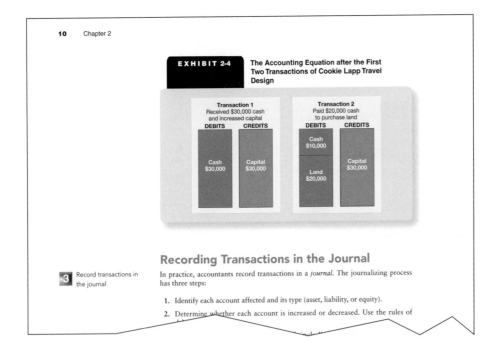

EXHIBIT 2-4   The Accounting Equation after the First Two Transactions of Cookie Lapp Travel Design

Recording Transactions in the Journal

3   Record transactions in the journal

In practice, accountants record transactions in a *journal*. The journalizing process has three steps:

1. Identify each account affected and its type (asset, liability, or equity).
2. Determine whether each account is increased or decreased. Use the rules of

INSTRUCTOR SUPPLEMENTS

Instructor's Edition Featuring *Instructor Demo Docs*

▶ **The New Look of the Instructor's Edition**

We've asked a lot of instructors how we can help them successfully implement new course-delivery methods (e.g. online) while maintaining their regular campus schedule of classes and academic responsibilities. In response, we developed a system of instruction for those of you who are long on commitment and expertise—but short on time and assistance.

The primary goal of the Instructor's Edition is **ease of implementation, using any delivery method**—traditional, self-paced, or online. That is, the Instructor's Edition quickly answers for you, the professor, the question "What must the student do?" Likewise, the Instructor's Edition quickly answers for the student "What must I do?," offers time-saving tips with "best of" categories for in class discussion, and strong examples to illustrate difficult concepts to a wide variety of students. The Instructor's Edition also offers a quick one-shot cross-reference at the exact point of importance with key additional teaching resources, so everything is in one place. The Instructor's Edition includes summaries and teaching tips, pitfalls for new students, and "best of" practices from instructors from across the world.

▶ **The Instructor's Edition also includes *Instructor Demo Docs***

In **Instructor Demo Docs**, we walk the students through how to solve a problem as if it were the first time they've seen it. There are no lengthy passages of text. Instead, bits of expository text are woven into the steps needed to solve the problem, in the exact sequence—for you to provide at the teachable ***"I get it!"*** moment. This is the point at which the student has a context within which he or she can understand the concept. We provide conversational text around each of the steps so the student stays engaged in solving the problem. We provide notes to the instructor for key teaching points around the Demo Docs, and "best of" practice tid-bits before each **Instructor Demo Doc**.

The **Instructor Demo Docs** are written with all of your everyday classroom realities in mind—and trying to save your time in prepping new examples each time your book changes. Additionally, algorithmic versions of these Demo Docs are provided to students in their student guide. We keep the terminology consistent with the text, so there are no surprises for students as they try and work through a problem the first time.

Solutions Transparencies

These transparency masters are the **Solutions Manual** in an easy-to-use format for class lectures.

Instructor's Resource Center CD or www.prenhall.com/horngren

The password-protected site and resource CD includes the following:
- **The Instructor's Edition with *Instructor Demo Docs***
- **Problem Set C**

- **Solutions Manual with Interactive Excel Solutions**

  The Solutions Manual contains solutions to all end-of-chapter questions, multiple-choice questions, short exercises, exercise sets, problems sets, and Internet exercises. The Solutions Manual is available in Microsoft Excel, Microsoft Word, and in print. You can access the solutions in MS Excel and MS Word formats by visiting the Instructor's Resource Center on the Prentice Hall catalog site at www.prenhall.com/horngren or on the Instructor's CD. You will need a Pearson Educator username and password to retrieve materials from the Web site.

  Solutions to select end-of-chapter exercises and problems are available in **interactive MS Excel format** so that instructors can present material in dynamic, step-by-step sequences in class. The interactive solutions were prepared by Kathleen O'Donnell of the State University of New York, Onondaga Community College.

- **Test Bank**

The test item file includes more than 2,000 questions:
  - Multiple Choice
  - Matching
  - True/False
  - Computational Problems
  - Essay

- **Test Bank** is formatted for use with WebCT, Blackboard, and Course Compass.

- **PowerPoints (instructor and student)** summarize and reinforce key text materials. They capture classroom attention with original problems and solved step-by-step exercises. These walk-throughs are designed to help facilitate classroom discussion and demonstrate where the numbers come from and what they mean to the concept at hand. There are approximately 35 slides per chapter. PowerPoints are available on the Instructor's CD and can be downloaded from www.prenhall.com/horngren.

New *MyAccountingLab* Online Homework and Assessment Manager

The **"I get it!"** moment meets *the power of practice*. The power of repetition when you "get it" means learning happens. **MyAccountingLab** is about helping students at their teachable moments, whether it's 1 P.M. or 1 A.M.

MyAccountingLab is an online homework and assessment tool, packed with algorithmic versions of every text problem, because practice makes perfect. It's also packed with the exact same end-of-chapter material that you're used to assigning for homework. Additionally, **MyAccountingLab** includes:

1. A **Demo Doc** for each of the end-of-chapter exercises and problems that students can refer to as they work through the questions.

2. A **Guided Solution** to the exact problem they are working on. It helps students when they're trying to solve a problem the way it was demonstrated in class.

3. A full **e-book** so the students can reference the book at the point of practice.

4. New **topic specific videos** that walk students through difficult concepts.

Companion Web Site–www.prenhall.com/Horngren

The book's Web site at www.prenhall.com/horngren—contains the following:

- Self-study quizzes—interactive study guide for each chapter
- MS Excel templates that students can use to complete homework assignments for each chapter (e-working papers)
- Samples of the Flash Demo Docs for students to work through the accounting cycle

Online Courses with WebCT/BlackBoard/Course Compass

Prentice Hall offers a link to MyAccountingLab through the Bb and WebCT Course Management Systems.

Classroom Response Systems (CRS)

CRS is an exciting new wireless polling technology that makes large and small classrooms even more interactive, because it enables instructors to pose questions to their students, record results, and display those results instantly. Students can easily answer questions using compact remote-control–type transmitters. Prentice Hall has partnerships with leading classroom response-systems providers and can show you everything you need to know about setting up and using a CRS system. Prentice Hall will provide the classroom hardware, text-specific PowerPoint slides, software, and support.

Visit **www.prenhall.com/crs** to learn more.

STUDENT SUPPLEMENTS

Runners Corporation PT Lab Manual

Containing numerous simulated real-world examples, the **Runners Corporation** practice set is available complete with data files for Peachtree, QuickBooks, and PH General Ledger. Each practice set also includes business stationery for manual entry work.

A-1 Photography-Manual PT Lab Manual

Containing numerous simulated real-world examples, the **A-1 Photography** practice set is available complete with data files for Peachtree, QuickBooks, and PH General Ledger. Each set includes business stationery for manual entry work.

Study Guide including Demo Docs and e-Working Papers

Introductory accounting students consistently tell us, "When doing homework, I get stuck trying to solve problems the way they were demonstrated in class." Instructors consistently tell us, "I have so much to cover in so little time; I can't afford to go backwards and review homework in class." Those challenges inspired us to develop Demo Docs. Demo Docs are comprehensive worked-through problems available for nearly every chapter of our introductory accounting text to help students when they are trying to solve exercises and problems on their own. The idea is to help students duplicate the classroom experience outside of class. Entire problems that mirror end-of-chapter material are shown solved and annotated with explanations written in a conversational style, essentially imitating what an instructor might say if standing over a student's shoulder. All Demo Docs will be available in the Study Guide—in print and on CD in Flash, so students can easily refer to them when they need them. The Study Guide also includes a summary overview of key topics and multiple-choice and short-answer questions for students to test their knowledge. Free electronic working papers are included on the accompanying CD.

MyAccountingLab Online Homework and Assessment Manager

The **"I get it!"** moment meets **power of practice**. The power of repetition when you "get it" means that learning happens. **MyAccountingLab** is about helping students at their teachable moment, whether that is 1 P.M. or 1 A.M.

MyAccountingLab is an online homework and assessment tool, packed with algorithmic versions of every text problem because practice makes perfect. It's also packed with the exact same end-of-chapter that you're used to assigning for homework. Additionally, **MyAccountingLab** includes:

1. A **Demo Doc** for each of the end-of-chapter exercises and problems that students can refer to as they work through the question.

2. A **Guided Solution** to the exact problem they are working on. It helps students when they're trying to solve a problem the way it was demonstrated in class.

3. A full **e-book** so the students can reference the book at the point of practice.

4. New **topic specific videos** that walk students through difficult concepts.

PowerPoints

For student use as a study aide or note-taking guide, these PowerPoint slides may be downloaded at the companion Web site at www.prenhall.com/horngren.

Companion Web Site–www.prenhall.com/Horngren

The book's Web site at www.prenhall.com/horngren—contains the following:

- Self-study quizzes—interactive study guide for each chapter
- MS Excel templates that students can use to complete homework assignments for each chapter (e-working papers)
- Samples of the Flash Demo Docs for students to work through the accounting cycle.

Classroom Response Systems (CRS)

CRS is an exciting new wireless polling technology that makes large and small classrooms even more interactive because it enables instructors to pose questions to their students, record results, and display those results instantly. Students can easily answer questions using compact remote-control-type transmitters. Prentice Hall has partnerships with leading classroom response-systems providers and can show you everything you need to know about setting up and using a CRS system. Prentice Hall will provide the classroom hardware, text-specific PowerPoint slides, software, and support.

Visit **www.prenhall.com/crs** to learn more.

- **VangoNotes in MP3 Format**

  Students can study on the go with VangoNotes, chapter reviews in downloadable
  MP3 format that offer brief audio segments for each chapter:

  - Big Ideas: the vital ideas in each chapter
  - Practice Test: lets students know if they need to keep studying
  - Key Terms: audio "flashcards" that review key concepts and terms
  - Rapid Review: a quick drill session—helpful right before tests

  Students can learn more at **www.vangonotes.com**

vang**o**
notes

In partnership with **Audible** Education

Hear it. Get It.

Study on the go with VangoNotes.

Just download chapter reviews from your text and listen to them on any mp3 player. Now wherever you are-- whatever you're doing--you can study by listening to the following for each chapter of your textbook:

Big Ideas: Your "need to know" for each chapter

Practice Test: A gut check for the Big Ideas--tells you if you need to keep studying

Key Terms: Audio "flashcards" to help you review key concepts and terms

Rapid Review: A quick drill session--use it right before your test

VangoNotes.com

Acknowledgments

We'd like to thank the following contributors:

Florence McGovern *Bergen Community College*
Sherry Mills *New Mexico State University*

Suzanne Oliver *Okaloosa Walton Junior College*
Helen Brubeck *San Jose State University*

We'd like to extend a special thank you to the following members of our advisory panel:

Jim Ellis *Bay State College, Boston*
Mary Ann Swindlehurst *Carroll Community College*
Andy Williams *Edmonds Community College*
Donnie Kristof-Nelson *Edmonds Community College*
Joan Cezair *Fayetteville State University*
David Baglia *Grove City College*

Anita Ellzey *Harford Community College*
Cheryl McKay *Monroe County Community College*
Todd Jackson *Northeastern State University*
Margaret Costello Lambert *Oakland Community College*
Al Fagan *University of Richmond*

We'd also like to thank the following reviewers:

Shi-Mu (Simon) Yang *Adelphi University*
Thomas Stolberg *Alfred State University*
Thomas Branton *Alvin Community College*
Maria Lehoczky *American Intercontinental University*
Suzanne Bradford *Angelina College*
Judy Lewis *Angelo State University*
Roy Carson Anne *Arundel Community College*
Paulette Ratliff-Miller *Arkansas State University*
Joseph Foley *Assumption College*
Jennifer Niece *Assumption College*
Bill Whitley *Athens State University*
Shelly Gardner *Augustana College*

Becky Jones *Baylor University*
Betsy Willis *Baylor University*
Michael Robinson *Baylor University*
Kay Walker-Hauser *Beaufort County Community College, Washington*
Joe Aubert *Bemidji State University*
Calvin Fink *Bethune Cookman College*
Michael Blue *Bloomsburg University*
Scott Wallace *Blue Mountain College*
Lloyd Carroll *Borough Manhattan Community College*
Ken Duffe *Brookdale Community College*
Chuck Heuser *Brookdale Community College*
Shafi Ullah *Broward Community College South*
Lois Slutsky *Broward Community College South*
Ken Koerber *Bucks County Community College*

Julie Browning *California Baptist University*
Richard Savich *California State University—San Bernardino*
David Bland *Cape Fear Community College*
Robert Porter *Cape Fear Community College*
Vickie Campbell *Cape Fear Community College*
Cynthia Thompson *Carl Sandburg College—Carthage*

Liz Ott *Casper College*
Joseph Adamo *Cazenovia College*
Julie Dailey *Central Virginia Community College*
Jeannie Folk *College of DuPage*
Lawrence Steiner *College of Marin*
Dennis Kovach *Community College Allegheny County—Allegheny*
Norma Montague *Central Carolina Community College*
Debbie Schmidt *Cerritos College*
Janet Grange *Chicago State University*
Bruce Leung *City College of San Francisco*
Pamela Legner *College of DuPage*
Bruce McMurrey *Community College of Denver*
Martin Sabo *Community College of Denver*
Jeffrey Jones *Community College of Southern Nevada*
Tom Nohl *Community College of Southern Nevada*
Christopher Kelly *Community College of Southern Nevada*
Patrick Rogan *Cosumnes River College*
Kimberly Smith *County College of Morris*

Jerold Braun *Daytona Beach Community College*
Greg Carlton *Davidson County Community College*
Irene Bembenista *Davenport University*
Thomas Szczurek *Delaware County Community College*
Charles Betts *Delaware Technical and Community College*
Patty Holmes *Des Moines Area Community College—Ankeny*
Tim Murphy *Diablo Valley College*

Phillipe Sammour *Eastern Michigan University*
Saturnino (Nino) Gonzales *El Paso Community College*
Lee Cannell *El Paso Community College*
John Eagan *Erie Community College*

Ron O'Brien *Fayetteville Technical Community College*
Patrick McNabb *Ferris State University*
John Stancil *Florida Southern College*
Lynn Clements *Florida Southern College*
Alice Sineath *Forsyth Technical Community College*
James Makofske *Fresno City College*
Marc Haskell *Fresno City College*
James Kelly *Ft. Lauderdale City College*

Christine Jonick *Gainesville State College*
Bruce Lindsey *Genesee Community College*
Constance Hylton *George Mason University*
Cody King *Georgia Southwestern State University*
Lolita Keck *Globe College*
Kay Carnes *Gonzaga University, Spokane*
Carol Pace *Grayson County College*
Rebecca Floor *Greenville Technical College*
Geoffrey Heriot *Greenville Technical College*
Jeffrey Patterson *Grove City College*
Lanny Nelms *Gwinnet Technical College*
Chris Cusatis *Gwynedd Mercy College*

Tim Griffin *Hillsborough Community College*
Clair Helms *Hinds Community College*
Michelle Powell *Holmes Community College*
Greg Bischoff *Houston Community College*
Donald Bond *Houston Community College*
Marina Grau *Houston Community College*
Carolyn Fitzmorris *Hutchinson Community College*

Susan Koepke *Illinois Valley Community College*
William Alexander *Indian Hills Community College—Ottumwa*
Dale Bolduc *Intercoast College*
Thomas Carr *International College of Naples*
Lecia Berven *Iowa Lakes Community College*
Nancy Schendel *Iowa Lakes Community College*
Michelle Cannon *Ivy Tech*
Vicki White *Ivy Tech*
Chuck Smith *Iowa Western Community College*

Stephen Christian *Jackson Community College*
DeeDee Daughtry *Johnston Community College*
Richard Bedwell *Jones County Junior College*

Ken Mark *Kansas City Kansas Community College*
Ken Snow *Kaplan Education Centers*
Charles Evans *Keiser College*
Bunney Schmidt *Keiser College*
Amy Haas *Kingsborough Community College*

Jim Racic *Lakeland Community College*
Doug Clouse *Lakeland Community College*

Patrick Haggerty *Lansing Community College*
Patricia Walczak *Lansing Community College*
Humberto M. Herrera *Laredo Community College*
Christie Comunale *Long Island University*
Ariel Markelevich *Long Island University*
Randy Kidd *Longview Community College*
Kathy Heltzel *Luzerne County Community College*
Lori Major *Luzerne County Community College*

Fred Jex *Macomb Community College*
Glenn Owen *Marymount College*
Behnaz Quigley *Marymount College*
Penny Hanes *Mercyhurst College, Erie*
John Miller *Metropolitan Community College*
Denise Leggett *Middle Tennessee State University*
William Huffman *Missouri Southern State College*
Ted Crosby *Montgomery County Community College*
Beth Engle *Montgomery County Community College*
David Candelaria *Mount San Jacinto College*
Linda Bolduc *Mount Wachusett Community College*

Barbara Gregorio *Nassau Community College*
James Hurat *National College of Business and Technology*
Denver Riffe *National College of Business and Technology*
Asokan Anandarajan *New Jersey Institute of Technology*
Robert Schoener *New Mexico State University*
Stanley Carroll *New York City Technical College of CUNY*
Audrey Agnello *Niagara County Community College*
Catherine Chiang *North Carolina Central University*
Karen Russom *North Harris College*
Dan Bayak *Northampton Community College*
Elizabeth Lynn Locke *Northern Virginia Community College*
Debra Prendergast *Northwestern Business College*
Nat Briscoe *Northwestern State University*
Tony Scott *Norwalk Community College*

Deborah Niemer *Oakland Community College*
John Boyd *Oklahoma City Community College*
Kathleen O'Donnell *Onondaga Community College*
J.T. Ryan *Onondaga Community College*

Toni Clegg *Palm Beach Atlantic College*
David Forsyth *Palomar College*
John Graves *PCDI*
Carla Rich *Pensacola Junior College*
Judy Grotrian *Peru State College*
Judy Daulton *Piedmont Technical College*
John Stone *Potomac State College*
Betty Habershon *Prince George's Community College*

Kathi Villani *Queensborough Community College*

William Black *Raritan Valley Community College*
Verne Ingram *Red Rocks Community College*
Paul Juriga *Richland Community College*
Patty Worsham *Riverside Community College*
Margaret Berezewski *Robert Morris College*
Phil Harder *Robert Morris College*
Shifei Chung *Rowan University of New Jersey*

Charles Fazzi *Saint Vincent College*
Lynnette Yerbuy *Salt Lake Community College*
Susan Blizzard *San Antonio College*
Hector Martinez *San Antonio College*
Audrey Voyles *San Diego Miramar College*
Margaret Black *San Jacinto College*
Merrily Hoffman *San Jacinto College*
Randall Whitmore *San Jacinto College*
Carroll Buck *San Jose State University*
Cynthia Coleman *Sandhills Community College*
Barbara Crouteau *Santa Rosa Junior College* \
Pat Novak *Southeast Community College*
Susan Pallas *Southeast Community College*
Al Case *Southern Oregon University*
Gloria Worthy *Southwest Tennessee Community College*
Melody Ashenfelter *Southwestern Oklahoma State University*
Douglas Ward *Southwestern Community College*
Brandi Shay *Southwestern Community College*
John May *Southwestern Oklahoma State University*
Jeffrey Waybright *Spokane Community College*
Renee Goffinet *Spokane Community College*
Susan Anders *ST Bonaventure University*
John Olsavsky *SUNY at Fredonia*
Peter Van Brunt *SUNY College of Technology at Delhi*

David L. Davis *Tallahassee Community College*
Kathy Crusto-Way *Tarrant County Community College*
Sally Cook *Texas Lutheran University*
Bea Chiang *The College of New Jersey*
Matt Hightower *Three Rivers Community College*

Susan Pope *University of Akron*
Joe Woods *University of Arkansas*
Allen Blay *University of California, Riverside*

Barry Mishra *University of California, Riverside*
Laura Young *University of Central Arkansas*
Jane Calvert *University of Central Oklahoma*
Bambi Hora *University of Central Oklahoma*
Joan Stone *University of Central Oklahoma*
Kathy Terrell *University of Central Oklahoma*
Harlan Etheridge *University of Louisiana*
Pam Meyer *University of Louisiana*
Sandra Scheuermann *University of Louisiana*
Tom Wilson *University of Louisiana*
Lawrence Leaman *University of Michigan*
Larry Huus *University of Minnesota*
Brian Carpenter *University of Scranton*
Ashraf Khallaf *University of Southern Indiana*
Tony Zordan *University of St. Francis*
Gene Elrod *University of Texas, Arlington*
Cheryl Prachyl *University of Texas, El Paso*
Karl Putnam *University of Texas, El Paso*
Stephen Rockwell *University of Tulsa*
Chula King *University of West Florida*
Charles Baird *University of Wisconsin – Stout*

Mary Hollars *Vincennes University*
Lisa Nash *Vincennes University*
Elaine Dessouki *Virginia Wesleyan College*

Sueann Hely *West Kentucky Community and Technical College*
Darlene Pulliam *West Texas A&M University, Canyon*
Judy Beebe *Western Oregon University*
Michelle Maggio *Westfield State College*
Kathy Pellegrino *Westfield State College*
Nora McCarthy *Wharton County Junior College*
Sally Stokes *Wilmington College*
Maggie Houston *Wright State University*

Gerald Caton *Yavapai College*
Chris Crosby *York Technical College*
Harold Gellis *York College of CUNY*

About the Authors

Charles T. Horngren is the Edmund W. Littlefield Professor of Accounting, Emeritus, at Stanford University. A graduate of Marquette University, he received his M.B.A. from Harvard University and his Ph.D. from the University of Chicago. He is also the recipient of honorary doctorates from Marquette University and DePaul University.

A Certified Public Accountant, Horngren served on the Accounting Principles Board for six years, the Financial Accounting Standards Board Advisory Council for five years, and the Council of the American Institute of Certified Public Accountants for three years. For six years, he served as a trustee of the Financial Accounting Foundation, which oversees the Financial Accounting Standards Board and the Government Accounting Standards Board.

Horngren is a member of the Accounting Hall of Fame.

A member of the American Accounting Association, Horngren has been its President and its Director of Research. He received its first annual Outstanding Accounting Educator Award.

The California Certified Public Accountants Foundation gave Horngren its Faculty Excellence Award and its Distinguished Professor Award. He is the first person to have received both awards.

The American Institute of Certified Public Accountants presented its first Outstanding Educator Award to Horngren.

Horngren was named Accountant of the Year, Education, by the national professional accounting fraternity, Beta Alpha Psi.

Professor Horngren is also a member of the Institute of Management Accountants, from whom he has received its Distinguished Service Award. He was a member of the Institute's Board of Regents, which administers the Certified Management Accountant examinations.

Horngren is the author of other accounting books published by Prentice-Hall: *Cost Accounting: A Managerial Emphasis*, Twelfth Edition, 2006 (with Srikant Datar and George Foster); *Introduction to Financial Accounting*, Ninth Edition, 2006 (with Gary L. Sundem and John A. Elliott); *Introduction to Management Accounting*, Thirteenth Edition, 2005 (with Gary L. Sundem and William Stratton); *Financial Accounting*, Sixth Edition, 2006 (with Walter T. Harrison, Jr.).

Horngren is the Consulting Editor for Prentice-Hall's Charles T. Horngren Series in Accounting.

Walter T. Harrison, Jr. is Professor Emeritus of Accounting at the Hankamer School of Business, Baylor University. He received his B.B.A. degree from Baylor University, his M.S. from Oklahoma State University, and his Ph.D. from Michigan State University.

Professor Harrison, recipient of numerous teaching awards from student groups as well as from university administrators, has also taught at Cleveland State Community College, Michigan State University, the University of Texas, and Stanford University.

A member of the American Accounting Association and the American Institute of Certified Public Accountants, Professor Harrison has served as Chairman of the Financial Accounting Standards Committee of the American Accounting Association, on the Teaching/Curriculum Development Award Committee, on the Program Advisory

Committee for Accounting Education and Teaching, and on the Notable Contributions to Accounting Literature Committee.

Professor Harrison has lectured in several foreign countries and published articles in numerous journals, including *Journal of Accounting Research*, *Journal of Accountancy*, *Journal of Accounting and Public Policy*, *Economic Consequences of Financial Accounting Standards*, *Accounting Horizons*, *Issues in Accounting Education*, and *Journal of Law and Commerce*.

He is co-author of *Financial Accounting*, Sixth Edition, 2006 (with Charles T. Horngren), published by Prentice Hall. Professor Harrison has received scholarships, fellowships, and research grants or awards from PriceWaterhouse Coopers, Deloitte & Touche, the Ernst & Young Foundation, and the KPMG Foundation.

accounting

7e

1 Accounting and the Business Environment

What You Probably Already Know

You want to purchase a cell phone and service plan. It would be easy to visit the closest store and buy the phone and company service plan the salesperson recommends. But would that necessarily be the selection that best services your needs with the least cost? Perhaps not. Before making this decision, it might make sense to:

1. gather information from reliable sources;
2. identify the various options and relevant costs;
3. evaluate the cost/benefit relationship of the different plans; and
4. make the decision.

Financial decisions require thoughtful analysis utilizing accurate, reliable, and relevant information. The choice may be finding the best investment for your savings, deciding to purchase or lease a car, or choosing the optimal cell phone service plan. The process that is undertaken to manage our personal financial lives is the same as that employed by managers and owners of businesses. This chapter will explain the importance of accounting to the many users of financial information and how such data are accumulated and reported.

Learning Objectives

1 Use accounting vocabulary.

Accounting is an information system that measures business activities, processes that information into reports, and communicates the results to decision makers. It is often referred to as the language of business. It's important as you begin your study of accounting to understand the basic accounting vocabulary. Make sure you review the first three sections in Chapter 1 of the textbook carefully, as well as the list of interchangeable terms commonly used in accounting. *Review Exhibit 1-3 (p. 7) in the main text to observe the flow of information between accounting and related organizations and users. Compare the three forms of business organization in Exhibit 1-4 (p. 9).*

2   Apply accounting concepts and principles.

The basic accounting concepts and principles include the entity concept, the reliability (objectivity) principle, the cost principle, the going-concern principle, and the stable-monetary-unit concept. Make sure you understand these concepts and principles and how they are applied in the business world.

3   Use the accounting equation.

It is critical to understand each of the basic components of the **accounting equation:**

$$\text{ASSETS = LIABILITIES + OWNER'S EQUITY}$$

Review carefully "The Accounting Equation" section of the main text to understand these important components. Owner's equity can be confusing. Pay special attention to Exhibit 1-6 (p. 12), which summarizes the four types of transactions that affect owner's equity.

4   Analyze business transactions.

A business **transaction** is an event that can be measured and affects any of the components of the accounting equation: assets, liabilities, or owner's equity. Use the accounting equation to record the effects of each business transaction. **Make sure that the amount of the increase or decrease on the left side of the equation (assets) is the same as that on the right side (liabilities and owner's equity.)** *This is a simple but crucial concept to understand. Review the analysis of transactions in Exhibit 1-7 (p. 18).*

5   Prepare the financial statements.

Business transactions are analyzed, recorded, classified, and reported in the financial statements. Financial statements are commonly prepared on a monthly, quarterly, or annual basis and include the income statement, statement of owner's equity, balance sheet, and statement of cash flows. *Refer to Exhibit 1-8 (p. 20) for examples of the four financial statements.*

6   Evaluate business performance.

Financial statements communicate important information necessary for users to make business decisions. Together the financial statements provide useful information to evaluate business performance.

Demo Doc 1

Basic Transactions

Learning Objectives 1–6

Rick Baldwin opened Rick's Delivery Service on August 1, 2008. He is the sole proprietor of the business. During the month of August, Rick had the following transactions:

a. Rick invested $6,000 of his personal funds in the business.

b. The business paid $650 cash for supplies.

c. The business purchased bicycles, paying $1,000 in cash and putting $2,000 on account.

d. The business paid $700 on the accounts to the bicycle store.

e. The business performed delivery services for customers totaling $1,200. These customers paid in cash.

f. The business performed delivery services for customers on account, totaling $2,400.

g. The business collected $550 on account.

h. The business paid rent (for the month of August) of $850.

i. The business paid employees $1,800 for the month of August.

j. Rick purchased groceries for his own use, paying $100 cash from his personal bank account.

k. The business received a telephone bill for $175. As of August 31, 2008, it had not been paid.

l. Rick withdrew $900 cash from the business for personal use.

Requirements

1. Analyze the preceding transactions in terms of their effects on the accounting equation of Rick's Delivery Service.

2. Prepare the income statement, statement of owner's equity, and balance sheet of the business as of August 31, 2008.

3. Was the delivery service profitable for the month of August? Given this level of profit or loss, do you think the withdrawal of $900 was appropriate?

Demo Doc 1 Solutions

Requirement 1

Analyze the preceding transactions in terms of their effects on the accounting equation of Rick's Delivery Service.

Part 1	Part 2	Part 3	Part 4	Part 5	Demo Doc Complete

1 Use accounting vocabulary

2 Apply accounting concepts and principles

3 Use the accounting equation

4 Analyze business transactions

The accounting equation is:

$$\text{Assets} = \text{Liabilities} + \text{Owner's Equity}$$

It is critical to understand each of these basic components:

Assets are economic resources that should benefit the business in the future. Common examples of these would be cash, inventory, equipment, and furniture.

Liabilities are debts or obligations to outsiders. The most common liability is an account payable, an amount owed to a supplier for goods or services. A note payable is a written promise of future payment and usually requires the payment of interest in addition to the repayment of the debt, unlike accounts payable.

Owner's equity represents the owner's interest in the business. It is the amount remaining after subtracting liabilities from assets.

Transaction analysis is a critical first step in understanding how individual transactions are treated in accounting.

a. Rick invested $6,000 of his personal funds in the business.

Rick is using his own money, but he is giving it *to the business*. This means that the business is involved and it is a recordable transaction.

From the business's perspective, this increases Cash (an asset) by $6,000 and increases Rick Baldwin, Capital (owner's equity) by $6,000.

b. The business paid $650 cash for supplies.

The supplies are an asset that increased by $650. Because they were paid for with cash, the Cash account (an asset) is decreased by $650.

c. The business purchased bicycles, paying $1,000 in cash and putting $2,000 on account.

The Bicycles account (an asset) is increasing. But by how much? What is the cost of the bicycles? If $1,000 is paid in cash and $2,000 is bought on account, the *total cost* is $1,000 + $2,000 = $3,000. Why? This is the total amount that the business will (eventually) end up paying in order to acquire the bicycles. This is consistent with the cost principle.

So the Bicycles account (an asset) is increased by $3,000, whereas the Cash account (an asset) is decreased by $1,000.

The $2,000 on account relates to accounts *pay*able (because it will have to be *paid* later). Because we now have *more* money that has to be paid later, it is an increase in Accounts Payable (a liability) of $2,000.

The end result is that Bicycles (an asset) is increased by $3,000, Cash (an asset) is decreased by $1,000, and Accounts Payable (a liability) is increased by $2,000.

d. The business paid $700 on the payable to the bicycle store.

Think of Accounts Payable (a liability) as a list of companies to which the business owes money. In other words, it is a list of companies to which the business will *pay* money at some future time. In this particular problem, the business owes money to the company from which it purchased bicycles on account (see transaction **c**). When the business *pays* the money in full, it can cross this company off the list of companies to which it owes money. Right now, the business is paying only part of the money owed to the bicycle store. This decreases Accounts Payable (a liability) by $700 and decreases Cash (an asset) by $700.

e. The business performed delivery services for customers totaling $1,200. These customers paid in cash.

When the business *performs services,* it means that it is doing work for customers. Doing work for customers is the way that the business makes money. By performing services, the business is earning revenues.

This means that Service Revenues is increased (which increases owner's equity) by $1,200. Because the business receives the cash the customers paid, Cash is also increased (an asset) by $1,200.

f. The business performed delivery services for customers on account, totaling $2,400.

Again, the delivery service is performing services for customers, which means that it is earning revenues. This results in an increase in Service Revenues (owner's equity) of $2,400.

However, this time the customers charged the services on account. This is money that the business will *receive* in the future (when the customers eventually pay) so it is called accounts *receiv*able. Accounts Receivable (an asset) is increased by $2,400.

g. The business collected $550 on account.

Think of Accounts Receivable (an asset) as a list of customers from whom the business will collect money. In other words, it is a list of customers from whom the business will *receive* money at some future time. In this particular situation, these customers received services but did not pay at that time (see transaction **f**). Later, when the business collects (*receives*) the cash in full from any particular customer, it can cross that customer off the list. This is a decrease to Accounts Receivable (an asset) of $550.

Because the cash is received, Cash (an asset) is increased by $550.

h. The business paid rent (for the month of August) of $850.

The rent has *already been used.* By the end of August, the service has been operating and using the space for the entire month. This means that the *benefit* of the rent has already been received or used up. This means that this is a rent *expense.* [Note that if the rent was paid for *September,* it would not yet be used up and would still be a *future* benefit (an asset) and *not* an expense. This issue will be discussed in Chapter 3.]

So Rent Expense is increased by $850, which is a decrease to owner's equity. The question states that the rent was *paid*. This means it was *paid in cash*. Therefore, Cash (an asset) is decreased by $850.

i. The business paid employees $1,800 for the month of August.

Again, the transaction states that the business *paid* the employees, meaning that it *paid in cash*. Therefore, Cash (an asset) is decreased by $1,800.

The work the employees have given to the business has *already been used*. By the end of August, the delivery service has had the employees working and delivering for customers for the entire month. This means that the *benefit* of the work has already been received, so it is a salary *expense*. Salary Expense is increased by $1,800, which is a decrease to owner's equity.

j. Rick purchased groceries for his own use, paying $100 cash from his personal bank account.

These groceries were purchased with Rick's *personal* money for Rick's *personal* use. Therefore, this purchase does not relate to the business and is not a recordable transaction for the delivery service.

k. The business received a telephone bill for $175. As of August 31, 2008, it had not been paid.

Utilities (such as water, gas, electricity, phone, and Internet service) are generally not billed until *after* they have been used. If these utilities have already been used, then they are utilities *expenses*. So, Utility Expense is increased by $175, which is a decrease to owner's equity.

Because the bill has not yet been *paid* as of August 31, it is an account *pay*able. This increases Accounts Payable (a liability) by $175.

l. Rick withdrew $900 cash from the business for personal use.

Although Rick is taking the money, the cash is coming from the *business,* so this is a recordable transaction for the business. There is a decrease of $900 to Cash (an asset). Because Rick is the owner, this results in an increase of $900 to Owner Withdrawals, which is a decrease to owner's equity.

Requirement 2

Prepare the income statement, statement of owners equity, and balance sheet of the business as of August 31, 2008.

Part 1	**Part 2**	Part 3	Part 4	Part 5	Demo Doc Complete

3 Use the accounting equation

Here's how the transactions from Requirement 1 look in the accounting equation:

		ASSETS				LIABILITIES +	OWNER'S EQUITY	TYPE OF OWNER'S EQUITY TRANSACTION
	Cash +	Accounts Receivable	+ Supplies +	Bicycles		Accounts Payable	Rick Baldwin, Capital	
a.	+$6,000						+$6,000	Owner investment
b.	−650		+$650					
c.	−1,000			+$3,000		+$2,000		
d.	−700					−700		
e.	+1,200				=		+1,200	Service revenue
f.		+$2,400					−2,400	Service revenue
g.	+550	−550						
h.	−850						−850	Rent expense
i.	−1,800						−1,800	Salary expense
j.	Not a transaction of the business.							
k.						+175	−175	Utilities expense
l.	−900						−900	Owner withdrawal
	$1,850	$1,850	$650	$3,000		$1,475	$5,875	
		$7,350					$7,350	

5 Prepare the financial statements

Remember that financial statements communicate important information necessary for users to make business decisions. An overview of the financial statements is as follows:

- **Income Statement**—Lists the revenues and expenses to determine net income or net loss for a period. Net income results if revenues exceed expenses; the reverse results in a net loss.
- **Statement of Owner's Equity**—Shows the changes in owner's equity during the period. Investments from owners and net income increase equity; owner withdrawals and net losses decrease equity.
- **Balance Sheet**—Lists the assets, liabilities, and owner's equity at a point in time, usually at the end of a month.
- **Statement of Cash Flows**—Report of cash receipts (inflows) and cash payments (outflows) for a period of time. (The statement of cash flow is covered in Chapter 17.)

The income statement is the first statement that should be prepared because the other financial statements rely on the net income number calculated on the income statement.

The income statement lists all revenues and expenses. It uses the following formula to calculate net income:

$$\text{Revenues} - \text{Expenses} = \text{Net income}$$

So, to create an income statement, we only need to list the revenue accounts and then subtract the list of expense accounts to calculate net income.

We can read these amounts from the accounting equation work sheet.

There are two transactions impacting service revenue: **e** and **f**. Transaction **e** increases service revenue by $1,200 and transaction **f** increases service revenue by $2,400. This means that total service revenue for the month was:

$$\$1,200 + \$2,400 = \$3,600$$

Rent expense of $850, salary expense of $1,800, and utilities expense of $175 were recorded in transactions **h**, **i**, and **k** (respectively).

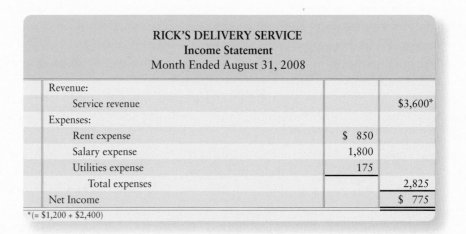

RICK'S DELIVERY SERVICE
Income Statement
Month Ended August 31, 2008

Revenue:		
Service revenue		$3,600*
Expenses:		
Rent expense	$ 850	
Salary expense	1,800	
Utilities expense	175	
Total expenses		2,825
Net Income		$ 775

*(= $1,200 + $2,400)

Part 1	Part 2	**Part 3**	Part 4	Part 5	Demo Doc Complete

Net income is used on the statement of owner's equity to calculate the new balance in the Capital account. This calculation uses the following formula:

Beginning capital amount
+ Owner investments
+ Net income
– Owner withdrawals
= Ending capital amount

Again, we just have to recreate this formula on the statement:

RICK'S DELIVERY SERVICE
Statement of Owner's Equity
Month Ended August 31, 2008

Rick Baldwin, capital, August 1, 2008	$ 0
Add: Investment by owner	6,000
Net income for month	775
	6,775
Less: Withdrawals by owner	(900)
Rick Baldwin, capital, August 31, 2008	$5,875

Part 1	Part 2	Part 3	**Part 4**	Part 5	Demo Doc Complete

The ending capital amount is used on the balance sheet. The balance sheet is just a listing of all assets, liabilities, and equity, with the accounting equation verified at the bottom:

RICK'S DELIVERY SERVICE
Balance Sheet
August 31, 2008

Assets		Liabilities	
Cash	$1,850	Accounts payable	$1,475
Accounts receivable	1,850		
Supplies	650	**Equity**	
Bicycles	3,000	Rick Baldwin, capital	5,875
Total assets	$7,350	Total liabilities and equity	$7,350

Requirement 3

Was the delivery service profitable for the month of August? Given this level of profit or loss, do you think the withdrawal of $900 was appropriate?

Part 1	Part 2	Part 3	Part 4	**Part 5**	Demo Doc Complete

Evaluate business performance

Evaluating business performance is critical to making sound business decisions. For example, reviewing the income statement shows the results of operations, how much the business generated in net income, or if it incurred a net loss. The statement of owner's equity indicates what caused the change in owner's equity for the period. The balance sheet is a statement of financial condition or financial position, which includes the ending owner's equity. The statement of cash flows would identify the cash receipts and cash payments from operating, investing, and financing activities.

From the income statement prepared in Requirement 2, we can see that the delivery service earned $775 of profit during the month of August. The level of withdrawals ($900) seems high given that it is more than the amount of profit earned during the month.

| Part 1 | Part 2 | Part 3 | Part 4 | Part 5 | Demo Doc Complete |

Quick Practice Questions

True/False

_____ 1. Financial accounting produces financial information and reports to be used by managers inside a business.

_____ 2. An audit is a financial examination performed by independent accountants.

_____ 3. The top financial position in private accounting is the rank of partner.

_____ 4. Professional accounting organizations and most companies have standards of ethical behavior.

_____ 5. A corporation's owners are called shareholders.

_____ 6. An advantage of the partnership form of business is that the life of the entity is indefinite.

_____ 7. The life of a sole proprietorship is limited to the owner's choice or death.

_____ 8. The entity concept separates business transactions from personal transactions.

_____ 9. A business has a net loss when total revenues are greater than total expenses.

_____ 10. The statement of owner's equity reports the cash coming in and going out.

Multiple Choice

1. **What is the private organization that is primarily responsible for formulating accounting standards?**
   a. The Internal Revenue Service
   b. The Securities and Exchange Commission
   c. The American Institute of Certified Public Accountants
   d. The Financial Accounting Standards Board

2. **What is the watchdog agency created by the Sarbanes-Oxley Act?**
   a. The American Institute of Certified Public Accountants
   b. The Public Companies Accounting Oversight Board
   c. The Internal Revenue Service
   d. The Financial Accounting Standards Board

3. **Financial accounting provides financial statements and financial information that are intended to be used by whom?**
   a. Management of the company
   b. Potential investors
   c. Employees of the company
   d. The board of directors

4. What is the purpose of financial accounting information?
   a. Help managers plan and control business operations
   b. Comply with the IRS rules
   c. Help investors, creditors, and others make decisions
   d. Provide information to employees

5. What characteristic is necessary for information to be useful?
   a. Relevance
   b. Reliability
   c. Comparability
   d. All of the above

6. Sue Mason owns a bagel shop as a sole proprietorship. Sue includes her personal home, car, and boat on the books of her business. Which of the following is violated?
   a. Entity concept
   b. Going-concern concept
   c. Cost principle
   d. Reliability principle

7. Which of the following is the accounting equation?
   a. Assets − Liabilities = Owner's equity
   b. Assets + Liabilities = Owner's equity
   c. Assets = Liabilities + Owner's equity
   d. Assets + Liabilities = Net income

8. If the assets of a business are $410,000 and the liabilities total $200,000, how much is the owner's equity?
   a. $150,000
   b. $160,000
   c. $210,000
   d. $610,000

9. Which financial statement contains a listing of assets, liabilities, and owner's equity?
   a. Balance sheet
   b. Statement of owner's equity
   c. Income statement
   d. Statement of cash flows

10. What is the claim of a business owner to the assets of the business called?
    a. Liabilities
    b. Owner's equity
    c. Revenue
    d. Withdrawals

Quick Exercises

1-1. Fill in the statements that follow with the correct type of business organization.

a. A _____ is a separate legal entity approved by the state.
b. A _____ is an entity with one owner where the business and not the owner is liable for the company's debts.
c. A _____ is an entity with two or more owners who are personally liable for the company's debts.

1-2.   Match the following terms with the best description.

Terms

    a. Entity concept
    b. Reliability principle
    c. Cost principle
    d. Going-concern concept
    e. Stable-monetary-unit concept

Description

_____ An organization or part of an organization is separate from other organizations and individuals.

_____ An item should be recorded at the actual amount paid.

_____ An entity is expected to remain in business in the future.

_____ Assumption that the dollar's purchasing power is constant.

_____ Accounting data should be neutral, unbiased information that can be confirmed by others.

1-3.   Determine the missing amounts:

    a. Assets = $50,000; Liabilities = $30,000; Owner's Equity = _____?
    b. Liabilities = $35,000; Owner's Equity = $75,000; Assets = _____?
    c. Assets = $105,000; Owner's Equity = $50,000; Liabilities = _____?

1-4.   Write a brief explanation for the following transactions:

	ASSETS				LIABILITIES	+	OWNER'S EQUITY
	Cash	+ Accounts Receivable	+ Supplies		Accounts Payable		Capital
a.	20,000						20,000
b.			1,000	=	1,000		
c.	−2,500						−2,500
d.		5,200					5,200
e.	3,000	−3,000					

    a. _____
    b. _____
    c. _____
    d. _____
    e. _____

1-5.   On which of the following three financial statements would you expect to find the items (a)–(f)?

Income Statement (IS)
Balance Sheet (BS)
Statement of Cash Flows (CF)

    a. _____ Accounts Payable
    b. _____ Service Revenue
    c. _____ Collections from Customer
    d. _____ Utilities Expense
    e. _____ Office Supplies
    f. _____ Payments to Suppliers

Do It Yourself! Question 1

Jennifer Hill opened a Laundromat business on October 1, 2008. She is the sole proprietor of the business.

Requirement

1. For each transaction of the business during the month of October, analyze the transaction in terms of its effect on the accounting equation of Jennifer's Laundromat.

a. Jennifer invested $10,000 of her personal funds in the business.

b. The Laundromat purchased washing machines, paying $4,000 in cash and putting another $5,000 on account.

c. Jennifer purchased a washing machine for use in her home costing $2,100 on her personal account.

d. The business paid $500 cash for supplies.

e. The Laundromat performed cleaning services for customers totaling $2,500. These customers paid in cash.

f. The Laundromat also performed cleaning services for customers on account totaling $3,700.

g. The Laundromat paid rent (for the month of October) of $1,000.

h. The business paid employees $1,500 for the month of October.

i. The Laundromat received a utility bill for $750. As of October 31, 2008, it had not been paid.

j. Jennifer withdrew $2,000 cash from the business for personal use.

k. The Laundromat collected $2,250 on account.

l. The amount of $2,400 was paid on the account to the washing machine store.

2. Prepare the income statement, statement of owner's equity, and balance sheet of the business as of October 31, 2008.

<u>Assets</u> = <u>Liabilities</u> + <u>Equity</u> <u>Type of Owners Equity Transaction</u>

a. _____

b. _____

c. _____

d. _____

e. _____

f. _____

g. _____

h. _____

i. _____

j. _____

k. _____

l. _____

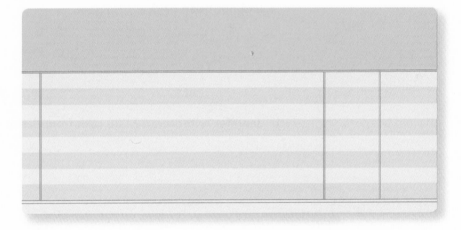

Quick Practice Solutions

True/False

  F   1. Financial accounting produces financial information and reports to be used by managers inside a business.

       False—Financial accounting produces information for people *outside* the company. (p. 5)

  T   2. An audit is a financial examination performed by independent accountants (p. 6).

  F   3. The top financial position in private accounting is the rank of partner.

       False—The top financial position in private accounting is the *chief financial officer*. (p. 6)

  T   4. Professional accounting organizations and most companies have standards of ethical behavior. (p. 7)

  T   5. A corporation's owners are called shareholders. (p. 8)

  F   6. An advantage of the partnership form of business is that the life of the entity is indefinite.

       False—The life of a partnership is limited by the owners' choices or death. (p. 9)

  F   7. The owner of a sole proprietorship is not personally liable for the debts of the business.

       False—The owner of a sole proprietorship *is* personally liable for the debts of the business. (p. 9)

  T   8. The entity concept separates business transactions from personal transactions. (p. 9)

  F   9. A business has a net loss when total revenues are greater than total expenses.

       False—A business has *net income* when total revenues are greater than total expenses. (p. 19)

  F 10. The statement of owner's equity reports the cash coming in and going out.

       False—The statement of owner's equity shows the changes in owner's equity during a time period. The *statement of cash flows* reports cash coming in and going out. (p. 19)

Multiple Choice

1. What is the private organization that is primarily responsible for formulating accounting standards? (p. 6)
   a. The Internal Revenue Service
   b. The Securities and Exchange Commission
   c. The American Institute of Certified Public Accountants
   d. The Financial Accounting Standards Board

2. What is the watchdog agency created by the Sarbanes-Oxley Act? (p. 7)
   a. The American Institute of Certified Public Accountants
   b. The Public Companies Accounting Oversight Board
   c. The Internal Revenue Service
   d. The Financial Accounting Standards Board

3. Financial accounting provides financial statements and financial information that are intended to be used by whom? (p. 17)
   a. Management of the company
   b. Potential investors
   c. Employees of the company
   d. The board of directors

4. What is the purpose of financial accounting information? (p. 17)
   a. To help managers plan and control business operations
   b. To comply with the IRS rules
   c. To help investors, creditors, and others make decisions
   d. To provide information to employees

5. What characteristic is necessary for information to be useful? (p. 9)
   a. Relevance
   b. Reliability
   c. Comparability
   d. All of the above

6. Sue Mason owns a bagel shop as a sole proprietorship. Sue includes her personal home, car, and boat on the books of her business. Which of the following is violated? (p. 9)
   a. Entity concept
   b. Going-concern concept
   c. Cost principle
   d. Reliability principle

7. Which is the accounting equation? (p. 11)
   a. Assets − Liabilities = Owner's equity
   b. Assets + Liabilities = Owner's equity
   c. Assets = Liabilities + Owner's equity
   d. Assets + Liabilities = Net income

8. If the assets of a business are $410,000 and the liabilities total $200,000, how much is the owner's equity? (p. 11)
   a. $150,000
   b. $160,000
   c. $210,000
   d. $610,000

9. Which financial statement contains a listing of assets, liabilities, and owner's equity? (p. 19)
   a. Balance sheet
   b. Statement of owner's equity
   c. Income statement
   d. Statement of cash flows

10. What is the claim of a business owner to the assets of the business called? (p. 11)
    a. Liabilities
    b. Owner's equity
    c. Revenue
    d. Withdrawals

Quick Exercises

1-1. Fill in the statements that follow with the correct type of business organization. (p. 8)

   a. A corporation is a separate legal entity approved by the state.
   b. A limited-liability corporation is an entity with one owner where the business and not the owner is liable for the company's debts.
   c. A partnership is an entity with two or more owners who are personally liable for the company's debts.

1-2. Match the following terms with the best description. (p. 9)

Terms

   a. Entity concept
   b. Reliability principle
   c. Cost principle
   d. Going-concern concept
   e. Stable-monetary-unit concept

Description

   a An organization or part of an organization is separate from other organizations and individuals.
   c An item should be recorded at the actual amount paid.
   d An entity is expected to remain in business in the future.
   e Assumption that the dollar's purchasing power is constant.
   b Accounting data should be neutral, unbiased information that can be confirmed by others.

1-3. Determine the missing amounts: (p. 11)

   a. Assets = $50,000; Liabilities = $30,000; Owner's Equity = $20,000 ($50,000 − $30,000)
   b. Liabilities = $35,000; Owner's Equity = $75,000; Assets = $110,000 ($35,000 + $75,000)
   c. Assets = $105,000; Owner's Equity = $50,000; Liabilities = $55,000 ($105,000 − $50,000)

1-4. Write a brief explanation for the following transactions: (p. 13)

	ASSETS				LIABILITIES	+	OWNER'S EQUITY
	Cash	+ Accounts Receivable +	Supplies		Accounts Payable		Capital
a.	20,000						20,000
b.			1,000	=	1,000		
c.	−2,500						−2,500
d.		5,200					5,200
e.	3,000	−3,000					

   a. The owner invested $20,000 cash in the business.
   b. Purchased $1,000 of supplies on account.
   c. Paid $2,500 for an expense *or* the owner withdrew $2,500 for personal use.
   d. Performed services for customer on account, $5,200.
   e. Received $3,000 cash from customers on account.

1-5. On which of the following three financial statements would you expect to find the items (a)–(f)? (p. 19)

Income Statement (IS)
Balance Sheet (BS)
Statement of Cash Flows (CF)

   a. _BS_ Accounts Payable
   b. _IS_ Service Revenue
   c. _CF_ Collections from Customer
   d. _IS_ Utilities Expense
   e. _BS_ Office Supplies
   f. _CF_ Payments to Suppliers

Do It Yourself! Question 1 Solutions

Requirement

1. For each transaction of the business during the month of October, analyze and describe the transaction in terms of its effect on the accounting equation of Jennifer's Laundromat.

a. Jennifer invested $10,000 of her personal funds in the business.

Cash (an asset) is increased by $10,000 and Jennifer Hill, Capital (owner's equity) is increased by $10,000.

b. The Laundromat purchased washing machines, paying $4,000 in cash and putting another $5,000 on account.

Washing Machines (an asset) is increased by $9,000, whereas Cash (an asset) is decreased by $4,000. Accounts Payable (a liability) is increased by $5,000.

c. Jennifer purchased a washing machine for use in her home costing $2,100 on her personal account.

This does not relate to the business and is not a recordable transaction for the Laundromat.

d. The business paid $500 cash for supplies.

Supplies (an asset) is increased by $500 and Cash (an asset) is decreased by $500.

e. The Laundromat performed cleaning services for customers totaling $2,500. These customers paid in cash.

Service Revenues (owner's equity) is increased by $2,500. Cash (an asset) is increased by $2,500.

f. The Laundromat also performed cleaning services for customers on account totaling $3,700.

Service Revenues (owner's equity) is increased by $3,700. Accounts Receivable (an asset) is increased by $3,700.

g. The Laundromat paid rent (for the month of October) of $1,000.

Rent Expense is increased by $1,000, which is a decrease to owner's equity. Cash (an asset) is decreased by $1,000.

h. The business paid employees $1,500 for the month of October.

Salary Expense is increased by $1,500, which is a decrease to owner's equity. Cash (an asset) is decreased by $1,500.

i. **The Laundromat received a utility bill for $750. As of October 31, 2008, it had not been paid.**

Utility Expense is increased by $750, which is a decrease to owner's equity. Accounts Payable (a liability) is increased by $750.

j. **Jennifer withdrew $2,000 cash from the business for personal use.**

This is a recordable transaction for the business. Cash (an asset) is decreased by $2,000. This results in an increase of $2,000 to Owner Withdrawals, which is a decrease to owner's equity.

k. **The Laundromat collected $2,250 of accounts receivable.**

Accounts Receivable (an asset) is decreased by $2,250. Because the cash is received, Cash is increased (an asset) by $2,250.

l. **The amount of $2,400 was paid on the accounts payable to the washing machine store.**

Accounts Payable (a liability) is decreased by $2,400 and Cash (an asset) is decreased by $2,400.

2. Prepare the income statement, balance sheet, and statement of owner's equity of the business as of October 31, 2008.

	Assets					Liabilities +	Owner's Equity	Type of Owner's Equity Transaction
	Cash	+ Accounts Receivable	+ Supplies	+ Washing Machines	=	Accounts Payable	+ Jennifer Hill, Capital	
a.	+$10,000						+ $10,000	*Owner investment*
b.	− 4,000			+ $9,000		+ $5,000		
c. Not a transaction of the business.								
d.	− $500		+ $500					
e.	+ 2,500						+ 2,500	*Service revenue*
f.		+ $3,700					+ 3,700	*Service revenue*
g.	− 1,000						− 1,000	*Rent expense*
h.	− 1,500						− 1,500	*Salary expense*
i.						+ 750	− 750	*Utilities expense*
j.	− 2,000						− 2,000	*Owner withdrawal*
k.	+ 2,250	− 2,250						
l.	− 2,400					− 2,400		
	$3,350	$1,450	$500	$9,000		$3,350	$10,950	
	$14,300					$14,300		

JENNIFER'S LAUNDROMAT
Income Statement
Month Ended October 31, 2008

Revenue:		
Service revenue		$6,200*
Expenses:		
Salary expense	$1,500	
Rent expense	1,000	
Utilities expense	750	
Total expenses		3,250
Net income		$2,950

*(= $2,500 + $3,700)

JENNIFER'S LAUNDROMAT
Statement of Owner's Equity
Month Ended October 31, 2008

Jennifer Hill, capital, October 1, 2008	$ 0
Add: Investment by owner	10,000
Net income for month	2,950
	12,950
Less: Withdrawals by owner	(2,000)
Jennifer Hill, capital, October 31, 2008	$10,950

JENNIFER'S LAUNDROMAT
Balance Sheet
October 31, 2008

Assets		Liabilities	
Cash	$ 3,350	Accounts payable	$ 3,350
Accounts receivable	1,450		
Supplies	500	**Equity**	
Washing machines	9,000	Jennifer Hill, capital	10,950
Total assets	$14,300	Total liabilities and equity	$14,300

The Power of Practice

For more practice using the skills learned in this chapter, visit MyAccountingLab. There you will find algorithmically generated questions that are based on these Demo Docs and your main textbook's Review and Assess Your Progress sections.

Go to MyAccountingLab and follow these steps:

1. Direct your URL to www.myaccountinglab.com.
2. Log in using your name and password.
3. Click the MyAccountingLab link.
4. Click Study Plan in the left navigation bar.
5. From the table of contents, select Chapter 1, Accounting and the Business Environment.
6. Click a link to work tutorial exercises.

2 Recording Business Transactions

WHAT YOU PROBABLY ALREADY KNOW

If you have a checking account, you know that once a month you receive a statement from the bank. The statement shows the beginning cash balance, increases, decreases, and the ending cash balance. The account balance is the amount that the bank *owes* you, their customer. Your balance represents a *liability* to the bank. The deposits you make *increase* the bank's liability to you. The withdrawals or checks you write *decrease* that liability. Instead of using the terms increase and decrease, businesses have used a system of accounting for over 500 years with debits and credits. Either a debit *or* a credit may signify an increase to the account, *depending upon the type of account:* **asset**, **liability**, or **owner's equity**. Your checking account balance is a **liability** to your bank; does a debit or credit indicate an increase? When you take money out of the bank, it *decreases* the bank's liability to you because you've received back a portion of your account balance and is shown as a *debit* on the bank statement. When you deposit money into your account, it *increases* the banks' liability to you and is reflected as a *credit* on the bank statement. So, you can see that you probably already know that the rule for a liability account is that increases are shown as credits and decreases as debits.

Learning Objectives

 Use accounting terms.

You learned in Chapter 1 that accounting is known as the language of business. The first several chapters contain many new terms that are used in the remaining chapters and are important for you to understand. These terms include the journal, account, ledger, trial balance, and chart of accounts. It is crucial that you understand these terms now before you proceed with your study of accounting. Also, carefully review the detailed description of the various specific asset, liability, and owner's equity accounts in Chapter 1 of the main text.

Apply the rules of debit and credit.

A business transaction affects two or more specific accounts. There are two sides to an account, the left (debit) side, and the right (credit) side. Remember that *debit only means left* and *credit only means right*. Increases are recorded on one side and decreases on the other. Depending on the type of account, a debit may indicate an increase **or** a decrease. Assets are on the left side of the equation; they increase on the left (debit) side. Liabilities and owner's equity are on the right side of the equation; they increase on the right (credit) side. *This is a basic concept, but crucial to understand. Review Exhibit 2-8 (p. 68) for the debit and credit rules.*

3 **Record transactions in the journal.**

Remember the five steps in transaction analysis. You will practice this in Demo Doc 1. The more you practice this, the easier it will be to understand.

4 **Post from the journal to the ledger.**

The journal shows the accounts that are debited and credited to record business transactions in chronological order. Debits and credits *only* reflect increases and decreases to the accounts. To obtain a specific account balance, it is helpful to collect the debit and credit information recorded in the journal in one place. Posting, copying the debits and credits from the journal into the account ledger, provides this information. The difference between the total debits and total credits in each account is the balance. The balance is shown on the larger side, normally the side to record the increase. *Review the posting process in Exhibits 2-6 (p. 68) and 2-10 (p. 70). Observe in Exhibit 2-11 (p. 77) that the entries on the increase side of each account balance exceed those on the decrease side. Note that the account balances are on the side where the increases are recorded.*

5 **Prepare and use a trial balance.**

After transactions are recorded in the journal and posted to the ledger, a trial balance is prepared. The trial balance is a listing of all of the accounts with their balances. In a manual accounting system, it is useful as a check to determine that the total debits equal the total credits. If they are unequal, an error has been made and must be investigated before proceeding. *Review the trial balance in Exhibit 2-12 (p. 77).*

Demo Doc 1

Debit/Credit Transaction Analysis

Learning Objectives 1–5

Knight Airlines provides private plane transportation for businesspeople. Knight had the following trial balance on April 1, 2008:

KNIGHT AIRLINES
Trial Balance
April 1, 2008

		Account Title	Debit	Credit
		Cash	$50,000	
		Accounts receivable	8,000	
		Accounts payable		$16,000
		Maureen Knight, capital		42,000
		Total	$58,000	$58,000

During April, the business had the following transactions:

a. **Purchased a new airplane for $50,000. Knight paid $10,000 down and signed a note payable for the remainder.**

b. **Purchased supplies worth $1,000 on account.**

c. **Paid $5,000 on account.**

d. **Transported customers on its planes for fees totaling $25,000. The amount of $7,500 was received in cash with the remainder on account.**

e. **Received $18,000 on account.**

f. **Paid the following in cash: interest, $1,200; rent, $2,300; salaries, $7,000.**

g. **Received a bill for airplane repair costs of $3,500 that will be paid next month.**

h. **Maureen Knight withdrew $6,000 for personal use.**

Requirements

1. Open the following accounts, with the balances indicated, in the ledger of Knight Airlines. Use the T-account format.

- **Assets**—Cash, $50,000; Accounts Receivable, $8,000; Supplies, no balance; Airplanes, no balance
- **Liabilities**—Accounts Payable, $16,000; Notes Payable, no balance
- *Owner's Equity*—Maureen Knight, Capital, $42,000; Maureen Knight, Withdrawals, no balance
- **Revenues**—Service Revenue, no balance
- **Expenses**—(none have balances) Interest Expense, Rent Expense, Salary Expense, Repairs Expense

2. Journalize each transaction. Key journal entries by transaction letter.

3. Post to the ledger.

4. Prepare the trial balance of Knight Airlines at April 30, 2008.

Demo Doc 1 Solutions

Requirement 1

Open the following accounts, with the balances indicated, in the ledger of Knight Airlines. Use the T-account format.

- **Assets**—Cash, $50,000; Accounts Receivable, $8,000; Supplies, no balance; Airplanes, no balance
- **Liabilities**—Accounts Payable, $16,000; Notes Payable, no balance
- **Owner's Equity**—Maureen Knight, Capital, $42,000; Maureen Knight, Withdrawals, no balance
- **Revenues**—Service Revenue, no balance
- **Expenses**—(none have balances) Interest Expense, Rent Expense, Salary Expense, Repairs Expense

Part 1	Part 2	Part 3	Part 4	Demo Doc Complete

Remember, an **account** is a record showing increases, decreases, and the balance of a particular asset, liability, or owner's equity. A T-account is a visual diagram of the additions and subtractions made to the accounts. A **chart of accounts** is a list of all of the business's account titles and account numbers assigned to those titles. A chart of accounts does not include account balances. Review the sample chart of accounts in Exhibit 2-2 (p. 63) of the main text.

Opening a T-account simply means drawing a blank account (the "T") and putting the account title on top. To help find the accounts later, they are usually organized into assets, liabilities, owner's equity, revenue, and expenses (in that order). If the account has a starting balance, it *must* be put in on the correct side.

Remember that debits are always on the left side of the T-account and credits are always on the right side. This is true for *every* account.

The correct side is the side of *increase* in the account (unless you are specifically told differently in the question). This is because we expect all accounts to have a *positive* balance (that is, more increases than decreases).

For assets, an increase is a debit, so we would expect all assets to have a debit balance. For liabilities and owner's equity, an increase is a credit, so we would expect all of these accounts to have a credit balance. By the same reasoning, we expect revenues to have a credit balance and expenses and withdrawals to have a debit balance.

The balances listed in Requirement 1 are simply the amounts from the starting trial balance. We actually did not need to be told how much to put in each account because we could have read the numbers directly from the April 1 trial balance.

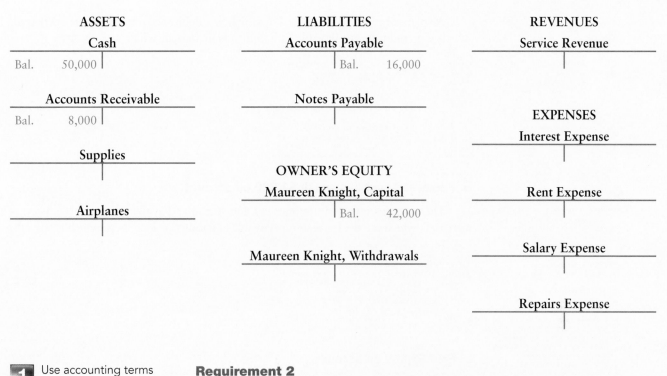

ASSETS

Cash

Bal. | 50,000 |

Accounts Receivable

Bal. | 8,000 |

Supplies

Airplanes

LIABILITIES

Accounts Payable

| Bal. | 16,000

Notes Payable

OWNER'S EQUITY

Maureen Knight, Capital

| Bal. | 42,000

Maureen Knight, Withdrawals

REVENUES

Service Revenue

EXPENSES

Interest Expense

Rent Expense

Salary Expense

Repairs Expense

1 Use accounting terms

2 Apply the rules of debit and credit

3 Record transactions in the journal

Requirement 2

Journalize each transaction. Key journal entries by transaction letter.

| Part 1 | **Part 2** | Part 3 | Part 4 | Demo Doc Complete |

Feel free to reference Exhibit 2-2 (p. 63 in text) for help in completing this exercise.

The business transactions discussed in Chapter 1 are recorded in chronological order in a **journal**. Similar to journaling that you may do for a class or at home, it provides a history of events that have taken place over a period of time. The recorded data in the journal are copied into the two or more specific accounts affected by the business transaction.

Remember, the steps to analyzing a transaction are (1) identify the accounts affected and the type of account, and (2) determine whether the account is increased or decreased and apply the rules for debits and credits.

After you've done this analysis, the third and final step to record transactions in the journal is to (3) enter the debit account followed by indenting the credit account in the journal. Include a brief explanation of the transaction below the journal entry.

a. Purchased a new airplane for $50,000. Knight paid $10,000 down and signed a note payable for the remainder.

The accounts involved are Airplanes, Cash, and Notes Payable. The airplane cost $50,000 and $10,000 was paid in cash, so that means that the note payable was for $50,000 − $10,000 = $40,000.

Airplanes (an asset) is increased, which is a debit. Cash (an asset) is decreased, which is a credit. Notes Payable (a liability) is increased, which is a credit.

a.	Airplanes	50,000	
	Cash		10,000
	Notes Payable ($50,000 – $10,000)		40,000
	Purchased airplane.		

b. Purchased supplies worth $1,000 on account.

The accounts involved are Supplies and Accounts Payable. Supplies (an asset) is increased, which is a debit. Accounts Payable (a liability) is increased, which is a credit.

b.	Supplies	1,000	
	Accounts Payable		1,000
	Purchased supplies.		

c. Paid $5,000 on account.

The accounts involved are Accounts Payable and Cash. Accounts Payable (a liability) is decreased, which is a debit. Cash (an asset) is decreased, which is a credit.

c.	Accounts Payable	5,000	
	Cash		5,000
	Paid on account.		

d. Transported customers on its planes for fees totaling $25,000. Cash of $7,500 was received with the remainder on account.

Knight's business is flying customers to where they want to go. This means that transporting customers is "performing services" and the business earned service revenue. The other accounts involved are Cash (because cash was received) and Accounts Receivable (because some customers charged to their accounts). The total revenue was $25,000 and $7,500 was paid in cash. This means that $25,000 – $7,500 = $17,500 was charged to the customers' accounts.

Service Revenue (revenues) is increased, which is a credit. Cash (an asset) is increased, which is a debit. Accounts Receivable (an asset) is increased, which is a debit.

d.	Cash	7,500	
	Accounts Receivable ($25,000 – $7,500)	17,500	
	Service Revenue		25,000
	Performed services on account and for cash.		

e. Received $18,000 on account.

The accounts involved are Cash and Accounts Receivable. Cash (an asset) is increased, which is a debit. Accounts Receivable (an asset) is decreased, which is a credit.

e.	Cash	18,000	
	Accounts Receivable		18,000
	Received cash on account.		

f. Paid the following in cash: interest, $1,200; rent, $2,300; salaries, $7,000.

The accounts involved are Interest Expense, Rent Expense, Salary Expense, and Cash.

Interest Expense, Rent Expense, and Salary Expense (all expenses) are all increased, which are debits. Cash (an asset) is decreased, which is a credit.

f.	Interest Expense	1,200	
	Rent Expense	2,300	
	Salary Expense	7,000	
	Cash		10,500
	Paid expenses.		

g. Received a bill for airplane repair costs of $3,500 that will be paid next month.

Repairs are not billed until *after* they have been performed. So the bill received was for repairs made *in the past*. This means that it is a *past* benefit and should be recorded as an expense. So the accounts involved are Repairs Expense and Accounts Payable.

Repairs Expense (an expense) is increased, which is a debit. Accounts Payable (a liability) is increased, which is a credit.

g.	Repairs Expense	3,500	
	Accounts Payable		3,500
	Received repair bill.		

h. Maureen Knight withdrew $6,000 for personal use.

The accounts involved are Maureen Knight, Withdrawals and Cash. Maureen Knight, Withdrawals is increased, which is a debit. This results in a *decrease to owner's equity,* which is a debit. Cash (an asset) is decreased, which is a credit.

h.	Maureen Knight, Withdrawals	6,000	
	Cash		6,000
	Owner withdrawal.		

4 Post from the journal to the ledger

Requirement 3

Post to the ledger.

Part 1	Part 2	**Part 3**	Part 4	Demo Doc Complete

The entire group of accounts is called the **ledger**. A manual system would have a book of account pages and a computerized system would have a printout of all of the accounts. Review Exhibit 2-1 (p. 63) in the main text to follow the flow of accounts into the ledger.

All amounts in the journal entries are put into the individual ledger T-accounts. Debits go on the left side and credits go on the right side.

To add up a T-account, total the debit/left side and total the credit/right side. Subtract the smaller number from the bigger number and put the difference on the side of the bigger number. This gives the *balance* in the T-account (the *net* total of both sides combined).

For example, with Accounts Receivable, the two numbers on the left side total $8,000 + $17,500 = $25,500. The credit/right side totals $18,000. The difference is $25,500 − $18,000 = $7,500. We put the $7,500 on the debit side because that was the side of the bigger number of $25,500.

Another way to think of computing the balance of T-accounts is:

Beginning balance in T-account
+ Increases to T-account
− Decreases to T-account
T-account balance (total)

ASSETS

Cash

Bal.	50,000			
		a.		10,000
		c.		5,000
d.	7,500			
e.	18,000			
		f.		10,500
		h.		6,000
	44,000			

Accounts Receivable

Bal.	8,000		
d.	17,500		
		e.	18,000
	7,500		

Supplies

b.	1,000		
	1,000		

Airplanes

a.	50,000		
	50,000		

LIABILITIES

Accounts Payable

		Bal.	16,000
		b.	1,000
c.	5,000		
		g.	3,500
			15,500

Notes Payable

	a.	40,000
		40,000

OWNER'S EQUITY

Maureen Knight, Capital

	Bal.	42,000
		42,000

Maureen Knight, Withdrawals

h.	6,000	
	6,000	

REVENUES

Service Revenue

	d.	25,000
		25,000

EXPENSES

Interest Expense

f.	1,200	
	1,200	

Rent Expense

f.	2,300	
	2,300	

Salary Expense

f.	7,000	
	7,000	

Repairs Expense

g.	3,500	
	3,500	

Requirement 4

5 Prepare and use a trial balance

Prepare the trial balance of Knight Airlines at April 30, 2008.

Part 1	Part 2	Part 3	**Part 4**	Demo Doc Complete

All of the debits and credits are now listed for the **trial balance**. A trial balance is a list of all of the account titles with their balances at the end of an accounting period. Review the illustration of a trial balance in Exhibit 2-12 (p. 77) of the main text. Again, the accounts are listed in the order of assets, liabilities, equity, revenues, and expenses for consistency.

KNIGHT AIRLINES
Trial Balance
April 30, 2008

Account Title	Balance Debit	Balance Credit
Cash	$ 44,000	
Accounts receivable	7,500	
Supplies	1,000	
Airplanes	50,000	
Accounts payable		$ 15,500
Notes payable		40,000
Maureen Knight, capital		42,000
Maureen Knight, withdrawals	6,000	
Service revenue		25,000
Interest expense	1,200	
Rent expense	2,300	
Salary expense	7,000	
Repairs expense	3,500	
Total	$122,500	$122,500

Part 1	Part 2	Part 3	Part 4	Demo Doc Complete

Quick Practice Questions

True/False

_____ 1. A ledger is a chronological record of transactions.

_____ 2. A chart of accounts lists all of the accounts and their balances.

_____ 3. An asset is an economic resource that will benefit the business in the future.

_____ 4. A note receivable is a written pledge that the customer will pay a fixed amount of money by a certain date.

_____ 5. Posting is the process of transferring information from the trial balance to the financial statements.

_____ 6. Prepaid expenses are listed as expenses on the income statement.

_____ 7. When an owner withdraws cash from the business, assets and owner's equity decrease.

_____ 8. When a business makes a payment on account, assets decrease and liabilities increase.

_____ 9. Every transaction affects only two accounts.

_____ 10. T-accounts help to summarize transactions.

Multiple Choice

1. **A business transaction is first recorded in which of the following?**
   a. Chart of accounts
   b. Journal
   c. Ledger
   d. Trial balance

2. **A trial balance is which of the following?**
   a. A record holding all the accounts
   b. A detailed record of the changes in a particular asset, liability, or owner's equity account
   c. A chronological record of transactions
   d. A list of all the accounts with their balances

3. **Which sequence of actions correctly summarizes the accounting process?**
   a. Prepare a trial balance, journalize transactions, post to the accounts
   b. Post to the accounts, journalize the transactions, prepare a trial balance
   c. Journalize transactions, post to the accounts, prepare a trial balance
   d. Journalize transactions, prepare a trial balance, post to the accounts

4. **Which of the following accounts increase with a credit?**
   a. Cash
   b. Owner's Capital
   c. Accounts Payable
   d. Both (b) and (c) increase when credited

5. A business makes a cash payment of $12,000 to a creditor. Which of the following occurs?
   a. Cash is credited for $12,000.
   b. Cash is debited for $12,000.
   c. Accounts Payable is credited for $12,000.
   d. Both (a) and (c).

6. Liabilities are which of the following?
   a. Debts or obligations owed to creditors
   b. Economic resources that will benefit the entity in the future
   c. Owner's claim to the assets of the business
   d. Amounts earned by providing products or services

7. Which account would normally have a debit balance?
   a. Accrued Liabilities
   b. Notes Payable
   c. Owner's Capital
   d. Accounts Receivable

8. Which of the following is the correct journal entry for a purchase of equipment for $50,000 cash?

		Accounts	Dr	Cr
a.		Equipment	50,000	
		Cash		50,000
b.		Equipment	50,000	
		Owner's Capital		50,000
c.		Accounts Receivable	50,000	
		Equipment		50,000
d.		Cash	50,000	
		Equipment		50,000

9. Which of the following is the correct journal entry for purchasing $5,000 worth of supplies on account?

		Accounts	Dr	Cr
a.		Supplies	5,000	
		Cash		5,000
b.		Accounts Payable	5,000	
		Supplies		5,000
c.		Supplies	5,000	
		Accounts Payable		5,000
d.		Cash	5,000	
		Supplies		5,000

10. Which of the following is the correct journal entry for providing $20,000 worth of consulting services for cash?

	Accounts	Dr	Cr
a.	Service Revenue	20,000	
	Cash		20,000
b.	Accounts Receivable	20,000	
	Service Revenue		20,000
c.	Accounts Receivable	20,000	
	Cash		20,000
d.	Cash	20,000	
	Service Revenue		20,000

Quick Exercises

2-1. Indicate whether a debit or credit is required to record an increase for each of these accounts.

_____Cash   _____Prepaid Rent

_____Owner, Withdrawals   _____Notes Payable

_____Salaries Expense   _____Land

_____Service Revenue   _____Utilities Expense

2-2. Write a brief explanation for the following transactions:

Accounts	Debit	Credit
Cash	10,000	
Owner, Capital		10,000

Accounts	Debit	Credit
Supplies	500	
Accounts Payable		500

Accounts	Debit	Credit
Cash	3,000	
Service Revenue		3,000

Accounts	Debit	Credit
Accounts Receivable	2,000	
Service Revenue		2,000

Accounts	Debit	Credit
Accounts Payable	300	
Cash		300

2-3. Identify the following as an asset, liability, owner's equity, revenue, or expense account. Also indicate the normal balance as a debit or credit.

	Account	Normal Balance
a. Building	_____	_____
b. Accounts Payable	_____	_____
c. Cash	_____	_____
d. Accounts Receivable	_____	_____
e. Prepaid Insurance	_____	_____
f. Supplies	_____	_____
g. Utilities Expense	_____	_____
h. Owner, Capital	_____	_____
i. Owner, Withdrawals	_____	_____

2-4. Journalize the following transactions for the Reid Public Relations Company using these accounts: Cash, Accounts Receivable, Notes Receivable, Supplies, Prepaid Insurance, Accounts Payable, Notes Payable, Reid Capital, Reid Withdrawals, Service Revenue, Salaries Expense, Rent Expense, Insurance Expense.

March 1   J. Reid invested $25,000 cash to begin her public relations company.

Date	Accounts	Debit	Credit

March 2   **Paid $3,000 for March rent.**

Date	Accounts	Debit	Credit

March 4   **Purchased $825 of supplies on account.**

Date	Accounts	Debit	Credit

March 5   **Performed $10,000 of services for a client on account.**

Date	Accounts	Debit	Credit

March 8   **Paid salaries of $2,500.**

Date	Accounts	Debit	Credit

March 15   **Paid the semiannual insurance premium of $1,800 for the period March 15 to September 15.**

Date	Accounts	Debit	Credit

March 20   Signed a bank note and borrowed $20,000 cash.

Date	Accounts	Debit	Credit

March 25   Received $10,000 from customers on account. (See March 5.)

Date	Accounts	Debit	Credit

2-5.   Find the errors in the trial balance shown here and prepare a corrected trial balance using the form on the next page.

COLEMAN COPY CENTER
Trial Balance
March 31, 2008

Account Title	Balance Debit	Credit
Cash	$30,000	
Accounts receivable		$ 2,000
Supplies	600	
Land	50,000	
Accounts payable	2,600	
Note payable		35,000
Jo Coleman, capital		42,550
Jo Coleman, withdrawals		2,400
Service revenue		9,300
Salary expense		2,500
Rent expense		1,200
Interest expense		500
Utilities expense		250
Total	$83,200	$95,700

COLEMAN COPY CENTER
Trial Balance
March 31, 2008

		Account Title	Balance	
			Debit	Credit
		Cash		
		Accounts receivable		
		Supplies		
		Land		
		Accounts payable		
		Note payable		
		Jo Coleman, capital		
		Jo Coleman, withdrawals		
		Service revenue		
		Salary expense		
		Rent expense		
		Interest expense		
		Utilities expense		
		Total		

Do It Yourself! Question 1

Debit/Credit Transaction Analysis

Ted's Repair Shop had the following trial balance on September 1, 2008:

TED'S REPAIR SHOP
Trial Balance
September 1, 2008

Account Title		Balance Debit	Credit
Cash		$6,000	
Accounts receivable		1,200	
Accounts payable			$ 700
Ted Johnson, capital			6,500
Total		$7,200	$7,200

Requirements

1 Use accounting terms

1. Journalize each of the following transactions. Key journal entries by transaction letter.

2 Apply the rules of debit and credit

3 Record transactions in the journal

a. Performed repairs for customers and earned $800 in cash and $1,500 of revenue on account.

Date	Accounts	Debit	Credit

b. Paid $200 cash for supplies.

Date	Accounts	Debit	Credit

c. **Took out a loan of $2,000 cash from City Bank.**

Date	Accounts	Debit	Credit

d. **Paid $3,000 cash to purchase repair tools.**

Date	Accounts	Debit	Credit

e. **Paid the following in cash: interest, $75; rent, $825; salaries, $1,000.**

Date	Accounts	Debit	Credit

f. **Received a telephone bill of $100 that will be paid next month.**

Date	Accounts	Debit	Credit

g. Paid $500 on account.

Date	Accounts	Debit	Credit

h. Received $1,100 on account.

Date	Accounts	Debit	Credit

i. Ted withdrew $1,300 for personal use.

Date	Accounts	Debit	Credit

2. Open the following accounts, with the balances indicated, in the ledger of Ted's Repair Shop. Use the T-account format.

- **Assets**—Cash, $6,000; Accounts Receivable, $1,200; Supplies, no balance; Repair Tools, no balance
- **Liabilities**—Accounts Payable, $700; Loans Payable, no balance
- **Owner's Equity**—Ted Johnson, Capital, $6,500; Ted Johnson, Withdrawals, no balance
- **Revenues**—Service Revenue, no balance
- **Expenses**—(none have balances) Interest Expense, Rent Expense, Salary Expense, Utilities Expense

4 Post from the journal to the ledger

3. Post all transactions in Requirement 1 to the ledger.

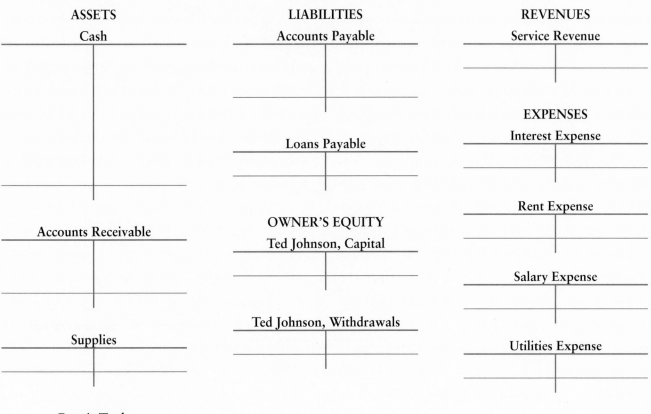

ASSETS

Cash

Accounts Receivable

Supplies

Repair Tools

LIABILITIES

Accounts Payable

Loans Payable

OWNER'S EQUITY

Ted Johnson, Capital

Ted Johnson, Withdrawals

REVENUES

Service Revenue

EXPENSES

Interest Expense

Rent Expense

Salary Expense

Utilities Expense

Prepare and use a trial balance

4. Prepare the trial balance of Ted's Repair Shop at September 30, 2008.

		Account Title	Balance	
			Debit	Credit

TED'S REPAIR SHOP
Trial Balance
September 30, 2008

Quick Practice Solutions

True/False

  F   1. A ledger is a chronological record of transactions.

         False—A journal contains a chronological record of transactions. A ledger is a collection of the accounts and summarizes their balances. (p. 60)

  F   2. A chart of accounts lists all of the accounts and their balances.

         False—A chart of accounts lists all of the accounts along with *account numbers*. A trial balance lists all accounts and their *balances*. (p. 62)

  T   3. An asset is an economic resource that will benefit the business in the future. (p. 60)

  T   4. A note receivable is a written pledge that the customer will pay a fixed amount of money by a certain date. (p. 61)

  F   5. Posting is the process of transferring information from the trial balance to the financial statements.

         False—Posting is the process of transferring information from the *journal to the ledger*. (p. 67)

  F   6. Prepaid expenses are listed as expenses on the income statement.

         False—Prepaid expenses are *assets* and are listed on the *balance sheet*. Can you name an example of a prepaid expense? (p. 61).

  T   7. When an owner withdraws cash from the business, assets and owner's equity decrease. (p. 62)

  F   8. When a business makes a payment on account, assets decrease and liabilities increase.

         False—When a business makes a payment on account, assets *decrease* and liabilities *decrease*. (p. 75)

  F   9. Every transaction affects only two accounts.

         False—Every transaction affects *at least* two accounts. Watch the wording here! Notice that the question uses the word *only* instead of *at least*. Can you describe a transaction that affects more than two accounts? (p. 64)

  T 10. T-accounts help to summarize transactions. (p. 65)

Multiple Choice

1. **A business transaction is first recorded in which of the following?** (p. 60)
   a. Chart of accounts
   b. Journal
   c. Ledger
   d. Trial balance

2. **A trial balance is which of the following?** (p. 60)
   a. A record holding all the accounts
   b. A detailed record of the changes in a particular asset, liability, or owner's equity
   c. A chronological record of transactions
   d. A list of all the accounts with their balances

3. **Which sequence of actions correctly summarizes the accounting process?** (p. 60)
   a. Prepare a trial balance, journalize transactions, post to the accounts
   b. Post to the accounts, journalize the transactions, prepare a trial balance
   c. Journalize transactions, post to the accounts, prepare a trial balance
   d. Journalize transactions, prepare a trial balance, post to the accounts

4. **Which of the following accounts increase with a credit?** (p. 65)
   a. Cash
   b. Owner's Capital
   c. Accounts Payable
   d. Both (b) and (c) increase when credited

5. **A business makes a cash payment of $12,000 to a creditor. Which of the following occurs?** (p. 64)
   a. Cash is credited for $12,000.
   b. Cash is debited for $12,000.
   c. Accounts Payable is credited for $12,000.
   d. Both (a) and (c).

6. **Liabilities are which of the following?** (p. 61)
   a. Debts or obligations owed to creditors
   b. Economic resources that will benefit the entity in the future
   c. Owner's claim to the assets of the business
   d. Amounts earned by providing products or services

7. **Which account would normally have a debit balance?** (p. 69)
   a. Accrued Liabilities
   b. Notes Payable
   c. Owner's Capital
   d. Accounts Receivable

8. Which of the following is the correct journal entry for a purchase of equipment for $50,000 cash? (p. 64)

		Accounts	Dr	Cr
a.		Equipment	50,000	
		Cash		50,000
b.		Equipment	50,000	
		Owner's Capital		50,000
c.		Accounts Receivable	50,000	
		Equipment		50,000
d.		Cash	50,000	
		Equipment		50,000

9. Which of the following is the correct journal entry for purchasing $5,000 worth of supplies on account? (p. 72)

		Accounts	Dr	Cr
a.		Supplies	5,000	
		Cash		5,000
b.		Accounts Payable	5,000	
		Supplies		5,000
c.		Supplies	5,000	
		Accounts Payable		5,000
d.		Cash	5,000	
		Supplies		5,000

10. Which of the following is the correct journal entry for providing $20,000 worth of consulting services for cash? (p. 73)

		Accounts	Dr	Cr
a.		Service Revenue	20,000	
		Cash		20,000
b.		Accounts Receivable	20,000	
		Service Revenue		20,000
c.		Accounts Receivable	20,000	
		Cash		20,000
d.		Cash	20,000	
		Service Revenue		20,000

Quick Exercise

2-1. Indicate whether a debit or credit is required to record an increase for each of these accounts. (p. 65)

_Dr_ Cash   _Dr_ Prepaid Rent

_Dr_ Owner, Withdrawals   _Cr_ Notes Payable

_Dr_ Salaries Expense   _Dr_ Land

_Cr_ Service Revenue   _Dr_ Utilities Expense

2-2. Write a brief explanation for the following transactions: (p. 67)

	Accounts	Debit	Credit
	Cash	10,000	
	Owner, Capital		10,000

   a. Owner investment of cash.

	Accounts	Debit	Credit
	Supplies	500	
	Accounts Payable		500

   b. Purchased supplies on account.

	Accounts	Debit	Credit
	Cash	3,000	
	Service Revenue		3,000

   c. Received cash for services performed.

	Accounts	Debit	Credit
	Accounts Receivable	2,000	
	Service Revenue		2,000

   d. Performed services on account.

Accounts	Debit	Credit
Accounts Payable	300	
Cash		300

e. Paid cash on account.

2-3. Identify the following as an asset, liability, owner's equity, revenue, or expense account. Also indicate the normal balance as a debit or a credit. (p. 63)

	Account	Normal Balance
a. Building	Asset	Debit
b. Accounts Payable	Liability	Credit
c. Cash	Asset	Debit
d. Accounts Receivable	Asset	Debit
e. Prepaid Insurance	Asset	Debit
f. Supplies	Asset	Debit
g. Utilities Expense	Expense	Debit
h. Owner, Capital	Owner's Equity	Credit
i. Owner, Withdrawals	Owner's Equity	Debit

2-4. Journalize the transactions for the Reid Public Relations Company using these accounts: Cash, Accounts Receivable, Notes Receivable, Supplies, Prepaid Insurance, Accounts Payable, Notes Payable, Reid Capital, Reid Withdrawals, Service Revenue, Salaries Expense, Rent Expense, Insurance Expense. (p. 70–76)

March 1   J. Reid invested $25,000 cash to begin her public relations company.

Date	Accounts	Debit	Credit
Mar. 1	Cash	25,000	
	Reid Capital		25,000

March 2   Paid $3,000 for March rent.

Date	Accounts	Debit	Credit
Mar. 2	Rent Expense	3,000	
	Cash		3,000

March 4   Purchased $825 of supplies on account.

Date	Accounts	Debit	Credit
Mar. 4	Supplies	825	
	Accounts Payable		825

March 5   Performed $10,000 of services for a client on account.

Date	Accounts	Debit	Credit
Mar. 5	Accounts Receivable	10,000	
	Service Revenue		10,000

March 8   Paid salaries of $2,500.

Date	Accounts	Debit	Credit
Mar. 8	Salaries Expense	2,500	
	Cash		2,500

March 15   Paid the semiannual insurance premium of $1,800 for the period March 15 to September 15.

Date	Accounts	Debit	Credit
Mar. 15	Prepaid Insurance	1,800	
	Cash		1,800

March 20   **Signed a bank note and borrowed $20,000 cash.**

Date	Accounts	Debit	Credit
Mar. 20	Cash	20,000	
	Notes Payable		20,000

March 25   **Received $10,000 from customers on account. (See March 5.)**

Date	Accounts	Debit	Credit
Mar. 25	Cash	10,000	
	Accounts Receivable		10,000

2-5.   Find the errors in the trial balance that follows and prepare a corrected trial balance. (p. 78)

COLEMAN COPY CENTER
Trial Balance
March 31, 2008

Account Title	Balance Debit	Credit
Cash	$30,000	
Accounts receivable	2,000	
Supplies	600	
Land	50,000	
Accounts payable		$ 2,600
Note payable		35,000
Jo Coleman, capital		42,550
Jo Coleman, withdrawals	2,400	
Service revenue		9,300
Salary expense	2,500	
Rent expense	1,200	
Interest expense	500	
Utilities expense	250	
Total	$89,450	$89,450

Do It Yourself! Question 1 Solutions

Debit/Credit Transaction Analysis

Requirements

1. Journalize each of the following transactions. Key journal entries by transaction letter.

		Accounts Title	Debit	Credit
a.		Cash	800	
		Accounts Receivable	1,500	
		Service Revenue		2,300
		Performed services on account and for cash.		

		Accounts Title	Debit	Credit
b.		Supplies	200	
		Cash		200
		Purchased supplies.		

		Accounts Title	Debit	Credit
c.		Cash	2,000	
		Loans Payable		2,000
		Took out a loan for cash.		

		Accounts Title	Debit	Credit
d.		Repair Tools	3,000	
		Cash		3,000
		Purchased repair tools.		

		Accounts Title	Debit	Credit
e.		Interest Expense	75	
		Rent Expense	825	
		Salary Expense	1,000	
		Cash		1,900
		Purchased repair tools.		

		Accounts Title	Debit	Credit
f.		Utilities Expense	100	
		Accounts Payable		100
		Received utility bill.		

		Accounts Title	Debit	Credit
g.		Accounts Payable	500	
		Cash		500
		Paid on account.		

		Accounts Title	Debit	Credit
h.		Cash	1,100	
		Accounts Receivable		1,100
		Received cash on account.		

		Accounts Title	Debit	Credit
i.		Ted Johnson, Withdrawals	1,300	
		Cash		1,300
		Owner withdrawal.		

2. Open the following accounts, with the balances indicated, in the ledger of Ted's Repair Shop. Use the T-account format.

- **Assets**—Cash, $6,000; Accounts Receivable, $1,200; Supplies, no balance; Repair Tools, no balance
- **Liabilities**—Accounts Payable, $700; Loans Payable, no balance
- **Owner's Equity**—Ted Johnson, Capital, $6,500; Ted Johnson, Withdrawals, no balance
- **Revenues**—Service Revenue, no balance
- **Expenses**—(none have balances) Interest Expense, Rent Expense, Salary Expense, Utilities Expense

3. Post all transactions in Requirement 1 to the ledger.

ASSETS

Cash

Bal.	6,000		
a.	800		
		b.	200
c.	2,000		
		d.	3,000
		e.	1,900
		g.	500
h.	1,100		
		i.	1,300
	3,000		

Accounts Receivable

Bal.	1,200		
a.	1,500		
		h.	1,100
	1,600		

Supplies

b.	200	
	200	

Repair Tools

d.	3,000	
	3,000	

LIABILITIES

Accounts Payable

		Bal.	700
		f.	100
g.	500		
			300

Loans Payable

		c.	2,000
			2,000

OWNER'S EQUITY

Ted Johnson, Capital

		Bal.	6,500
			6,500

Ted Johnson, Withdrawals

i.	1,300	
	1,300	

REVENUES

Service Revenue

		a.	2,300
			2,300

EXPENSES

Interest Expense

e.	75	
	75	

Rent Expense

e.	825	
	825	

Salary Expense

e.	1,000	
	1,000	

Utilities Expense

f.	100	
	100	

4. Prepare the trial balance of Ted's Repair Shop at September 30, 2008.

TED'S REPAIR SHOP
Trial Balance
September 30, 2008

Account Title	Balance Debit	Balance Credit
Cash	$ 3,000	
Accounts receivable	1,600	
Supplies	200	
Repair tools	3,000	
Accounts payable		$ 300
Loans payable		2,000
Ted Johnson, capital		6,500
Ted Johnson, withdrawals	1,300	
Service revenue		2,300
Interest expense	75	
Rent expense	825	
Salary expense	1,000	
Utilities expense	100	
Total	$11,100	$11,100

The Power of Practice

For more practice using the skills learned in this chapter, visit MyAccountingLab. There you will find algorithmically generated questions that are based on these Demo Docs and your main textbook's Review and Assess Your Progress sections.

Go to MyAccountingLab and follow these steps:

1. Direct your URL to www.myaccountinglab.com.
2. Log in using your name and password.
3. Click the MyAccountingLab link.
4. Click Study Plan in the left navigation bar.
5. From the table of contents, select Chapter 2, Recording Business Transactions.
6. Click a link to work tutorial exercises.

3 The Adjusting Process

When you receive your car insurance bill, the period of coverage is always in the future. The bill may indicate that your payment must be received no later than 12:01 a.m. on the day after your current coverage expires to maintain your policy. Your payment is actually a *prepayment*, Prepaid Insurance. Prepaid Insurance is an asset because the insurance coverage is a future benefit. But every day that the car is protected by the insurance policy, part of the benefit is used up. When an asset is used up, it becomes an expense. Technically, every day you are incurring an expense of 1/365 of your annual premium. Assume that you paid $730 for an annual insurance policy in December 2007 for the period covering January 1–December 31, 2008. Each day beginning January 1, you are using up $2 ($730/365 days) of the prepaid insurance and incurring an expense or benefit of $2. At the end of January 1, what is your future benefit? It is $728 because you've benefited from the insurance coverage service you received that day. Technically, you have prepaid insurance with a reduced value of $728 and an expense of $2; the total $730 payment is split between the two accounts. Each day there is an additional $2 expense and $2 less future value in the asset account. Although it would be too cumbersome to "adjust" these accounts on a daily basis, businesses will make adjustments to their records whenever financial statements are prepared.

Learning Objectives

1 Distinguish accrual-basis accounting from cash-basis accounting.

Consider this example: Assume that you have a pet care business; you care for pets in their owners' absence. You had a customer who went away the last week of December and returned on January 1. You charge $140 for the weekly service and are paid on January 1.

- If you are using **cash-basis accounting**, how much revenue would you record in December? In January? Because the cash is **received** in January, $140 would be recorded as revenue in January and none in December.

- If you are using **accrual-basis accounting**, how much revenue would you record in December? In January? Because the revenue is **earned** in December when you performed the services, that is the month you would record $140 of revenue and none in January.

Review Exhibit 3-1 (p. 127) in the main text to reinforce the difference between the two methods of accounting.

2 Apply the revenue and matching principles.

Consider this example: Assume that the Cool Clothing store opened for business on May 15 and pays employees on the 1st and 15th of each month. Employees who worked May 15–31 will be paid on June 1; no payroll payments are made in May. Does this mean that there should be no wage or salary expense for the month of May? Is it fair that Cool Clothing reports the revenue from selling clothing without the related payroll expense? Customers would not be able to view and purchase the clothing without employees to stock the shelves and check out the customers. It makes sense to **match** the payroll expense for the month of May with the sales revenue. *This is a basic concept that is crucial to understand. See Exhibit 3-2 (p. 128) in the main text for a sample business transaction illustrating the appropriate revenue recognition timing. Exhibit 3-3 (p. 129) illustrates the matching principle.*

3 Make adjusting entries.

The following two-step process will facilitate preparing the adjusting journal entries:

1. Determine whether a revenue account needs to be recorded (credited) or an expense account needs to be recorded (debited.)

2. The other account in the entry **MUST** be *either* an asset or a liability account.

If you have determined that revenue needs to be credited, then an asset account must be debited (increased) or a liability account must be debited (decreased). If you have determined that an expense needs to be debited, then an asset account must be credited (decreased) or a liability must be credited (increased). **WATCH OUT:** Cash will **NEVER** be included in an adjusting journal entry. *Review Exhibits 3-7 through 3-10 (pp. 140–143) carefully for a review of the adjusting journal entry process.*

4 Prepare an adjusted trial balance.

Business transactions are journalized and posted; then a trial balance is prepared. After the adjusting journal entries are journalized, they are posted and an adjusted trial balance is prepared. The list of updated account balances is prepared to determine that debits equal credits before preparing the financial statements. *Exhibit 3-10 (p. 143) shows the flow of information from the trial balance to the adjusted trial balance on the work sheet.*

5 Prepare the financial statements from the adjusted trial balance.

Follow the flow of data from the adjusted trial balance in Exhibit 3-10 (p. 143) to the financial statements in *Exhibits 3-11 through 3-13 (p. 145).*

Demo Doc 1

Adjusting Entries for Accrual Accounting

Learning Objectives 1–5

Wood's Restaurant's December 31 (year-end) trial balance (before adjustments) is as follows:

			Balance	
	Account Title		**Debit**	**Credit**
	Cash		$10,600	
	Accounts receivable		14,000	
	Supplies		1,200	
	Prepaid rent		3,000	
	Furniture		15,000	
	Accumulated depreciation—furniture			$ 4,500
	Accounts payable			2,600
	Salary payable			0
	Daniel Wood, capital			40,000
	Daniel Wood, withdrawals		11,500	
	Service revenue			24,000
	Rent expense		5,000	
	Salary expense		10,000	
	Depreciation expense		0	
	Supplies expense		800	
	Total		$71,100	$71,100

WOOD'S RESTAURANT
Trial Balance
Year Ended December 31, 2008

Requirements

1. Open the T-accounts and enter their unadjusted balances.

2. Journalize the following adjusting entries at December 31, 2008. Key the entries by letter.

a. Employees are paid $200 every Friday for the previous five days of work. December 31, 2008, is a Wednesday.

b. Depreciation on the furniture is $1,500 for the year.

c. Supplies on hand at December 31, 2008, are $400.

d. Six months of rent ($3,000) was paid in advance on November 1, 2008. No adjustment has been made to the Prepaid Rent account since then.

e. Accrued revenue of $1,800 must be recorded.

3. Post the adjusting entries.

4. Write the trial balance on a work sheet, enter the adjusting entries, and prepare an adjusted trial balance.

5. Prepare the income statement, statement of owner's equity, and balance sheet for Wood's Restaurant.

6. Would any of these entries be made under the cash basis of accounting? Why or why not?

Demo Doc 1 Solutions

Requirement 1

Open the T-accounts and enter their unadjusted balances.

Part 1	Part 2	Part 3	Part 4	Part 5	Part 6	Part 7	Part 8	Demo Doc Complete

ASSETS

Cash

Bal. 10,600 |

Accounts Receivable

Bal. 14,000 |

Supplies

Bal. 1,200 |

Prepaid Rent

Bal. 3,000 |

Furniture

Bal. 15,000 |

Accumulated Depreciation—Furniture

| Bal. 4,500

LIABILITIES

Accounts Payable

| Bal. 2,600

Salary Payable

|

OWNER S EQUITY

Daniel Wood, Capital

| Bal. 40,000

Daniel Wood, Withdrawals

Bal. 11,500 |

REVENUES

Service Revenue

| Bal. 24,000

EXPENSES

Rent Expense

Bal. 5,000 |

Salary Expense

Bal. 10,000 |

Depreciation Expense

|

Supplies Expense

Bal. 800 |

Requirement 2

Journalize the following adjusting entries at December 31, 2008. Key the entries by letter.

There are five general types of adjusting entries.

- **Prepaid expenses** are assets that are paid for in advance and will be used up in the future like supplies, prepaid rent (see transaction **d**), and insurance. As the asset is used up, the asset account is reduced and an expense is recorded.
- **Depreciation** is the allocation of the plant asset cost over its useful life (see transaction **b**). All plant assets used in the operation of the business, except land, are depreciated. The asset loses usefulness over time and is reduced. The cost of the plant asset is not reduced directly. Accumulated Depreciation, a contra asset account, is used to record the loss of asset usefulness. Depreciation expense matches the revenue generated from sales made possible from the use of these assets that are depreciated.

- **Accrued Expenses** are expenses the business has incurred but not yet paid. Common examples may be salaries (see transaction **a**) and utilities.
- **Accrued Revenue** is a revenue that has been earned but not collected in cash (see transaction **e**).
- **Unearned Revenue** is a liability that results from receiving cash before earning it. The company owes the customer a product or a service in the future. When the product is sold or the service is performed, the liability is reduced and the revenue is earned.

2 Apply the revenue and matching principles

3 Make adjusting entries

a. Employees are paid $200 every Friday for the previous five days of work. December 31, 2008, is a Wednesday.

Part 1	**Part 2**	Part 3	Part 4	Part 5	Part 6	Part 7	Part 8	Demo Doc Complete

If employees are paid $200 for five days of work, then they are paid $200/5 = $40 per day. By the end of the day on Wednesday, December 31, the employees have worked for three days and have not been paid. This means that Wood owes employees $40 × 3 = $120 of salary at December 31.

If the salaries have not been paid, then they are pay*able* (or in other words, they are *owed*). This means that they must be recorded as some kind of payable account. Normally, we might consider using Accounts Payable, but this account is usually reserved for *bills* received. The employees do not send Wood a bill. They simply expect to be paid and Wood knows that the salaries are owed. This means that we put this into another payable account. In this case, Salary Payable is most appropriate.

Because salary is not owed until work is performed, we know that Wood's employees have already worked. This is a *past* benefit, which means that we need to record an expense (in this case, Salary Expense).

There is an increase to Salary Expense (a debit) and an increase to the liability Salary Payable (a credit) of $120.

a.	Salary Expense (3 days × $200/5 days)	120	
	Salary Payable		120
	To accrue salary expense.		

3 Make adjusting entries

b. Depreciation on the furniture is $1,500 for the year.

The entry to record depreciation expense is *always* the same. It is only the *number* (dollar amount) in the entry that changes. There is always an increase to Depreciation Expense (a debit) and an increase to the contra asset account of Accumulated Depreciation (a credit). Because we are given the depreciation expense of $1,500, we simply write the entry with that amount.

b.	Depreciation Expense	1,500	
	Accumulated Depreciation—Furniture		1,500
	To record depreciation expense.		

Apply the revenue and matching principles

 Make adjusting entries

c. Supplies on hand at December 31, 2008, are $400.

Before adjustments, there is $1,200 in the Supplies account. If only $400 of supplies remains, then the other $800 must have been used ($1,200 − $400 = $800).

Supplies are an asset, a *future* benefit to Wood. Once the supplies are used, they are a *past* benefit. This means that they are no longer assets, so the Supplies asset must be decreased by $800 (a credit). *Past* benefits are expenses, so Supplies Expense must be increased (a debit).

c.	Supplies Expense ($1,200 − $400)	800	
	Supplies		800
	To record supplies used.		

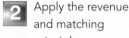 Apply the revenue and matching principles

 Make adjusting entries

d. Six months of rent ($3,000) was paid in advance on November 1, 2008. No adjustment has been made to the Prepaid Rent account since then.

Wood prepaid $3,000 for six months of rent on November 1. This means that Wood pays $3,000/6 = $500 a month for rent. At December 31, two months have passed since the prepayment, so two months of the prepayment have been used. The amount of rent used is 2 × $500 = $1,000.

When something is prepaid, it is a *future* benefit (an asset) because the business is now entitled to receive goods or services. Once those goods or services are received (in this case, once Wood has occupied the building being rented), this becomes a *past* benefit and, therefore, an expense. This means that Rent Expense must be increased (a debit) and the Prepaid Rent (an asset) must be decreased (a credit).

d.	Rent Expense ($3,000 × 2 months/6 months)	1,000	
	Prepaid Rent		1,000
	To record insurance expense.		

 Apply the revenue and matching principles

Make adjusting entries

e. Accrued revenue of $1,800 must be recorded.

Accrued revenue is another way of saying "accounts receivable" (or payment in the future). If accrued revenue is recorded, it means that accounts receivable are also recorded (that is, customers received goods or services from the business, but the business has not yet received the cash). The business is entitled to these receivables because the revenue has been earned.

Note that not all revenue is *accrued* revenue. This is *only* the revenue that is earned but not immediately received from the customer (that is, the accounts receivable). Revenues that are earned and received immediately in cash are *not* accrued revenues.

Service Revenue must be increased by $1,800 (a credit) and the Accounts Receivable asset must be increased by $1,800 (a debit).

e.	Accounts Receivable	1,800	
	Service Revenue		1,800
	To accrue revenue earned.		

Requirement 3

Post the adjusting entries.

Part 1	Part 2	**Part 3**	Part 4	Part 5	Part 6	Part 7	Part 8	Demo Doc Complete

ASSETS

Cash

Bal.	10,600	

Accounts Receivable

	14,000		
e.	1,800		
Bal.	15,800		

Supplies

	1,200		
		c.	800
Bal.	400		

Prepaid Rent

	3,000		
		d.	1,000
Bal.	2,000		

Furniture

Bal.	15,000	

Accumulated Depreciation—Furniture

			4,500
		b.	1,500
		Bal.	6,000

LIABILITIES

Accounts Payable

		Bal.	2,600

Salary Payable

		a.	120
		Bal.	120

OWNER'S EQUITY

Daniel Wood, Capital

		Bal.	40,000

Daniel Wood, Withdrawals

Bal.	11,500	

REVENUES

Service Revenue

			24,000
		e.	1,800
		Bal.	25,800

EXPENSES

Rent Expense

	5,000		
d.	1,000		
Bal.	6,000		

Salary Expense

	10,000		
a.	120		
Bal.	10,120		

Depreciation Expense

b.	1,500		
Bal.	1,500		

Supplies Expense

	800		
c.	800		
Bal.	1,600		

Prepare an adjusted trial balance

Requirement 4

Write the trial balance on a work sheet, enter the adjusting entries, and prepare an adjusted trial balance.

| Part 1 | Part 2 | Part 3 | **Part 4** | Part 5 | Part 6 | Part 7 | Part 8 | Demo Doc Complete |

WOOD'S RESTAURANT
Preparation of Adjusted Trial Balance
Year Ended December 31, 2008

Account Title	Trial Balance Debit	Trial Balance Credit	Adjustments Debit	Adjustments Credit	Adjusted Trial Balance Debit	Adjusted Trial Balance Credit
Cash	$10,600				$10,600	
Accounts receivable	14,000		e. $1,800		15,800	
Supplies	1,200			c. 800	400	
Prepaid rent	3,000			d. 1,000	2,000	
Furniture	15,000				15,000	
Accumulated depreciation—furniture		$ 4,500		b. 1,500		$ 6,000
Accounts payable		2,600				2,600
Salary payable		0		a. 120		120
Daniel Wood, capital		40,000				40,000
Daniel Wood, withdrawals	11,500				11,500	
Service revenue		24,000		e. 1,800		25,800
Rent expense	5,000		d. 1,000		6,000	
Salary expense	10,000		a. 120		10,120	
Depreciation expense	0		b. 1,500		1,500	
Supplies expense	800		c. 800		1,600	
Total	$71,100	$71,100	$5,220	$5,220	$74,520	$74,520

Prepare the financial statements from the adjusted trial balance.

Requirement 5

Prepare the income statement, statement of owner's equity, and balance sheet for Wood's Restaurant.

| Part 1 | Part 2 | Part 3 | Part 4 | **Part 5** | Part 6 | Part 7 | Part 8 | Demo Doc Complete |

WOOD'S RESTAURANT
Income Statement
Year Ended December 31, 2008

Revenue			
Service revenue			$25,800
Expenses:			
Salary expense		$10,120	
Rent expense		6,000	
Supplies expense		1,600	
Depreciation expense		1,500	
Total expenses			19,220
Net income			$ 6,580

| Part 1 | Part 2 | Part 3 | Part 4 | Part 5 | **Part 6** | Part 7 | Part 8 | Demo Doc Complete |

Remember, the one account that has not yet been updated is Daniel Wood, Capital. The amount of $40,000 in this account is the amount from the beginning of the year (January 1). To update the account, we need to prepare the statement of owner's equity.

| Part 1 | Part 2 | Part 3 | Part 4 | Part 5 | Part 6 | **Part 7** | Part 8 | Demo Doc Complete |

WOOD'S RESTAURANT
Statement of Owner's Equity
Year Ended December 31, 2008

Daniel Wood, capital, January 1, 2008	$ 40,000
Add: Net income for month	6,580
	46,580
Less: Withdrawals by owner	(11,500)
Daniel Wood, capital, December 31, 2008	$ 35,080

We use this updated Daniel Wood, Capital amount on the balance sheet.

WOOD'S RESTAURANT
Balance Sheet
December 31, 2008

Assets			Liabilities	
Cash		$10,600	Accounts payable	$ 2,600
Accounts receivable		15,800	Salary payable	120
Prepaid rent		400	Total liabilities	2,720
Supplies		2,000		
Furniture	$15,000			
Less: Accumulated			Equity	
depreciation	(6,000)	9,000	Daniel Wood, capital	35,080
Total assets		$37,800	Total liabilities and equity	$37,800

1
Distinguish accrual accounting from cash-basis accounting

Requirement 6

Would any of these entries be made under the cash basis of accounting? Why or why not?

Part 1	Part 2	Part 3	Part 4	Part 5	Part 6	Part 7	**Part 8**	Demo Doc Complete

Cash-basis accounting *only* records a journal entry when cash is involved. This means that there must be a line for cash in the journal entry in order for it to be recorded under the cash basis of accounting.

Because none of these adjusting entries deal with cash, none of them are relevant (that is, none of them would be recorded) under the cash basis of accounting.

On the other hand, accrual-basis accounting records revenue when it is earned and expenses when they are incurred. Revenue is earned when services are performed or goods are sold. Expenses are incurred when the service is received or the asset is used up. This method is in accordance with generally accepted accounting principles.

Part 1	Part 2	Part 3	Part 4	Part 5	Part 6	Part 7	Part 8	**Demo Doc Complete**

Quick Practice Questions

True/False

_____ 1. Revenue is recorded when it is earned, usually when a good or service has been delivered to the customer.

_____ 2. The time-period concept provides for periodic reporting at regular intervals.

_____ 3. An accounting year that ends on a date other than December 31 is called an interim year.

_____ 4. The revenue principle requires that a cash deposit for future construction be recorded as revenue.

_____ 5. Adjusting journal entries are made at the end of the period.

_____ 6. The income statement is the first financial statement that should be prepared.

_____ 7. Every adjusting journal entry affects one income statement account and one balance sheet account.

_____ 8. An accrual is an expense that is recorded after it is paid.

_____ 9. Accumulated Depreciation is a liability account.

_____ 10. Unearned Service Revenue appears on the income statement.

Multiple Choice

1. **What items should be matched according to the matching principle?**
   a. Debits with credits
   b. Assets with liabilities
   c. Expenses with revenues
   d. Accruals with prepaids

2. **When is revenue recorded under the cash-basis system of accounting?**
   a. When cash is received
   b. When revenue is earned
   c. When cash is received only if related expenses have been incurred
   d. In the period the related expenses are paid

3. **What do adjusting entries properly measure?**
   a. Net income for the period
   b. The assets, liabilities, and owner's equity on the balance sheet
   c. Both a and b
   d. Neither a nor b

4. Which of the following entities would most likely have an Unearned Revenue account?
    a. A local pizza store
    b. An accounting firm
    c. A department store
    d. A magazine publisher

5. Georgia Industries paid $48,000 for two years of insurance coverage on July 1, 2007. The company prepares financial statements on July 31, 2007. What is the amount of insurance expense on July 31?
    a. $48,000
    b. $ 2,000
    c. $24,000
    d. $46,000

6. Using the information from question 5, what is the adjusted balance in Prepaid Insurance on December 31, 2007?
    a. $36,000
    b. $24,000
    c. $12,000
    d. $38,000

7. *Sports Illustrated* receives $120,000 on September 1, 2008, for one year's worth of magazine subscriptions for the year beginning September 1, 2008. What is the journal entry to record the prepaid subscriptions?

	Accounts	Debit	Credit
a.	Accounts Receivable	120,000	
	Unearned Subscription Revenue		120,000
b.	Cash	120,000	
	Subscription Revenue		120,000
c.	Cash	120,000	
	Unearned Subscription Revenue		120,000
d.	Accounts Receivable	120,000	
	Subscription Revenue		120,000

8. Which of the following accounts is depreciated?
    a. Building
    b. Land
    c. Supplies
    d. Prepaid Insurance

9. What is book value?
    a. The sum of all the depreciation recorded for the asset
    b. The cost of the depreciable asset
    c. The cost of the depreciable asset divided by the useful life
    d. The cost of the depreciable asset minus Accumulated Depreciation

10. Mason Company has a weekly payroll of $5,000. Wages are paid every Friday for the work performed Monday through Friday of that week. Assuming that the accounting period ends on a Tuesday, what amount of Wages Expense should be recorded on that date?
   a. $1,000
   b. $2,000
   c. $3,000
   d. $4,000

Quick Exercises

3-1.   Central University received $840,000 in tuition from students in August 2007. The tuition is for the four-month semester, September–December 2007. What is the amount of revenue that should be recorded for the month of September?

   a. $_____ assuming the cash basis of accounting.
   b. $_____ assuming the accrual basis of accounting.

3-2.   For each of the following situations, indicate if an expense or revenue should be recorded and the amount of the adjustment at the end of the month on January 31, 2008.

	Revenue or Expense	Adjustment Amount
a. $1,500 of supplies is purchased during January. On January 31, there is $800 of supplies remaining.	_____	_____
b. The five-day weekly payroll is $6,000. Employees worked the last two days of January and have not been paid by January 31.	_____	_____
c. $750 of Unearned Revenue has been earned in January.	_____	_____
d. Depreciation on equipment is $3,600 for the year.	_____	_____
e. Services of $2,300 were performed on January 31 and have not been recorded.	_____	_____

3-3.   Journalize the required adjusting journal entries using the information in 3-2.

   a.

Date	Accounts	Debit	Credit

b.

Date	Accounts	Debit	Credit

c.

Date	Accounts	Debit	Credit

d.

Date	Accounts	Debit	Credit

e.

Date	Accounts	Debit	Credit

3-4.   Following is the trial balance for Coleman Copy Center:

COLEMAN COPY CENTER
Trial Balance
March 31, 2008

		Balance	
Account Title		Debit	Credit
Cash		$30,000	
Accounts receivable		2,000	
Supplies		600	
Land		50,000	
Accounts payable			$ 2,600
Note payable			35,000
Jo Coleman, capital			42,550
Jo Coleman, withdrawals		2,400	
Service revenue			9,300
Salary expense		2,500	
Rent expense		1,200	
Interest expense		500	
Utilities expense		250	
Total		$89,450	$89,450

Prepare (a) an income statement and (b) a statement of owner's equity for the month ending March 31, 2008.

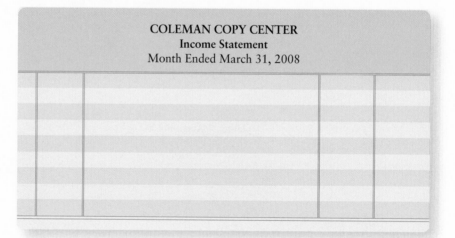

COLEMAN COPY CENTER
Income Statement
Month Ended March 31, 2008

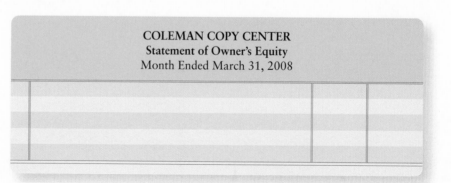

COLEMAN COPY CENTER
Statement of Owner's Equity
Month Ended March 31, 2008

3-5.   Using the trial balance for Coleman Copy Center in 3-4, prepare the balance sheet at March 31, 2008.

COLEMAN COPY CENTER Balance Sheet March 31, 2008			

Do It Yourself! Question 1

Angela's Business Services has the following balances on its December 31 (year-end) trial balance (before adjustments):

	Account Title	Balance Debit	Balance Credit
	ANGELA'S BUSINESS SERVICES Trial Balance December 31		
	Cash	$ 40,400	
	Prepaid insurance	4,800	
	Supplies	13,000	
	Office equipment	25,000	
	Accumulated depreciation—equipment		$ 7,500
	Accounts payable		5,300
	Salary payable		
	Unearned revenue		6,800
	Angela Waring, capital		60,000
	Angela Waring, withdrawals	8,000	
	Service revenue		80,000
	Insurance expense	13,200	
	Salary expense	45,000	
	Depreciation expense		
	Supplies expense	10,200	
	Total	$159,600	$159,600

Requirements

1. Open the T-accounts and enter the unadjusted balances.

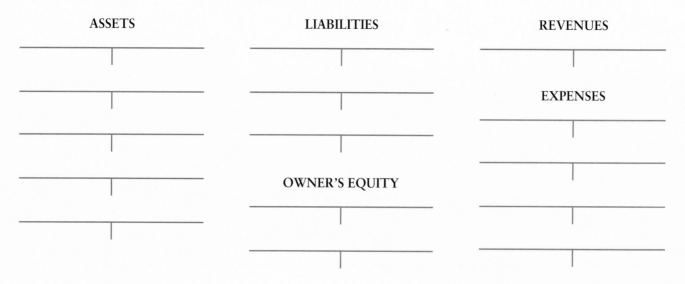

ASSETS

LIABILITIES

REVENUES

EXPENSES

OWNER'S EQUITY

2. Journalize the following adjusting entries at December 31, 2008. Key the entries by letter.

 Apply the revenue and matching principles

3 Make adjusting entries

a. Only $1,500 of the unearned revenue remains unearned.

Date	Accounts	Debit	Credit

b. Depreciation on the office equipment is $2,500 for the year.

Date	Accounts	Debit	Credit

c. Employees earned salaries of $4,000 that have not been paid.

Date	Accounts	Debit	Credit

d. $5,100 of supplies have been used.

Date	Accounts	Debit	Credit

e. Four months of insurance ($4,800) was paid in advance on December 1, 2008. No adjustment has been made to the Prepaid Insurance account since then.

Date	Accounts	Debit	Credit

3. Post the adjusting entries.

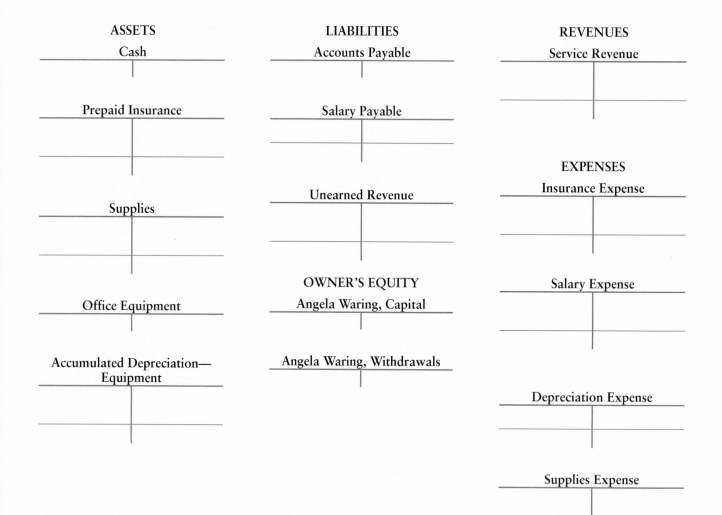

ASSETS
Cash

Prepaid Insurance

Supplies

Office Equipment

Accumulated Depreciation—
Equipment

LIABILITIES
Accounts Payable

Salary Payable

Unearned Revenue

OWNER'S EQUITY
Angela Waring, Capital

Angela Waring, Withdrawals

REVENUES
Service Revenue

EXPENSES
Insurance Expense

Salary Expense

Depreciation Expense

Supplies Expense

Prepare an adjusted
trial balance

4. Write the trial balance on a work sheet, enter the adjusting entries, and prepare an adjusted trial balance.

 Prepare the financial
statements from the
adjusted trial balance

5. Prepare the income statement, statement of owner's equity, and balance sheet for Angela's Business Services.

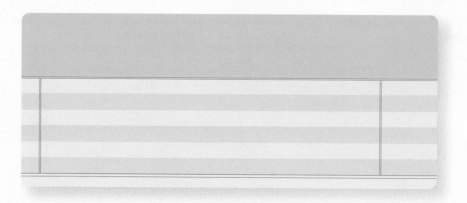

Do It Yourself! Question 2

Everly Industries is preparing its financial statements for the year ended December 31, 2009. Three accounting issues have been discovered.

Requirement

1. Make the necessary adjusting entry for each situation.

a. **Employees work five days a week (Monday through Friday) and are paid $7,500 for the previous week of work each Friday. December 31, 2009, falls on a Thursday.**

Date	Accounts	Debit	Credit

b. **The T-account for supplies shows an unadjusted balance of $1,000. However, there is only $350 of supplies on hand at December 31, 2009.**

Date	Accounts	Debit	Credit

c. **The company has forgotten to record four months of interest expense ($80 per month) that has been incurred but not yet paid.**

Date	Accounts	Debit	Credit

Quick Practice Solutions

True/False

___T___ 1. Revenue is recorded when it is earned, usually when a good or service has been delivered to the customer. (p. 127)

___T___ 2. The time-period concept provides for periodic reporting at regular intervals. (p. 129)

___F___ 3. An accounting year that ends on a date other than December 31 is called an interim year.

   False—An accounting year that ends on a date other than December 31 is called a *fiscal* year. (p. 127)

___F___ 4. The revenue principle requires that a cash deposit for future construction be recorded as revenue.

   False—The revenue principle requires that revenue be recorded when it has been *earned*. The cash received for future construction has not been earned yet. (p. 128)

___T___ 5. Adjusting journal entries are made at the end of the period. (p. 130)

___T___ 6. The income statement is the first financial statement that should be prepared. (p. 144)

___T___ 7. Every adjusting journal entry affects one income statement account and one balance sheet account. (p. 131)

___F___ 8. An accrual is an expense that is recorded after it is paid.

   False—An accrual is an expense that is recorded *before* it is paid. (p. 131)

___F___ 9. Accumulated Depreciation is a liability account.

   False—Accumulated Depreciation is a *contra asset* account. (p. 134)

___F___ 10. Unearned Service Revenue appears on the income statement.

   False—Unearned Service Revenue is a liability and appears on the *balance sheet*. (p. 139)

Multiple Choice

1. **What items should be matched according to the matching principle?** (p. 129)
   a. Debits with credits
   b. Assets with liabilities
   c. Expenses with revenues
   d. Accruals with prepaids

2. **When is revenue recorded under the cash-basis system of accounting?** (p. 127)
   a. When cash is received
   b. When revenue is earned
   c.. When cash is received only if related expenses have been incurred
   d. In the period the related expenses are paid

3. **What do adjusting entries properly measure?** (p. 131)
   a. Net income for the period
   b. The assets, liabilities, and owner's equity on the balance sheet
   c. Both a and b
   d. Neither a nor b

4. **Which of the following entities would most likely have an Unearned Revenue account?** (p. 138)
   a. A local pizza store
   b. An accounting firm
   c. A department store
   d. A magazine publisher

5. **Georgia Industries paid $48,000 for two years of insurance coverage on July 1, 2007. The company prepares financial statements on July 31, 2007. What is the amount of insurance expense on July 31?** (p. 131)
   a. $48,000
   b. $ 2,000
   c. $24,000
   d. $46,000

6. **Using the information from question 5, what is the adjusted balance in Prepaid Insurance on December 31, 2007?** (p. 131)
   a. $36,000
   b.. $24,000
   c. $12,000
   d. $38,000

7. *Sports Illustrated* **receives $120,000 on September 1, 2008, for one year's worth of magazine subscriptions for the year beginning September 1, 2008. What is the journal entry to record the prepaid subscriptions?** (p. 138)

	Accounts	Debit	Credit
a.	Accounts Receivable	120,000	
	Unearned Subscription Revenue		120,000
b.	Cash	120,000	
	Subscription Revenue		120,000
c.	Cash	120,000	
	Unearned Subscription Revenue		120,000
d.	Accounts Receivable	120,000	
	Subscription Revenue		120,000

8. Which of the following accounts is depreciated? (p. 133)
   a. Building
   b. Land
   c. Supplies
   d. Prepaid Insurance

9. What is book value? (p. 134)
   a. The sum of all the depreciation recorded for the asset
   b. The cost of the depreciable asset
   c. The cost of the depreciable asset divided by the useful life
   d. The cost of the depreciable asset minus Accumulated Depreciation

10. Mason Company has a weekly payroll of $5,000. Wages are paid every Friday for the work performed Monday through Friday of that week. Assuming that the accounting period ends on a Tuesday, what amount of Wages Expense should be recorded on that date? (p. 136)
    a. $1,000
    b. $2,000
    c. $3,000
    d. $4,000

Quick Exercise

3-1.   Central University received $840,000 in tuition from students in August 2007. The tuition is for the four-month semester, September–December 2007. What is the amount of revenue that should be recorded for the month of September? (p. 138)

   a. $ 840,000 assuming the cash basis of accounting.
   b. $ 210,000 assuming the accrual basis of accounting.

3-2.   For each of the following situations, indicate if an expense or revenue needs to be recorded and the amount of the adjustment at the end of the month on January 31, 2008. (p. 131)

	Revenue or Expense	Adjustment Amount
a. $1,500 of supplies is purchased during January. On January 31 there is $800 of supplies remaining.	Expense	$700
b. The five-day weekly payroll is $6,000. Employees worked the last two days of January and have not been paid by January 31.	Expense	$2,400
c. $750 of Unearned Revenue has been earned in January.	Revenue	$750
d. Depreciation on equipment is $3,600 for the year.	Expense	$300
e. Services of $2,300 were performed on January 31 and have not been recorded.	Revenue	$2,300

3-3. Journalize the required adjusting journal entries using the information in
      3-2. (p. 131)

a.

Date	Accounts	Debit	Credit
1/31/08	Supplies Expense	700	
	Supplies		700

b.

Date	Accounts	Debit	Credit
1/31/08	Salary Expense	2,400	
	Salary Payable		2,400

c.

Date	Accounts	Debit	Credit
1/31/08	Unearned Revenue	750	
	Service Revenue		750

d.

Date	Accounts	Debit	Credit
1/31/08	Depreciation—Equipment	300	
	Accumulated Depreciation—Equipment		300

e.

Date	Accounts	Debit	Credit
1/31/08	Accounts Receivable	2,300	
	Service Revenue		2,300

3-4. Following is the trial balance for Coleman Copy Center:

		Account Title	Debit	Credit
		COLEMAN COPY CENTER		
		Trial Balance		
		March 31, 2008		
			Balance	
		Account Title	**Debit**	**Credit**
		Cash	$30,000	
		Accounts receivable	2,000	
		Supplies	600	
		Land	50,000	
		Accounts payable		$ 2,600
		Note payable		35,000
		Jo Coleman, capital		42,550
		Jo Coleman, withdrawals	2,400	
		Service revenue		9,300
		Salary expense	2,500	
		Rent expense	1,200	
		Interest expense	500	
		Utilities expense	250	
		Total	$89,450	$89,450

Prepare (a) an income statement and (b) a statement of owner's equity for the month ending March 31, 2008. (p. 144)

a.

		COLEMAN COPY CENTER		
		Income Statement		
		Month Ended March 31, 2008		
		Revenue:		
		Service revenue		$9,300
		Expenses:		
		Salary expense	2,500	
		Rent expense	1,200	
		Interest expense	500	
		Utilities expense	250	
		Total expenses	4,450	
		Net income		$4,850

b.

COLEMAN COPY CENTER
Statement of Owner's Equity
Month Ended March 31, 2008

Liz Violet, capital, May 1, 2008	$42,550
Add: Net income	4,850
	47,400
Less: Withdrawals	(2,400)
Jo Coleman, capital, May 31, 2008	$45,000

3-5. Using the trial balance for Coleman Copy Center in 3-4, prepare the balance sheet at March 31, 2008. (p. 144)

COLEMAN COPY CENTER
Balance Sheet
March 31, 2008

Assets		Liabilities	
Cash	$30,000	Accounts payable	$ 2,600
Accounts receivable	2,000	Note payable	35,000
Supplies	600	Total liabilities	37,600
Land	50,000		
		Owner's Equity	
		Jo Coleman, capital	45,000
		Total liabilities and	
Total assets	$82,600	owner's equity	$82,600

Do It Yourself! Question 1 Solutions

Requirements

1. Open the ledger accounts with the unadjusted balances.

ASSETS	LIABILITIES	REVENUES

Cash

Bal.   40,400

Prepaid Insurance

Bal.   4,800

Supplies

Bal.   13,000

Office Equipment

Bal.   25,000

Accumulated Depreciation— Equipment

Bal.   7,500

Accounts Payable

Bal.   5,300

Salary Payable

Unearned Revenue

Bal.   6,800

OWNER'S EQUITY

Angela Waring, Capital

Bal.   60,000

Angela Waring, Withdrawals

Bal.   8,000

Service Revenue

Bal.   80,000

EXPENSES

Insurance Expense

Bal. 13,200

Salary Expense

Bal. 45,000

Depreciation Expense

Supplies Expense

Bal. 10,200

2. Journalize the following adjusting entries at December 31, 2008. Key the entries by letter.

a. Only $1,500 of the unearned revenue remains unearned.

a.	Unearned Revenue ($6,800 – $1,500)	5,300	
	Service Revenue		5,300
	To record service revenue collected in advance.		

b. Depreciation on the office equipment is $2,500 for the year.

b.	Depreciation Expense	2,500	
	Accumulated Depreciation—Equipment		2,500
	To record depreciation expense.		

c. Employees earned salaries of $4,000 that have not been paid.

c.	Salary Expense	4,000	
	Salary Payable		4,000
	To accrue salary expense.		

d. $5,100 of supplies have been used.

d.	Supplies Expense	5,100	
	Supplies		5,100
	To record supplies used.		

e. Four months of insurance ($4,800) was paid in advance on December 1, 2008. No adjustment has been made to the Prepaid Insurance account since.

e.	Insurance Expense ($4,800 × 1 month/4 months)	1,200	
	Prepaid Insurance		1,200
	To record insurance expense.		

3. Post the adjusting entries.

ASSETS

Cash

Bal.	40,400	

Prepaid Insurance

	4,800		
		e.	1,200
Bal.	3,600		

Supplies

	13,000		
		d.	5,100
Bal.	7,900		

Office Equipment

Bal.	25,000	

Accumulated Depreciation— Equipment

			7,500
		b.	2,500
		Bal.	10,000

LIABILITIES

Accounts Payable

		Bal.	5,300

Salary Payable

		c.	4,000
		Bal.	4,000

Unearned Revenue

			6,800
a.	5,300		
		Bal.	1,500

OWNER'S EQUITY

Angela Waring, Capital

		Bal.	60,000

Angela Waring, Withdrawals

Bal.	8,000	

REVENUES

Service Revenue

			80,000
		a.	5,300
		Bal.	85,300

EXPENSES

Insurance Expense

	13,200	
e.	1,200	
Bal.	14,400	

Salary Expense

	45,000	
c.	4,000	
Bal.	49,000	

Depreciation Expense

b.	2,500	
Bal.	2,500	

Supplies Expense

	10,200	
d.	5,100	
Bal.	15,300	

4. Write the trial balance on a work sheet, enter the adjusting entries, and prepare an adjusted trial balance.

ANGELA'S BUSINESS SERVICES
Preparation of Adjusted Trial Balance
Year Ended December 31, 2008

Account Title	Trial Balance Debit	Trial Balance Credit	Adjustments Debit	Adjustments Credit	Adjusted Trial Balance Debit	Adjusted Trial Balance Credit
Cash	$ 40,400				$ 40,400	
Prepaid insurance	4,800			(e)$ 1,200	3,600	
Supplies	13,000			(d) 5,100	7,900	
Office equipment	25,000				25,000	
Accumulated depreciation—equipment		$ 7,500		(b) 2,500		$ 10,000
Accounts payable		5,300				5,300
Salary payable				(c) 4,000		4,000
Unearned revenue		6,800	(a)$ 5,300			1,500
Angela Waring, capital		60,000				60,000
Angela Waring, withdrawals	8,000				8,000	
Service revenue		80,000		(a) 5,300		85,300
Insurance expense	13,200		(e) 1,200		14,400	
Salary expense	45,000		(c) 4,000		49,000	
Depreciation expense			(b) 2,500		2,500	
Supplies expense	10,200		(d) 5,100		15,300	
Total	$159,600	$159,600	$18,100	$18,100	$166,100	$166,100

5. Prepare the income statement, statement of owner's equity, and balance sheet for Angela's Business Services.

ANGELA'S BUSINESS SERVICES
Income Statement
Year Ended December 31, 2008

Revenue:		
Service revenue		$85,300
Expenses:		
Salary expense	$49,000	
Supplies expense	15,300	
Insurance expense	14,400	
Depreciation expense	2,500	
Total expenses		81,200
Net income		$ 4,100

ANGELA'S BUSINESS SERVICES
Statement of Owner's Equity
Year Ended December 31, 2008

Angela Waring, capital, January 1, 2008	$60,000
Add: Net income for month	4,100
	64,100
Less: Withdrawals by owner	(8,000)
Angela Waring, capital, December 31, 2008	$56,100

ANGELA'S BUSINESS SERVICES
Balance Sheet
December 31, 2008

Assets			Liabilities	
Cash		$40,400	Accounts payable	$ 5,300
Prepaid insurance		3,600	Salary payable	4,000
Supplies		7,900	Unearned revenue	1,500
Office equipment	$25,000		Total liabilities	10,800
Less: Accumulated			**Equity**	
depreciation	(10,000)	15,000	Angela Waring, capital	56,100
Total assets		$66,900	Total liabilities and equity	$66,900

Do it Yourself! Question 2 Solutions

Requirement

1. Make the necessary adjusting entry for each situation.

a. **Employees work five days a week (Monday through Friday) and are paid $7,500 for the previous week of work each Friday. December 31, 2009, falls on a Thursday.**

$7,500/5 days = $1,500 salary per day of work

Monday through Thursday = 4 days of work

4 × $1,500 = $6,000

Salary Expense ($7,500 × 4 days/5 days)		6,000	
Salary Payable			6,000
To accrue salary expense.			

b. **The T-account for supplies shows an unadjusted balance of $1,000. However, there is only $350 of supplies on hand at December 31, 2009.**

$1,000 − $350 = $650 of supplies used

Supplies Expense ($1,000 – $350)		650	
Supplies			650
To record supplies used.			

c. **The company has forgotten to record four months of interest expense ($80 per month) that has been incurred but not yet paid.**

4 months × $80 per month = $320

Interest Expense (4 months × $80)		320	
Interest Payable			320
To accrue interest expense.			

The Power of Practice

For more practice using the skills learned in this chapter, visit MyAccountingLab. There you will find algorithmically generated questions that are based on these Demo Docs and your main textbook's Review and Assess Your Progress sections.

Go to MyAccountingLab and follow these steps:

1. Direct your URL to www.myaccountinglab.com.
2. Log in using your name and password.
3. Click the MyAccountingLab link.
4. Click Study Plan in the left navigation bar.
5. From the table of contents, select Chapter 3, The Adjusting Process.
6. Click a link to work tutorial exercises.

4 Completing the Accounting Cycle

WHAT YOU PROBABLY ALREADY KNOW

If you work, you have probably noticed that your pay stub includes year-to-date earnings. When a new year begins, the year-to-date totals from last year are gone and the year-to-date earnings include only the current year. Last year's records are not erased or unimportant. Earnings from last year are reported for each employee on a W-2 form, Wage and Tax Statement. This form is sent to employees in the new year to attach to their income tax return. The year-to-date earnings are zeroed out to be ready to accumulate earnings in the new year. The same thing happens in a business. At the end of the accounting year, the earnings and revenue accounts are zeroed out to get ready for the new year.

Learning Objectives

1 Prepare an accounting work sheet.

A **work sheet** is a multicolumned document or spreadsheet that is used to summarize accounting data at the end of the period. In Chapter 3, Exhibit 3-10 (p. 143) illustrated the first of three columns of data in the work sheet: the trial balance, adjusting journal entries, and the adjusted trial balance. The adjusted balances are brought forward to one of the last two sets of columns, either the income statement columns or the balance sheet columns. The income statement debit column includes expenses and the credit column includes revenue accounts. The balance sheet debit column includes assets and withdrawals; the credit column includes liabilities, owner's equity, and accumulated depreciation accounts. *Review Exhibits 4-2 through 4-6 (p. 198) to understand the flow of steps in preparing the work sheet.*

2 Use the work sheet.

The work sheet is a working document. It helps to make the adjusting entries, prepare financial statements, and close out the temporary accounts. *Review Exhibits 4-2 through 4-7 (p. 198 and 202) to understand the flow of information from the work sheet to the financial statements.*

Close the revenue, expense, and withdrawal accounts.

The revenue, expense, and withdrawal accounts are temporary accounts; the account balances are zeroed (closed) out at the end of the year to get ready for journalizing transactions in the new year. Income Summary is a temporary account that is used only for this process. The closing process also updates the ending Capital account balance for the net income or net loss and withdrawals during the year. *Review Exhibits 4-9 and 4-10 (pp. 204–205) to enhance your understanding of the closing process.*

 Classify assets and liabilities as current or long-term.

It's important to remember that a liability (such as a mortgage or car loan) may be split between current and long-term liability classification on the balance sheet, such as when an installment on a loan is due within one year, but future installments are due thereafter.

Refer to Exhibits 4-12 or 4-13 (p. 209) to review the classified balance sheet.

5 Use the current ratio and the debt ratio to evaluate a company.

The current ratio is a key liquidity measure. It indicates the amount of current assets that is available for each dollar of current liabilities. A higher ratio is usually considered to be preferable.

The debt ratio is an indicator of the entity's ability to pay its debt. It measures the portion of assets that is financed with debt.

Demo Doc 1

Closing Entries

Learning Objectives 1–5

This question continues on from the Wood's Restaurant problem given in Demo Doc 1 of Chapter 3 (see p. 69 of your Study Guide).

Use the data from Wood's Restaurant's adjusted trial balance at December 31, 2008:

WOOD'S RESTAURANT Adjusted Trial Balance December 31, 2008				
			Adjusted Trial Balance	
	Account Title		**Debit**	**Credit**
	Cash		$10,600	
	Accounts receivable		15,800	
	Supplies		400	
	Prepaid rent		2,000	
	Furniture		15,000	
	Accumulated depreciation—furniture			$ 6,000
	Accounts payable			2,600
	Salary payable			120
	Daniel Wood, capital			40,000
	Daniel Wood, withdrawals		11,500	
	Service revenue			25,800
	Rent expense		6,000	
	Salary expense		10,120	
	Depreciation expense		1,500	
	Supplies expense		1,600	
	Total		$74,520	$74,520

Requirements

1. Prepare Wood's accounting work sheet showing the adjusted trial balance, the income statement accounts, and the balance sheet accounts.

2. Journalize and post the closing entries.

3. Which assets are current? Which assets are long-term?

4. Which liabilities are current? Which liabilities are long-term?

5. Calculate Wood's current and debt ratios.

Demo Doc 1 Solutions

Requirement 1

Prepare Wood's accounting work sheet showing the adjusted trial balance, the income statement accounts, and the balance sheet accounts.

Part 1	Part 2	Part 3	Part 4	Part 5	Part 6	Part 7	Part 8	Demo Doc Complete

1 Prepare an accounting work sheet

2 Use the work sheet

The revenues and expenses belong on the income statement. All other accounts listed belong on the balance sheet.

Net income is calculated by subtracting the expenses from the revenues:

$$\$25,800 - \$19,220 = \$6,580$$

Net income is added to the credit side of the balance sheet to make total debits equal total credits. This is because net income increases the Capital account (as seen in Requirement 2 of this question, in which the closing entries are journalized).

	WOOD'S RESTAURANT Work Sheet December 31, 2008						
	Adjusted Trial Balance		Income Statement		Balance Sheet		
Account Title	**Debit**	**Credit**	**Debit**	**Credit**	**Debit**	**Credit**
Cash	$10,600				$10,600	
Accounts receivable	15,800				15,800	
Supplies	400				400	
Prepaid rent	2,000				2,000	
Furniture	15,000				15,000	
Accumulated depreciation—furniture		$ 6,000				$ 6,000
Accounts payable		2,600				2,600
Salary payable		120				120
Daniel Wood, capital		40,000				40,000
Daniel Wood, withdrawals	11,500				11,500	
Service revenue		25,800		$25,800		
Rent expense	6,000		$ 6,000			
Salary expense	10,120		10,120			
Depreciation expense	1,500		1,500			
Supplies expense	1,600		1,600			
Total	$74,520	$74,520	$19,220	$25,800	$55,300	$48,720
Net income			$ 6,580			$ 6,580
			$25,800	$25,800	$55,300	$55,300

Close the revenue, expense, and withdrawal accounts

Requirement 2

Journalize and post the closing entries.

Part 1	**Part 2**	Part 3	Part 4	Part 5	Part 6	Part 7	Part 8	Demo Doc Complete

There are two reasons to prepare closing entries. First, we need to clear out the revenue, expense, and withdrawal accounts to a zero balance. This is because they need to begin the next year empty. Second, we need to update the Capital account.

In Chapter 1, we discussed the formula to calculate the balance in the Capital account:

Beginning capital amount
+ Owner investments
= Adjusted capital amount
+ Net income (or − net loss)
− Owner withdrawals
= Ending capital amount

Capital

| | Beginning Capital Amount |
	Investments
	Adjusted Capital Amount
	Net Income
Withdrawals	
	Ending Capital Amount

This formula is the key to preparing the closing entries. We will use this formula, but we will do it *inside* the Capital account T-account.

What is in the Capital account right now? From the trial balance, we can see that there is a balance of $40,000. But where did that balance come from? It is the adjusted capital amount. In this particular problem, because there are no investments (as seen from the problem in Chapter 3), it is also the ending balance from last period.

So we have an advantage: The first component of the formula (adjusted capital amount) is already in the T-account.

The next component is net income. This is *not* already in the Capital account. We do not have a T-account with net income in it, but we can *create* one.

We will create a new T-account called Income Summary. We will place in there all the components of net income and come out with the net income number at the bottom. From Chapter 1, remember the formula for net income:

Revenues − Expenses = Net income

This means that we need to get all of the revenues and expenses into the Income Summary account.

Let's look at the Service Revenue T-account:

Service Revenue	
	Bal. 25,800

Remember the first reason to prepare closing entries: We need to clear out the income statement accounts so that they are empty to begin the next year. What do we need to do to bring the Service Revenue account to zero? It has a *credit* balance of $25,800, so to bring that to zero, we need to *debit* $25,800.

This means that we have part of our first closing entry:

1.	Service Revenue	25,800	
	???		25,800

What is the credit side of this entry? The reason we were looking at Service Revenue to begin with was to help calculate net income using the Income Summary. So the other side of the entry must go to the Income Summary:

1.	Service Revenue	25,800	
	Income Summary		25,800

Service Revenue		
		25,800
1.	25,800	
		Bal. 0

The next part of net income is the expenses. In this case, we have four different expenses:

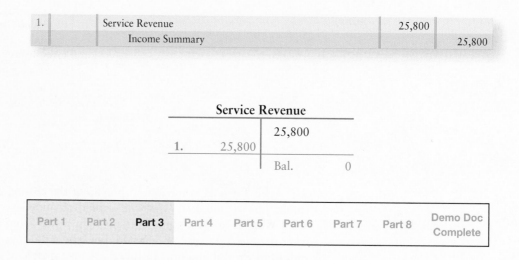

Rent Expense		
Bal.	6,000	

Depreciation Expense		
Bal.	1,500	

Salary Expense		
Bal.	10,120	

Supplies Expense		
Bal.	1,600	

Each of these expenses has a *debit* balance. In order to bring these accounts to zero, we must *credit* them. The balancing debit will go to the Income Summary account:

2.	Income Summary	19,220	
	Rent Expense		6,000
	Salary Expense		10,120
	Depreciation Expense		1,500
	Supplies Expense		1,600

Rent Expense

6,000			
	2.		6,000
Bal.	0		

Depreciation Expense

1,500			
	2.		1,500
Bal.	0		

Salary Expense

10,120			
	2.		10,120
Bal.	0		

Supplies Expense

1,600			
	2.		1,600
Bal.	0		

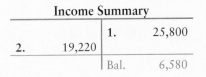

| Part 1 | Part 2 | Part 3 | **Part 4** | Part 5 | Part 6 | Part 7 | Part 8 | Demo Doc Complete |

Now let's look at the Income Summary account:

Income Summary

			1.	25,800
2.	19,220			
			Bal.	6,580

The purpose of creating this account was to get a net income number. (If you did the Chapter 3 problem, note that this balance is the same net income number that appears on the income statement.)

We can now take this number and put it into the Capital account. How do we remove it from the Income Summary? The Income Summary has a *credit* balance of $6,580, which is the net income, so to remove this number, we must *debit* the Income Summary for $6,580:

3.	Income Summary	6,580	
	???		6,580

What is the credit side of this entry? The reason we created the Income Summary account to begin with was to help calculate the profit or loss for the Capital account. So the credit side of the entry must go to Daniel Wood, Capital:

3.	Income Summary	6,580	
	Daniel Wood, Capital		6,580

This adds the net income to the Capital account. Note that it also brings the Income Summary account to a zero balance.

Income Summary

			1.	25,800
2.	19,220			
			Bal.	6,580
3.	6,580			
			Bal.	0

Part 1	Part 2	Part 3	Part 4	**Part 5**	Part 6	Part 7	Part 8	Demo Doc Complete

The last component of the Capital account formula is withdrawals. There is already a Withdrawals account that exists:

Daniel Wood, Withdrawals

Bal.	11,500	

What do we need to do to bring the Withdrawals account to zero? It has a *debit* balance of $11,500, so to bring that to zero we need to *credit* $11,500. The balancing debit will go to the Daniel Wood, Capital account:

4.	Daniel Wood, Capital	11,500	
	Daniel Wood, Withdrawals		11,500

This subtracts the withdrawals from the Capital account.
The Capital account now has the following transactions:

Daniel Wood, Capital

					40,000	Beginning Capital Amount
			3.		6,580	Net Income
Withdrawals	4.	11,500				
			Bal.		35,080	Ending Capital Amount

The formula to update the capital amount has been recreated inside the Capital T-account.

Daniel Wood, Withdrawals

	11,500		
		4.	11,500
Bal.	0		

Daniel Wood, Capital

			40,000
		3.	6,580
4.	11,500		
		Bal.	35,080

Notice that all temporary accounts (that is, the revenue, the expense, the withdrawals, and the Income Summary accounts) now have a zero balance.

4 Classify assets and liabilities as current or long-term

Requirement 3

Which assets are current? Which assets are long-term?

Part 1	Part 2	Part 3	Part 4	Part 5	**Part 6**	Part 7	Part 8	Demo Doc Complete

Current assets are assets whose benefit will be realized within one year (or reporting period, whichever is longer). Typical current assets include cash, accounts receivable, prepaid expenses, and inventory. In this problem, the current assets are:

Cash—Cash is used constantly and its benefits are immediate.

Accounts Receivable—Generally, customers pay what they owe to the company in less than one year (reporting period).

Supplies—Supplies are usually purchased close to the time of use (benefit)—well within one year or reporting period.

Prepaid Rent—Generally, prepayments are not made more than one year (period) in advance. This means that the prepayments (benefits) will be used within one year (reporting period).

Total current assets =

Cash	+	Accounts Receivable	+	Supplies	+	Prepaid Rent	=	
$10,600	+	$15,800	+	$400	+	$2,000	=	$28,800

Long-term assets are assets whose benefit will be realized in more than one year (or reporting period). Long-term assets include all asset accounts except for current assets. Some of the categories include long-term investments and property, plant, and equipment. In this problem, the only long-term asset is the **furniture.**

The furniture will be used (benefited from) for many years. We know this because the use of the furniture is represented as depreciation, which is being taken over many years.

$$\text{Total long-term assets} = \text{Furniture(net)} =$$

Furniture	–	Accumulated Depreciation	=
$15,000	–	$6,000	= $9,000

Requirement 4

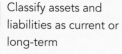

4 Classify assets and liabilities as current or long-term

Which liabilities are current? Which liabilities are long-term?

Part 1	Part 2	Part 3	Part 4	Part 5	Part 6	**Part 7**	Part 8	Demo Doc Complete

Current liabilities are liabilities that will be paid (that is, obligations met) within one year (or reporting period, whichever is longer). In this problem, the current liabilities are:

Accounts Payable—Accounts Payable generally consists of bills from suppliers (such as utilities, providers of raw materials, and inventory). It is rare that such suppliers would be willing to wait a year (or reporting period) for payment. Most often, such bills are due within 30 days.

Salary Payable—Generally, employees are not willing to wait longer than a month to be paid.

$$\text{Total current liabilities} =$$

Accounts Payable	+	Salary Payable	=
$2,600	+	$120	= $2,720

Long-term liabilities include all obligations other than those classified as current liabilities. There are no long-term liabilities in this problem.

$$\text{Total long-term liabilities} = \$0$$

Requirement 5

Calculate Wood's current and debt ratios.

5   Use the current ratio and the debt ratio to evaluate a company

Part 1	Part 2	Part 3	Part 4	Part 5	Part 6	Part 7	**Part 8**	Demo Doc Complete

$$\text{Current ratio} = \frac{\text{Current assets}}{\text{Current liabilities}}$$

$$= \frac{\$28,800}{\$2,720} = 10.59$$

$$\text{Debt ratio} = \frac{\text{Total liabilities}}{\text{Total assets}}$$

$$= \frac{\$2,720 + \$0}{\$28,800 + \$9,000}$$

$$= \frac{\$2,720}{\$37,800} = 7.20\%$$

Part 1	Part 2	Part 3	Part 4	Part 5	Part 6	Part 7	Part 8	**Demo Doc Complete**

Quick Practice Questions

True/False

_____ 1. The last step in the accounting cycle is preparing the financial statements.

_____ 2. The adjusted trial balance columns of a work sheet contain the account balances that appear on the financial statements.

_____ 3. If the sum of the work sheet income statement debit column is greater than the income statement credit column, there is net income.

_____ 4. Capital, revenue, expenses, and withdrawals are closed out at the end of the year.

_____ 5. The postclosing trial balance contains only balance sheet accounts.

_____ 6. A lower debt ratio is preferable to a higher debt ratio.

_____ 7. Long-term liabilities are debts that are not due for at least six months.

_____ 8. The capital in the balance sheet credit column of a work sheet represents the beginning capital amount plus any additional capital investments during the period.

_____ 9. Permanent accounts include revenue and expenses.

_____ 10. The difference between the debit and credit totals of the balance sheet columns of the work sheet is net income or net loss.

Multiple Choice

1. **What is a work sheet?**
   a. A formal statement issued to investors
   b. A document required by the Internal Revenue Service
   c. A replacement for the general journal
   d. A multicolumn document used by accountants to aid in the preparation of the financial statements

2. **Which of the following accounts would appear in the balance sheet credit column of the work sheet?**
   a. Equipment
   b. Salary Payable
   c. Rent Revenue
   d. Insurance Expense

3. **Which of the following accounts is not closed out?**
   a. Accumulated Depreciation
   b. Service Revenue
   c. Depreciation Expense
   d. Owner's Withdrawals

4. What is the measure of how quickly an item can be converted into cash?
   a. Contribution margin
   b. Liquidity
   c. Profitability
   d. Leverage

5. What type of asset is expected to be converted to cash, sold, or consumed during the next 12 months or within the businesss no rmal operating cycle if longer than a year?
   a. Permanent assets
   b. Quick assets
   c. Current assets
   d. Cash-equivalent assets

6. What is the time span during which cash is used to acquire goods and services that are sold to customers and collected in cash?
   a. Operating cycle
   b. Cash-to-cash cycle
   c. Liquidity cycle
   d. Receivables-to-cash cycle

7. In what category would Inventory appear on a classified balance sheet?
   a. Long-term liability
   b. Plant asset
   c. Current asset
   d. Current liability

Use the following account balances for Philip's Rentals as of December 31, 2008, to answer questions 8–10:

Cash	$10,300	Prepaid Rent	$ 3,600
Accounts Payable	7,800	Equipment	15,000
Accumulated Depreciation	2,000	Supplies	1,200
Philip Browning, Capital	9,300	Unearned Revenue	1,600
Philip Browning, Withdrawals	2,200	Notes Payable (due 12/31/2010)	7,500

8. What is the current ratio for Philip's Rentals?
   a. 1.61
   b. 1.03
   c. 1.29
   d. 1.38

9. What is the debt ratio for Philip's Rentals?
   a. 0.60
   b. 0.73
   c. 0.67
   d. 1.16

10. What are the total current assets and total assets, respectively, for Philip's Rentals?
    a. $15,100 and $30,100
    b. $13,900 and $27,100
    c. $15,100 and $28,100
    d. $13,700 and $30,100

Quick Exercises

4-1. For each of the following accounts, indicate whether it (a) normally has a debit or credit balance and (b) appears in the income statement or balance sheet columns of the work sheet.

	Normal Debit or Credit Balance	Income Statement or Balance Sheet
a. Equipment	_____	_____
b. Salary Expense	_____	_____
c. Unearned Revenue	_____	_____
d. Accumulated Depreciation	_____	_____
e. Accounts Payable	_____	_____
f. Service Revenue	_____	_____

4-2. Complete the work sheet information in the adjusted trial balance columns.

Account Title	Trial Balance Debit	Trial Balance Credit	Adjustments Debit	Adjustments Credit	Adjusted Trial Balance Debit	Adjusted Trial Balance Credit
Cash	$30,800					
Accounts receivable	5,800		(a)$ 6,000			
Prepaid insurance	2,400			(b)$ 1,200		
Building	17,000					
Accumulated depreciation—building		$ 8,000		(c) 500		
Accounts payable		1,600				
Salary payable		1,000		(d) 2,400		
Daniel Wood, capital		50,320				
Daniel Wood, withdrawals	7,500					
Service revenue		25,800		(a) 6,000		
Insurance expense	2,500		(b) 1,200			
Rent expense	5,500					
Salary expense	11,120		(d) 2,400			
Depreciation expense	2,000		(c) 500			
Supplies expense	2,100					
Total	$86,720	$86,720	$10,100	$10,100		

4-3. Complete the remainder of the following work sheet:

Account Title	Adjusted Trial Balance Debit	Adjusted Trial Balance Credit	Income Statement Debit	Income Statement Credit	Balance Sheet Debit	Balance Sheet Credit
Cash	8,400					
Accounts receivable	10,100					
Supplies	2,400					
Prepaid rent	4,000					
Furniture	24,400					
Accumulated depreciation—furniture		4,000				
Accounts payable		3,100				
Unearned revenue		2,420				
Daniel Wood, capital		42,000				
Daniel Wood, withdrawals	8,000					
Service revenue		25,000				
Rent expense	6,000					
Salary expense	9,820					
Depreciation expense	1,500					
Supplies expense	1,900					
Total	$76,520	$76,520				
Net Income						

4-4. Given the following adjusted account balances, journalize the closing entries for Sports Unlimited on December 31, 2007.

Joseph Golf, capital	$ 85,000
Service revenue	104,400
Depreciation expense—building	2,000
Salary expense	28,000
Supplies expense	8,500
Interest revenue	15,400
Rent expense	15,000
Joseph Golf, withdrawals	3,000

Date	Accounts	Debit	Credit

Date	Accounts	Debit	Credit

Date	Accounts	Debit	Credit

Date	Accounts	Debit	Credit

4-5. Given the following adjusted account balances at 12/31/07, calculate total (a) current assets, (b) current liabilities, (c) long-term assets, and (d) long-term liabilities.

Cash	$ 25,000
Accounts Receivable	12,500
Land	100,000
Joseph Golf, Capital	75,000
Accounts Payable	15,200
Building	245,000
Accumulated Depreciation—Bldg.	70,000
Salaries Payable	1,500
Notes Payable—due 12/31/09	39,000

Do It Yourself! Question 1

This question continues on from the Angela's Business Services problem given in Chapter 3.

Use the data from Angela's Business Services adjusted trial balance at December 31, 2008:

		Account Title	Debit	Credit
		ANGELA'S BUSINESS SERVICES		
		Adjusted Trial Balance		
		December 31, 2008		
			Adjusted Trial Balance	
		Account Title	**Debit**	**Credit**
		Cash	$ 40,400	
		Prepaid insurance	3,600	
		Supplies	7,900	
		Office equipment	25,000	
		Accumulated depreciation—equipment		$ 10,000
		Accounts payable		5,300
		Salary payable		4,000
		Unearned revenue		1,500
		Angela Waring, capital		60,000
		Angela Waring, withdrawals	8,000	
		Service revenue		85,300
		Insurance expense	14,400	
		Salary expense	49,000	
		Depreciation expense	2,500	
		Supplies expense	15,300	
		Total	$166,100	$166,100

3 Close the revenue, expense, and withdrawal accounts

Requirement

1. Journalize and post the closing entries.

	Date	Accounts	Debit	Credit
1.				

	Date	Accounts	Debit	Credit
2.				

	Date	Accounts	Debit	Credit
3.				

	Date	Accounts	Debit	Credit
4.				

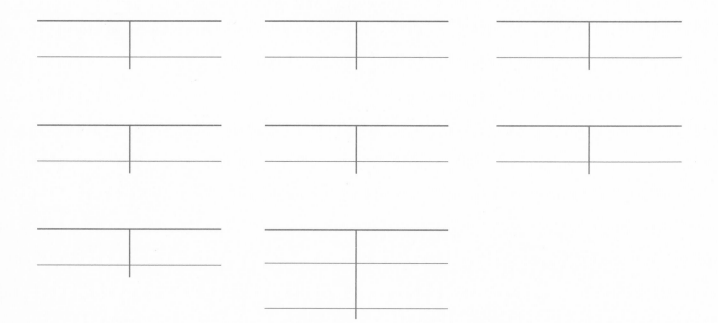

Do It Yourself! Question 2

Krake Theaters has the following data for 2008:

Total revenues	$10,000
Total expenses	13,000
Owner withdrawals	1,600
Owner investments	4,000

The Capital account had a balance of $8,200 at January 1, 2008.

Requirement

3 Close the revenue, expense, and withdrawal accounts

1. Journalize and post the closing entries.

	Date	Accounts	Debit	Credit
1.				

	Date	Accounts	Debit	Credit
2.				

	Date	Accounts	Debit	Credit
3.				

	Date	Accounts	Debit	Credit
4.				

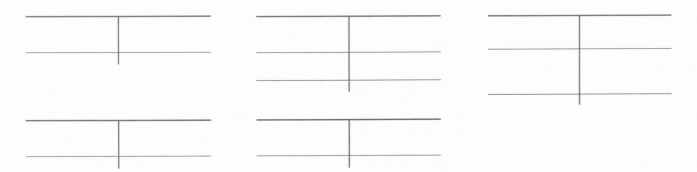

Quick Practice Solutions

True/False Question

  F   1. The last step in the accounting cycle is preparing the financial statements.

              False—The last step in the accounting cycle is preparing the *postclosing trial balance*. (p. xx)

  T   2. The adjusted trial balance columns of a work sheet contain the account balances that appear on the financial statements. (p. xx)

  F   3. If the sum of the work sheet income statement debit column is greater than the income statement credit column, there is net income.

              False—If the sum of the work sheet income statement debit column is greater than the income statement credit column, there is net *loss*. (p. xx)

  F   4. Capital, revenue, expense, and withdrawals are closed out at the end of the year.

              False—The revenue, expense, and withdrawals are closed out at the end of the year. *Capital* is a permanent account and is not closed out. (p. xx)

  T   5. The post closing trial balance contains only balance sheet accounts. (p. xx)

  T   6. A lower debt ratio is preferable to a higher debt ratio. (p. xx)

  F   7. Long-term liabilities are debts that are not due for at least six months.

              False—Long-term liabilities are those due *beyond a year.* (p. xx)

  T   8. The capital in the balance sheet credit column of a work sheet represents the beginning capital amount plus any additional capital investments during the period. (p. xx)

  F   9. Permanent accounts include revenue and expenses.

              False—Permanent accounts include assets, liabilities, and owner's equity. Revenue and expenses are *temporary* accounts. (p. xx)

  T   10. The difference between the debit and credit totals of the balance sheet columns of the work sheet is net income or net loss. (p. xx)

Multiple Choice Question

1. **What is a work sheet?** (p. xx)
   a. A formal statement issued to investors
   b. A document required by the Internal Revenue Service.
   c. A replacement for the general journal
   d. A multicolumn document used by accountants to aid in the preparation of the financial statements

2. Which of the following accounts would appear in the balance sheet credit column of the work sheet? (p. xx)
   a. Equipment
   b. Salary Payable
   c. Rent Revenue
   d. Insurance Expense

3. Which of the following accounts is not closed out? (p. xx)
   a. Accumulated Depreciation
   b. Service Revenue
   c. Depreciation Expense
   d. Owner's Withdrawals

4. What is the measure of how quickly an item can be converted into cash? (p. xx)
   a. Contribution margin
   b. Liquidity
   c. Profitability
   d. Leverage

5. What type of asset is expected to be converted to cash, sold, or consumed during the next 12 months or within the business's normal operating cycle if longer than a year? (p. xx)
   a. Permanent assets
   b. Quick assets
   c. Current assets
   d. Cash-equivalent assets

6. What is the time span during which cash is used to acquire goods and services that are sold to customers and collected in cash? (p. xx)
   a. Operating cycle
   b. Cash-to-cash cycle
   c. Liquidity cycle
   d. Receivables-to-cash cycle

7. In what category would Inventory appear on a classified balance sheet? (p. xx)
   a. Long-term liability
   b. Plant asset
   c. Current asset
   d. Current liability

   Use the following account balances for Philip's Rentals as of December 31, 2008, to answer questions 8–10:

Cash	$10,300	Prepaid Rent	$ 3,600
Accounts Payable	7,800	Equipment	15,000
Accumulated Depreciation	2,000	Supplies	1,200
Philip Browning, Capital	9,300	Unearned Revenue	1,600
Philip Browning, Withdrawals	2,200	Notes Payable (due 12/31/2010)	7,500

8. What is the current ratio for Philip's Rentals? (p. xx)
   a. 1.61
   b. 1.03
   c. 1.29
   d. 1.38

9. What is the debt ratio for Philip's Rentals? (p. xx)
   a. 0.60
   b. 0.73
   c. 0.67
   d. 1.16

10. What are the total current assets and total assets, respectively, for Philip's Rentals? (p. xx)
    a. $15,100 and $30,100
    b. $13,900 and $27,100
    c. $15,100 and $28,100
    d. $13,700 and $30,100

Quick Exercises

4-1. For each of the following accounts, indicate whether it (a) normally has a debit or credit balance and (b) appears in the income statement or balance sheet columns of the work sheet. (p. xx)

	Normal Debit (Dr.) or Credit (Cr.) Balance	Income Statement (I/S) or Balance Sheet (B/S)
a. Equipment	Dr.	B/S
b. Salary Expense	Dr.	I/S
c. Unearned Revenue	Cr.	B/S
d. Accumulated Depreciation	Cr.	B/S
e. Accounts Payable	Cr.	B/S
f. Service Revenue	Cr.	I/S

4-2. Complete the work sheet information that follows through the adjusted trial balance columns. (p. xx)

Account Title	Trial Balance Debit	Trial Balance Credit	Adjustments Debit	Adjustments Credit	Adjusted Trial Balance Debit	Adjusted Trial Balance Credit
Cash	$30,800				$30,800	
Accounts receivable	5,800		(a)$ 6,000		11,800	
Prepaid insurance	2,400			(b)$ 1,200	1,200	
Building	17,000				17,000	
Accumulated depreciation—building		$ 8,000		(c) 500		$ 8,500
Accounts payable		1,600				1,600
Salary payable		1,000		(d) 2,400		3,400
Daniel Wood, capital		50,320				50,320
Daniel Wood, withdrawals	7,500				7,500	
Service revenue		25,800		(a) 6,000		31,800
Insurance expense	2,500		(b) 1,200		3,700	
Rent expense	5,500				5,500	
Salary expense	11,120		(d) 2,400		13,520	
Depreciation expense	2,000		(c) 500		2,500	
Supplies expense	2,100				2,100	
Total	$86,720	$86,720	$10,100	$10,100	$95,620	$95,620

4-3. Complete the remainder of the following work sheet: (p. xx)

Account Title	Adjusted Trial Balance Debit	Adjusted Trial Balance Credit	Income Statement Debit	Income Statement Credit	Balance Sheet Debit	Balance Sheet Credit
Cash	$ 8,400				$ 8,400	
Accounts receivable	10,100				10,100	
Supplies	2,400				2,400	
Prepaid rent	4,000				4,000	
Furniture	24,400				24,400	
Accumulated depreciation—furniture		$ 4,000				$ 4,000
Accounts payable		3,100				3,100
Unearned revenue		2,420				2,420
Daniel Wood, capital		42,000				42,000
Daniel Wood, withdrawals	8,000				8,000	
Service revenue		25,000		$25,000		
Rent expense	6,000		$ 6,000			
Salary expense	9,820		9,820			
Depreciation expense	1,500		1,500			
Supplies expense	1,900		1,900			
Total	$76,520	$76,520	$19,220	$25,000	$57,300	$51,520
Net income			$ 5,780			$ 5,780
			$25,000	$25,000	$57,300	$57,300

4-4. Given the following adjusted account balances, journalize the closing entries for Sports Unlimited on December 31, 2007. (p. xx)

Joseph Golf, capital	$ 85,000
Service revenue	104,400
Depreciation expense—building	2,000
Salary expense	28,000
Supplies expense	8,500
Interest revenue	15,400
Rent expense	15,000
Joseph Golf, withdrawals	3,000

Date	Accounts	Debit	Credit
12/31/07	Service Revenue	104,400	
	Interest Revenue	15,400	
	Income Summary		119,800
	To close out revenue accounts into Income Summary.		

Date	Accounts	Debit	Credit
	Income Summary	53,500	
	Depreciation expense—building		2,000
	Salary expense		28,000
	Supplies expense		8,500
	Rent expense		15,000
	To close out expense accounts into Income Summary.		

Date	Accounts	Debit	Credit
	Income Summary	66,300	
	Joseph Golf, Capital		66,300
	To close out Income Summary into Capital.		

Date	Accounts	Debit	Credit
	Joseph Golf, Withdrawals	3,000	
	Joseph Golf, Capital		3,000
	To close out Withdrawals into Capital.		

4-5. Given the following adjusted account balances at 12/31/07, calculate total (a) current assets, (b) current liabilities, (c) long-term assets, and (d) long-term liabilities. (p. xx)

Cash	$ 25,000
Accounts Receivable	12,500
Land	100,000
Joseph Golf, Capital	75,000
Accounts Payable	15,200
Building	245,000
Accumulated Depreciation—Bldg.	70,000
Salaries Payable	1,500
Notes Payable—due 12/31/09	39,000

a. Cash	$ 25,000
Accounts Receivable	12,500
Total Current Assets	$ 37,500
b. Accounts Payable	$ 15,200
Salaries Payable	1,500
Total Current Liabilities	$ 16,700
c. Land	$ 100,000
Building	245,000
Less: Accumulated Dep.—Bldg.	(70,000)
Total Long-Term Assets	$ 275,000
d. Notes Payable—due 12/31/09	$ 39,000
Total Long-Term Liabilities	$ 39,000

Do It Yourself! Question 1 Solutions

Requirement

1. Journalize and post the closing entries.

	Date	Accounts	Debit	Credit
1.		Accounts Receivable	85,300	
		Unearned Subscription Revenue		85,300

	Date	Accounts	Debit	Credit
2.		Income Summary	81,200	
		Insurance Expense		14,400
		Salary Expense		49,000
		Depreciation Expense		2,500
		Supplies Expense		15,300

	Date	Accounts	Debit	Credit
3.		Income Summary	4,100	
		Angela Waring, Capital		4,100

	Date	Accounts	Debit	Credit
4.		Angela Waring, Capital	8,000	
		Angela Waring, Withdrawals		8,000

Service Revenue		
		85,300
1.	85,300	
	Bal.	0

Depreciation Expense		
2,500		
	2.	2,500
Bal.	0	

Angela Waring, Withdrawals		
8,000		
	4.	8,000
Bal.	0	

Insurance Expense		
14,400		
	2.	14,400
Bal.	0	

Supplies Expense		
15,300		
	2.	15,300
Bal.	0	

Angela Waring, Capital		
		60,000
	3.	4,100
4.	8,000	
	Bal.	56,100

Salary Expense		
49,000		
	2.	49,000
Bal.	0	

Income Summary		
	1.	85,300
2.	81,200	
	Bal.	4,100
3.	4,100	
	Bal.	0

Do It Yourself! Question 2 Solutions

Requirement

1. Journalize and post the closing entries.

	Date	Accounts	Debit	Credit
1.		Revenues	10,000	
		Income Summary		10,000

	Date	Accounts	Debit	Credit
2.		Income Summary	13,000	
		Expenses		13,000

	Date	Accounts	Debit	Credit
3.		Capital	3,000	
		Income Summary		3,000

	Date	Accounts	Debit	Credit
4.		Capital	1,600	
		Withdrawals		1,600

Revenues

			10,000
1.	10,000		
		Bal.	0

Expenses

13,000			
		2.	13,000
Bal.	0		

Income Summary

		1.	10,000
2.	13,000		
Bal.	3,000		
		3.	3,000
Bal.	0		

Withdrawals

1,600			
		4.	1,600
Bal.	0		

Capital

				8,200	Beginning Capital Amount
				4,000	Owner Investments
			Bal.	12,200	Ending Capital Amount
Net Loss	3.	3,000			
Withdrawals	4.	1,600			
			Bal.	7,600	Ending Capital Amount

The Power of Practice

For more practice using the skills learned in this chapter, visit MyAccountingLab. There you will find algorithmically generated questions that are based on these Demo Docs and your main textbook's Review and Assess Your Progress sections.

Go to MyAccountingLab and follow these steps:

1. Direct your URL to www.myaccountinglab.com.
2. Log in using your name and password.
3. Click the MyAccountingLab link.
4. Click Study Plan in the left navigation bar.
5. From the table of contents, select Chapter 4, Completing the Accounting Cycle.
6. Click a link to work tutorial exercises.

5 Merchandising Operations

You want to order a pair of pants from a mail-order catalog. The price listed in the catalog is $50. There is a 10% off coupon in the catalog for first-time customers that you plan to use. You also see that there will be a $6.95 shipping and handling charge for an order of this size. How much will the pair of pants cost you? Although the selling price listed is $50, that is not the cost to you. The 10% coupon results in a $5 discount ($50 × .10) *decreasing* the cost to $45 ($50 − 5). However, the shipping and handling charge of $6.95 *adds* to the cost of the pants. The required cost for the pants is $51.95 ($50.00 − 5.00 + 6.95).

Businesses calculate the cost of assets purchased in the same manner. When inventory is acquired, the cost is calculated as

1. the purchase price on the invoice
2. *plus* the cost of shipping or freight
3. *less* discounts taken

Learning Objectives

1 Account for the purchase of inventory.

There are **two inventory accounting systems** that a business may use:

- **Periodic system**—Periodically a physical inventory count is taken to determine the amount of inventory on hand. The inventory (asset) balance is not continually updated for the increase in inventory owing to purchases or the decrease in inventory owing to sales. The Purchases (expense) account is debited when inventory is purchased. This system has become increasingly less popular as the cost of technology and optical-scanning cash registers has decreased.

- **Perpetual system**—Continuously updates the inventory account and cost of goods sold for purchases and sales. The Inventory (asset) account is debited to record the purchase of inventory. A physical inventory count is still performed to verify the accuracy of the inventory balance.

Review the "Inventory Systems: Perpetual and Periodic" section in the main text.

2 Account for the sale of inventory.

Two entries must be recorded when inventory is sold under a perpetual system. One entry records the revenue amount charged to the customer and the cash or accounts receivable. The other records the cost of goods sold expense and the decrease in the cost of inventory. Sales Discounts and Sales Returns and Allowances are contra revenue, debit balance accounts. *Review the "Sale of Inventory" section of the main text.*

3 Adjust and close the accounts of a merchandising business.

The Inventory account should be adjusted, as necessary, to the actual amount of inventory on hand. Cost of Goods Sold will be affected by the inventory adjustment. The closing entries are similar to those studied in Chapter 4. All of the temporary accounts will be closed out, including the new ones introduced in this chapter: Sales, Sales Discounts, Sales Returns and Allowances and Cost of Goods Sold. *Review the closing entries in Exhibit 5-6 (p. 628).*

4 Prepare a merchandiser's financial statements.

The income statement of a merchandiser may be prepared in two formats. A single-step income statement lists all revenues followed by all expenses to determine net income or loss. The multi-step income statement shows various subtotals as gross profit and income from operations. The other statements are very similar to those for a service company. *Review a merchandiser's multi-step income statement in Exhibit 5-7 and a single-step statement in Exhibit 5-8 (pp. 270–271).*

5 Use gross profit percentage and inventory turnover to evaluate a business.

Two ratios that provide important information for a merchandiser are the gross profit percentage and inventory turnover. *Review the "Two Ratios for Decision Making" section in the main text.*

6 Compute cost of goods sold in a periodic inventory system.

The cost of goods sold expense must be computed in a periodic inventory system because it is not recorded as each item of inventory is sold. The inventory inputs must equal the outputs.

Beginning inventory + Net purchases + Freight-in = Cost of goods available
Cost of goods available − Ending inventory = Cost of goods sold

Review the measurement of cost of goods sold in Exhibit 5-11 (p. 274).

Demo Doc 1

Inventory Transaction Analysis (perpetual system)

Learning Objectives 1–6

Danner Inc. began operations on January 1, 2008. Danner had the following transactions during the year:

Jan. 1   Purchased inventory for $400 with credit terms of 2/15 net 30.

Jan. 12 Paid for the January 1 purchase in full.

Feb. 1   Sold 10 units costing $21 each to a customer for $360 on account. This sale had credit terms of 1/15 net 30.

Feb. 9   Customer returned three units from his February 1 order because he did not like the color of the goods.

Feb. 18 Customer paid for the February 1 order (less returns) in full.

May 5   Purchased inventory for $250 with credit terms of 2/10 net 30.

May 6   Paid special freight costs of $30 on the May 5 inventory purchase in cash.

May 14   Found that 15% of the goods purchased on May 5 were defective. Danner returned these goods.

Jun. 1   Paid for the May 5 purchase (less returns) in full.

Oct. 1   Sold $160 of goods to a customer for $220 with credit terms of 1/20 net 40.

Oct. 19 Received cash payment in full for the October 1 sale.

Requirements

1. Journalize these transactions using the perpetual method. Explanations are not required.

2. Show the Inventory and COGS T-accounts for the year.

3. Inventory on hand at December 31, 2008 (as per count) was $325. Make any necessary adjustments.

4. Use the COGS formula to calculate COGS for the year.

5. Prepare the top portion of Danner's 2008 income statement (ending with gross profit).

6. Calculate Danner's inventory turnover for 2008.

Demo Doc 1 Solutions

Requirement 1

Journalize these transactions using the perpetual method. Explanations are not required.

Part 1	Part 2	Part 3	Part 4	Part 5	Part 6	Demo Doc Complete

 Account for the purchase of inventory

Jan. 1   Purchased inventory for $400 with credit terms of 2/15 net 30.

The Inventory account is involved here because inventory was purchased. Inventory is increased by $400 (a debit). Because the inventory was not paid for in cash (it was purchased on account), Accounts Payable must also be increased by $400 (a credit).

Note that the actual credit terms do not matter at this point, only that the purchase was not made in cash.

However, note that 2/15 net 30 means that the customer will get a 2% discount if the full amount is paid within 15 days. Otherwise, full payment is due in 30 days.

Jan. 1	Inventory	400	
	Accounts Payable		400

Account for the purchase of inventory

Jan. 12   Paid for the January 1 purchase in full.

Remember that 2/15 means that if full payment is made within 15 days, the customer gets a 2% discount.

We are paying the supplier, so we can decrease our Accounts Payable by $400 (a debit). Cash also decreases (a credit). But by how much? January 12 is within 15 days of the original purchase, so Danner is entitled to take the discount. Therefore, Danner only has to pay 100% − 2% = 98% of the purchase price to satisfy the debt owed. So the cash paid is:

$$98\% \times \$400 = \$392$$

The difference is an adjustment to the Inventory account. The cost principle says that we should record assets at cost. The true cost of the inventory is now less than we originally thought. So Inventory is decreased (a credit) by this difference.

Jan. 12	Accounts Payable	400	
	Inventory (to balance*)		8
	Cash [(100% − 2%) × $400]		392

*$400 − $392 = $8

The amount of the adjustment to Inventory was made to balance the entry. In all journal entries, total debits = total credits.

The amount of the adjustment to Inventory is the amount needed to make the total debits in the entry equal to the total credits in the entry. In this case, a credit of 400 − 392 = 8 is required.

Account for the sale of inventory

Feb. 1 **Sold 10 units costing $21 each to a customer for $360 on account. This sale had credit terms of 1/15 net 40.**

There are two parts to this transaction. First, Danner is earning sales revenue of $360. This will cause an increase to Sales Revenue (a credit) and (because it is not paid for in cash but rather sold on account) an increase to Accounts Receivable (a debit).

Second, Danner is also selling inventory. This means that Inventory will decrease (a credit) and COGS will increase (a debit) by:

$$10 \times \$21 = \$210$$

Remember that 1/15 net 40 means that the customer will get a 1% discount if the full amount is paid within 15 days. Otherwise, full payment is due in 40 days.

Feb. 1	Accounts Receivable	360	
	Sales Revenue		360
	COGS (10 units × $21)	210	
	Inventory		210

 Account for the sale of inventory

Feb. 9 **Customer returned three units from his February 1 order because he did not like the color of the goods.**

Because the customer is returning goods (and the goods are not defective) to the company, Danner's Inventory will increase (a debit) by 3 × $21 = $63. This then causes the COGS to decrease (a credit) by $63.

The customer has not yet paid, so this will decrease the amount of Accounts Receivable Danner can collect from the customer (a credit) by (3/10) × $360 = $108. Instead of decreasing Sales Revenue, we will increase Sales Returns and Allowances (a debit) by $108. This allows Danner to keep track of sales returns and make better business decisions.

Feb. 9	Inventory (3 × $21)	63	
	COGS		63
	Sales Returns and Allowances ([3/10] × $360)	108	
	Accounts Receivable		108

Account for the sale of inventory

Feb. 18 **Customer paid for the February 1 order (less returns) in full.**

Remember that 1/15 means that if full payment is made within 15 days, the customer gets a 1% discount.

However, the customer is paying 18 days after the sale, which is longer than the 15 days the discount allows. Therefore, the customer must pay the *full* amount.

Cash is increased (a debit) by $360 − $108 = $252 (original sale of $360 less the sales return of $108). Because the customer is paying Danner, Accounts Receivable is also decreased (a credit) by $252.

Feb. 18	Cash ($360 – $108)	252	
	Accounts Receivable		252

Account for the
purchase of inventory

May 5   Purchased inventory for $250 with credit terms of 2/10 net 30.

Inventory is increasing by $250 (a debit). Because the inventory was not paid for in cash but rather on account, Accounts Payable must also be increased by $250 (a credit).

Remember that 2/10 net 30 means that the customer will get a 2% discount if the full amount is paid within 10 days. Otherwise, full payment is due in 30 days.

May 5	Inventory	250	
	Accounts Payable		250

May 6   Paid special freight costs of $30 on the May 5 inventory purchase in cash.

The *total cost* of the inventory is the purchase price *plus* any additional purchasing costs (such as shipping or taxes). Therefore, we include the extra $30 of freight as part of the cost of the inventory.

Inventory is increased by $30 (a debit). Because these costs are being paid in cash, the Cash account is decreased (a credit) by $30.

May 6	Inventory	30	
	Cash		30

 Account for the
purchase of inventory

May 14   Found that 15% of the goods purchased on May 5 were defective. Danner returned these goods.

When the goods are returned to the supplier, they are taken out of inventory. This decreases Inventory (a credit) by 15% × $250 = $37.50. Because Danner has not yet paid for the goods, Accounts Payable is decreased for the related amount (a debit).

May 14	Accounts Payable (15% × $250)	37.50	
	Inventory		37.50

 Account for the
purchase of inventory

Jun. 1   Paid for the May 5 purchase (less returns) in full.

Remember that 2/10 means that if full payment is made within 10 days, the customer gets a 2% discount.

Accounts Payable decreases by the original payable less returns made: $250 − $37.50 = $212.50 (a debit). Cash also decreases (a credit). June 1 is 27 days after the original purchase. This is within the deadline for payment of 30 days, but it is *not* early enough to take the discount. Therefore, the cash paid is the full amount of $212.50. In order for Danner to be entitled to take the discount, the payment would have had to have been made on May 15 (May 5 plus 10 days).

June 1	Accounts Payable	212.50	
	Cash		212.50

2 Account for the sale
of inventory

Oct. 1   **Sold $160 of goods to a customer for $220 with credit terms of 1/20 net 40.**

The company is earning sales revenue of $220. This will cause an increase to Sales Revenue (a credit) and (because it is not paid for in cash) an increase to Accounts Receivable (a debit).

The company is also selling inventory. This means that Inventory will decrease (a credit) and COGS will increase (a debit) by $160.

Note that the actual credit terms do not matter at this point, only that the sale was not made in cash.

However, note that 1/20 net 40 means that the customer will get a 1% discount if the full amount is paid within 20 days. Otherwise, full payment is due in 40 days.

Even though the sale was on account, the actual sale must be recorded at this time.

Oct. 1	Accounts Receivable		220	
	Sales Revenue			220
	COGS		160	
	Inventory			160

2 Account for the sale
of inventory

Oct. 19   **Received cash for payment in full of the October 1 sale.**

This payment is within the 20-day period, so the customer is entitled to take the discount. The customer will pay 100% − 1% = 99% of the receivable amount, or 99% × $220 = $217.80.

Accounts Receivable will be decreased by the *full* amount of $220 (a credit) because the bill has been paid and no more can be collected from the customer. Cash will increase by $217.80 (a debit) and the difference (the amount to balance) will go to Sales Discounts.

Oct. 19	Cash [(100% − 1%) × $220]		217.80	
	Sales Discounts (to balance*)		2.20	
	Accounts Receivable			220

* 220 − 217.80 = 2.20

Requirement 2

3 Adjust and close the accounts of a merchandising business

Show the Inventory and COGS T-accounts for the year.

Part 1	**Part 2**	Part 3	Part 4	Part 5	Part 6	Demo Doc Complete

The entries are posted into the T-accounts (just as in previous chapters). However, for this question, we only want to see the Inventory and COGS T-accounts in detail:

Inventory			
Jan. 1	400		
		Jan. 12	8
		Feb. 1	210
Feb. 9	63		
May 5	250		
May 6	30		
		May 14	37.50
		Oct. 1	160
Bal.	327.50		

COGS			
Feb. 1	210		
		Feb. 9	63
Oct. 1	160		
Bal.	307		

Requirement 3

3 Adjust and close the accounts of a merchandising business

Inventory on hand at December 31, 2008 (as per count) was $325. Make any necessary adjustments.

Part 1	Part 2	**Part 3**	Part 4	Part 5	Part 6	Demo Doc Complete

The balance of Inventory in the T-account is $327.50. Because the count shows less, there must be inventory shrinkage.

The number for Inventory on the balance sheet must *always* be the number from the actual physical *count*. This means that we need to adjust the Inventory balance to the count number of $325. This will require a decrease (credit) of $327.50 − $325 = $2.50 to Inventory. The balance to this entry is an increase (debit) to COGS for $2.50.

Dec. 31	COGS ($327.50 – $325)		2.50	
	Inventory			2.50

The updated Inventory and COGS T-accounts are:

Inventory				
Jan. 1	400			
		Jan. 12	8	
		Feb. 1	210	
Feb. 9	63			
May 5	250			
May 6	30			
		May 14	37.50	
		Oct. 1	160	
Bal.	327.50			
		Dec. 31	2.50	
Bal.	325			

COGS				
Feb. 1	210			
		Feb. 9	63	
Oct. 1	160			
Bal.	307			
Dec. 31	2.50			
Bal.	309.50			

Requirement 4

 Compute cost of goods sold in a periodic inventory system

Use the COGS formula to calculate COGS for the year.

Part 1	Part 2	Part 3	**Part 4**	Part 5	Part 6	Demo Doc Complete

We can use the COGS formula to calculate COGS:

$$COGS = \underset{\text{inventory}}{\text{Beginning}} + \underset{\text{purchases}}{\text{Inventory}} - \underset{\text{inventory}}{\text{Ending}}$$

$$COGS = 0 + ([400 - 8] + [250 + 30 - 37.50]) - 325$$

$$COGS = 0 + (392 + 242.50) - 325$$

$$COGS = 0 + 634.50 - 325 = 309.50$$

Requirement 5

4 Prepare a merchandiser's financial statements

Prepare the top portion of Danner's 2008 income statement (ending with gross profit).

Part 1	Part 2	Part 3	Part 4	**Part 5**	Part 6	Demo Doc Complete

Sales Discounts and Sales Returns and Allowances are *contra accounts* to Sales Revenue. As we did with Accumulated Depreciation, these contra accounts must be shown on the financial statements, then combined with their associated account to create the *net* value (in this case, net sales revenue).

DANNER CORP.
Income Statement
Year Ended December 31, 2008

Sales revenue			$580.00*	
Less: Sales discounts		$ (2.20)		
Sales returns and allowances		(108.00)	(110.20)	
Net sales revenue				$469.80
Cost of goods sold				(309.50)
Gross profit				160.30

*$360 + $220 = $580

Requirement 6

Use gross profit percentage and inventory turnover to evaluate a business

Calculate Danner's inventory turnover for 2008.

| Part 1 | Part 2 | Part 3 | Part 4 | Part 5 | **Part 6** | Demo Doc Complete |

Inventory turnover = COGS/Average inventory

Average (when used in a financial ratio) generally means the beginning balance plus the ending balance divided by 2.

> 2008 Inventory turnover
> = $309.50/[($0 + $325)/2]
> = $309.50/$162.50
> = **1.9 times**

| Part 1 | Part 2 | Part 3 | Part 4 | Part 5 | Part 6 | **Demo Doc Complete** |

Quick Practice Questions

True/False

_____ 1. Cost of Goods Sold is included in a merchandiser's income statement but excluded from a service company income statement.

_____ 2. Under the periodic inventory system, the only way to determine the cost of goods sold is to take a physical count of the merchandise on hand.

_____ 3. Most businesses use the periodic inventory system because it offers management more control over inventory.

_____ 4. A sales return requires two entries to be journalized if the seller uses a perpetual inventory system.

_____ 5. Sales Returns and Allowances is an expense account.

_____ 6. The single-step income statement shows gross profit and income from operations.

_____ 7. An inventory count is not performed if the perpetual inventory system is used.

_____ 8. Advertising expenses would be considered general expenses on the income statement.

_____ 9. A higher inventory turnover is preferable to a lower turnover.

_____ 10. A company with a gross profit percentage of 40% must have a higher net income than one with a gross profit percentage of 30%.

Multiple Choice

1. **What do credit terms 1/10 n/30 indicate?**
   a. A 10% discount is available if payment is made within 30 days
   b. A 1% discount is available if payment is made within 10 days
   c. A 1% discount is available if payment is made within 30 days
   d. A 30% discount is available if payment is made within 10 days

2. **Which of the following is necessary to record the purchase of merchandise on account under a perpetual inventory system?**
   a. A credit to Cash
   b. A debit to Accounts Payable
   c. A credit to Inventory
   d. A debit to Inventory

3. **What account is credited when a discount is taken for prompt payment under a perpetual inventory system?**
   a. Accounts Payable
   b. Accounts Receivable
   c. Purchase Discounts
   d. Inventory

4. What is the entry required to record the payment of a $200 freight bill, assuming the shipping terms are FOB shipping point, under a perpetual inventory system?
   a. Debit Inventory and credit Cash
   b. Debit Accounts Payable and credit Inventory
   c. Debit Inventory and credit Purchase Discounts
   d. Debit Purchase Discounts and credit Inventory

5. How does the purchaser account for transportation charges when goods are shipped to them FOB destination?
   a. No journal entry would be recorded for the transportation charges.
   b. Debit Delivery Expense for the amount of the transportation charges.
   c. Debit Freight-in for the amount of the transportation charges.
   d. Debit Inventory for the amount of the transportation charges.

6. Which of the following accounts has a normal debit balance?
   a. Sales Revenue
   b. Sales Returns and Allowances
   c. Net Sales Revenue
   d. Gross Profit

7. When the seller is liable for the shipping costs, what account is debited when payment is made?
   a. Delivery Expense
   b. Freight-in
   c. Inventory
   d. Cash

8. Which of the following is necessary to record an adjustment to account for inventory shrinkage under a perpetual system?
   a. A credit to Miscellaneous Expense
   b. A credit to Cost of Goods Sold
   c. A credit to Inventory
   d. A debit to Miscellaneous Expense

9. Which of the following accounts should be closed to Income Summary?
   a. Beginning Inventory
   b. Sales Returns and Allowances
   c. Owner Withdrawals
   d. Ending Inventory

10. What does inventory turnover indicate?
    a. How quickly inventory is received from the supplier after the order is placed
    b. How many days it takes the inventory to travel between the seller's warehouse and the buyer's warehouse
    c. How rapidly inventory is sold
    d. How many days it takes from the time an order is received until the day it is shipped

Quick Exercises

5-1.   Werner Company purchased $11,000 of merchandise. The purchase invoice is for $11,200, which includes transportation charges of $200. The company returned $2,900 of the goods received before paying the invoice. The company paid the invoice within the discount terms, 2/10 n/30.

Requirement

1. Compute the following amounts:

    a. The amount of the discount

    b. The total amount for the merchandise recorded in the Inventory account

    c. The amount that the purchaser would remit if paid after the discount period

5-2.   Select whether the following accounts are:

    (A) Closed out with a debit to the account
    (B) Closed out with a credit to the account
    (C) Not closed out at all

a.	_____	Sales Revenue
b.	_____	Sales Returns and Allowances
c.	_____	Salary Expense
d.	_____	Inventory
e.	_____	Depreciation Expense
f.	_____	Accumulated Depreciation
g.	_____	Accounts Receivable
h.	_____	Interest Revenue
i.	_____	Interest Expense
j.	_____	Cost of Goods Sold

5-3.   The following data are for the Griswold Corporation, which uses the periodic inventory system.

Sales revenue	$600,000
Freight-in	42,000
Beginning inventory	77,000
Purchase discounts	19,000
Sales returns and allowances	33,000
Ending inventory	81,000
Inventory purchases	415,000
Sales discounts	35,000
Purchase returns and allowances	39,000

Requirements

1. Calculate Net Sales Revenue.

2. Calculate the Cost of Goods Available.

3. Calculate the Cost of Goods Sold.

5-4. Moyer Company had the following transactions during August 2007. Assuming that the perpetual inventory system is used, prepare the journal entries to record these transactions.

Aug. 5 Purchased $2,900 of merchandise on account from Ryan Company, terms 3/15 n/60.

Aug. 9 Paid transportation cost of $440 directly to the trucking company for the August 5 purchase.

Aug. 10 Returned $600 of unwanted merchandise purchased on August 5.

Aug. 15 Paid for the August 5 purchase, less the return and the discount.

Date	Accounts	Debit	Credit

Date	Accounts	Debit	Credit

Date	Accounts	Debit	Credit

Date	Accounts	Debit	Credit

5-5.   Prepare the necessary journal entries for Ryan Company using the transactions in 5-4. Assume that the cost of goods sold is 50% of the sales price.

Date	Accounts	Debit	Credit

Date	Accounts	Debit	Credit

Date	Accounts	Debit	Credit

Date	Accounts	Debit	Credit

Date	Accounts	Debit	Credit

Date	Accounts	Debit	Credit

Do It Yourself! Question 1

Franco Bros. began operations on January 1, 2008. Franco had the following transactions during the year:

Jan. 1   Purchased inventory for $150 under credit terms 2/10 net 30.

Jan. 8   Paid for the January 1 purchase in full.

Mar. 1   Purchased inventory for $240 under credit terms 2/20 net 45.

Apr. 1   Paid for the March 1 purchase in full.

July 1   Sold $80 worth of goods to a customer for $120 under credit terms 5/15 net eom (end of month).

July 12   Received cash payment in full for the July 1 sale.

Sept. 1   Found that 10% of the goods purchased on March 1 were defective. Franco Bros. returned these goods.

Oct. 1   Received cash refund for the goods returned on September 1.

Dec. 1   Sold $210 worth of goods to a customer for $320 under credit terms 1/15 net eom (end of month).

Dec. 6   Customer returned 20% of his December 1 order because he did not like the color of the goods.

Dec. 12   Customer paid for the December 1 order (less returns) in full.

Requirements

1. Account for the purchase of inventory

2. Account for the sale of inventory

1. Journalize these transactions using the perpetual system. Explanations are not required.

Date	Accounts	Debit	Credit
Jan. 1			

Date	Accounts	Debit	Credit
Jan. 8			

Date	Accounts	Debit	Credit
Mar. 1			

Date	Accounts		Debit	Credit
Apr. 1				

Date	Accounts		Debit	Credit
July 1				

Date	Accounts		Debit	Credit
July 12				

Date	Accounts		Debit	Credit
Sept. 1				

Date	Accounts		Debit	Credit
Oct. 1				

Date	Accounts		Debit	Credit
Dec. 1				

Date	Accounts		Debit	Credit
Dec. 6				

Date	Accounts		Debit	Credit
Dec. 12				

Adjust and close the accounts of a merchandising business

2. Show the Inventory and COGS T-accounts for the year.

Adjust and close the accounts of a merchandising business

3. Inventory on hand at December 31, 2008 (as per count) was $110. Make any necessary adjustments.

Date	Accounts	Debit	Credit

Prepare a merchandiser's financial statements

4. Prepare the top portion of Franco's 2008 income statement (ending with gross profit).

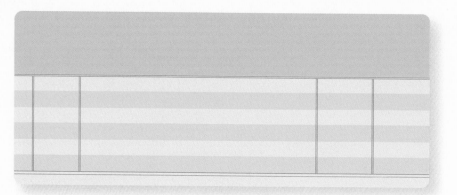

Quick Practice Solutions

True/False

T 1. Cost of Goods Sold is included in a merchandiser's income statement but excluded from a service company income statement. (p. 254)

T 2. Under the periodic inventory system, the only way to determine the cost of goods sold is to take a physical count of the merchandise on hand. (p. 256)

F 3. Most businesses use the periodic inventory system because it offers management more control over inventory.

   False—The *perpetual* inventory system offers management more control over inventory and is the system most businesses use. (p. 256)

T 4. A sales return requires two entries to be recorded if the seller uses a perpetual inventory system. (p. 262)

F 5. Sales Returns and Allowances is an expense account.

   False—Sales Returns and Allowances is a *contra account* to Sales Revenue. (p. 262)

F 6. The single-step income statement shows gross profit and income from operations.

   False—The *multistep* income statement shows gross profit and income from operations. (p. 271)

F 7. An inventory count is not performed if the perpetual inventory system is used.

   False—Inventory counts are performed for *all* inventory systems. (p. 256)

F 8. Advertising expenses would be considered general expenses on the income statement.

   False—Advertising would be considered a *selling* expense on the income statement. (p. 269)

T 9. A higher inventory turnover is preferable to a lower turnover. (p. 273)

F 10. A company with a gross profit percentage of 40% must have a higher net income than one with a gross profit percentage of 30%.

   False—The gross profit percentage indicates the amount of gross profit per dollar of sales. It does not consider the operating expenses, which are deducted from gross profit to determine net income. (p. 272)

Multiple Choice

1. **What do credit terms 1/10 n/30 indicate?** (p. 258)
    a. A 10% discount is available if payment is made within 30 days
    b. A 1% discount is available if payment is made within 10 days
    c. A 1% discount is available if payment is made within 30 days
    d. A 30% discount is available if payment is made within 10 days

2. Which of the following is necessary to record the purchase of merchandise on account under a perpetual inventory system? (p. 257)
   a. A credit to Cash
   b. A debit to Accounts Payable
   c. A credit to Inventory
   d. A debit to Inventory

3. What account is credited when a discount is taken for prompt payment under a perpetual inventory system? (p. 258)
   a. Accounts Payable
   b. Accounts Receivable
   c. Purchase Discounts
   d. Inventory

4. What is the entry required to journalize the payment of a $200 freight bill, assuming the shipping terms are FOB shipping point, under a perpetual inventory system? (p. 259)
   a. Debit Inventory and credit Cash
   b. Debit Accounts Payable and credit Inventory
   c. Debit Inventory and credit Purchase Discounts
   d. Debit Purchase Discounts and credit Inventory

5. How does the purchaser account for transportation charges when goods are shipped to the FOB destination? (p. 258)
   a. No journal entry would be recorded for the transportation charges.
   b. Debit Delivery Expense for the amount of the transportation charges.
   c. Debit Freight-in for the amount of the transportation charges.
   d. Debit Inventory for the amount of the transportation charges.

6. Which of the following accounts has a normal debit balance? (p. 262)
   a. Sales Revenue
   b. Sales Returns and Allowances
   c. Net Sales Revenue
   d. Gross Profit

7. When the seller is liable for the shipping costs, what account is debited when payment is made? (p. 260)
   a. Delivery Expense
   b. Freight-in
   c. Inventory
   d. Cash

8. Which of the following is necessary to record an adjustment to account for inventory shrinkage under a perpetual system? (p. 267)
   a. A credit to Miscellaneous Expense
   b. A credit to Cost of Goods Sold
   c. A credit to Inventory
   d. A debit to Miscellaneous Expense

9. Which of the following accounts should be closed to Income Summary? (p. 267)
   a. Beginning Inventory
   b. Sales Returns and Allowances
   c. Owner Withdrawals
   d. Ending Inventory

10. **What does inventory turnover indicate?** (p. 272)
   a. How quickly inventory is received from the supplier after the order is placed
   b. How many days it takes the inventory to travel between the seller's warehouse and the buyer's warehouse
   c. How rapidly inventory is sold
   d. How many days it takes from the time an order is received until the day it is shipped

Quick Exercises

5-1. Werner Company purchased $11,000 of merchandise. The purchase invoice is for $11,200, which includes transportation charges of $200. The company returned $2,900 of the goods received before paying the invoice. The company paid the invoice within the discount terms, 2/10 n/30. (p. 258)

Requirement

1. Compute the following amounts.

a. The amount of the discount

$$\$11,000 - 2,900 = \$8,100 \text{ net sales}$$
$$\$8,100 \times .02 = \$162$$

b. The total amount for the merchandise recorded in the Inventory account

$$\$11,200 - 2,900 - \$162 = \$8,138$$

c. The amount that the purchaser would remit if paid after the discount period

$$\$11,200 - 2,900 = \$8,300$$

5-2. Select whether the following accounts are (p. 257):

(A) Closed out with a debit to the account
(B) Closed out with a credit to the account
(C) Not closed out at all

a. _A_ Sales Revenue
b. _B_ Sales Returns and Allowances
c. _B_ Salary Expense
d. _C_ Inventory
e. _B_ Depreciation Expense
f. _C_ Accumulated Depreciation
g. _C_ Accounts Receivable
h. _A_ Interest Revenue
i. _B_ Interest Expense
j. _B_ Cost of Goods Sold

5-3. The following data are for the Griswold Corporation, which uses the periodic inventory system. (p. 273)

Sales revenue	$600,000
Freight-in	42,000
Beginning inventory	77,000
Purchase discounts	19,000
Sales returns and allowances	33,000
Ending inventory	81,000
Inventory purchases	415,000
Sales discounts	35,000
Purchase returns and allowances	39,000

Requirements

1. Calculate Net Sales Revenue

$600,000 - 33,000 - 35,000 = $532,000

2. Calculate the Cost of Goods Available

$77,000 + 415,000 + 42,000 - 19,000 - 39,000 = $476,000

3. Calculate the Cost of Goods Sold.

$476,000 - 81,000 = $395,000

5-4. Moyer Company had the following transactions during August 2007. Assuming that the perpetual inventory system is used, prepare the journal entries to record these transactions. (p. 256)

Aug. 5 Purchased $2,900 of merchandise on account from Ryan Company, terms 3/15 n/60.

Aug. 9 Paid transportation cost of $440 directly to the trucking company for the August 5 purchase.

Aug. 10 Returned $600 of unwanted merchandise purchased on August 5.

Aug. 15 Paid for the August 5 purchase, less the return and the discount.

Date	Accounts	Debit	Credit
Aug. 5	Inventory	2,900	
	Accounts Payable		2,900

Date	Accounts	Debit	Credit
Aug. 9	Inventory	440	
	Cash		440

Date	Accounts	Debit	Credit
Aug. 10	Accounts Payable	600	
	Inventory		600

Date	Accounts	Debit	Credit
Aug. 15	Accounts Payable	2,300	
	Inventory		69
	Cash		2,231

5-5. Prepare the necessary journal entries for Ryan Company using the transactions in 5-4. Assume that the cost of good sold is 50% of the sales price. (p. 256)

Date	Accounts	Debit	Credit
Aug. 5	Accounts Receivable	2,900	
	Sales		2,900

Date	Accounts	Debit	Credit
Aug. 5	Cost of Goods Sold	1,450	
	Inventory		1,450

Date	Accounts	Debit	Credit
Aug. 9	No Entry Required		

Date	Accounts	Debit	Credit
Aug. 10	Sales Returns and Allowances	600	
	Accounts Receivable		600

Date	Accounts	Debit	Credit
Aug. 10	Inventory	300	
	Cost of Goods Sold		300

Date	Accounts	Debit	Credit
Aug. 15	Cash	2,231	
	Sales Discounts	69	
	Accounts Receivable		2,300

Do It Yourself! Question 1 Solutions

Requirements

1. Journalize these transactions. Explanations are not required.

Date	Accounts	Debit	Credit
Jan. 1	Inventory	150	150
	Accounts Payable		

Date	Accounts	Debit	Credit
Jan. 8	Accounts Payable	150	
	Inventory (to balance*)		3
	Cash [(100% − 2%) × $150]		147

* = $150 − $147 = 3

Date	Accounts	Debit	Credit
Mar. 1	Inventory	240	
	Accounts Payable		240

Date	Accounts	Debit	Credit
Apr.1	Accounts Payable	240	
	Cash		240

Date	Accounts	Debit	Credit
July 1	Accounts Receivable	120	
	Sales Revenue		120
	COGS	80	
	Inventory		80

Date	Accounts	Debit	Credit
July 12	Cash [(100% − 5%) × $120]	114	
	Sales Discounts (to balance*)	6	
	Accounts Receivable		120

* = $120 − $114 = 6

Date	Accounts	Debit	Credit
Sept. 1	Accounts Receivable (10% × $240)	24	
	Inventory		24

Date	Accounts	Debit	Credit
Oct. 1	Cash	24	
	Accounts Receivable		24

Date	Accounts	Debit	Credit
Dec. 1	Accounts Receivable	320	
	Sales Revenue		320
	COGS	210	
	Inventory		210

Date	Accounts	Debit	Credit
Dec. 6	Inventory (20% × $210)	42	
	COGS		42
	Sales Returns and Allowances (20% × $320)	64	
	Accounts Receivable		64

Date	Accounts	Debit	Credit
Dec. 12	Cash ($320 – $64)	256	
	Accounts Receivable		256

2. Show the Inventory and COGS T-accounts for the year.

Inventory

Jan. 1	150		
		Jan. 8	3
Mar. 1	240		
		July 1	80
		Sept. 1	24
		Dec. 1	210
Dec. 6	42		
Bal.	115		

COGS

July 1	80		
Dec. 1	210		
		Dec. 6	42
Bal.	248		

3. Inventory on hand at December 31, 2008 (as per count) was $110. Make any necessary adjustments.

Dec. 31	COGS ($115 – $110)	5	
	Inventory		5

Inventory

Jan. 1	150		
		Jan. 8	3
Mar. 1	240		
		July 1	80
		Sept. 1	24
		Dec. 1	210
Dec. 6	42		
Bal.	115		
		Dec. 31	5
Bal.	110		

COGS

July 1	80		
Dec. 1	210		
		Dec. 6	42
Bal.	248		
Dec. 31	5		
Bal.	253		

4. Prepare the top portion of Franco's 2008 income statement (ending with gross profit).

FRANCO BROS.
Income Statement
Year Ended December 31, 2008

Sales revenue			$440*	
Less: Sales discounts		$ (6)		
Sales returns and allowances		(64)	(70)	
Net sales revenue				$370
Cost of goods sold				(253)
Gross profit				$117

*$120 + $320 = $440

The Power of Practice

For more practice using the skills learned in this chapter, visit MyAccountingLab. There you will find algorithmically generated questions that are based on these Demo Docs and your main textbook's Review and Assess Your Progress sections.

Go to MyAccountingLab and follow these steps:

1. Direct your URL to www.myaccountinglab.com.
2. Log in using your name and password.
3. Click the MyAccountingLab link.
4. Click Study Plan in the left navigation bar.
5. From the table of contents, select Chapter 5, Merchandising Operations.
6. Click a link to work tutorial exercises.

6 Merchandise Inventory

WHAT YOU PROBABLY ALREADY KNOW

Assume that you want to invest in the stock market. You purchase 100 shares of a stock mutual fund in January at $24/share, another 100 shares in February at $27/share, and another 100 shares in April at $30/share. In December, you decide to sell 200 shares of stock to purchase a used car. The market value of the stock at the date of sale is $35/share. You know that you will receive $7,000 (200 shares × $35/share) and that the market price of the shares is higher than what you paid, so you have a gain. To compute the amount of the gain you will have to report on your tax return, you must determine the cost of the shares. Because there were purchases over a period of time at several different prices, how is the cost computed for the 200 shares sold? Can we assume that the shares sold were the first 100 shares purchased at $24/share plus the next 100 shares purchased at $27/share for a total cost of $5,100, that is, (100 shares × $24) + (100 shares × $27)? Can we calculate the cost using an average? Yes, either of these methods is allowed by the Internal Revenue Service. The same problem exists for businesses to determine the cost of the inventory units sold when the unit cost varies. Generally accepted accounting principles (GAAP) also allows a choice from several methods to calculate the cost of goods sold.

Learning Objectives

1 Account for inventory by the FIFO, LIFO, and average-cost methods.

The inventory cost method selected for use is an *assumed* outflow of goods to determine the cost of goods sold expense and ending inventory; the actual physical outflow of goods sold may differ. **FIFO** is a popular method that *assumes the oldest goods are sold first leaving the newest goods in ending inventory.* **LIFO** is the opposite assumption; it *assumes that the newest goods are sold first leaving the oldest goods in ending inventory.* **Average cost** assumes that the goods sold as well as those in ending inventory have the same cost.

$$\frac{\text{Total cost of goods available for sale (Beginning inventory + Purchases)}}{\text{Total quantity of goods available for sale}} = \frac{\text{Average cost}}{\text{per unit of inventory}}$$

Review the inventory records and journal entries for these methods in Exhibits 6-2 through 6-6 (pp. 313–319).

2 Compare the effects of FIFO, LIFO, and average cost.

The cost of goods sold will usually be different for each of the methods. However, the sum of the cost of goods sold plus the cost of ending inventory will equal the cost of goods available for sale for all methods. In times of inflation, FIFO will result in higher net income and higher ending inventory amounts than LIFO. The average-cost method falls between FIFO and LIFO results. *Review the comparative results of these methods in Exhibit 6-8 (p. 320).*

3 Apply the lower-of-cost-or-market rule to inventory.

The inventory amount on the balance sheet is reduced to the market value if that amount is lower than the cost. This is an application of the conservatism concept. *Review the "Lower-of-Cost-or-Market Rule" section in the main text (p. 325). Note the required journal entry and balance sheet presentation.*

4 Measure the effects of inventory errors.

When measuring the effects of inventory errors, it is helpful to remember that:

Cost of goods sold + Cost of ending inventory = Cost of goods available

The cost of goods available is a defined amount. Therefore, if the cost of ending inventory is understated, the cost of goods sold must be overstated by the same amount to compensate for the error. **Understating ending inventory results in an understatement of net income.** The reverse is also true; **overstating ending inventory results in an overstatement of net income.**

The ending inventory for one period becomes the beginning inventory for the next. An error in ending inventory is carried over into the succeeding period. **Whatever effect the ending inventory error had on the income statement in the initial period causes the opposite effect on net income in the next period.** *Review the impact of ending inventory errors in Exhibits 6-9 and 6-10 (p. 327).*

5 Estimate ending inventory by the gross profit method.

Sometimes a business may need to estimate its ending inventory. If there is a natural disaster and the inventory is destroyed, an estimate must be determined for insurance purposes.

To calculate the estimate of inventory:

a.   Determine the cost of goods available for sale (Beginning inventory + Purchases).

b.   Estimate the cost of goods sold; Net sales − (Normal gross profit rate × Net sales).

c.   Subtract the estimate of cost of goods sold (b) from the cost of goods available for sale (a) to determine the *estimated cost of ending inventory.*

Review the gross profit method of estimating inventory in Exhibit 6-11 (p. 328).

Demo Doc 1

Inventory Costing Methods and Lower of Cost or Market

Learning Objectives 1–3

Collins Industries' inventory records show the following data for 2008:

Inventory at January 1	400 units	@	$2 each
Inventory Purchases, March	200 units	@	$3 each
Sales, May	160 units		
Inventory Purchases, July	100 units	@	$4 each
Sales, September	460 units		
Inventory Purchases, November	250 units	@	$5 each

Assume there is no inventory shrinkage.

Requirements

1. Calculate COGS for the year ended December 31, 2008, and inventory at December 31, 2008, under each of the following assumptions:

- FIFO (same for both periodic and perpetual)
- Periodic LIFO
- Perpetual LIFO
- Weighted Average (periodic average cost)
- Moving Average (perpetual average cost)

2. Sales revenues were $4,000 for 2008. Calculate gross profit under each method.

3. Now assume that Collins has a periodic inventory system. Which method would maximize net income? Which method would minimize income taxes?

4. Assume that Collins is using FIFO. The ending inventory has a market price of $4.50 per unit. Calculate the lower of cost or market and make any necessary adjustment.

Demo Doc 1 Solutions

Calculate COGS for the year ended December 31, 2008, and inventory at December 31, 2008, under each of the following assumptions.

- FIFO (same for both periodic and perpetual)
- Periodic LIFO
- Perpetual LIFO
- Weighted Average (periodic average cost)
- Moving Average (perpetual average cost)

Part 1	Part 2	Part 3	Part 4	Part 5	Part 6	Part 7	Part 8	Part 9	Demo Doc Complete

Before doing any costing calculations, it is important to determine the goods available for sale (both in units and dollars). We must also determine the number of units that were sold and the number of units in ending inventory.

$$\text{Goods available for sale} = \text{Beginning inventory} + \text{Purchases}$$

Beginning Inventory

	400 units	@	$2	=	$ 800

Inventory Purchases

	200 units	@	$3	=	600
	100 units	@	$4	=	400
	250 units	@	$5	=	1,250
	950 units				**$3,050**

= Goods Available for Sale

Number of units sold = 160 in May + 460 in September

= 620 units for the year

$$\text{COGS} = \text{Beginning inventory} + \text{Inventory purchases} - \text{Ending inventory}$$

OR

$$\text{COGS} = \text{Goods available for sale} - \text{Ending inventory}$$

This formula is expressed in *dollars*, but it also works in *units*:

$$\text{Units sold} = \text{Units in beginning inventory} + \text{Units purchased} - \text{Units in ending inventory}$$

OR

$$\text{Units sold} = \text{Units available for sale} - \text{Units in ending inventory}$$

$$620 \text{ units} = 950 \text{ units} - \text{Units in ending inventory}$$

$$\text{Units in ending inventory} = 330$$

1 Account for inventory by the FIFO, LIFO, and average-cost methods

2 Compare the effects of FIFO, LIFO, and average cost

FIFO

Part 1	**Part 2**	Part 3	Part 4	Part 5	Part 6	Part 7	Part 8	Part 9	Demo Doc Complete

It turns out that FIFO has the same mathematical results whether the calculations are done under the perpetual or the periodic method. Because the periodic method calculations are a little easier, we will save ourselves some work and assume periodic FIFO. Remember, the answer will be the same even if we are using perpetual FIFO.

We are using the FIFO method. This means *first in, first out*. In other words, we always sell the *oldest* item we have. So what is left in inventory? The *newest* units.

There were 620 units sold. Under FIFO, these are the *oldest* inventory items. The oldest inventory is the beginning inventory of 400 units @ $2/unit. They must be part of COGS.

There are 620 − 400 = 220 other units that were sold. Some of these must be from the next oldest inventory: the March purchase of 200 units @ $3/unit.

There are 220 − 200 = 20 other units that were also sold (that were not part of beginning inventory or the March purchase).

These other units must have come from the July purchase of 100 units @ $4/unit (the next oldest units).

So we can calculate COGS as:

From beginning inventory:		
400 units × $2 per unit	=	$ 800
From March purchase:		
200 units × $3 per unit	=	600
From July purchase:		
20 units × $4 per unit	=	80
COGS		**$1,480**

There are 330 units in ending inventory. These are the 330 *newest* units the company has.

The newest units are the ones purchased in November of 250 units @ $5 per unit. They must be part of the ending inventory.

There are 330 − 250 = 80 other units that are also part of ending inventory (that were not from the November purchase). These other units must have come from the July purchase of 100 units @ $4 per unit (the next newest units). So we can calculate ending inventory as:

From November purchase:

250 units × $5 per unit	=	$1,250

From July purchase:

80 units × $4 per unit	=	320
Ending Inventory		**$1,570**

We can use the inventory formula to check our calculation:

$$COGS = \$800 + \$2,250 − \$1,570 = \$1,480$$

OR

$$COGS = \$3,050 − \$1,570 = \$1,480$$

So under FIFO (whether using the periodic or perpetual method), COGS = $1,480 and inventory at December 31, 2008 = $1,570.

Periodic LIFO

Account for inventory by the FIFO, LIFO, and average-cost methods

Compare the effects of FIFO, LIFO, and average cost

Part 1	Part 2	**Part 3**	Part 4	Part 5	Part 6	Part 7	Part 8	Part 9	Demo Doc Complete

What differs under LIFO is the *dollar* amount of ending inventory and COGS. Notice that the number of *units* sold and the number of *units* in ending inventory are still the same at 620 and 330 units, respectively.

We are using the LIFO method. This means last-in-first-out. In other words, we always sell the *newest* item we have. So what is left in inventory? The *oldest* items.

There were 620 units sold. Under LIFO, COGS is made up of the *newest* inventory items.

The newest inventory is the November purchase of 250 units @ $5 per unit. These units must be part of COGS.

There are 620 − 250 = 370 other units that were sold. Some of these must be from the next newest inventory: the July purchase of 100 units @ $4 per unit.

There are 370 − 100 = 270 other units that were also sold (that were not part of the November or July purchases). Some of these must be from the next newest inventory: the March purchase of 200 units @ $3 per unit.

There are 270 − 200 = 70 other units that were also sold (that were not part of the November, July, or March purchases). These other units must have come from the beginning inventory of 400 units @ $2 per unit (the next newest units).

So we can calculate COGS as:

From November purchase:			
250 units × $5 per unit	=	$1,250	
From July purchase:			
100 units × $4 per unit	=	400	
From March purchase:			
200 units × $3 per unit	=	600	
From beginning inventory:			
70 units × $2 per unit	=	140	
COGS		**$2,390**	

Under the LIFO method, we always sell the *newest* items we have. So what is left in inventory? The *oldest* units. Ending inventory must be the 330 oldest units the company has.

The oldest units are the ones in beginning inventory: 400 units @ $2 per unit. All 330 units in ending inventory must have come from the beginning inventory.

So we can calculate ending inventory as 330 units × $2 per unit = $660.

We can use the inventory formula to check our calculations:

$$COGS = \$800 + \$2,250 - \$660 = \$2,390$$

OR

$$COGS = \$3,050 - \$660 = \$2,390$$

 Account for inventory by the FIFO, LIFO, and average-cost methods

 Compare the effects of FIFO, LIFO, and average cost

Perpetual LIFO

| Part 1 | Part 2 | Part 3 | **Part 4** | Part 5 | Part 6 | Part 7 | Part 8 | Part 9 | Demo Doc Complete |

While we are still working under LIFO and selling the newest units, we must track *each sale individually* with the perpetual recording system. It is also important to remember that under perpetual inventory recording, we are keeping up-to-date track of inventory. We cannot sell units that *we have not yet acquired.*

The first sale is in May when 160 units are sold. At this time, what were the newest units in stock? The 200 units @ $3 per unit purchased in March. So the 160 units sold must have come from this group. This means that:

$$\text{May COGS} = 160 \times \$3 = \$480$$

The second sale was in September when 460 units were sold. At that time, what were the newest units in stock? The 100 units @ $4 per unit purchased in July. But this is not enough to cover the entire sale. There were another 460 − 100 = 360 units sold.

Some of these other units must have come from the next newest group, the 200 units @ $3 per unit purchased in March. However, there are only 40 of these units left after the sale in May. There were another 360 − 40 = 320 units sold.

These other units must come from the beginning inventory of 400 units @ $2 per unit. This means that September COGS is calculated as:

From July purchase:

100 units × $4 per unit	=	$ 400
From March purchase:		
40 units × $3 per unit	=	120
From beginning inventory:		
320 units × $2 per unit	=	640
September COGS		$1,160

Total COGS for the period is the COGS for all sales added together:

May COGS	+	September COGS	=	Total COGS
$480	+	$1,160	=	$1,640

Inventory at December 31 is whatever remains.

There were 400 − 320 = 80 units of the beginning inventory (@ $2 per unit) that were not sold.

The entire March purchase of 200 units @ $3 per unit was sold in May (160 units) and September (40 units), so there is none of this inventory left unsold.

The entire July purchase of 100 units @ $4 per unit was sold in September.

None of the units from the November purchase of 250 units @ $5 per unit were sold. This means that all of these units are part of ending inventory. So we can calculate ending inventory as:

From beginning inventory:

80 units × $2 per unit	=	$ 160
From November purchase:		
250 units × $5 per unit	=	1,250
Ending Inventory		**$ 1,410**

We can use the inventory formula to check our calculations:

$$COGS = \$800 + \$2,250 - \$1,410 = \$1,640$$

OR

$$COGS = \$3,050 - \$1,410 = \$1,640$$

These same calculations can also be done in chart format:

	Purchases			Cost of Goods Sold			Inventory on Hand		
Date	Quantity	Unit Cost	Total Cost	Quantity	Unit Cost	Total Cost	Quantity	Unit Cost	Total Cost
January							400	$2	$ 800
March	200	$3	$ 600				400	$2	$ 800
							200	$3	$ 600
May				160	$3	$ 480	400	$2	$ 800
							40	$3	$ 120
July	100	$4	$ 400				400	$2	$ 800
							40	$3	$ 120
							100	$4	$ 400
September				100	$4	$ 400			
				40	$3	$ 120			
				320	$2	$ 640	80	$2	$ 160
November	250	$5	$1,250				80	$2	$ 160
							250	$5	$ 1,250
December				600		$1,640	330		$ 1,410

So under perpetual LIFO, COGS = $1,640 and inventory at December 31, 2008 = $1,410.

Account for inventory by the FIFO, LIFO, and average-cost methods

Compare the effects of FIFO, LIFO, and average cost

Weighted Average (periodic average cost)

Part 1	Part 2	Part 3	Part 4	**Part 5**	Part 6	Part 7	Part 8	Part 9	Demo Doc Complete

Under the average-cost method, we must calculate the average cost per unit of inventory. Because weighted average uses the periodic recording method, we only need to calculate this once for the entire period. Using the data calculated for the FIFO part of this problem:

$$\text{Average cost per unit} = \frac{\text{Goods available for sale}}{\text{Units available for sale}}$$

We know goods available for sale are the $800 (400 units) in beginning inventory + $2,250 (550 units) in inventory purchases = $3,050 (950 units). So the average cost per unit is:

$$\text{Average cost per unit} = \frac{\$3,050}{950 \text{ units}} = \$3.21 \text{ per unit}$$

We know that there are 330 units left in ending inventory, so inventory at December 31 is:

$$330 \text{ units} \times \$3.21 = \$1,060$$

We know that there were 620 units sold during the period, so:

$$\text{COGS} = 620 \text{ units} \times \$3.21 \text{ per unit} = \$1,990$$

We can check our calculations using the inventory formula:

$$\text{COGS} = \$800 + \$2,250 - \$1,060 = \$1,990$$

OR

$$\text{COGS} = \$3,050 - \$1,060 = \$1,990$$

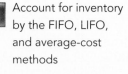

Account for inventory by the FIFO, LIFO, and average-cost methods

Compare the effects of FIFO, LIFO, and average cost

Moving Average (perpetual average cost)

Part 1	Part 2	Part 3	Part 4	Part 5	**Part 6**	Part 7	Part 8	Part 9	Demo Doc Complete

This method is the same as the weighted-average method, only it is under the perpetual system. This means that we need to recalculate the average cost per unit with *every* sale.

The first sale is in May. At that time in inventory, we have:

400 units × $2 per unit	=	$ 800
200 units × $3 per unit	=	600
600 units		$1,400

So at this time, the average cost per unit is:

$$\frac{\text{Average cost}}{\text{per unit}} = \frac{\text{Cost of units in inventory}}{\text{Units in inventory}}$$

$$\frac{\text{Average cost}}{\text{per unit}} = \frac{\$1,400}{600 \text{ units}} = \frac{\$2.33 \text{ per}}{\text{unit}}$$

The COGS for the May sale is:

$$160 \text{ units} \times \$2.33 \text{ per unit} = \$373$$

We have 600 units − 160 units = 440 units left in inventory @ $2.33 per unit = $1,025.

The next sale is in September. At this time in inventory, we have:

440 units × $2.33 per unit	=	$1,025
100 units × $4 per unit	=	400
540 units		$1,425

So at this time, the average cost per unit is:

$$\text{Average cost per unit} = \frac{\$1,425}{540 \text{ units}} = \$2.64 \text{ per unit}$$

$$\text{September COGS} = 460 \text{ units} \times \$2.64 \text{ per unit} = \$1,214$$

There are now 540 units − 460 units = 80 units left in inventory at the average cost of \$2.64 = \$211.

Total COGS for the period is the COGS for all sales added together:

$$\begin{array}{ccccc} \text{May COGS} & + & \text{September COGS} & = & \text{Total COGS} \\ \$373 & + & \$1,214 & = & \$1,587 \end{array}$$

Inventory at December 31, 2008, is the units left over after the September sale plus those purchased in November:

80 units × \$2.64 per unit	=	\$ 211
250 units × \$5 per unit	=	1,250
330 units in ending inventory		\$1,461

We can check our calculations using the inventory formula:[*]

$$\text{COGS} = \$800 + \$2,250 - \$1,461 = \$1,589$$

OR

$$\text{COGS} = \$3,050 - \$1,461 = \$1,589$$

[*]Note that the \$2 difference is due to rounding the per-unit cost under the moving average method.

These same calculations can also be done in chart format:

	Purchases			Cost of Goods Sold			Inventory on Hand		
Date	Quantity	Unit Cost	Total Cost	Quantity	Unit Cost	Total Cost	Quantity	Unit Cost	Total Cost
January				400	\$2.00	\$800			
March	200	\$3	\$ 600				400	\$2.00	\$ 800
							200	\$3.00	\$ 600
May				160	\$2.33	\$ 373	440	\$2.33	\$1,025
July	100	\$4	\$ 400				440	\$2.33	\$1,025
							100	\$4.00	\$ 400
September				460	\$2.64	\$1,214	80	\$2.64	\$ 211
November	250	\$5	\$1,250				80	\$2.64	\$ 211
							250	\$5.00	\$1,250
December				620		\$1,587	330		\$1,461

So under moving average, COGS = \$1,587 and inventory at December 31, 2008 = \$1,461.

Requirement 2

2 Compare the effects of FIFO, LIFO, and average cost

Sales revenues were $4,000 for 2008. Calculate gross profit under each method.

| Part 1 | Part 2 | Part 3 | Part 4 | Part 5 | Part 6 | **Part 7** | Part 8 | Part 9 | Demo Doc Complete |

Gross profit = Sales revenue − COGS

	FIFO	Periodic LIFO	Perpetual LIFO	Weighted Average	Moving Average
Sales Revenue	$4,000	$4,000	$4,000	$4,000	$4,000
− COGS	1,480	2,390	1,640	1,990	1,587
Gross Profit	$2,520	$1,610	$2,360	$2,010	$2,413

Requirement 3

2 Compare the effects of FIFO, LIFO, and average cost

Now assume that Collins has a periodic inventory system. Which method would maximize net income? Which method would minimize income taxes?

| Part 1 | Part 2 | Part 3 | Part 4 | Part 5 | Part 6 | Part 7 | **Part 8** | Part 9 | Demo Doc Complete |

For the *periodic* methods, we have the following COGS:

FIFO	$1,480
LIFO	2,390
Weighted Average	1,990

Of these, FIFO is the lowest and LIFO is the highest. Note that FIFO and LIFO will usually be the extremes with average cost being somewhere in the middle.

FIFO gives the lowest COGS, which means that it gives the highest gross profit. You can see this result in Requirement 2 of this question. This means that FIFO would maximize net income.

LIFO gives the highest COGS, which means that it gives the lowest gross profit. You can also see this result in Requirement 2 of this question. This means that LIFO would minimize net income, which in turn would minimize income taxes.

Note that if prices are decreasing over time (such as for high-tech items that quickly become obsolete), then the reverse of this analysis is true (FIFO gives highest COGS).

Requirement 4

Apply the lower-of-cost-or-market rule to inventory

Assume that Collins is using FIFO. The ending inventory has a market price of $4.50 per unit. Calculate the lower of cost or market and make any necessary adjustment.

Part 1	Part 2	Part 3	Part 4	Part 5	Part 6	Part 7	Part 8	**Part 9**	Demo Doc Complete

We have already determined that there are 330 units in ending inventory. Under FIFO, the cost of these units is $1,570. The market price of these units is:

$$330 \text{ units} \times \$4.50 \text{ per unit} = \$1,485$$

If cost is $1,570 and market price is $1,485, the lower of cost or market is $1,485 (the market value of the inventory).

The balance in the inventory T-account is currently the cost of $1,570. Therefore, Inventory must be decreased to the market value of $1,485. So Inventory is decreased (a credit) by $1,570 − $1,485 = $85. The other side of the journal entry is an adjustment to COGS. This will have to be a debit to balance out the credit to Inventory.

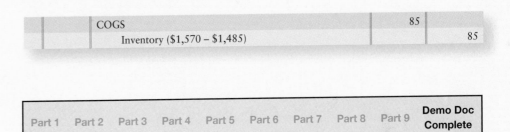

	COGS	85	
	Inventory ($1,570 − $1,485)		85

Part 1	Part 2	Part 3	Part 4	Part 5	Part 6	Part 7	Part 8	Part 9	**Demo Doc Complete**

Demo Doc 2

Gross Profit Method and Inventory Errors

Learning Objectives 4, 5

On December 31, 2008, Talon Corp.'s warehouse and accounting records were destroyed in a flood. For insurance purposes, Talon must estimate the value of the inventory lost.

   Through records from its bank and suppliers, Talon has been able to compile the following information:

Sales Revenue for 2008	$20,000
Inventory at December 31, 2007	6,000
Inventory Purchases for 2008	23,000

Talon has historically had gross profit of 10%.

Requirements

1. Estimate Talon's ending inventory value for 2008 using the gross profit method.

2. Assume that the actual value of inventory lost was $12,000. What is Talon's true COGS? Is COGS overstated or understated? How will this impact Talon's estimate of net income for 2008?

Demo Doc 2 Solutions

 Estimate ending inventory by the gross profit method

Requirement 1

Estimate Talon's ending inventory value for 2008 using the gross profit method.

Part 1	Part 2	Demo Doc Complete

The gross profit method uses the COGS formula:

$$\text{COGS} = \begin{matrix}\text{Beginning}\\\text{inventory}\end{matrix} + \begin{matrix}\text{Inventory}\\\text{purchases}\end{matrix} - \begin{matrix}\text{Ending}\\\text{inventory}\end{matrix}$$

We are given information about purchases and beginning inventory, but to calculate ending inventory we will need an estimate for COGS.

The formula for the gross profit percentage is:

$$\begin{matrix}\text{Gross profit}\\\text{percentage}\end{matrix} = \frac{\text{Gross profit}}{\text{Sales revenue}} = \frac{\text{Sales} - \text{COGS}}{\text{Sales}}$$

So we know that 10% = ($20,000 − COGS)/$20,000.
From this, we can calculate COGS = $18,000. Using this in the COGS formula:

$$\$18,000 = \$6,000 + \$23,000 - \text{Ending inventory}$$

From this, we can calculate ending inventory = $11,000.

Requirement 2

 Measure the effects of inventory errors

Assume that the actual value of inventory lost was $12,000. What is Talon's true COGS? Is COGS overstated or understated? How will this impact Talon's estimate of net income for 2008?

Part 1	Part 2	Demo Doc Complete

Using the actual value of $12,000 for ending inventory, we can recalculate COGS.

$$\text{COGS} = \$6,000 + \$23,000 - \$12,000 = \$17,000$$

Because Talon is estimating COGS of $18,000, COGS is overstated by $18,000 − $17,000 = $1,000. If Talon uses the wrong COGS number of $18,000 to calculate net income, then net income will be understated by $1,000.

Part 1	Part 2	Demo Doc Complete

Quick Practice Questions

True/False

_____ 1. Under FIFO, the ending inventory cost comes from the oldest purchases.

_____ 2. FIFO is the opposite of LIFO.

_____ 3. The LIFO method can result in misleading inventory costs on the balance sheet because the oldest prices are left in ending inventory.

_____ 4. When inventory costs are rising, LIFO will result in the lowest gross profit.

_____ 5. When using a perpetual inventory system, a business will debit Inventory and credit Cost of Goods Sold each time a sale is recorded.

_____ 6. If a company had 10 units of beginning inventory with a unit cost of $10 and a subsequent purchase of 15 units with a unit cost of $12, the average cost of one unit sold would be $11.

_____ 7. When applying lower-of-cost-or-market rules to ending inventory valuation, market value generally refers to the company's current selling price for its inventory.

_____ 8. Understating beginning inventory in the current year will understate cost of goods sold in the current year.

_____ 9. Overstating ending inventory in 2007 will overstate net income for 2008.

_____ 10. The gross profit method is an estimate of inventory that can be used to estimate losses for insurance claims due to a fire or natural disaster.

Multiple Choice

1. Anticipating no gains but providing for all probable losses can be most closely associated with which of the following?
   a. Conservatism
   b. Disclosure principle
   c. Consistency principle
   d. Materiality concept

2. Which of the following are required to record the sale of merchandise on credit under a perpetual inventory system?
   a. Debit Accounts Receivable; credit Sales Revenue
   b. Debit Cost of Goods Sold; credit Purchases
   c. Debit Cost of Goods Sold; credit Inventory
   d. Both (a) and (c) are necessary entries

3. What is the effect of using FIFO during a period of rising prices under a perpetual inventory system?
   a. Less net income than LIFO
   b. Less operating expenses than LIFO
   c. Higher gross profit than LIFO
   d. Higher cost of goods sold than average costing

4. Which of the following is NOT a reason for choosing the LIFO method?
   a. LIFO reports the most up-to-date inventory values on the balance sheet.
   b. LIFO uses more current costs in calculating cost of goods sold.
   c. LIFO allows owners and managers to manage reported income.
   d. LIFO generally results in lower income taxes paid.

5. Which of the following is true for ending inventory when prices are falling and the LIFO inventory system is used?
   a. LIFO ending inventory is less than FIFO.
   b. LIFO ending inventory is greater than FIFO.
   c. LIFO ending inventory is equal to FIFO.
   d. LIFO ending inventory is equally likely to be higher or lower than FIFO.

6. The following data are for Daisy's Florist Shop for the first seven months of its fiscal year:

Beginning inventory	$53,500
Purchases	75,500
Net sales revenue	93,700
Normal gross profit percent	30%

   What is the estimated inventory on hand as determined by the gross profit method?
   a. $28,110
   b. $63,410
   c. $65,590
   d. $100,890

7. Which of the following statements is true about a company making an accounting change in its financial statements?
   a. It is generally entitled to make one accounting change per year.
   b. It must report the change in accounting method.
   c. Companies can never make accounting changes because of the consistency principle.
   d. It must petition the Financial Accounting Standards Board for permission to make the change.

8. When is an item considered material?
   a. When it facilitates comparison with the financial statements of another company in the same industry
   b. When its inclusion in the financial statements would cause a statement user to change a decision
   c. When its dollar value is greater than 10% of net income
   d. When it is accounted for using a treatment that is not normally allowed by generally accepted accounting principles

9. Ending inventory for Commodity X consists of 20 units. Under the FIFO method, the cost of the 20 units is $5 each. Current replacement cost is

$4.50 per unit. Using the lower-of-cost-or-market rule to value inventory, the balance sheet would show ending inventory at what amount?
a. $4.75
b. $5.00
c. $90.00
d. $100.00

10. Inventory at the end of the current year is overstated by $20,000. What effect will this error have on the following year's net income?
a. Net income will be overstated $20,000.
b. Net income will be understated $20,000.
c. Net income will be correctly stated.
d. Net income will be understated $40,000.

Quick Exercises

6-1. Compute the missing income statement amounts for each of the following independent companies:

Company	Net Sales	Beginning Inventory	Purchases	Ending Inventory	Cost of Goods Sold	Gross Profit
A	$93,000	$14,600	$65,000	(a)	$58,300	(b)
B	(c)	$31,600	(d)	$23,600	$96,200	$52,500
C	$89,300	$23,600	$54,000	(f)	(e)	$23,900
D	$105,000	$11,200	(h)	$9,400	(g)	$48,200

6-2. Which inventory method would best meet the specific goal of management stated below? Show your answer by inserting the proper letter beside each statement.

a. Specific unit cost
b. LIFO
c. FIFO
d. Average cost

_____ 1. Management desires to properly match net sales revenue with the most recent cost of goods.
_____ 2. Management desires to minimize the company's ending inventory balance during a period of falling prices.
_____ 3. The company sells rare antique items.
_____ 4. Management desires to show the current value of inventory on the balance sheet.
_____ 5. Management desires to minimize the company's tax liability during a period of rising prices.

6-3. The following data are available for the month of March:

March 1 balance 20 units at $16 each

March 10 purchase 40 units at $18 each

March 17 purchase 30 units at $20 each

March 30 purchase 25 units at $21 each

On March 31, 35 units are on hand.

Requirement:

1. Calculate cost of goods sold under the following methods:

    a. FIFO

    b. LIFO

    c. Average cost (round the per-unit cost to the nearest cent; round the final answer to the nearest dollar)

6-4.   Plastic Products Company lost some of its inventory due to a flood and needs to determine the amount of the inventory lost. The following data are available for 2008:

Sales revenue	$400,000
Estimated gross profit rate	35%
January 1, beginning inventory	11,600
Net purchases	275,000
Inventory on hand, after flood	6,500

Requirements

1. Compute what the estimated ending inventory should be using the gross profit method.

2. Calculate the amount of the inventory loss.

6-5.   Determine the effect on cost of goods sold and net income for the current year of the following inventory errors. Indicate your answer with either a + (overstated) or a − (understated).

Item	Error	Effect on Cost of Goods Sold	Effect on Net Income
1	Beginning inventory is understated.		
2	Ending inventory is understated.		
3	Beginning inventory is overstated.		
4	Ending inventory is overstated.		

Do It Yourself! Question 1

Sam Inc.'s inventory records show the following data for July 2008:

Inventory at July 1	10 units	@	$1 each
Inventory Purchases, July 5	80 units	@	$2 each
Sales, July 10	50 units		
Inventory Purchases, July 15	20 units	@	$3 each
Sales, July 20	40 units		
Inventory Purchases, July 25	30 units	@	$4 each

Assume there is no inventory shrinkage.

Requirements

 Account for inventory by the FIFO, LIFO, and average-cost methods

1. Calculate COGS for the month ended July 31, 2008, and inventory at July 31, 2008, using the FIFO costing method.

2. Calculate COGS for the month ended July 31, 2008, and inventory at July 31, 2008, using the periodic LIFO costing method.

Compare the effects of FIFO, LIFO, and average cost

3. Calculate COGS for the month ended July 31, 2008, and inventory at July 31, 2008, using the perpetual LIFO costing method.

Account for inventory by the FIFO, LIFO, and average-cost methods

4. Calculate COGS for the month ended July 31, 2008, and inventory at July 31, 2008, using the weighted average (periodic average cost) costing method.

Compare the effects of FIFO, LIFO, and average cost

5. Calculate COGS for the month ended July 31, 2008, and inventory at July 31, 2008, using the moving average (perpetual average cost) costing method.

Compare the effects of FIFO, LIFO, and average cost

6. Sales revenues were $500 for July 2008. Calculate gross profit under each method.

Apply the lower-of-cost-or-market rule to inventory

7. The market value of ending inventory is $130. If Sam Inc. uses perpetual LIFO, give any necessary adjustment for the lower-of-cost-or-market rule.

Do It Yourself! Question 2

On December 31, 2008, Virga Brothers lost all of its inventory during a hurricane. Virga was able to gather the following information.

Inventory at January 1, 2008	$ 40,000
Inventory Purchases for 2008	90,000
Sales Revenue for 2008	180,000

Historically, Virga has had gross profit of 40%.

Requirement

1. Estimate the value of Virga's lost inventory.

Quick Practice Solutions

True/False

_F_ 1. Under FIFO, the ending inventory cost comes from the oldest purchases.

False—FIFO leaves in ending inventory the last or *newest* costs. (p. 314)

_T_ 2. FIFO is the opposite of LIFO. (p. 314)

_T_ 3. The LIFO method can result in misleading inventory costs on the balance sheet because the oldest prices are left in ending inventory. (p. 314)

_T_ 4. When inventory costs are rising, LIFO will result in the lowest gross profit. (p. 320)

_F_ 5. When using a perpetual inventory system, a business will debit Inventory and credit Cost of Goods Sold each time a sale is recorded.

False—Using a perpetual inventory system, a business will *debit* Cost of Goods Sold and *credit* Inventory each time a sale is recorded. (p. 315)

_F_ 6. If a company had 10 units of beginning inventory with a unit cost of $10 and a subsequent purchase of 15 units with a unit cost of $12, the average cost of one unit sold would be $11.

False—Average cost is determined by dividing the cost of goods available, (10 units × $10) + (15 units $12) = $280, by the number of units available, (10 + 15 = 25). $280/25 = $11.20. (p. 318)

_F_ 7. When applying lower-of-cost-or-market rules to ending inventory valuation, market value generally refers to the company's current selling price for its inventory.

False—Market value generally means current *replacement* cost. (p. 325)

_T_ 8. Understating beginning inventory in the current year will understate cost of goods sold in the current year. (p. 326)

_F_ 9. Overstating ending inventory in 2007 will overstate net income for 2008.

False—Overstating ending inventory in 2007 will *understate* net income for 2008. (p. 326)

_T_ 10. The gross profit method is an estimate of inventory that can be used to estimate losses for insurance claims due to a fire or natural disaster. (p. 328)

Multiple Choice

1. **Anticipating no gains but providing for all probable losses can be most closely associated with which of the following?** (p. 324)
   a. Conservatism
   b. Disclosure principle
   c. Consistency principle
   d. Materiality concept

2. Which of the following are required to record the sale of merchandise on credit under a perpetual inventory system? (p. 316)
   a. Debit Accounts Receivable; credit Sales Revenue
   b. Debit Cost of Goods Sold; credit Purchases
   c. Debit Cost of Goods Sold; credit Inventory
   d. Both (a) and (c) are necessary entries

3. What is the effect of using FIFO during a period of rising prices under a perpetual inventory system? (p. 320)
   a. Less net income than LIFO
   b. Less operating expenses than LIFO
   c. Higher gross profit than LIFO
   d. Higher cost of goods sold than average costing

4. Which of the following is NOT a reason for choosing the LIFO method? (p. 317)
   a. LIFO reports the most up-to-date inventory values on the balance sheet.
   b. LIFO uses more current costs in calculating cost of goods sold.
   c. LIFO allows owners and managers to manage reported income.
   d. LIFO generally results in lower income taxes paid.

5. Which of the following is true for ending inventory when prices are falling and the LIFO inventory system is used? (p. 320)
   a. LIFO ending inventory is less than FIFO.
   b. LIFO ending inventory is greater than FIFO.
   c. LIFO ending inventory is equal to FIFO.
   d. LIFO ending inventory is equally likely to be higher or lower than FIFO.

6. The following data are for Daisy's Florist Shop for the first seven months of its fiscal year:

Beginning inventory	$53,500
Purchases	75,500
Net sales revenue	93,700
Normal gross profit percent	30%

   What is the estimated inventory on hand as determined by the gross profit method? (p. 328)
   a. $28,110
   b. $63,410
   c. $65,590
   d. $100,890

7. Which of the following statements is true about a company making an accounting change in its financial statements? (p. 324)
   a. It is generally entitled to make one accounting change per year.
   b. It must report the change in accounting method.
   c. Companies can never make accounting changes because of the consistency principle.
   d. It must petition the Financial Accounting Standards Board for permission to make the change.

8. When is an item considered material? (p. 324)
    a. When it facilitates comparison with the financial statements of another company in the same industry
    b. When its inclusion in the financial statements would cause a statement user to change a decision
    c. When its dollar value is greater than 10% of net income
    d. When it is accounted for using a treatment that is not normally allowed by generally accepted accounting principles

9. Ending inventory for Commodity X consists of 20 units. Under the FIFO method, the cost of the 20 units is $5 each. Current replacement cost is $4.50 per unit. Using the lower-of-cost-or-market rule to value inventory, the balance sheet would show ending inventory at what amount? (p. 325)
    a. $4.75
    b. $5.00
    c. $90.00
    d. $100.00

10. Inventory at the end of the current year is overstated by $20,000. What effect will this error have on the following year's net income? (p. 326)
    a. Net income will be overstated $20,000.
    b. Net income will be understated $20,000.
    c. Net income will be correctly stated.
    d. Net income will be understated $40,000.

Quick Exercise

6-1. Compute the missing income statement amounts for each of the following independent companies: (p. 315)

Company	Net Sales	Beginning Inventory	Purchases	Ending Inventory	Cost of Goods Sold	Gross Profit
A	$ 93,000	$14,600	$65,000	(a)	$58,300	(b)
B	(c)	$31,600	(d)	$23,600	$96,200	$52,500
C	$ 89,300	$23,600	$54,000	(f)	(e)	$23,900
D	$105,000	$11,200	(h)	$ 9,400	(g)	$48,200

(a) $14,600 + $65,000 − $58,300 = $21,300
(b) $93,000 − $58,300 = $34,700
(c) $96,200 + $52,500 = $148,700
(d) $23,600 + $96,200 − $31,600 = $88,200
(e) $89,300 − $23,900 = $65,400
(f) $23,600 + $54,000 − $65,400 = $12,200
(g) $105,000 − $48,200 = $56,800
(h) $9,400 + $56,800 − $11,200 = $55,000

6-2.   Which inventory method would best meet the specific goal of management stated below? Show your answer by inserting the proper letter beside each statement. (p. 315)

   a.   Specific unit cost
   b.   LIFO
   c.   FIFO

   __b__ 1. Management desires to properly match net sales revenue with the most recent cost of goods.
   __c__ 2. Management desires to minimize the company's ending inventory balance during a period of falling prices.
   __a__ 3. The company sells rare antique items.
   __c__ 4. Management desires to show the current value of inventory on the balance sheet.
   __b__ 5. Management desires to minimize the company's tax liability during a period of rising prices.

6-3.   The following data are available for the month of March: (p. 315)

   March 1 balance 20 units at $16 each

   March 10 purchase 40 units at $18 each

   March 17 purchase 30 units at $20 each

   March 30 purchase 25 units at $21 each

   On March 31, 35 units are on hand.

Requirement

1. Calculate cost of goods sold under the following methods:

   a.   FIFO
        115 units available − 35 ending units = 80 units sold
        Cost of goods sold:
        (20 × $16) + (40 × $18) + (20 × $20) = $320 + $720 + $400 = $1,440
   b.   LIFO
        (25 × $21) + (30 × $20) + (25 × $18) = $525 + $600 + 450 = $1,575
   c.   Average cost (round the per-unit cost to the nearest cent, round the final answer to the nearest dollar)
        (20 × $16) + (40 × $18) + (30 × $20) + (25 × $21) = $320 + $720 + $600 + $525 = $2,165
        $2,165/115 units = $18.83
        $18.83 × 80 = $1,506

6-4.   Plastic Products Company lost some of its inventory due to a flood and needs to determine the amount of the inventory lost. The following data are available for 2008: (p. 328)

Net sales revenue	$400,000
Estimated gross profit rate	35%
January 1, beginning inventory	11,600
Net purchases	275,000
Inventory on hand, after flood	6,500

Requirements

1. Compute what the estimated ending inventory should be using the gross profit method.

Beginning inventory		$ 11,600
Net purchases		275,000
Cost of goods available		286,600
Estimated cost of goods sold:		
Net sales revenue	400,000	
Less: Estimated gross profit of 35%	(140,000)	
Estimated cost of goods sold		260,000
Estimated cost of ending inventory		$ 26,600

2. Calculate the amount of the inventory loss.

Estimated cost of ending inventory	$ 26,600
Less: Inventory on hand, after flood	6,500
Amount of inventory loss	$ 20,100

6-5. Determine the effect on cost of goods sold and net income for the current year of the following inventory errors. Indicate your answer with either a + (overstated) or a − (understated). (p. 326)

Item	Error	Effect on Cost of Goods Sold	Effect on Net Income
1	Beginning inventory is understated.	−	+
2	Ending inventory is understated.	+	−
3	Beginning inventory is overstated.	+	−
4	Ending inventory is overstated.	−	+

Do It Yourself! Question 1 Solutions

Requirements

1. Calculate COGS for the month ended July 31, 2008, and inventory at July 31, 2008, using the FIFO costing method.

Beginning Inventory	10 units	@ $1 per unit	= $	10
Inventory Purchases				
July 5	80 units	@ $2 per unit	=	160
July 15	20 units	@ $3 per unit	=	60
July 25	30 units	@ $4 per unit	=	120
Goods Available for Sale	130 units			$350

Number of units sold

= 50 on July 10 + 40 on July 20 = 90 units

90 units = 10 units + 130 units − Units in ending inventory

OR

90 units = 140 units − Units in ending inventory

Units in ending inventory = 50 units

From beginning inventory:

10 units × $1 per unit	=	$ 10
From July 5 purchase:		
80 units × $2 per unit	=	160
COGS		$170

From July 25 purchase:

30 units × $4 per unit	=	$120
From July 15 purchase:		
20 units × $3 per unit	=	60
Ending Inventory		$180

Check:

COGS = $10 + $340 − $180 = $170

OR

COGS = $350 − $180 = $170

2. Calculate COGS for the month ended July 31, 2008, and inventory at July 31, 2008, using the periodic LIFO costing method.

From July 25 purchase:

30 units × $4 per unit	=	$120
From July 15 purchase:		
20 units × $3 per unit	=	60
From July 5 purchase:		
40 units × $2 per unit	=	80
COGS		$260

From beginning inventory:

10 units × $1 per unit	=	$ 10
From July 5 purchase:		
40 units × $2 per unit	=	80
Ending Inventory		$ 90

Check:

$$COGS = \$10 + \$340 - \$90 = \$260$$

OR

$$COGS = \$350 - \$90 = \$260$$

3. Calculate COGS for the month ended July 31, 2008, and inventory at July 31, 2008, using the perpetual LIFO costing method.

$$\text{July 10 COGS} = 50 \times \$2 \text{ (from July 5 purchase)} = \$100$$

From July 15 purchase:

20 units × $3 per unit	=	$ 60
From July 5 purchase:		
20 units × $2 per unit	=	40
July 20 COGS		$100

July 10 COGS	+	July 20 COGS	=	Total COGS
$100	+	$100	=	$200

From beginning inventory:

10 units $\times$ \$1 per unit	=	\$ 10	

From July 5 purchase:

10 units $\times$ \$2 per unit	=	20	

From July 25 purchase:

30 units $\times$ \$4 per unit	=	120	
Ending Inventory		\$150	

Check:

$$COGS = \$10 + \$340 - \$150 = \$200$$

OR

$$COGS = \$350 - \$150 = \$200$$

These same calculations can also be done in chart format:

	Purchases			Cost of Goods Sold			Inventory on Hand		
Date	Quantity	Unit Cost	Total Cost	Quantity	Unit Cost	Total Cost	Quantity	Unit Cost	Total Cost
July 1							10	\$1	\$ 10
July 5	80	\$2	\$ 160				10	\$1	\$ 10
							80	\$2	\$160
July 10				50	\$2	\$100	10	\$1	\$ 10
							30	\$2	\$ 60
July 15	20	\$3	\$ 60				10	\$1	\$ 10
							30	\$2	\$ 60
							20	\$3	\$ 60
July 20				20	\$3	\$ 60	10	\$1	\$ 10
				20	\$2	\$ 40	10	\$2	\$ 20
July 25	30	\$4	\$ 120				10	\$1	\$ 10
							10	\$2	\$ 20
							30	\$4	\$120
July 31				90	\$200		50		\$150

4. Calculate COGS for the month ended July 31, 2008, and inventory at July 31, 2008, using the weighted average (periodic average cost) costing method.

$$\frac{\text{Average cost}}{\text{per unit}} = \frac{\$10 + \$340}{10 \text{ units} + 130 \text{ units}} = \frac{\$350}{140 \text{ units}}$$

$= \$2.50$ per unit

Ending inventory $= 50$ units $\times \$2.50 = \$125$

COGS $= 90$ units $\times \$2.50$ per unit $= \$225$

Check:

$$\text{COGS} = \$10 + \$340 - \$125 = \$225$$

OR

$$\text{COGS} = \$350 - \$125 = \$225$$

5. Calculate COGS for the month ended July 31, 2008, and inventory at July 31, 2008, using the moving average (perpetual average cost) costing method.

July 9 Inventory:

10 units $\times \$1$ per unit	=	$\$ \ 10$
80 units $\times \$2$ per unit	=	$\underline{\ 160}$
90 units		$\$170$

For July 10 Sale:

$$\frac{\text{Average cost}}{\text{per unit}} = \frac{\$170}{90 \text{ units}} = \frac{\$1.89}{\text{per unit}}$$

July 10 COGS = 50 units $\times \$1.89$ per unit = $94

Inventory after July 10 sale = 40 units $\times \$1.89$ per unit = $76

July 19 Inventory:

40 units $\times \$1.89$ per unit	=	$\$ \ 76$
20 units $\times \$3$ per unit	=	$\underline{\ 60}$
60 units		$\$136$

For July 20 Sale:

$$\text{Average cost per unit} = \frac{\$136}{60 \text{ units}} = \$2.27 \text{ per unit}$$

July 20 COGS = 40 units $\times$ $2.27 per unit = $91

Inventory after July 20 sale = 20 units $\times$ $2.27 per unit = $45

July 10 COGS + July 20 COGS = Total COGS

  $94 + $91 = $185

Remaining inventory after previous sale:

20 units $\times$ $2.27 per unit	=	$ 45
From July 25 Purchase		
30 units $\times$ $4 per unit	=	120
Ending Inventory		$165

Check:

$$\text{COGS} = \$10 + \$340 - \$165 = \$185$$

OR

$$\text{COGS} = \$350 - \$165 = \$185$$

These same calculations can also be made in chart format:

	Purchases			Cost of Goods Sold			Inventory on Hand		
Date	Quantity	Unit Cost	Total Cost	Quantity	Unit Cost	Total Cost	Quantity	Unit Cost	Total Cost
July 1							10	$1.00	$ 10
July 5	80	$2.00	$160				10	$1.00	$ 10
							80	$2.00	$160
July 10				50	$1.89	$ 94	40	$1.89	$ 76
July 15	20	$3.00	$ 60				40	$1.89	$ 76
							20	$3.00	$ 60
July 20				40	$2.27	$ 91	20	$2.27	$ 45
July 25	30	$4.00	$120				20	$2.27	$ 45
							30	$4.00	$120
July 31				90		$185	50		$165

6. Sales revenues were $500 for 2008. Calculate gross profit under each method.

	FIFO	Periodic LIFO	Perpetual LIFO	Weighted Average	Moving Average
Sales Revenue	$500	$500	$500	$500	$500
−COGS	170	260	200	225	185
Gross Profit	$330	$240	$300	$275	$315

7. The market value of ending inventory is $130. If Sam Inc. uses perpetual LIFO, give any necessary adjustment for the lower-of-cost-or-market rule.

Cost (under perpetual LIFO) = $150   Market = $130

Lower of cost or market   = $130

COGS		20	
Inventory ($150 − $130)			20

Do It Yourself! Question 2 Solutions

Requirement

1. Estimate the value of Virga's lost inventory.

$$\frac{\text{Gross profit}}{\text{percentage}} = \frac{\text{Gross profit}}{\text{Sales revenue}} = \frac{\text{Sales} - \text{COGS}}{\text{Sales}}$$

$$40\% = (\$180,000 - \text{COGS}) / \$180,000$$

$$\text{COGS} = \$108,000$$

$$\text{COGS} = \frac{\text{Beginning}}{\text{inventory}} + \frac{\text{Inventory}}{\text{purchases}} - \frac{\text{Ending}}{\text{inventory}}$$

$$\$108,000 = \$40,000 + \$90,000 - \text{Ending inventory}$$

$$\text{Ending inventory} = \$22,000$$

The Power of Practice

For more practice using the skills learned in this chapter, visit MyAccountingLab. There you will find algorithmically generated questions that are based on these Demo Docs and your main textbook's Review and Assess Your Progress sections.

Go to MyAccountingLab and follow these steps:

1. Direct your URL to www.myaccountinglab.com.
2. Log in using your name and password.
3. Click the MyAccountingLab link.
4. Click Study Plan in the left navigation bar.
5. From the table of contents, select Chapter 6, Merchandise Inventory.
6. Click a link to work tutorial exercises.

7 Accounting Information Systems

What You Probably Already Know

If you enroll in four classes this semester, you know that you will need to take notes and organize them efficiently. You could purchase several large notebooks and enter your notes in the order in which you attend each class Monday through Friday throughout the semester. This would be similar to the general journal. But it would be more efficient to group your notes in chronological order *by task or class*. Organizing your notes in this manner facilitates the review of what has transpired in the past and action that may be required related only to that specific class. This is similar to special journals, which group transactions by task.

Learning Objectives

1 Describe an effective accounting information system.

Four essential characteristics of an effective accounting information system are:

a. **Control**—Controls must be in place to monitor all aspects of the business.
b. **Compatibility**—The information system must work well for your business structure and personnel.
c. **Flexibility**—The system must be able to accommodate change as the business evolves.
d. **Good Cost/Benefit Relationship**—Consider the cost of an initiative compared to the benefit to be derived. Select the most economical option.

2 Understand both computerized and manual accounting systems.

Computerized and manual accounting systems both have the same basic elements: inputs (invoices, checks, and faxes), processing, and outputs (financial reporting outputs for decision making). In a computerized system, transactions are processed by function, such as cash payments. There are updates to the ledger account balances after the **online** or **batch processing** is completed. In a manual system, each function that occurs with regularity is grouped into a special journal just for that particular task. **Special journals** group certain types of transactions and facilitate the recordkeeping. Common special journals used in addition to the general journal include the following:

- Sales Journal—records sales on account

- Cash Receipts Journal—records all cash receipts for any reason

- Purchases Journal—records purchases of anything on account

- Cash Payments Journal—records all cash payments for any reason

NOTE: There MUST be equal debit and credit entries recorded in the journal columns for each transaction. *Review Exhibits 7-1 through 7-4 (pp. 355–357).*

3 **Understand how spreadsheets are used in accounting.**

A **spreadsheet** is a grid with rows and columns. Each **cell** is a specific row and column combination that can represent a number, word, or formula. Spreadsheets are used extensively in accounting because the impact of a change in one piece of information is calculated automatically. *Observe the cell B4 in Exhibit 7-5 (p. 359) and the operation symbols in Exhibit 7-6 (p. 359).*

4 **Use the sales journal, the cash receipts journal, and the accounts receivable ledger.**

Sales journal: Recall that sales on account require two entries. When the sale is made, Accounts Receivable is debited and Sales Revenue is credited for the amount of the sale; Cost of Goods Sold is debited and Inventory is credited for the cost of the inventory sold. Accordingly, the sales journal contains two columns to record both of these amounts for each sale. *Review the sales journal in Exhibit 7-8, Panel A (p. 364).*

Cash receipts journal: Review the cash receipts journal in Exhibit 7-9, Panel A (p. 365).

Accounts receivable ledger: Review the posting from the cash receipts journal to the control account and to the accounts receivable subsidiary ledger in Exhibits 7-8 and 7-9, Panel B (pp. 362–365).

5 **Use the purchases journal, the cash payments journal, and the accounts payable ledger.**

Purchases journal: Review the purchases journal in Exhibit 7-10, Panel A (p. 367).

Cash payments journal: The cash payments journal is much like the cash receipts journal you will see in Demo Doc 1, except all items in the cash payments journal decrease cash and are recorded in the Cash credit column. *Review the cash payments journal in Exhibit 7-11, Panel A (p. 371).*

Accounts payable ledger: The accounts payable ledger is much like the accounts receivable ledger you will see in Demo Doc 1, except that whenever Accounts *Payable* is debited or credited in the ledger, the subsidiary ledger for the suppliers affected must be debited or credited as well. *Review the posting from the cash payments journal to the control account and to the accounts payable subsidiary ledger in Exhibits 7-10 and 7-11, Panel B (pp. 367–369).*

Demo Doc 1

Bookkeeping Ledgers

Learning Objectives 1, 2, 4

Juniper Corp. had the following transactions during November 2008:

Nov. 4	Received $3,300 on a note receivable from Harry Stevenson. This amount includes the $3,000 note receivable plus interest revenue.
12	Borrowed $8,000 from National Bank by signing a note payable.
18	Received $1,800 on account from Lisa Henders. Collection was received after the sales discount period lapsed.
26	Received $2,400 on account from Peter Wilkins. The full invoice amount was $2,500, but Peter paid within the discount period to gain the $100 discount.
29	Received $4,000 on a cash sale to a customer (cost $2,700).

The general ledger showed the following balances at October 31, 2008:

Account	Post Ref	Amount
Cash	10	$1,300
Accounts Receivable	20	6,700
Notes Receivable	30	7,400
Inventory	40	4,000
Notes Payable	50	0
Sales Revenues	60	0
Sales Discounts	70	0
COGS	80	0
Interest Revenue	90	0

The accounts receivable subsidiary ledger at October 31, 2008, showed:

Lisa Henders	$3,200
Jennifer Collins	1,000
Peter Wilkins	2,500
Total	$6,700

(This is the same as the total in the Accounts Receivable general ledger account.)

Requirements

1. Record the transactions in the cash receipts journal (ledger page 10). Compute the column totals at November 30, 2008. Show that total debits equal total credits.

2. Post to the general ledger and the accounts receivable ledger. Check that the total of the customer balances in the subsidiary ledger equals the general ledger balance in accounts receivable.

3. The employee at Juniper who opens the mail and physically collects the cash is the same person who updates the cash receipts journal. Does this create any problems?

Demo Doc 1 Solutions

Requirement 1

Use the sales journal, the cash receipts journal, and the accounts receivable ledger

Record the transactions in the cash receipts journal (ledger page 10). Compute the column totals at November 30, 2008. Show that total debits equal total credits.

Part 1	Part 2	Part 3	Part 4	Part 5	Demo Doc Complete

Remember that the debits and credits in these transactions are *exactly* the same as we have done in previous chapters. It is only the format of recording the entries that has changed.

Remember also that the *totals* in the columns are the same amounts as the *ending balances* in the T-accounts that we are used to dealing with.

All transactions in the cash receipts journal increase cash and are included in the Cash debit column of the journal. Routine transactions in this journal might include cash sales and cash receipts from customers on account. A Sales and Accounts Receivable credit column is in the journal to fully record these transactions. Whatever other accounts are normally affected when cash is received should be listed in the remaining columns.

Notice that it is not possible to have a column for *every* account. The Other Account column is for accounts that are not used often (and so are not listed separately).

Use the sales journal, the cash receipts journal, and the accounts receivable ledger

Nov. 4   Received $3,300 on a note receivable from Harry Stevenson. This amount includes the $3,000 note receivable plus interest revenue.

This is an increase to Cash (debit) of $3,300. Notes Receivable decreases (credit) by $3,000. The difference of $3,300 − $3,000 = $300 is an increase to Interest Revenue (credit).

Cash	3,300	
Notes Receivable		3,000
Interest Revenue		300

Use the sales journal, the cash receipts journal, and the accounts receivable ledger

Nov. 12 Borrowed $8,000 from National Bank by signing a note payable.

This is an increase to Cash (debit) and an increase to Notes Payable (credit) of $8,000.

Cash	8,000	
Notes Payable		8,000

Use the sales journal, the cash receipts journal, and the accounts receivable ledger

Nov. 18 Received $1,800 on account from Lisa Henders. Collection was received after the sales discount period lapsed.

This is an increase to Cash (debit) and a decrease to Accounts Receivable (credit) of $1,800. Because the collection is after the discount period has lapsed, sales discounts are not applicable.

Cash	1,800	
Accounts Receivable		1,800

 Use the sales journal, the cash receipts journal, and the accounts receivable ledger

Nov. 26 Received $2,400 on account from Peter Wilkins. The full invoice amount was $2,500, but Peter paid within the discount period to gain the $100 discount.

This is an increase to Cash (debit) of $2,400. However, Accounts Receivable decreases (credit) by $2,500. The difference of $100 is an increase to Sales Discounts (debit).

Cash	2,400	
Sales Discounts	100	
Accounts Receivable		2,500

 Use the sales journal, the cash receipts journal, and the accounts receivable ledger

Nov. 29 Received $4,000 on a cash sale to a customer (cost $2,700).

This is an increase to Cash (debit) and an increase to Sales Revenue (credit) of $4,000. We also need to record an increase to COGS (debit) and a decrease to Inventory (credit) of $2,700.

Cash	4,000	
Sales Revenue		4,000

COGS	2,700	
Inventory		2,700

Part 1	**Part 2**	Part 3	Part 4	Part 5	Demo Doc Complete

 Use the sales journal, the cash receipts journal, and the accounts receivable ledger

Because all of these transactions involved cash receipts (debits to cash), they are all posted in the cash receipts ledger. Amounts are put in the appropriate column for debits or credits. Posting references are used to help track the transaction through the various ledgers.

Cash Receipts Journal   Page 10

| | Debits | | Credits | | | | | | |
| | | | | | Other Accounts | | | | |
Date	Cash	Sales Discounts	Accounts Receivable	Sales Revenue	Account Title	Post Ref	Amount	COGS Debit Inventory Credit	
Nov. 4	3,300				Notes Receivable	30	3,000		
					Interest Revenue	90	300		
12	8,000				Notes Payable	50	8,000		
18	1,800		1,800		Lisa Henders	✔			
26	2,400	100	2,500		Peter Wilkins	✔			
29	4,000			4,000				2,700	
30	19,500	100	4,300	4,000	Total		11,300	2,700	
	(10)	(70)	(20)	(60)			(X)	(80/40)	

Total Dr. = 19,600   Total Cr. = 19,600

We can see that the total debits (cash and sales discounts) are the same as the total credits (all other accounts). This is because all of the transactions recorded in the cash receipts journal had equal debits and credits.

Requirement 2

Post to the general ledger and the accounts receivable ledger. Check that the total of the customer balances in the subsidiary ledger equals the general ledger balance in accounts receivable.

Part 1	Part 2	**Part 3**	Part 4	Part 5	Demo Doc Complete

4 Use the sales journal, the cash receipts journal, and the accounts receivable ledger

First, the individual accounts in the accounts receivable ledger are adjusted by posting any accounts receivable transactions.

Some general ledger accounts, like Accounts Receivable, need to have support for the balance. These accounts are called control accounts. The accounts receivable ledger, which contains each individual customer's name and balance, is called a subsidiary ledger. Whenever Accounts Receivable is debited or credited in the ledger, the subsidiary ledger for the individual customers affected must be debited or credited as well. *The total of the subsidiary ledger must always equal the control account balance.*

Accounts Receivable Ledger

Lisa Henders

Date	Journal Ref	Debit	Credit	Balance
Oct. 31	✔			3,200
Nov. 18	CR.10		1,800	1,400

Jennifer Collins

Date	Journal Ref	Debit	Credit	Balance
Oct. 31	✔			1,000

Peter Wilkins

Date	Journal Ref	Debit	Credit	Balance
Oct. 31	✔			2,500
Nov. 26	CR.10		2,500	—

The amounts are then combined to get a total accounts receivable balance.

Accounts Receivable Subsidiary

Customer	Balance
Lisa Henders	$1,400
Jennifer Collins	1,000
Total	$2,400

This is the same total that should appear for the Accounts Receivable in the general ledger.

Part 1	Part 2	Part 3	**Part 4**	Part 5	Demo Doc Complete

The totals/balances from the cash receipts ledger are now brought to the general ledger. This includes any amounts in the Other Accounts column that need to be brought forth to specific accounts in the general ledger.

The balance in each account is updated. Notice that the setup for each account is basically a T-account laid out *completely horizontally!*

The balance in each general ledger account is now updated by adding the cash receipts journal transactions to the previous balance. This becomes the new balance in the general journal for that account.

For example, the cash journal had a balance of $1,300 debit on October 31. The cash receipts journal shows an overall debit of $19,500 to cash. This total is entered in a separate line into the general ledger.

The Cash account is then totaled as the beginning balance of $1,300 debit plus the $19,500 debit of activity for November from the cash receipts journal. Therefore, the Cash account in the general ledger has a total of $20,800 on November 30.

The other accounts are updated and totaled in the same manner.

Cash   No. 10

Date	Journal Ref	Debit	Credit	Balance
Oct. 31	✔			1,300
Nov. 30	CR.10	19,500		20,800

Accounts Receivable   No. 20

Date	Journal Ref	Debit	Credit	Balance
Oct. 31	✔			6,700
Nov. 30	CR.10		4,300	2,400

Notes Receivable   No. 30

Date	Journal Ref	Debit	Credit	Balance
Oct. 31	✔			7,400
Nov. 4	CR.10		3,000	4,400

Inventory   No. 40

Date	Journal Ref	Debit	Credit	Balance
Oct. 31	✔			4,000
Nov. 30	CR.10		2,700	1,300

Notes Payable   No. 50

Date	Journal Ref	Debit	Credit	Balance
Nov. 12	CR.10		8,000	8,000

Sales Revenues   No. 60

Date	Journal Ref	Debit	Credit	Balance
Nov. 30	CR.10		4,000	4,000

Sales Discounts   No. 70

Date	Journal Ref	Debit	Credit	Balance
Nov. 30	CR.10	100		100

COGS   No. 80

Date	Journal Ref	Debit	Credit	Balance
Nov. 30	CR.10	2,700		2,700

Interest Revenue   No. 90

Date	Journal Ref	Debit	Credit	Balance
Nov. 4	CR.10		300	300

Notice that the total in the accounts receivable general ledger account ($2,400) is the same as in the subsidiary schedule ($2,400). This is a good check to make sure all of the transactions were posted correctly.

Requirement 3

1   Describe an effective accounting information system

The employee at Juniper who opens the mail and physically collects the cash is the same person who updates the cash receipts journal. Does this create any problems?

Part 1	Part 2	Part 3	Part 4	**Part 5**	Demo Doc Complete

If an employee collects the cash *and* records the receipt of the cash in the accounting system, then there is an opportunity for fraud. The employee could steal the cash and delay recording the cash receipt or perhaps never record the cash receipt.

To avoid this problem, most internal control systems require <u>separation of duties</u>; that is, the employees who handle cash (both receipts and payments) are *not* the same employees who maintain the accounting records.

Part 1	Part 2	Part 3	Part 4	Part 5	**Demo Doc Complete**

Demo Doc 2

Purchases Journal

Learning Objective 5

5 Use the purchases journal, the cash payments journal, and the accounts payable ledger

During the month of March 2008, Sanders Corp. purchased $7,600 of inventory on account from Iain Brothers on March 12 and $4,200 of inventory on account from Stevenson Inc. on March 24.

On March 18, Sanders also purchased $1,100 of supplies from Quattrix Inc. on account.

Requirement

1. Record these transactions in Sanders's purchases journal.

Demo Doc 2 Solutions

Requirement 1

Record these transactions in Sanders's purchases journal.

Part 1	Demo Doc Complete

All items in the purchases journal increase accounts payable and are included in the Accounts Payable credit column. Routine transactions in this journal might include the purchase of inventory or supplies on account. Inventory and Supplies debit columns are in the journal to fully record these transactions. An Other Accounts column may also be provided for nonroutine transactions that are on account and do not impact one of the established columns.

In this case, for each purchase, a line is filled out in the purchases journal. Because the purchases are on account, Accounts Payable is impacted, and the associated amount is put into this column.

The purchases that relate to inventory (March 12 and 24) are also entered into the Inventory column.

The purchase that relates to supplies (March 18) is also entered into the Supplies column.

Notice that the purchases are recorded in chronological order (that is, by date).

Purchases Journal

Date	Account Credited	Accounts Payable	Inventory	Supplies
March 12	Iain Bros.	7,600	7,600	
18	Quattrix	1,100		1,100
24	Stevenson	4,200	4,200	
31	Total	12,900	11,800	1,100

Part 1	Demo Doc Complete

Quick Practice Questions

True/False

_____ 1. When special journals are used in a manual system, there is no need for a general journal.

_____ 2. Control and flexibility are important only in a manual accounting system.

_____ 3. The chart of accounts numbering design is usually ordered beginning with assets followed by liabilities, owner's equity, revenues, and expenses.

_____ 4. Enterprise resource planning systems combine all of the entity's information in one place to better manage the data.

_____ 5. A typical spreadsheet formula may look like the following: =D*C.

_____ 6. A special journal records only a specific type of transaction.

_____ 7. For every subsidiary ledger, there must be a control account in the general ledger.

_____ 8. Using documents as sales invoices to serve as a sales journal eliminates the need to maintain an accounts receivable subsidiary ledger.

_____ 9. When a customer returns merchandise to the seller, the company issues a debit memo to the customer.

_____ 10. At the end of the period, the total in the accounts payable ledger balance should equal the total in the accounts payable subsidiary ledger.

Multiple Choice

1. **What is an element of an effective accounting information system?**
   a. Allows employees flexibility in setting the working hours
   b. Should be designed to meet all the requirements of management, regardless of the costs involved
   c. Includes control, compatibility, flexibility, and a favorable cost/benefit relationship
   d. Includes all of the above

2. **What is known as the set of programs that drive the computer?**
   a. The server
   b. Software
   c. Input
   d. Output

3. The Hide and Seek Company has retail outlets at both large and small strip malls throughout the United States. Its accounting information system is able to track total revenues by store, type of mall, store size, state, and region. This is an example of which feature of an effective accounting information system?
   a. Flexibility
   b. Favorable cost/benefit relationship
   c. Control
   d. Compatibility

4. Inputs of an accounting system would include which of the following?
   a. Purchase invoices
   b. Income statement
   c. Balance sheet
   d. None of the above

5. The design of an accounting system begins with which of the following?
   a. Chart of accounts
   b. General ledger
   c. Previous year's financial statements
   d. Beginning year's trial balance

6. Which of the following is recorded in the sales journal?
   a. Return of merchandise purchased for cash
   b. Sale of merchandise for cash
   c. Sale of merchandise on account
   d. Return of merchandise purchased on account

7. Suppose you borrowed $80,000 from the bank by signing a note payable. In which journal would this be recorded?
   a. Sales journal
   b. Purchases journal
   c. Cash receipts journal
   d. Cash payments journal

8. The sale of equipment in exchange for a promissory note would be recorded in which journal?
   a. Sales journal
   b. Cash payments journal
   c. Cash receipts journal
   d. General journal

9. The payment of a purchase on account, within the discount period, would be recorded in which journal?
   a. Sales journal
   b. Cash payments journal
   c. Cash receipts journal
   d. General journal

10. The purchase of supplies on account would be recorded in which journal?
    a. Purchases journal
    b. Cash payments journal
    c. Cash receipts journal
    d. General journal

Quick Exercises

7-1. Record the following transactions in the sales journal for Jasper Corp. Total each of the journal columns.

Dec. 6	Sold $2,300 of merchandise on account to Peters Corp., invoice #124, terms 2/10 net 30. The cost of the merchandise was $920.
15	Sold $8,900 of merchandise on account to Rowan Corp., invoice #125, terms 2/10 net 30. The cost of the merchandise was $3,560.
27	Sold $5,200 of merchandise on account to Halpert Corp., invoice #126, terms 2/10 net 30. The cost of the merchandise was $2,080.

Sales Journal   Page 7

Date	Invoice No.	Customer Account Debited	Post Ref	Accounts Receivable Dr. Sales Revenue Cr.	Cost of Goods Sold Dr. Inventory Cr.
2008					

7-2. Record the following transactions in the cash receipts journal for Jasper Corp. Also total the journal and show that total debits equal total credits.

Dec. 5	Sold land for cost; $335,000 is received in cash.
8	Received $4,500 from Halpert Corp., the full invoice amount due on account. (The discount period lapsed.)
12	Received $2,254 from Peters Corp. The full invoice amount was $2,300, but payment was received within the discount period.
29	Received $7,000 on a cash sale to a customer (cost of inventory, $2,100).
31	Borrowed $45,000 from State Bank and signed a note.

Cash Receipts Journal   Page 2

	Debits		Credits					
					Other Accounts			
Date	Cash	Sales Discounts	Accounts Receivable	Sales Revenue	Account Title	Post Ref	Amount	COGS Debit Inventory Credit
2008								
							(X)	

Total Dr. =   Total Cr. =

7-3. Post the information from Quick Exercises 7-1 and 7-2 into the general ledger accounts. Indicate the account number in the journals for the posting to the account in the general ledger. Prepare a trial balance after posting to verify that debits equal credits. (Assume all of the accounts are normally balanced.)

Cash   No. 11

Date	Journal Ref	Debit	Credit	Balance
Nov. 30	✔			24,200

Accounts Receivable   No. 15

Date	Journal Ref	Debit	Credit	Balance
Nov. 30	✔			20,400

Inventory   No. 18

Date	Journal Ref	Debit	Credit	Balance
Nov. 30	✔			33,600

Land   No. 19

Date	Journal Ref	Debit	Credit	Balance
Nov. 30		335,000		335,000

Accounts Payable   No. 20

Date	Journal Ref	Debit	Credit	Balance
Nov. 30	✔			19,800

Notes Payable   No. 22

Date	Journal Ref	Debit	Credit	Balance

Jasper Capital   No. 30

Date	Journal Ref	Debit	Credit	Balance
Nov. 30	✔			360,100

Sales Revenues   No. 40

Date	Journal Ref	Debit	Credit	Balance
Nov. 30	✔			82,000

Sales Discounts   No. 43

Date	Journal Ref	Debit	Credit	Balance
Nov. 30	✔			1,200

COGS   No. 51

Date	Journal Ref	Debit	Credit	Balance
Nov. 30	✔			32,800

Salary Expense   No. 55

Date	Journal Ref	Debit	Credit	Balance
Nov. 30	✔			14,700

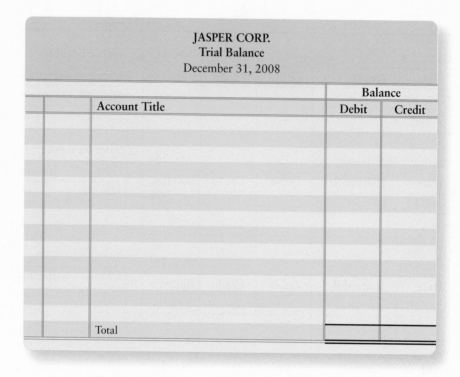

JASPER CORP.
Trial Balance
December 31, 2008

		Account Title	Balance Debit	Credit
		Total		

7-4. Post the accounts receivable information from the journals in Quick Exercises 7-1 and 7-2 into the accounts receivable subsidiary ledger. Summarize the accounts receivable balance by customer to make sure that it agrees with the accounts receivable balance in Quick Exercise 7-3.

Accounts Receivable Ledger

Halpert Corp.

Date	Journal Ref	Debit	Credit	Balance
Nov. 30	✔			4,500

Peters Corp.

Date	Journal Ref	Debit	Credit	Balance
Nov. 30	✔			7,700

Rowan Corp.

Date	Journal Ref	Debit	Credit	Balance
Nov. 30	✔			8,200

Customer Accounts Receivable

Customer	Balance
Total	

7-5. You have recorded your daily expenses for the past week in a spreadsheet. Write the spreadsheet formula to calculate:

    a. The total expenses for the week in cell D11.

    b. The average daily expense in cell D13.

	A	B	C	D
1	DAILY SPENDING:			
2				
3	DAY			AMOUNT
4	Sunday			$20
5	Monday			12
6	Tuesday			18
7	Wednesday			14
8	Thursday			6
9	Friday			25
10	Saturday			17
11	TOTAL			
12				
13	Average Daily Spending			

Do It Yourself! Question 1

Ore Company had the following transactions during April 2008:

Apr. 3	Received $900 on account from Winton Westerly. Collection was received after the sales discount period lapsed.
9	Borrowed $6,000 from City Bank by signing a note payable.
16	Received $1,200 on a cash sale to a customer (cost $800).
22	Received $1,000 on account from Yolanda Yupps. The full invoice amount was $1,050, but Yolanda paid within the discount period to gain the $50 discount.
25	Received $1,600 on a note receivable from Zach Ziff. This amount includes the $1,400 note receivable plus interest revenue.

The general ledger showed the following balances at March 31, 2008:

Account	Post Ref	Amount
Cash	5	$ 300
Accounts Receivable	10	5,000
Notes Receivable	15	1,600
Inventory	20	1,000
Notes Payable	25	0
Sales Revenues	30	0
Sales Discounts	35	0
COGS	40	0
Interest Revenue	50	0

The accounts receivable subsidiary ledger at March 31, 2008, showed:

Vinnie Voit	$2,300
Winton Westerly	900
Yolanda Yupps	1,800
Totals	$5,000

Requirements

4 Use the sales journal, the cash receipts journal, and the accounts receivable ledger

1. Record the transactions in the cash receipts journal (ledger page 9). Compute the column totals at April 30, 2008. Show that total debits equal total credits.

Cash Receipts Journal   Page 9

	Debits		Credits					
					Other Accounts			
Date	Cash	Sales Discounts	Accounts Receivable	Sales Revenue	Account Title	Post Ref	Amount	COGS Debit Inventory Credit
							(X)	

Total Dr. =   Total Cr. =

Use the sales journal, the cash receipts journal, and the accounts receivable ledger

2. Post to the general ledger and the accounts receivable ledger. Check that the total of the customer balances in the subsidiary ledger equals the general ledger balance in accounts receivable.

Accounts Receivable Ledger

Date	Journal Ref	Debit	Credit	Balance

Date	Journal Ref	Debit	Credit	Balance

Date	Journal Ref	Debit	Credit	Balance

Accounts Receivable Subsidiary

Customer	Balance

Cash   No. 5

Date	Journal Ref	Debit	Credit	Balance

Accounts Receivable   No. 10

Date	Journal Ref	Debit	Credit	Balance

Notes Receivable   No. 15

Date	Journal Ref	Debit	Credit	Balance

Inventory   No. 20

Date	Journal Ref	Debit	Credit	Balance

Notes Payable   No. 25

Date	Journal Ref	Debit	Credit	Balance

Sales Revenues   No. 30

Date	Journal Ref	Debit	Credit	Balance

Sales Discounts   No. 35

Date	Journal Ref	Debit	Credit	Balance

COGS   No. 40

Date	Journal Ref	Debit	Credit	Balance

Interest Revenue   No. 45

Date	Journal Ref	Debit	Credit	Balance

Quick Practice Solutions

True/False

___F___ 1. When special journals are used in a manual system, there is no need for a general journal.

    False—A general journal may still be required for those transactions that don't fit the special journals. (p. 360)

___F___ 2. Control and flexibility are important only in a manual accounting system.

    False—The features of an effective accounting system are necessary whether the accounting system is computerized or manual. (p. 354)

___T___ 3. The chart of accounts numbering design is usually ordered beginning with assets followed by liabilities, owner's equity, revenues, and expenses. (p. 356)

___T___ 4. Enterprise resource planning systems combine all of the entity's information in one place to better manage the data. (p. 358)

___F___ 5. A typical spreadsheet formula may look like the following: =D*C.

    False—Each cell is defined by a column designation that is alphabetic *and* a row designation that is numeric. An example would be =D4*C12. (p. 358)

___T___ 6. A special journal records only a specific type of transaction. (p. 360)

___T___ 7. For every subsidiary ledger, there must be a control account in the general ledger. (p. 363)

___F___ 8. Using documents as sales invoices to serve as a sales journal eliminates the need to maintain an accounts receivable subsidiary ledger.

    False—The information on each sales invoice would still be posted into the accounts receivable ledger. (p. 363)

___F___ 9. When a customer returns merchandise to the seller, the company issues a debit memo to the customer.

    False—When a customer returns merchandise to the seller, the company issues a *credit* memo to the customer. (p. 370)

___T___ 10. At the end of the period, the total in the accounts payable ledger balance should equal the total in the accounts payable subsidiary ledger. (p. 372)

Multiple Choice

1. **What is an element of an effective accounting information system?** (p. 354)
   a. Allows employees flexibility in setting the working hours
   b. Should be designed to meet all the requirements of management, regardless of the costs involved
   c. Includes control, compatibility, flexibility, and a favorable cost/benefit relationship
   d. Includes all of the above

2. What is known as the set of programs that drive the computer? (p. 355)
   a. The server
   b. Software
   c. Input
   d. Output

3. The Hide and Seek Company has retail outlets at both large and small strip malls throughout the United States. Its accounting information system is able to track total revenues by store, type of mall, store size, state, and region. This is an example of which feature of an effective accounting information system? (p. 354)
   a. Flexibility
   b. Favorable cost/benefit relationship
   c. Control
   d. Compatibility

4. Inputs of an accounting system would include which of the following? (p. 355)
   a. Purchase invoices
   b. Income statement
   c. Balance sheet
   d. None of the above

5. The design of an accounting system begins with which of the following? (p. 356)
   a. Chart of accounts
   b. General ledger
   c. Previous year's financial statements
   d. Beginning year's trial balance

6. Which of the following is recorded in the sales journal? (p. 357)
   a. Return of merchandise purchased for cash
   b. Sale of merchandise for cash
   c. Sale of merchandise on account
   d. Return of merchandise purchased on account

7. Suppose you borrowed $80,000 from the bank by signing a note payable. In which journal would this be recorded? (p. 364)
   a. Sales journal
   b. Purchases journal
   c. Cash receipts journal
   d. Cash payments journal

8. The sale of equipment in exchange for a promissory note would be recorded in which journal? (p. 357)
   a. Sales journal
   b. Cash payments journal
   c. Cash receipts journal
   d. General journal

9. The payment of a purchase on account, within the discount period, would be recorded in which journal? (p. 357)
   a. Sales journal
   b. Cash payments journal
   c. Cash receipts journal
   d. General journal

10. The purchase of supplies on account would be recorded in which journal?
   (p. 357)
   a. Purchases journal
   b. Cash payments journal
   c. Cash receipts journal
   d. General journal

Quick Exercises

7-1. Record the following transactions in the sales journal for Jasper Corp. Total each of the journal columns. (p. 362)

Dec. 6	Sold $2,300 of merchandise on account to Peters Corp., invoice #124, terms 2/10 net 30. The cost of the merchandise was $920.
15	Sold $8,900 of merchandise on account to Rowan Corp., invoice #125, terms 2/10 net 30. The cost of the merchandise was $3,560.
27	Sold $5,200 of merchandise on account to Halpert Corp., invoice #126, terms 2/10 net 30. The cost of the merchandise was $2,080.

Sales Journal   Page 7

Date	Invoice No.	Customer Account Debited	Post Ref	Accounts Receivable Dr. Sales Revenue Cr.	Cost of Goods Sold Dr. Inventory Cr.
2008					
Dec. 6	124	Peters Corp.		2,300	920
15	125	Rowan Corp.		8,900	3,560
27	126	Halpert Corp.		5,200	2,080
31		Total		16,400	6,560
				(15/40)	(51/18)

7-2. Record the following transactions in the cash receipts journal for Jasper Corp. Also total the journal and show that total debits equal total credits. (p. 365)

Dec. 5	Sold land for cost; $335,000 is received in cash.
8	Received $4,500 from Halpert Corp., the full invoice amount due on account. (The discount period lapsed.)
12	Received $2,254 from Peters Corp. The full invoice amount was $2,300, but payment was received within the discount period.
29	Received $7,000 on a cash sale to a customer (cost of inventory, $2,100).
31	Borrowed $45,000 from State Bank and signed a note.

Cash Receipts Journal   Page 2

Date	Cash	Sales Discounts	Accounts Receivable	Sales Revenue	Account Title	Post Ref	Amount	COGS Debit Inventory Credit
		Debits			Credits			
					Other Accounts			
2008								
Dec. 5	335,000				Land	19	335,000	
8	4,500		4,500					
12	2,254	46	2,300					
29	7,000			7,000				2,100
31	45,000				Note Payable	22	45,000	
	393,754	46	6,800	7,000			380,000	2,100
	(11)	(43)	(15)	(40)			(X)	(51/18)

Total Dr. = 395,900   Total Cr. = 395,900
(393,754 + 46 + 2,100)   (6,800 + 7,000 + 380,000 + 2,100)

7-3. Post the information from Quick Exercises 7-1 and 7-2 into the general ledger accounts. Indicate the account number in the journals for the posting to the account in the general ledger. Prepare a trial balance after posting to verify that debits equal credits. (Assume all of the accounts are normally balanced.)(pp. 362–365)

General Ledger

Cash No. 11

Date	Journal Ref	Debit	Credit	Balance
Nov. 30	✓			24,200
Dec. 31	CR.2	393,754		417,954

Accounts Receivable No. 15

Date	Journal Ref	Debit	Credit	Balance
Nov. 30	✓			20,400
Dec. 31	S.7	16,400		36,800
Dec. 31	CR.2		6,800	30,000

Inventory No. 18

Date	Journal Ref	Debit	Credit	Balance
Nov. 30	✓			33,600
Dec. 31	S.7		6,560	27,040
Dec. 31	CR.2		2,100	24,940

Land No. 19

Date	Journal Ref	Debit	Credit	Balance
Nov. 30	✓	335,000		335,000
Dec. 31	CR.2		335,000	0

Accounts Payable No. 20

Date	Journal Ref	Debit	Credit	Balance
Nov. 30	✓			19,800

Notes Payable No. 22

Date	Journal Ref	Debit	Credit	Balance
Dec. 31	CR.2		45,000	45,000

Jasper Capital No. 30

Date	Journal Ref.	Debit	Credit	Balance
Nov. 30	✓			360,100

Sales Revenues No. 40

Date	Journal Ref	Debit	Credit	Balance
Nov. 30	✓			82,000
Dec. 31	S.7		16,400	98,400
Dec. 31	CR.2		7,000	105,400

Sales Discounts No. 43

Date	Journal Ref	Debit	Credit	Balance
Nov. 30	✓			1,200
Dec. 31	CR.2	46		1,246

COGS No. 51

Date	Journal Ref	Debit	Credit	Balance
Nov. 30	✓			32,800
Dec. 31	S.7	6,560		39,360
Dec. 31	CR.2	2,100		41,460

Salary Expense No. 55

Date	Journal Ref	Debit	Credit	Balance
Nov. 30	✓			14,700

JASPER CORP.
Trial Balance
December 31, 2008

Account Title	Balance Debit	Balance Credit
Cash	$417,954	
Accounts receivable	30,000	
Inventory	24,940	
Accounts payable		$19,800
Note payable		45,000
Jasper, capital		360,100
Sales revenues		105,400
Sales discounts	1,246	
Cost of goods sold	41,460	
Salary expense	14,700	
Total	$530,300	$530,300

7-4. Post the accounts receivable information from the journals in Quick Exercises 7-1 and 7-2 into the accounts receivable subsidiary ledger. Summarize the accounts receivable balance by customer to make sure that it agrees with the accounts receivable balance in Quick Exercise 7-3. (pp. 362–365)

Accounts Receivable Ledger

Halpert Corp.

Date	Journal Ref	Debit	Credit	Balance
Nov. 30	✔			4,500
Dec. 8	CR.2		4,500	0
Dec. 27	S.7	5,200		5,200

Peters Corp.

Date	Journal Ref	Debit	Credit	Balance
Nov. 30	✔			7,700
Dec. 6	S.7	2,300		10,000
Dec. 12	CR.2		2,300	7,700

Rowan Corp.

Date	Journal Ref	Debit	Credit	Balance
Nov. 30	✔			8,200
Dec. 15	S.7	8,900		17,100

Customer Accounts Receivable

Customer	Balance
Halpert Corp.	$ 5,200
Peters Corp.	7,700
Rowan Corp.	17,100
Total	$30,000

7-5.   You have recorded your daily expenses for the past week in a spreadsheet. (p.359)

Write the spreadsheet formula to calculate:

    a.   The total expenses for the week in cell D11.
    b.   The average daily expense in cell D13.

	A	B	C	D
1	DAILY SPENDING:			
2				
3	DAY			AMOUNT
4	Sunday			$20
5	Monday			12
6	Tuesday			18
7	Wednesday			14
8	Thursday			6
9	Friday			25
10	Saturday			17
11	TOTAL			
12				
13	Average Daily Spending			

    a.   =SUM(D4:D10)
    b.   =D11/7

Do It Yourself! Question 1 Solutions

Requirements

1. Record the transactions in the cash receipts journal (ledger page 9). Compute the column totals at April 30, 2008. Show that total debits equal total credits.

Cash Receipts Journal

| | Debits | | Credits | | | | | |
| | | | | | Other Accounts | | | |
Date	Cash	Sales Discounts	Accounts Receivable	Sales Revenue	Account Title	Post Ref	Amount	COGS Debit Inventory Credit
Apr. 3	900		900		Winton Westerly	✔		
9	6,000				Notes Payable	25	6,000	
16	1,200			1,200				800
22	1,000	50	1,050		Yolanda Yupps	✔		
25	1,600				Notes Receivable	15	1,400	
					Interest Revenue	45	200	
30	10,700	50	1,950	1,200	Total		7,600	800
	(5)	(35)	(10)	(30)			(X)	(40/20)

Total Dr. = 10,750   Total Cr. = 10,750

2. Post to the general ledger and the accounts receivable ledger. Check that the total of the customer balances in the subsidiary ledger equals the general ledger balance in accounts receivable.

Accounts Receivable Ledger

Vinnie Voit

Date	Journal Ref	Debit	Credit	Balance
Mar. 31	✔			2,300

Winton Westerly

Date	Journal Ref	Debit	Credit	Balance
Mar. 31	✔			900
Apr. 3	CR.1		900	–

Yolanda Yupps

Date	Journal Ref	Debit	Credit	Balance
Mar. 31	✔			1,800
Apr. 22			1,050	750

Accounts Receivable Subsidiary

Customer	Balance
Vinnie Voit	$2,300
Yolanda Yupps	750
Total	$3,050

General Ledger

Cash   No. 5

Date	Journal Ref	Debit	Credit	Balance
Mar. 31	✔			300
Apr. 30	CR.5	10,700		11,000

Accounts Receivable   No. 10

Date	Journal Ref	Debit	Credit	Balance
Mar. 31	✔			5,000
Apr. 30	CR.5		1,950	3,050

Notes Receivable   No. 15

Date	Journal Ref	Debit	Credit	Balance
Mar. 31	✔			1,600
Apr. 25	CR.5		1,400	3,000

Inventory   No. 20

Date	Journal Ref	Debit	Credit	Balance
Mar. 31	✔			1,000
Apr. 30	CR.5		800	200

Notes Payable   No. 25

Date	Journal Ref	Debit	Credit	Balance
Apr. 3	CR.5		6,000	6,000

Sales Revenues   No. 30

Date	Journal Ref	Debit	Credit	Balance
Apr. 30	CR.5		1,200	1,200

Sales Discounts   No. 35

Date	Journal Ref	Debit	Credit	Balance
Apr. 30	CR.5	50		50

COGS   No. 40

Date	Journal Ref	Debit	Credit	Balance
Apr. 30	CR.5	800		800

Interest Revenue   No. 45

Date	Journal Ref	Debit	Credit	Balance
Apr. 25	CR.5		200	200

The Power of Practice

For more practice using the skills learned in this chapter, visit MyAccountingLab. There you will find algorithmically generated questions that are based on these Demo Docs and your main textbook's Review and Assess Your Progress sections.

Go to MyAccountingLab and follow these steps:

1. Direct your URL to www.myaccountinglab.com.
2. Log in using your name and password.
3. Click the MyAccountingLab link.
4. Click Study Plan in the left navigation bar.
5. From the table of contents, select Chapter 7, Accounting Information Systems.
6. Click a link to work tutorial exercises.

8 Internal Control and Cash

WHAT YOU PROBABLY ALREADY KNOW

When you shop in a department store, you have probably noticed that there are electronic tags on some of the goods. The cashier will remove the tag upon purchase to avoid sounding an alarm when exiting the store through the security gates. You may also have noticed that fine jewelry is likely displayed in a locked case that can only be opened by an employee. The employee will stay with you until the item is returned to the case and locked or purchased. Cartons of cigarettes are also usually secured behind locked doors or cabinets.

If you work as a cashier, it's likely that you have your own cash drawer. Periodically there may be times when cash is collected and deposited in a safe or taken to the bank. At the end of the shift, the cash is counted and compared to the sales rung up for the period to determine that the appropriate amount of cash is in the drawer. These observations are just a few of the procedures and policies that businesses employ to achieve a good system of internal control.

Learning Objectives

1 Define internal control.

Internal control is the entity's plan to safeguard assets, encourage employees to follow company policy, promote operational efficiency, and ensure accurate and reliable accounting records. Strong controls are more important than ever owing to the overstatement of net income that occurred in companies like Enron and WorldCom. As a result of these misstatements, public companies are now required to issue an internal control report and the outside auditor must evaluate the company's controls. *Review in the main text the provisions of the Sarbanes-Oxley Act, which has had a pervasive impact on public companies and their employees.*

2 Describe good internal control procedures.

Business owners and managers must be acutely aware of the need to have adequate policies and procedures in place to protect the company. Hiring competent, reliable, and ethical personnel and paying them a fair salary; assigning employees responsibilities and making them accountable; and separating responsibility for the custody of assets from the accounting and the operating departments are some of the ways employers address this need. They also engage in periodic internal and external audits, use prenumbered source documents, and use electronic devices to safeguard assets. *Review the "Internal Control Procedures" section of the main text carefully. This topic is critical for business owners and managers.*

3 Prepare bank reconciliations and the related journal entries.

Review the format of the bank reconciliation in Exhibit 8-6, Panel B (p. 420). Take note that the ending "Adjusted bank balance" and "Adjusted book balance" are the same amount. **These amounts represent the correct book balance.** As you review Exhibit 8-6, think about the objective of the bank reconciliation, which is to arrive at the correct book balance. This focus should help you to understand the rationale for why the various items are added to or subtracted from the balance per bank and the balance per books. When these balances differ, journal entries record all the items that appear between those two amounts to obtain the correct balance. Continue to review the journal entries related to Exhibit 8-6.

4 Apply internal controls to cash receipts.

The assignment and separation of employee responsibilities is important for handling cash. Cashiers should each use a separate drawer. The cash should be counted and checked against the sales register information. Remittances that are mailed in are opened and the checks and source documentation are forwarded to two separate individuals. A third party verifies that the amount deposited agrees with the source documentation. *Review the cash receipt controls in Exhibits 8-8 and 8-9 (pp. 425–426).*

5 Apply internal controls to cash payments.

Three documents are required to be in agreement and approved before a check will be disbursed: receiving report, purchase invoice, and purchase order. Separate individuals must be responsible for approving the purchase, verifying that the services or goods have been received, and approving the invoice for payment. *Review the description of these documents shown in Exhibit 8-11 (p. 427) and the process description in Exhibit 8-10 (p. 427) of the main text.*

6 Make ethical business judgments.

Ethical business practices have always been important, but they have taken on renewed emphasis due to the recent accounting scandals of Enron and other companies. Employees are often held to the code of ethics of their employers. Accountants are subject to higher standards than others and must comply with the code of ethics of various professional accounting associations.

Demo Doc 1

Bank Reconciliations

Learning Objectives 1–4

Hunter Corp. has the following information for July 2008:

Cash

July 1 Bal. 2,100		July 8	400
July 14	300	July 25	900
July 29	120	July 30	500
July 31 Bal. 720			

Bank Statement for July 2008

Balance, July 1, 2008		2,100
Deposits		
July 14		300
Checks		
July 8	400	
July 10	230*	
July 25	900	(1,530)
Other items:		
NSF check from Jim Andrews		(150)
Interest on account balance		25
EFT — collection of installment payments from customers		800
EFT — monthly rent expense		(700)
Service charges		(75)
Balance, July 31, 2008		770

*The July 10 check was *not* written by Hunter. It was written by another bank customer and taken from Hunter's account in error.

Hunter deposits all cash receipts and makes all payments by check.

Requirements

1. Prepare Hunter's bank reconciliation at July 31, 2008.

2. Journalize any entries required by Hunter and update Hunter's Cash T-account. Explanations are not required.

3. The employee at Hunter who opens the mail and physically collects the cash is the same person who updates the cash receipts journal and prepares the bank reconciliation. Is this a good internal control system?

Demo Doc 1 Solutions

Requirement 1

 Prepare a bank reconciliation and the related journal entries

Prepare Hunter's bank reconciliation at July 31, 2008.

Part 1	Part 2	Part 3	Part 4	Demo Doc Complete

When you receive a monthly bank statement, the cash balance on your records is often different from the amount on the bank statement. The bank reconciliation reconciles, or brings into agreement, the checking account balance on the depositor's records and the bank's records.

In this case, to prepare the bank reconciliation we need to add reconciling items to both the bank balance and Hunter's cash balance. First, we must determine what these adjustments are. To more easily calculate the impact of these adjustments, we begin with a work sheet.

Make three columns: one for Hunter, one for the bank, and one for reconciling items in the middle. Begin with the balance both sides have for cash at July 31, 2008.

Hunter	Reconciling Items	Bank
720	July 31 Balance	770

A reconciling item arises because a valid transaction has not been recorded by both parties. For example, if the bank records service charges and Hunter does not, a reconciling item is required to bring Hunter's cash balance to the correct amount.

For each reconciling item, we will describe it in the Reconciling Items column and add it to or subtract it from the column of the party that has *not* yet recorded that transaction/entry.

Deposits in Transit

 Prepare a bank reconciliation and the related journal entries

According to the Cash T-account, Hunter made two deposits.

Cash

July 1 Bal. 2,100			
		July 8	400
July 14	300		
		July 25	900
July 29	120		
		July 30	500
July 31 Bal. 720			

The two deposits are:

July 14	300
July 29	120

However, the bank statement only shows one (the July 14 deposit for $300). The July 29 deposit for $120 has not yet been recorded by the bank. This is a

<u>deposit in transit</u> and will *increase* the bank account when the bank processes and records the deposit.

Outstanding Checks and Bank Error

Prepare a bank reconciliation and the related journal entries

According to the Cash T-account, Hunter wrote three checks.

Cash			
July 1 Bal. 2,100		July 8	400
July 14	300	July 25	900
July 29	120	July 30	500
July 31 Bal. 720			

The three checks are:

July 8	400
July 25	900
July 30	500

The bank statement shows three checks; however, only two (the July 8 check for $400 and the July 25 check for $900) are valid.

The July 10 check for $230 shown on the bank statement is a bank error and does not relate to Hunter. This error needs to be corrected by the bank (it would be a good idea for Hunter to contact the bank to confirm that it is correcting this mistake). This is an *increase* to Cash on the bank's side.

The bank statement does not show the third valid check: The July 30 check for $500 has not yet been recorded by the bank. This is an <u>outstanding check</u> and will *decrease* the bank account when it is recorded. The bank will record this check in the (near) future when it is cashed.

NSF Check

Prepare a bank reconciliation and the related journal entries

A check deposited by Hunter for $150 was returned to the bank for insufficient funds. Hunter has not yet recorded the return of this customer check.

The $150 the customer owed has *not* been paid because Hunter was unable to cash the customer's check. The account receivable must be reinstated and Hunter's Cash account must be *decreased*.

Interest Earned

Prepare a bank reconciliation and the related journal entries

Interest revenue of $25 has been earned on Hunter's bank balance but has not yet been recorded by Hunter. This will *increase* Hunter's Cash account.

Installment Payments Received

Prepare a bank reconciliation and the related journal entries

Installment payments from customers of $800 have been collected by the bank via EFT but have not yet been recorded by Hunter. This will *increase* Hunter's Cash account.

Rent Expense

3 Prepare a bank reconciliation and the related journal entries

The rent payment of $700 was made by the bank (on Hunter's behalf) but has not yet been recorded by Hunter. This will *decrease* Hunter's Cash account.

Service Charges

3 Prepare a bank reconciliation and the related journal entries

Service charges of $75 have been incurred with the bank but have not yet been recorded by Hunter. This will *decrease* Hunter's Cash account.

Put all of these reconciling items into the work sheet.

Notice that the only items showing in the bank's column are deposits in transit, outstanding checks, and bank errors. Generally, these are the only reconciling items that will be on the bank's side of the reconciliation. Almost all other items will be on the company's side of the reconciliation. It is easier to remember potential reconciling items for the bank with the acronym DOE:

D	Deposits in Transit
O	Outstanding Checks
E	Bank Errors

Hunter	Reconciling Items	Bank
720	July 31 Balance	770
	Deposits in Transit	120
	Outstanding Checks	−500
	Bank Error (July 10 check)	230
−150	NSF Check	
25	Interest Earned	
800	Installment Payments Collected	
−700	Rent Payment	
−75	Service Charges	
620	**Total**	620

Notice that both columns in the work sheet have the same total. This is a good check to ensure that all calculations are correct. If these totals were not the same, there would be an error and/or some data would be missing.

Part 1	**Part 2**	Part 3	Part 4	Demo Doc Complete

We can now take these reconciling items and prepare the formal bank reconciliation. We list all additions and subtractions required for the bank and Hunter.

HUNTER CORP.
Bank Reconciliation
July 31, 2008

Bank:					
Balance, July 31, 2008					770
Add: July 29 deposit in transit					120
Bank error (July 10 check not belonging to Hunter)					230
					1,120
Less: July 30 outstanding check					(500)
Adjusted bank balance, July 31, 2008					620
Books:					
Balance, July 31, 2008					720
Add: Bank collection of installment payments					800
Interest earned on account					25
					1,545
Less: Rent payment			700		
NSF check			150		
Service charges			75		(925)
Adjusted book balance, July 31, 2008					620

Requirement 2

Prepare a bank reconciliation and the related journal entries

Journalize any entries required by Hunter and update Hunter's Cash T-account. Explanations are not required.

Part 1	Part 2	**Part 3**	Part 4	Demo Doc Complete

Any reconciling items on Hunter's side for the bank reconciliation should be journalized. Usually, these entries are made in the order in which they appear on the bank reconciliation.

Prepare a bank reconciliation and the related journal entries

Installment Payments

Cash increases (a debit) and Accounts Receivable decreases (a credit) by $800.

July 31	Cash	800	
	Accounts Receivable		800

Prepare a bank
reconciliation and the
related journal entries

Interest Earned

Cash increases (a debit) and Interest Revenue increases (a credit) by $25.

July 31	Cash		25	
	Interest Revenue			25

Prepare a bank
reconciliation and the
related journal entries

Rent Payment

Cash decreases (a credit) and Rent Expense increases (a debit) by $700.

July 31	Rent Expense		700	
	Cash			700

Prepare a bank
reconciliation and the
related journal entries

NSF Check

Cash decreases (a credit) and Accounts Receivable increases (a debit) by $150.

July 31	Accounts Receivable—J. Andrews		150	
	Cash			150

Prepare a bank
reconciliation and the
related journal entries

Service Charges

Cash decreases (a credit) and Misc. Expense increases (a debit) by $75.

July 31	Misc. Expense		75	
	Cash			75

Post these adjustments to the Cash T-account:

Cash			
July 31 Bal. 720			
800			
25			
	July 31	700	
		150	
		75	
July 31 Bal. 620			

The final cash balance is \$620, which is also the total on the bank reconciliation. Both totals must agree, so this is a good check to make sure that everything was done correctly.

Requirement 3

1 Define internal control

2 Describe good internal control procedures

4 Apply internal controls to cash receipts

The employee at Hunter who opens the mail and physically collects the cash is the same person who updates the cash receipts journal and prepares the bank reconciliation. Is this a good internal control system?

Part 1	Part 2	Part 3	**Part 4**	Demo Doc Complete

If an employee collects the cash *and* records the receipt of the cash *and* performs the bank reconciliation, then there is an opportunity for fraud.

The employee could steal the cash and delay recording the cash receipt or perhaps never record the cash receipt. The employee could hide his or her act for a long period of time by manipulating the bank reconciliations.

To avoid this problem, most internal control systems require separation of duties; that is, the employees who handle cash (both receipts and payments) are *not* the same employees who maintain the accounting records and prepare the bank reconciliations.

Part 1	Part 2	Part 3	Part 4	**Demo Doc Complete**

Demo Doc 2

Petty Cash _____

Learning Objectives 2, 5, 6

Young Brothers established a $300 petty cash fund on July 1, 2008. On July 31, 2008, the petty cash box contained $80 cash and the following receipts:

July 5	Travel Expenses	$80
July 12	Donuts for Board Meeting	50
July 23	Office Supplies	60
July 29	Delivery Charges	40

On August 1, 2008, the petty cash balance was replenished.

Requirements

1. Journalize the entry to establish the fund.

2. What is the total cash amount paid from petty cash in July? How does this compare to the amount remaining in the petty cash box?

3. What is the problem with petty cash in July? Why did this problem occur? How can it be fixed?

4. Journalize the entry to record the expenses incurred from petty cash during July. (Assume all charges are recorded as supplies expense, delivery expense, travel expense, or catering expense.) On what date(s) are these expenses recorded?

5. A Young employee notices that there have been several months in a row in which the petty cash has been short. Although the amounts involved are small (immaterial), the trend is consistent. What should the employee do?

Demo Doc 2 Solutions

Requirement 1

5 Apply internal controls to cash payments

Journalize the entry to establish the fund.

Part 1	Part 2	Part 3	Part 4	Part 5	Demo Doc Complete

When the fund is established, cash is withdrawn from Young's bank accounts and put into the petty cash box. This increases Petty Cash (a debit) and decreases Cash in Bank (a credit) by $300.

July 1	Petty Cash	300	
	Cash in Bank		300

Requirement 2

What is the total cash amount paid from petty cash in July? How does this compare to the amount remaining in the petty cash box?

Part 1	**Part 2**	Part 3	Part 4	Part 5	Demo Doc Complete

The receipts in the petty cash box total $80 + $50 + $60 + $40 = $230. This means that there should be $300 − $230 = $70 left in the petty cash box. However, there is actually $80 of cash remaining. This is a cash overage.

Requirement 3

5 Apply internal controls to cash payments

What is the problem with petty cash in July? Why did this problem occur? How can it be fixed?

Part 1	Part 2	**Part 3**	Part 4	Part 5	Demo Doc Complete

As stated in Requirement 2, there is a cash overage of $80 − $70 = $10. This could be because a receipt is in error or cash was put into petty cash and not recorded.

Young should implement some internal controls to better monitor petty cash. These could include requiring the use of petty cash tickets with an authorized signature (the person signing would presumably review the receipts for correctness).

Requirement 4

 Apply internal controls to cash payments

Journalize the entry to record the expenses incurred from petty cash during July. (Assume all charges are recorded as supplies expense, delivery expense, travel expense, or catering expense.) On what date(s) are these expenses recorded?

Part 1	Part 2	Part 3	**Part 4**	Part 5	Demo Doc Complete

These expenses are *not* recorded at the time they are incurred. The amounts involved are immaterial, so instead we can wait to record them until the petty cash is replenished:

Aug. 1	Supplies Expense	60	
	Delivery Expense	40	
	Travel Expense	80	
	Catering Expense	50	
	Cash Short (Over)		10
	Cash		220

The missing $10 is recorded as *Cash Short (Over)*. The amount is for an overage, so this account is credited (as if it were "revenue").

Requirement 5

Describe good internal control procedures

Make ethical business judgments

A Young employee notices that there have been several months in a row in which the petty cash has been short. Although the amounts involved are small (immaterial), the trend is consistent. What should the employee do?

Part 1	Part 2	Part 3	Part 4	**Part 5**	Demo Doc Complete

It is easy to have cash overages and shortages from month to month. Record-keeping for petty cash is often spotty because it is usually handled by someone who is not familiar with accounting. However, consistent shortages every month imply that there may be unethical behavior on the part of the petty cash handler.

Having someone review petty cash transactions periodically is a good internal control.

The employee who notices this trend should discuss it with the person responsible for petty cash. If the issue cannot be resolved, then the employee should report it to a supervisor.

Part 1	Part 2	Part 3	Part 4	Part 5	**Demo Doc Complete**

Quick Practice Questions

True/False

_____ 1. A deposit in transit has been recorded by the company but not by the bank.

_____ 2. An NSF check would be recorded on the books by debiting Accounts Receivable.

_____ 3. The AICPA Code of Professional Conduct and the Standards of Ethical Conduct for Management Accountants set the minimum standards of conduct for members of the AICPA and the IMA.

_____ 4. Only accountants are held to a code of ethics.

_____ 5. Different people should perform various accounting duties to minimize errors and the opportunities for fraud.

_____ 6. Funds disbursed from the petty cash fund will be recorded as a credit to the Petty Cash account.

_____ 7. The person who prepares checks for payment would be a suitable employee to reconcile the bank account.

_____ 8. Encryption helps to secure confidential information in e-commerce.

_____ 9. Outstanding checks would include only those checks written for the current month that have not cleared or been canceled by the bank.

_____10. It is a good control to have just one person open the checks and deposit them in the bank.

Multiple Choice

1. **Which of the following is not an objective of internal control?**
   a. Help safeguard the assets a business uses in its operations
   b. Guarantee a company will not go bankrupt
   c. Encourage adherence to company policies
   d. Promote operational efficiency

2. **Which of the following items used to reconcile cash does not require an adjusting entry?**
   a. Bank service charge
   b. Interest earned
   c. A note collected by the bank
   d. Deposits in transit

3. **Which of the following statements about bank reconciliations is correct?**
   a. Should not be prepared by an employee who handles cash transactions
   b. Is part of a sound internal control system
   c. Is a formal financial statement
   d. Both (a) and (b) are correct

4. Which of the following items does not cause a difference between the cash balance per bank and book?
   a. NSF checks
   b. Deposits in transit
   c. Outstanding checks
   d. Canceled checks

5. The following data are available for Wonder Boutique for October:

Book balance, October 31	$5,575
Outstanding checks	584
Deposits in transit	2,500
Service charges	75
Interest revenue	25

   What is the adjusted book balance on October 31 for Wonder Boutique based on the preceding data?
   a. $5,500
   b. $5,525
   c. $5,550
   d. $7,466

6. The bank statement lists a $700 deposit as $70. On a bank reconciliation, this will appear as which of the following?
   a. Addition to the book balance
   b. Deduction from the book balance
   c. Addition to the bank balance
   d. Deduction from the bank balance

7. When the Cash Short (Over) account has a credit balance, it is treated as what type of account?
   a. Expense
   b. Liability
   c. Revenue
   d. Equity

8. For which items must journal entries be prepared?
   a. Any errors made on the books revealed by the bank reconciliation
   b. Any errors made by the bank revealed by the bank reconciliation
   c. All items on the bank's side
   d. Only outstanding checks

9. Which of the following is *not* a control over petty cash?
   a. Keeping an unlimited amount of cash on hand
   b. Supporting all fund disbursements with a petty cash ticket
   c. Replenishing the fund through normal cash disbursement procedures
   d. Designating one employee to administer the fund

10. If the petty cash fund is not replenished on the balance sheet date, which of the following will be true?
    a. Assets will be overstated
    b. Income will be overstated
    c. Neither (a) nor (b)
    d. Both (a) and (b)

Quick Exercises

8-1. Classify each of the following reconciling items of the Bread and Butter Company as one of the following:

      a. An addition to the bank balance
      b. A deduction from the bank balance
      c. An addition to the book balance
      d. A deduction from the book balance
      e. Not a reconciling item

      _____ 1. Collection of note receivable plus interest revenue by bank
      _____ 2. Bookkeeper recorded check #849 as $557 instead of the correct amount of $755
      _____ 3. Bank service charges
      _____ 4. Bank credited the account for interest revenue
      _____ 5. Bank added deposit to Bread and Butter's account in error
      _____ 6. Deposits in transit
      _____ 7. Bank withdrew $1,270 from Bread and Butter's account for a check written for $12,700
      _____ 8. Bookkeeper failed to record a check that was returned with the bank statement
      _____ 9. Check deposited and returned by the bank marked NSF
      _____ 10. Outstanding checks

8-2. On November 1, 2008, Heather Station established a $300 petty cash fund. At the end of November the petty cash fund contained:

Cash on hand		$ 45.00
Petty cash tickets for:		
Postage	$73.50	
Office supplies	87.55	
Miscellaneous items	90.95	
		252.00
Total		$297.00

    a. Prepare the journal entry to establish the petty cash fund on November 1, 2008.
    b. Prepare the journal entry on November 30, 2008, to replenish the petty cash fund.

Journal				Page 1
Date	Accounts		Debit	Credit

Journal			Page 1	
Date	Accounts and Explanation		Debit	Credit

8-3. Using the following information, record the journal entries that would be necessary after preparing the bank reconciliation for Louis Brothers. Some items may not require an entry.

a. Outstanding checks total $1,533.25.
b. The bookkeeper recorded a $1,524 check as $15,240 in payment of the current month's rent.
c. A deposit of $300 from a customer was credited to Louis Brothers for $3,000 by the bank.
d. A customer's check for $1,380 was returned for nonsufficient funds.
e. The bank service charge based on the bank statement is $70.

Journal			Page 1	
Date	Accounts and Explanation		Debit	Credit

Journal			Page 1	
Date	Accounts and Explanation		Debit	Credit

Journal			Page 1	
Date	Accounts and Explanation		Debit	Credit

Journal			Page 1	
Date	Accounts and Explanation		Debit	Credit

Journal			Page 1	
Date	Accounts and Explanation		Debit	Credit

8-4. The following data have been gathered for Batter Company to assist you in preparing the September 30, 2008, bank reconciliation:

a. The September 30 bank balance was $5,460.
b. The bank statement included $30 of service charges.
c. There was an EFT deposit of $1,800 on the bank statement for the monthly rent due from a tenant.
d. Checks #541 and #543, for $205 and $420, respectively, were not among the canceled checks returned with the statement.
e. The September 30 deposit of $3,800 did not appear on the bank statement.
f. The bookkeeper had erroneously recorded a $500 check as $5,000. The check was payment for an amount due on account.
g. Included with the canceled checks was a check written by Bitter Company for $200, which was deducted from Batter Company's account.
h. The bank statement included an NSF check written by Tate Company for a $360 payment on account.
i. The Cash account showed a balance of $2,925 on September 30.

Prepare the September 30, 2008, bank reconciliation for Batter Company.

BATTER COMPANY
Bank Reconciliation
September 30, 2008

	Bank:		
	Balance, September 30, 2008		
	Add:		
	Less:		
	Adjusted bank balance, September 30, 2008		
	Books:		
	Balance, September 30, 2008		
	Add:		
	Less:		
	Adjusted book balance, September 30, 2008		

8-5. The following data have been gathered for Ragpicker Company. Calculate the correct cash balance on February 28, 2008, by performing the part of the bank reconciliation beginning with the balance per bank as shown. NOTE: Not all of the following information may be needed.

a. The service charges for February amount to $90.
b. Outstanding checks amount to $650.
c. The bank erroneously credited Ragpicker Company's account for $300 for a deposit made by another company.
d. Check #665 for $3,000 for the cash purchase of office equipment was erroneously recorded by the bookkeeper as $2,080.
e. A deposit ticket correctly prepared for $975 appeared on the bank statement as a deposit for $795.
f. A customer's check for $560 was returned with the bank statement and stamped NSF.
g. Check #650 for $125 for utilities expense was erroneously recorded by the bookkeeper as $1,250.

RAGPICKER COMPANY
Bank Reconciliation
February 28, 2008

	Bank:			
	Balance, February 28, 2008			$ 7,975
	Add:			
	Less:			
	Adjusted bank balance, February 28, 2008			

Do It Yourself! Question 1

Bank Reconciliations

Quint Inc. has the following information for May 2008:

Cash

May 1 Bal. 4,500		May 4	900
May 9	600	May 12	2,300
May 18	1,000	May 22	1,500
May 28	700	May 30	500
May 31 Bal. 1,600			

Bank Statement for May 2008

Balance, May 1, 2008		4,500
Deposits		
May 9	600	
May 18	1,000	1,600
Checks		
May 4	900	
May 12	2,300	
May 22	1,500	(4,700)
Other items:		
EFT — payment of loan payable		(1,300)
NSF check from Bennet Smith		(400)
Service charges		(100)
EFT — monthly rent collection		1,200
Interest on account balance		50
Balance, May 31, 2008		850

The loan payment includes principal of $950 and interest of $350.

The rent collection is from tenants leasing extra space in Quint's office building.

Quint deposits all cash receipts and makes all payments by check.

Requirements

1. Prepare Quint's bank reconciliation at May 31, 2008.

Reconciling Items
Total

2. Journalize any entries required by Quint and update Quint's Cash T-account. Explanations are not required.

Date	Accounts and Explanation	Debit	Credit

Date	Accounts and Explanation	Debit	Credit

Date	Accounts and Explanation	Debit	Credit

Date	Accounts and Explanation	Debit	Credit

Date	Accounts and Explanation	Debit	Credit

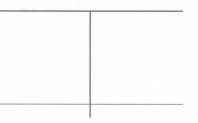

Do It Yourself! Question 2

Petty Cash

Xander Co. established a $400 petty cash fund on May 1, 2008. On May 31, 2008, the petty cash box contained $80 cash and the following receipts:

May 6	Office Supplies	$75
May 13	Delivery Charges	90
May 24	Pizza for Office Party	70
May 30	Office Supplies	85

On June 1, 2008, the petty cash balance was replenished.

Requirements

1. Journalize the entry to establish the fund.

Date	Accounts and Explanation	Debit	Credit

2. Journalize the entry to record the expenses incurred from petty cash during May. (Assume all charges are recorded as supplies expense, delivery expense, or catering expense.)

Date	Accounts and Explanation	Debit	Credit

Quick Practice Solutions

True/False

T   1. A deposit in transit has been recorded by the company but not by the bank. (p. 420)

T   2. An NSF check would be recorded on the books by debiting Accounts Receivable. (p. 421)

T   3. The AICPA Code of Professional Conduct and the Standards of Ethical Conduct for Management Accountants set the minimum standards of conduct for members of the AICPA and the IMA. (p. 431)

F   4. Only accountants are held to a code of ethics.

      False—*All* employees are usually held to a code of ethics. (p. 411)

T   5. Different people should perform various accounting duties to minimize errors and the opportunities for fraud. (p. 411)

F   6. Funds disbursed from the petty cash fund will be recorded as a credit to the Petty Cash account.

      False—When the petty cash fund is replenished, funds disbursed from the fund will be recorded as a credit to the *Cash* account. No entries affect Petty Cash for the disbursement of funds. (p. 430)

F   7. The person who prepares checks for payment would be a suitable employee to reconcile the bank account.

      False—Responsibilities for custody, approval, and accounting should be held by *separate* employees. (p. 411)

T   8. Encryption helps to secure confidential information in e-commerce. (p. 414)

F   9. Outstanding checks would include only those checks written for the current month that have not cleared or been canceled by the bank.

      False—Outstanding checks include *all* checks written that have not cleared the bank. They could be from the *current month or previous periods*. (p. 418)

F   10. It is a good control to have just one person open the checks and deposit them in the bank.

      False—*Separate* individuals should be assigned custody, approval, and accounting tasks. (p. 411)

Multiple Choice

1. Which of the following is not an objective of internal control? (p. 408)
   a. Help safeguard the assets a business uses in its operations
   b. Guarantee a company will not go bankrupt
   c. Encourage adherence to company policies
   d. Promote operational efficiency

2. Which of the following items used to reconcile cash does not require an adjusting entry? (p. 419)
   a. Bank service charge
   b. Interest earned
   c. A note collected by the bank
   d. Deposits in transit

3. Which of the following statements about bank reconciliations is correct? (p. 411)
   a. Should not be prepared by an employee who handles cash transactions
   b. Is part of a sound internal control system
   c. Is a formal financial statement
   d. Both (a) and (b) are correct

4. Which of the following items does not cause a difference between the cash balance per bank and book? (p. 411)
   a. NSF checks
   b. Deposits in transit
   c. Outstanding checks
   d. Canceled checks

5. The following data are available for Wonder Boutique for October:

Book balance, October 31	$5,575
Outstanding checks	584
Deposits in transit	2,500
Service charges	75
Interest revenue	25

   What is the adjusted book balance on October 31 for Wonder Boutique based on the preceding data? (p. 418)
   a. $5,500
   b. $5,525
   c. $5,550
   d. $7,466

6. The bank statement lists a $700 deposit as $70. On a bank reconciliation, this will appear as which of the following? (p. 418)
   a. Addition to the book balance
   b. Deduction from the book balance
   c. Addition to the bank balance
   d. Deduction from the bank balance

7. When the Cash Short (Over) account has a credit balance, it is treated as what type of account? (p. 430)
   a. Expense
   b. Liability
   c. Revenue
   d. Equity

8. **For which items must journal entries be prepared?** (p. 421)
   a. Any errors made on the books revealed by the bank reconciliation
   b. Any errors made by the bank revealed by the bank reconciliation
   c. All items on the bank's side
   d. Only outstanding checks

9. **Which of the following is *not* a control over petty cash?** (p. 428)
   a. Keeping an unlimited amount of cash on hand
   b. Supporting all fund disbursements with a petty cash ticket
   c. Replenishing the fund through normal cash disbursement procedures
   d. Designating one employee to administer the fund

10. **If the petty cash fund is not replenished on the balance sheet date, which of the following will be true?** (p. 429)
    a. Assets will be overstated
    b. Income will be overstated
    c. Neither (a) nor (b)
    d. Both (a) and (b)

Quick Exercises

8-1. Classify each of the following reconciling items of the Bread and Butter Company as one of the following: (p. 418)

    a. An addition to the bank balance
    b. A deduction from the bank balance
    c. An addition to the book balance
    d. A deduction from the book balance
    e. Not a reconciling item

c	1.	Collection of note receivable plus interest revenue by bank
d	2.	Bookkeeper recorded check #849 as $557 instead of the correct amount of $755
d	3.	Bank service charges
a	4.	Bank credited the account for interest revenue
b	5.	Bank added deposit to Bread and Butter's account in error
a	6.	Deposits in transit
b	7.	Bank withdrew $1,270 from Bread and Butter's account for a check written for $12,700
d	8.	Bookkeeper failed to record a check that was returned with the bank statement
d	9.	Check deposited and returned by the bank marked NSF
b	10.	Outstanding checks

8-2. On November 1, 2008, Heather Station established a $300 petty cash fund. At the end of November the petty cash fund contained: (p. 429)

Cash on hand	$ 45.00
Petty cash tickets for:	
Postage	$73.50
Office supplies	87.55
Miscellaneous items	90.95
	252.00
Total	$297.00

a. Prepare the journal entry to establish the petty cash fund on November 1, 2008.

b. Prepare the journal entry on November 30, 2008, to replenish the petty cash fund.

Journal			Page 1
Date	Accounts and Explanation	Debit	Credit
11/1/08	Petty Cash	300	
	Cash		300
	To establish the petty cash fund.		

Journal			Page 1
Date	Accounts and Explanation	Debit	Credit
11/30/08	Postage Expense	73.50	
	Office Supplies	87.55	
	Miscellaneous Expense	90.95	
	Cash Short and Over	3.00	
	Cash		255.00
	To replenish petty cash.		

8-3. Using the following information, record the journal entries that would be necessary after preparing the bank reconciliation for Louis Brothers on May 31, 2008. Not all items will require an entry. (p. 421)

  a. Outstanding checks total $1,533.25.
  b. The bookkeeper recorded a $1,524 check as $15,240 in payment of the current month's rent.
  c. A deposit of $300 from a customer was credited to Louis Brothers for $3,000 by the bank.
  d. A customer's check for $1,380 was returned for nonsufficient funds.
  e. The bank service charge based on the bank statement is $70.

Journal					Page 1
	Date	Accounts and Explanation		Debit	Credit
a.		No entry required.			

Journal					Page 1
	Date	Accounts and Explanation		Debit	Credit
b.	May 31	Cash		13,716	
		Rent Expense			13,716

Journal					Page 1
	Date	Accounts and Explanation		Debit	Credit
c.		No entry required.			

Journal					Page 1
	Date	Accounts and Explanation		Debit	Credit
d.	May 31	Accounts Receivable		1,380	
		Cash			1,380

Journal					Page 1
	Date	Accounts and Explanation		Debit	Credit
e.	May 31	Miscellaneous Expense		70	
		Cash			70

8-4.   The following data have been gathered for Batter Company to assist you in preparing the September 30, 2008, bank reconciliation: (p. 419)

a. The September 30 bank balance was $5,460.
b. The bank statement included $30 of service charges.
c. There was an EFT deposit of $1,800 on the bank statement for the monthly rent due from a tenant.
d. Checks #541 and #543, for $205 and $420, respectively, were not among the canceled checks returned with the statement.
e. The September 30 deposit of $3,800 did not appear on the bank statement.
f. The bookkeeper had erroneously recorded a $500 check as $5,000. The check was payment for an amount due on account.
g. Included with the canceled checks was a check written by Bitter Company for $200, which was deducted from Batter Company's account.
h. The bank statement included an NSF check written by Tate Company for a $360 payment on account.
i. The Cash account showed a balance of $2,925 on September 30.

Prepare the September 30, 2008, bank reconciliation for Batter Company.

BATTER COMPANY Bank Reconciliation September 30, 2008		
Bank:		
Balance, September 30, 2008		$5,460
Add: Deposit in transit	$3,800	
Bank error—Bitter Co. check	200	
		4,000
Less: Outstanding checks		
Check #541	205	
Check #543	420	
		(625)
Adjusted bank balance, September 30, 2008		$8,835
Books:		
Balance, September 30, 2008		$2,925
Add:		
EFT—Rent deposit	$1,800	
Bookkeeper error ($5,000 – 500)	4,500	
		6,300
Less:		
Bank service charge	30	
NSF check	360	
		(390)
Adjusted book balance, September 30, 2008		$8,835

8-5.   The following data have been gathered for Ragpicker Company. Calculate the correct cash balance on February 28, 2008, by performing the part of the bank reconciliation beginning with the balance per bank as shown. NOTE: Not all of the following information may be needed. (p. 419)

a. The service charges for February amount to $90.
b. Outstanding checks amount to $650.
c. The bank erroneously credited Ragpicker Company's account for $300 for a deposit made by another company.
d. Check #665 for $3,000 for the cash purchase of office equipment was erroneously recorded by the bookkeeper as $2,080.
e. A deposit ticket correctly prepared for $975 appeared on the bank statement as a deposit for $795.
f. A customer's check for $560 was returned with the bank statement and stamped NSF.
g. Check #650 for $125 for utilities expense was erroneously recorded by the bookkeeper as $1,250.

RAGPICKER COMPANY
Bank Reconciliation
February 28, 2008

Bank:		
Balance, February 28, 2008		$ 7,975
Add:		
Bank error—Deposit of $975 recorded as $795	$180	
		180
Less:		
Outstanding checks	650	
Bank Error	300	
		(950)
Adjusted bank balance, February 28, 2008		$7,205
NOTE: Remember that the adjusted bank balance is the correct book balance.		

Do It Yourself! Question 1 Solutions

Requirement

1. Prepare Quint's bank reconciliation at May 31, 2008.

Quint	Reconciling Items	Bank
1,600	May 31 Balance	850
	Deposits in Transit	700
	Outstanding Checks	(500)
(1,300)	Mortgage Payment	
(400)	NSF Check	
(100)	Service Charges	
1,200	Rent Collection	
50	Interest Earned	
1,050	Total	1,050

QUINT INC.
Bank Reconciliation
May 31, 2008

Bank:		
Balance, May 31, 2008		850
Add: May 28 deposit in transit		700
		1,550
Less: May 30 outstanding check		(500)
Adjusted bank balance, May 31, 2008		1,050
Books:		
Balance, May 31, 2008		1,600
Add: Bank collection of rent		1,200
Interest earned on account		50
		2,850
Less: Mortgage payment	1,300	
NSF check—B. Smith	400	
Service charges	100	(1,800)
Adjusted book balance, May 31, 2008		1,050

2. Journalize any entries required by Quint and update Quint's Cash T-account. Explanations are not required.

	May 31	Cash	1,200	
		Rent Revenue		1,200

	May 31	Cash	50	
		Interest Revenue		50

	May 31	Mortgage Payable	950	
		Interest Expense	350	
		Cash		1,300

	May 31	Accounts Receivable—Bennet Smith	400	
		Cash		400

	May 31	Miscellaneous Expense	100	
		Cash		100

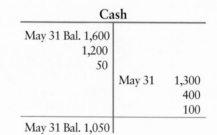

Cash

May 31 Bal. 1,600		
1,200		
50	May 31	1,300
		400
		100
May 31 Bal. 1,050		

Do It Yourself! Question 2 Solutions

Requirements

1. Journalize the entry to establish the fund.

May 1	Petty Cash		400	
	Cash in Bank			400

2. Journalize the entry to record the expenses incurred from petty cash during May.

June 1	Supplies Expense ($75 + $85)		160	
	Delivery Expense		90	
	Catering Expense		70	
	Cash			320

The Power of Practice

For more practice using the skills learned in this chapter, visit MyAccountingLab. There you will find algorithmically generated questions that are based on these Demo Docs and your main textbook's Review and Assess Your Progress sections.

Go to MyAccountingLab and follow these steps:

1. Direct your URL to www.myaccountinglab.com.
2. Log in using your name and password.
3. Click the MyAccountingLab link.
4. Click Study Plan in the left navigation bar.
5. From the table of contents, select Chapter 8, Internal Control and Cash.
6. Click a link to work tutorial exercises.

9 Receivables

You probably already know that if a friend borrows money from you, there is a *chance* you may not be repaid. You would not loan a friend money if you didn't believe that he or she is creditworthy and will likely repay the debt. However, until the money is received, there is no guarantee. If the friend asks to borrow more money before repaying the original loan, you may be more likely to refuse your friend because your risk of nonpayment is increased. There has been no history of successful repayment yet. If the friend never pays, you have incurred a loss equal to the amount of the loan.

The same concerns exist for a business. Sales on account are made only after a company has been approved by the credit department. Despite the most thorough investigation, there will always be some customers who may not pay the amount due. The uncollectible accounts receivable results in a reduction to the asset and to net income.

Learning Objectives

1 Design internal controls for receivables.

In Chapter 7, we learned that an important feature of a strong system of internal control is to separate responsibility for custody of assets from the accounting and operating departments. The individual handling cash should not be granting credit, nor should he or she be accounting for receivables.

2 Use the allowance method to account for uncollectibles.

The **allowance method** matches the sales revenues with the uncollectible accounts expense. An *estimate* of the uncollectible accounts expense must be made in the period of sale using either the aging of receivables or the percentage-of-sales methods. The entry required at the end of the period is:

Uncollectible Accounts Expense	X	
Allowance for Doubtful Accounts		X

The **Allowance for Doubtful Accounts** is a contra-asset account. This account is credited, rather than Accounts Receivable, because it is unknown on the entry date which specific customers will eventually not pay. When it is determined which customer's receivable is uncollectible, the Allowance account is reduced (debited) and the specific customer accounts receivable is reduced (credited). *Carefully review "Accounting for Uncollectibles (Bad Debts)" in the main text. This can be a challenging concept.*

3 **Understand the direct write-off method for uncollectibles.**

The **direct write-off method** is simple to employ, but the method is not in accordance with GAAP. No estimate of the uncollectible accounts expense is recorded. When it is determined which customer's receivable is uncollectible, the following entry is recorded:

Uncollectible Accounts Expense	X	
Accounts Receivable		X

Check out "The Direct Write-Off Method" in the main text.

4 **Account for notes receivable.**

A **note receivable** is a formal written promise to pay the amount borrowed by the debtor plus interest. Interest must be recorded for the period of indebtedness. *Study the key components of a note in Exhibit 9-4 (p. 470). Review "Computing Interest on a Note" in the main text and the interest revenue accrual journal entries that follow.*

5 **Report receivables on the balance sheet.**

The amount reported for accounts receivables on the balance sheet is the amount the business expects to collect. This can be reported in one of two ways:

a. Accounts receivable is on the face of the balance sheet, followed by the allowance for uncollectible accounts as a deduction, leaving net Accounts Receivable.
b. Accounts receivable may be shown at the net amount on the face of the balance sheet with parenthetical disclosure of the allowance balance or in the footnotes.

6 **Use the acid-test ratio and days' sales in receivables to evaluate a company.**

A measure of liquidity is the acid-test ratio. The current assets most quickly converted into cash are compared to the total current liabilities. A higher result is usually more favorable. The ratio is calculated as follows:

$$\text{Acid-test ratio} = \frac{\text{Cash} + \text{Short-term investments} + \text{Net current receivables}}{\text{Total current liabilities}}$$

The **days' sales in receivables** indicates the number of days it takes on average to collect from customers. The objective is to minimize the collection period.

Review the ratio computations in "Using Accounting Information for Decision Making" in the main text.

Demo Doc 1

Learning Objectives 1–3, 5, 6

Hart Inc.'s December 31, 2007, balance sheet reported:

Accounts Receivable	$800
Allowance for Uncollectible Accounts	(40)
Accounts Receivable (net)	$760

Requirements

1. Is Hart using the allowance method or the direct write-off method to account for uncollectible receivables? How much of the December 31, 2007, balance of accounts receivable did Hart expect to collect?

2. During 2008, Hart wrote off accounts receivable totaling $35 from Amanda Blake. Journalize these write-offs as one transaction. How does this transaction affect the net accounts receivable balance? How would this transaction have been recorded if the direct write-off method were being used?

3. During 2008, Hart earned $2,800 of service revenues, all on account. Journalize these revenues as one transaction.

4. During 2008, Hart collected $2,745 cash from customers. Journalize this transaction and calculate the gross accounts receivable balance at December 31, 2008.

5. Assume that Hart estimates uncollectible account expense to be 1.5% of revenues. Journalize the entry to adjust the allowance at December 31, 2008. What is the December 31, 2008, balance in the allowance?

6. Ignoring Requirement 5, assume that Hart estimates that 5% of accounts receivable will turn out to be uncollectible. Gross accounts receivable at December 31, 2008, were $825. Journalize the entry to adjust the allowance at December 31, 2008. What is the December 31, 2008, balance in the allowance?

7. Ignoring Requirements 5 and 6, assume that Hart has the following information at December 31, 2008:

Age	Gross Accounts Receivable	Percentage Estimated Uncollectible
< 30 days	$100	2%
30–60 days	500	4%
> 60 days	220	10%
Total	$820	

Journalize the entry to adjust the allowance at December 31, 2008. What is the December 31, 2008, balance in the allowance? Show how accounts receivable would be reported on the balance sheet at December 31, 2008.

8. In 2009, Hart wrote off $48 of accounts receivable. On June 30, 2009, Hart estimated uncollectible accounts expense was $10 for the first six months of the year, based on the percentage-of-sales method. Journalize these transactions.

9. At December 31, 2009, based on the percentage-of-receivables method, Hart estimated the allowance balance to be $35. Journalize Hart's entry to adjust the allowance for the year-end financial statements. (Assume the December 31, 2008, balance in the allowance was $30.) What is total uncollectible account expense for 2009?

10. Calculate Hart's days' sales in accounts receivable for 2008. (Assume Hart uses the aging-of-accounts method in Requirement 7.) What does this ratio mean?

11. The employee at Hart who opens the mail and physically collects the cash is the same person who updates the cash receipts journal and accounts receivable ledger. Is this a good internal control system?

Demo Doc 1 Solutions

Requirement 1

3 Understand the direct
write-off method for
uncollectibles

5 Report receivables on
the balance sheet

Is Hart using the allowance method or the direct write-off method to account for uncollectible receivables? How much of the December 31, 2007, balance of accounts receivable did Hart expect to collect?

Part 1	Part 2	Part 3	Part 4	Part 5	Part 6	Part 7	Part 8	Part 9	Part 10	Part 11	Demo Doc Complete

Hart is using the allowance method. We know this because an allowance for uncollectible accounts has been set up. If Hart were using the direct write-off method, there would be no allowance for uncollectible accounts.

Gross accounts receivable is the total amount of receivables that exist. For Hart, this is $800. The allowance is (by definition) the amount of receivables we do *not* expect to collect.

The total receivables minus the amount we do not expect to collect (that is, the gross accounts receivable minus the allowance) is the amount we *do* expect to collect (that is, the *net* accounts receivable).

Hart expects to collect $760 of the accounts receivable.

Requirement 2

2 Use the allowance
method to account for
uncollectibles

3 Understand the direct
write-off method for
uncollectibles

During 2008, Hart wrote off accounts receivable totaling $35 from Amanda Blake. Journalize these write-offs as one transaction. How does this transaction affect the net accounts receivable balance? How would this transaction have been recorded if the direct write-off method were being used?

Part 1	Part 2	Part 3	Part 4	Part 5	Part 6	Part 7	Part 8	Part 9	Part 10	Part 11	Demo Doc Complete

Writing off an account receivable means removing it from the accounting books/records because it has been determined that this specific amount will *not* be collected. This means that we have to reduce (credit) the Accounts Receivable. Additionally, now that we have found one of the accounts that will not be collected, we can take it out of our estimate of uncollectible accounts (the Allowance for Uncollectible Accounts). This results in a decrease to this account (a debit).

Allowance for Uncollectible Accounts	35	
Accounts Receivable—Amanda Blake		35

This is the standard format to write off Accounts Receivable when using the allowance method. The entry structure is always the same, only the amount changes.

Note that this entry does *not* change the *net* accounts receivable. Gross accounts receivable decreases, but so does the allowance. Overall the change is zero:

Gross Accounts Receivable	change of −$35
−Allowance for Uncollectible Accounts	(change of −$35)
Net Accounts Receivable	no change

The impact of this transaction is:

Gross Accounts Receivable	$800 − $35 = $765
−Allowance	($40 − $35 = $5)
Net Accounts Receivable	$760 − $0 = $760

There is no allowance under the direct write-off method, so the debit in the write-off entry is an increase to Uncollectible Accounts Expense.

Uncollectible Accounts Expense	35	
Accounts Receivable—Amanda Blake		35

Requirement 3

During 2008, Hart earned $2,800 of service revenues, all on account. Journalize these revenues as one transaction.

Part 1	Part 2	**Part 3**	Part 4	Part 5	Part 6	Part 7	Part 8	Part 9	Part 10	Part 11	Demo Doc Complete

When revenues are earned, we increase the Revenues account (a credit). In this case, we are not receiving cash, so instead we increase Accounts Receivable (a debit) to show that we intend to collect this amount later from our customer(s).

Accounts Receivable	2,800	
Service Revenue		2,800

Requirement 4

During 2008, Hart collected $2,745 cash from customers. Journalize this transaction and calculate the gross accounts receivable balance at December 31, 2008.

Part 1	Part 2	Part 3	**Part 4**	Part 5	Part 6	Part 7	Part 8	Part 9	Part 10	Part 11	Demo Doc Complete

When cash is collected, we increase the Cash account (a debit) and decrease Accounts Receivable (a credit).

Cash	2,745	
Accounts Receivable		2,745

From the initial data given in the question, we can see that *gross* accounts receivable had a balance of $800 at the beginning of the year ($760 is the *net* balance). Accounts Receivable increased in the year as revenues were earned. Accounts Receivable decreased when uncollectible accounts were written off and when cash was collected. Using this information, we can calculate the ending balance in (gross) Accounts Receivable:

Accounts Receivable

Dec. 31, 2007 Bal.	800		
2008 Revenues	2,800	2008 Write-Offs	35
		2008 Cash Collections	2,745
Dec. 31, 2008 Bal.	820		

Requirement 5

2 Use the allowance method to account for uncollectibles

Assume that Hart estimates uncollectible account expense to be 1.5% of revenues. Journalize the entry to adjust the allowance at December 31, 2008. What is the December 31, 2008, balance in the allowance?

Part 1	Part 2	Part 3	Part 4	**Part 5**	Part 6	Part 7	Part 8	Part 9	Part 10	Part 11	Demo Doc Complete

The problem states, "*Hart estimates uncollectible account expense to be 1.5% of revenues.*" The key phrase here is "*1.5% of revenues.*" This informs us that Hart is using the <u>percentage-of-sales</u> method to calculate the expense and allowance.

Under the percentage-of-sales method, the percentage of sales equals the uncollectible accounts expense. Therefore, we can calculate that 1.5% of $2,800 = $42 = the uncollectible accounts expense. This means that we record $42 of expense in our journal entry.

Recording the Uncollectible Accounts Expense increases that account (a debit) and also increases the total estimate of uncollectible accounts: the Allowance (a credit).

Uncollectible Accounts Expense ($2,800 $\times$ 1.5%)	42	
Allowance for Uncollectible Accounts		42

This is the standard journal entry format to record Uncollectible Accounts Expense and adjust the Allowance. The entry structure is always the same; only the amount changes.

The balance in the Allowance account must be calculated. The beginning balance in the allowance for 2008 is the ending balance for 2007 (the $40 shown at the beginning of the question, as shown in the balance sheet presentation on page 255). During the year, write-offs will decrease the allowance ($35, as in Requirement 2) and the year-end adjustment will increase it ($42, as in this requirement). We can fill in this information to calculate an ending balance of $47 in the Allowance account.

Allowance for Uncollectible Accounts

		Dec. 31, 2007 Bal. 40
2008 Write-Offs	35	
		2008 Uncollectible Accounts Expense Adjustment 42
		Dec. 31, 2008 Bal. 47

Requirement 6

2 Use the allowance method to account for uncollectibles

Ignoring Requirement 5, assume that Hart estimates that 5% of accounts receivable will turn out to be uncollectible. Gross accounts receivable at December 31, 2008, were $825. Journalize the entry to adjust the allowance at December 31, 2008. What is the December 31, 2008, balance in the allowance?

Part 1	Part 2	Part 3	Part 4	Part 5	**Part 6**	Part 7	Part 8	Part 9	Part 10	Part 11	Demo Doc Complete

The problem states, "*Hart estimates that 5% of accounts receivable will turn out to be uncollectible.*" The key phrase here is "*5% of accounts receivable.*"

This informs us that Hart is using the <u>percentage-of-receivables</u> method to calculate the allowance and *then* the expense.

Under the percentage-of-receivables method, the percentage of receivables equals the ending balance in the allowance. Therefore, we can calculate that 5% of $820 = $41 = the required (or target) ending balance in the allowance.

We need an additional credit in the T-account to make it balance (to make the total correct).

We can use the $41 target ending balance in the T-account (along with the beginning balance of $40 and the write-offs of $35) to calculate the Uncollectible Accounts Expense of $36 ($41 required balance −$5 current credit balance = $36). This is the amount that must be used in the journal entry.

Allowance for Uncollectible Accounts

		Dec. 31, 2007 Bal. 40
2008 Write-Offs	35	
		2008 Uncollectible Accounts Expense X
		Dec. 31, 2008 Bal. 41

$$So\ 40 - 35 + X = 41$$

$$X = 41 - 40 + 35 = 36$$

Uncollectible Accounts Expense		36	
Allowance for Uncollectible Accounts			36

This is the standard journal entry format to record Uncollectible Accounts Expense and adjust the Allowance. The entry structure is always the same; only the amount changes.

Requirement 7

Ignoring Requirements 5 and 6, assume that Hart has the following information at December 31, 2008:

Age	Gross Accounts Receivable	Percentage Estimated Uncollectible
< 30 days	$100	2%
30–60 days	500	4%
> 60 days	220	10%
Total	$820	

2 Use the allowance method to account for uncollectibles

Journalize the entry to adjust the allowance at December 31, 2008. What is the December 31, 2008, balance in the allowance? Show how accounts receivable would be reported on the balance sheet at December 31, 2008.

| Part 1 | Part 2 | Part 3 | Part 4 | Part 5 | Part 6 | **Part 7** | Part 8 | Part 9 | Part 10 | Part 11 | Demo Doc Complete |

The problem does not explicitly state which method is being used; however, the table clearly shows estimated uncollectible percentages of *accounts receivable*. This informs us that Hart is using the percentage-of-receivables (aging-of-accounts) method to calculate the allowance and *then* the expense. In fact, *all* aging-of-accounts methods are a subset of the percentage-of-receivable method.

Under the percentage-of-receivables (aging-of-accounts) method, the percentage of receivables equals the ending balance in the allowance. Therefore, we can calculate that (2% of $100) + (4% of $500) + (10% of $220) = $44 = the required (or target) ending balance in the allowance.

Age	Gross Accouts Receivable		Percentage Estimated Uncollectible		Amount Estimated Uncollectible
< 30 days	$100	×	2%	=	$ 2
30–60 days	500	×	4%	=	20
> 60 days	220	×	10%	=	22
Total	$820	×			$44

Ending Allowance Balance

We need an additional credit in the T-account to make it balance (to make the total correct).

We can use the $44 ending balance in the T-account (along with the beginning balance of $40 and the write-offs of $35) to calculate the Uncollectible Accounts Expense of $39. This is the amount that must be used in the journal entry ($44 required balance − $5 credit balance = $39 amount for journal entry).

 5 Report receivables on the balance sheet

Allowance for Uncollectible Accounts

2008 Write-Offs	35	Dec. 31, 2007 Bal.	40
		2008 Uncollectible Accounts Expense Adjustment	X
		Dec. 31, 2008 Bal.	44

So 40 − 35 + X = 44

X = 44 − 40 + 35 = 39

Uncollectible Accounts Expense		39	
Allowance for Uncollectible Accounts			39

This is the standard journal entry format to record Uncollectible Accounts Expense and adjust the Allowance. The entry structure is always the same; only the amount changes.

On the balance sheet, we would see the gross accounts receivable combined with the Allowance contra account:

Accounts Receivable	$820
Less Allowance for Uncollectible Accounts	(44)
Accounts Receivable (net)	$776

Requirement 8

 2 Use the allowance method to account for uncollectibles

In 2009, Hart wrote off $48 of accounts receivable. On June 30, 2009, Hart estimated uncollectible accounts expense was $10 for the first six months of the year, based on the percentage-of-sales method. Journalize these transactions.

Part 1	Part 2	Part 3	Part 4	Part 5	Part 6	Part 7	**Part 8**	Part 9	Part 10	Part 11	Demo Doc Complete

As in Requirement 2, we use the standard format to write off Accounts Receivable:

Allowance for Uncollectible Accounts	48	
Accounts Receivable		48

We also use the standard format to record the Uncollectible Accounts Expense:

Uncollectible Accounts Expense	10	
Allowance for Uncollectible Accounts		10

Requirement 9

Use the allowance method to account for uncollectibles

At December 31, 2009, based on the percentage-of-receivables method, Hart estimated the allowance balance to be $35. Journalize Hart's entry to adjust the allowance for the year-end financial statements. (Assume the December 31, 2008, balance in the allowance was $30.) What is total uncollectible account expense for 2009?

Part 1	Part 2	Part 3	Part 4	Part 5	Part 6	Part 7	Part 8	**Part 9**	Part 10	Part 11	Demo Doc Complete

Because we only have the target balance in the allowance, we need to analyze the Allowance T-account in order to determine how much Uncollectible Accounts Expense to record for the remaining three months of the year.

So far, the Allowance has been affected in 2009 by write-offs and the Uncollectible Accounts Expense recorded in June:

Allowance for Uncollectible Accounts

		Dec. 31, 2008 Bal.	30	
2009 Write-Offs	48	June 2009 Expense Adjustment	10	
Bal. Before Adj.	8			
		Dec. 31, 2009 Expense Adj.	X	
		Dec. 31, 2009 Bal.	35	

So X − 8 = 35

X = 35 + 8 = 43

So the additional expense recorded on December 31, 2009, is $43. Again, we use the standard format to record Uncollectible Accounts Expense:

Uncollectible Accounts Expense	43	
Allowance for Uncollectible Accounts		43

Requirement 10

6 Use the acid-test ratio and days' sales in receivables to evaluate a company

Calculate Hart's days' sales in accounts receivable for 2008. (Assume Hart uses the aging-of-accounts method in Requirement 7.) What does this ratio mean?

Part 1	Part 2	Part 3	Part 4	Part 5	Part 6	Part 7	Part 8	Part 9	**Part 10**	Part 11	Demo Doc Complete

The days' sales ratio is calculated as:

$$\frac{\text{Days' sales in average}}{\text{accounts receivable}} = \frac{\text{Average net accounts receivable} \times 365 \text{ days}}{\text{Net sales}}$$

From Requirement 3, we know that service revenues for 2008 are $2,800. From Requirement 7, we know that net accounts receivable were $760 on December 31, 2007, and $776 on December 31, 2008.

So for Hart:

$$\frac{\text{Days' sales in average}}{\text{accounts receivable}} = \frac{\frac{1}{2} \times [\$760 + \$776] \times 365 \text{ days}}{\$2,800}$$

$$\text{Day's sales in average accounts receivable} = 100.1 \text{ days}$$

The average amount of time that it takes Hart to collect an account receivable is 100.1 days (more than three months).

Requirement 11

1 Design internal controls for receivables

The employee at Hart who opens the mail and physically collects the cash is the same person who updates the cash receipts journal and accounts receivable ledger. Is this a good internal control system?

Part 1	Part 2	Part 3	Part 4	Part 5	Part 6	Part 7	Part 8	Part 9	Part 10	**Part 11**	Demo Doc Complete

If an employee collects the cash *and* records the receipt of the cash *and* updates the accounts receivable ledger, there is an opportunity for fraud. The employee could steal the cash and delay recording the cash receipt or perhaps never record the cash receipt. The employee could hide his or her act for a long period of time by manipulating the accounts receivable ledger.

To avoid this problem, most internal control systems require <u>separation of duties</u>; that is, the employees who handle cash (both receipts and payments) are *not* the same employees who maintain the accounting records.

Part 1	Part 2	Part 3	Part 4	Part 5	Part 6	Part 7	Part 8	Part 9	Part 10	Part 11	**Demo Doc Complete**

Demo Doc 2

Notes Receivable

On November 1, 2008, Jordan Inc. borrowed $1,800 cash from Donald Corp. Jordan signed a three-month, 10% note. Jordan paid the note plus interest in full on the due date. Both Jordan and Donald have December 31 year-ends.

Requirements

1. When is the note due? What is the total interest that will be paid on this note? What is its maturity value?

2. Prepare all journal entries for this note for both companies from November 1, 2008, through the due date. Explanations are not required.

Demo Doc 2 Solutions

Requirement 1

4 Account for notes
receivable

When is the note due? What is the total interest that will be paid on this
note? What is its maturity value?

	Part 1	Part 2	Demo Doc Complete

The note was issued on November 1, 2008. Because it is a three-month note, it is
due three months from that date on February 1, 2009.

The amount of interest incurred over the entire life of the note is calculated as:

$$\frac{\text{Interest}}{\text{incurred}} = \frac{\text{Amount}}{\text{of debt}} \times \frac{\text{Annual interest}}{\text{rate}} \times \frac{\text{Time elapsed}}{\text{(in years)}}$$

So in this case:

$$\frac{\text{Interest}}{\text{incurred}} = \$1,800 \times 10\% \times \frac{3 \text{ months}}{12 \text{ months}}$$

$$\text{Interest incurred} = \$45$$

The maturity value is calculated as:

$$\text{Maturity value} = \text{Principal} + \text{Interest incurred over life of the note}$$

So in this case:

$$\text{Maturity value} = \$1,800 + \$45 = \$1,845$$

Requirement 2

Prepare all journal entries for this note for both companies from November 1,
2008, through the due date. Explanations are not required.

	Part 1	Part 2	Demo Doc Complete

4 Account for notes
receivable

November 1, 2008: Jordan borrows $1,800 from Donald.

Jordan borrowed cash from Donald. This means that Donald has a decrease
(a credit) to Cash of $1,800. Because Donald can expect to get this money back
(that is, collect it) in the future, we can also set up a Notes Receivable asset (a
debit) for $1,800.

Donald:

Nov. 1	Notes Receivable	1,800	
	Cash		1,800

Jordan has an increase to Cash (a debit) and because the money must be paid back, we can set up a Notes Payable liability (a credit) for $1,800.

Jordan:

Nov. 1	Cash	1,800	
	Notes Payable		1,800

Account for notes receivable

December 31, 2008: Accrue 10% interest on note.

Both companies have a December 31 year-end. This means that they need to adjust their accounting information on this date. By this time, the note has been outstanding for two months. This means that interest has been incurred on the note.

The amount of interest incurred is calculated as:

$$\text{Interest incurred} = \text{Amount of debt} \times \text{Annual interest rate} \times \text{Time elapsed (in years)}$$

So in this case:

$$\text{Interest incurred} = \$1,800 \times 10\% \times \frac{2 \text{ months}}{12 \text{ months}}$$

$$\text{Interest incurred} = \$30$$

Note that *all* interest rates that are given are assumed to be *annual* rates, unless specifically stated otherwise.

Donald has earned Interest Revenue (a credit) of $30. Because the cash has not yet been received, we must also set up an Interest Receivable account (a debit) of $30.

Donald:

Dec. 31	Interest Receivable	30	
	Interest Revenue ($1,800 × 10% × 2/12)		30

Jordan has incurred Interest Expense (a debit) of $30. Because the cash has yet to be paid, we must also set up an Interest Payable account (a credit) of $30.

Jordan:

Dec. 31	Interest Expense	30	
	Interest Payable		30

February 1, 2009: Note and interest are paid in full.

On this day, the note and interest are fully paid. For Donald, this causes a decrease to Notes Receivable (a credit) of $1,800. Additionally, Donald is receiving the interest that was accrued on December 31, so there will also be a decrease to Interest Receivable of $30 (a credit).

However, there is *more* interest than this! Donald has also earned interest between December 31 and February 1 (one month):

$$\frac{\text{Interest}}{\text{incurred}} = \$1,800 \times 10\% \times \frac{1 \text{ month}}{12 \text{ months}}$$

$$\text{Interest incurred} = \$15$$

So Donald records Interest Revenue (a credit) of $15.

All of these amounts are being paid in cash, so Donald's Cash account will be increased (a debit) by $1,800 + $30 + $15 = $1,845 (the maturity value).

Donald:

Feb. 1	Cash (maturity value)	1,845	
	Notes Receivable		1,800
	Interest Receivable		30
	Interest Revenue ($1,800 × 10% × 1/12)		15

With payment of the note and interest, Jordan will decrease Notes Payable by $1,800 and Interest Payable by $30 (debits). Jordan will also record additional interest expense of $15 (a debit) and decrease Cash (a credit) by $1,845.

Jordan:

Feb. 1	Notes Payable	1,800	
	Interest Payable	30	
	Interest Expense	15	
	Cash		1,845

Part 1	Part 2	**Demo Doc Complete**

Demo Doc 3

Credit-Card Receivables

Learning Objective 5

Mack Corp. accepts credit-card payments from its customers. On May 4, 2008, a customer paid for $800 worth of services using his MasterCard credit card. MasterCard charges Mack a 3% fee to process the transaction. On May 10, 2008, Mack received the cash payment from MasterCard for this sale.

Requirements

1. Show Mack's journal entry to record the sale on May 4, 2008.

2. Show Mack's journal entry to record the cash receipt from MasterCard on May 10, 2008.

Demo Doc 3 Solutions

Requirement 1

 Report receivables on the balance sheet

Show Mack's journal entry to record the sale on May 4, 2008.

Part 1	Part 2	Demo Doc Complete

As with a non-credit-card sale, Mack will increase Accounts Receivable (a debit) and increase Service Revenue (a credit) by $800. However, the account receivable is not for the full $800, because not all of this amount will be collected. The 3% MasterCard fee must be deducted.

So Accounts Receivable = $800 × (1 − 3%) = $776.

The difference of $800 − $776 = $24 is recorded as an increase (debit) to Credit-Card Discount Expense.

Accounts Receivable—MasterCard ($800 × [1 – 3%])		776	
Credit-Card Discount Expense ($800 × 3%)		24	
Service Revenue			800

Requirement 2

 Report receivables on the balance sheet

Show Mack's journal entry to record the cash receipt from MasterCard on May 10, 2008.

Part 1	**Part 2**	Demo Doc Complete

The collection of the account receivable is similar to any other collection of an account receivable. Accounts Receivable is decreased (a credit) by $776 and Cash is increased (a debit) by $776.

Cash		776	
Accounts Receivable—MasterCard			776

Part 1	Part 2	**Demo Doc Complete**

Quick Practice Questions

True/False

_____ 1. The Allowance for Uncollectible Accounts is a contra account to Accounts Receivable.

_____ 2. Under the allowance method, the recovery of an account previously written off has no effect on net income.

_____ 3. Under the allowance method, the entry to write off an account that is determined to be uncollectible includes a credit to the Allowance for Uncollectible Accounts.

_____ 4. Under the allowance method, the entry to write off an account that has been deemed uncollectible has no effect on the total assets of the firm.

_____ 5. The direct write-off method is the preferred way to apply the accrual basis for measuring uncollectible accounts expense because it matches revenues and expenses on the income statement.

_____ 6. Under the direct write-off method, the entry to write off an account that has been deemed uncollectible has no effect on the total assets of the firm.

_____ 7. A written promise to pay a specified amount of money at a particular future date is referred to as a promissory note.

_____ 8. If the maker of a note does not pay at maturity, the maker is said to dishonor the note.

_____ 9. The acid-test ratio includes cash, inventory, and net accounts receivable in the numerator.

_____ 10. Nonbank credit-card sales are recorded as a debit to Accounts Receivable and a credit to Sales Revenue in the same amount.

Multiple Choice

1. **Chuck Battle's account of $5,000 must be written off. Which of the following would be journalized assuming that the allowance method is used?**
   a. A debit to Battle's Accounts Receivable and a credit to Allowance for Uncollectible Accounts
   b. A debit to Allowance for Uncollectible Accounts and a credit to Battle's Accounts Receivable
   c. A debit to Cash and a credit to Uncollectible Accounts Expense
   d. A debit to Cash and a credit to Battle's Accounts Receivable

2. **The current credit balance in Allowance for Uncollectible Accounts before adjustment is $658. An aging schedule reveals $3,700 of uncollectible**

accounts. What is the ending balance in the Allowance for Uncollectible Accounts?

a. $3,042
b. $3,700
c. $4,029
d. $4,358

3. The current debit balance in Allowance for Uncollectible Accounts before adjustment is $742. An aging schedule reveals $3,500 of uncollectible accounts. What is the amount of the journal entry for Estimated Uncollectible Accounts?

a. $742
b. $2,758
c. $3,500
d. $4,242

4. What is the type of account and normal balance of Allowance for Uncollectible Accounts?

a. Asset, debit
b. Contra asset, credit
c. Liability, credit
d. Contra liability, debit

5. If the direct write-off method is used for uncollectible receivables, what account is debited when writing off a customer's account?

a. Accounts Receivable
b. Allowance for Uncollectible Accounts
c. Uncollectible Accounts Expense
d. Sales Returns and Allowances

6. What is the effect on the financial statements of writing off an uncollectible account under the direct write-off method?

a. Increases expenses and decreases liabilities
b. Decreases net income and decreases assets
c. Decreases assets and increases owner's equity
d. Increases expenses and increases assets

7. Which of the following is not avoided when a company uses national credit cards?

a. Checking a customer's credit rating
b. Keeping an accounts receivable subsidiary ledger for each customer
c. Having to collect cash from customers
d. Paying a credit-card discount expense

8. A 90-day, 12% note for $20,000, dated July 10, is received from a customer. What is the maturity value of the note?

a. $20,000
b. $20,600
c. $21,200
d. $22,400

9. Carolina Supply accepted an 8-month, $16,000 note receivable, with 8% interest, from Reading Corporation on August 1, 2008. Carolina Supply's year-end is December 31. What is the amount of interest to be accrued on December 31, 2008?

a. $320
b. $533
c. $853
d. $1,280

10. Which of the following is recorded on the payee's books when a debtor dishonors a note receivable?
a. Debit Uncollectible Accounts Expense
b. Debit Accounts Receivable
c. No entry required
d. Debit Notes Receivable

Quick Exercises

9-1. Prepare the adjusting journal entry on December 31, 2008, for the following independent situations:

a. The Allowance for Uncollectible Accounts has a $700 credit balance prior to adjustment. Net credit sales during the year are $216,000 and 4% are estimated to be uncollectible.

Journal				Page 1
Date	Accounts		Debit	Credit

b. The Allowance for Uncollectible Accounts has a $500 credit balance prior to adjustment. An aging schedule prepared on December 31 reveals an estimated uncollectible accounts amount of $7,300.

Journal				Page 1
Date	Accounts		Debit	Credit

c. The Allowance for Uncollectible Accounts has a $525 debit balance prior to adjustment. An aging schedule prepared on December 31 reveals an estimated uncollectible accounts amount of $5,100.

Journal				Page 1
Date	Accounts		Debit	Credit

d. The Allowance for Uncollectible Accounts has an $800 credit balance prior to adjustment. Net credit sales during the year are $229,000 and 3.5% are estimated to be uncollectible.

Journal				Page 1
Date	Accounts		Debit	Credit

9-2.   Compute the ending balance in the Allowance for Uncollectible Accounts after the adjusting entries in 9-1 have been prepared for the four independent situations, a–d.

     a. _____

     b. _____

     c. _____

     d. _____

9-3.   Record the following independent transactions assuming the allowance method is used.

     a. August 5, 2008—Wrote off Jones Corp. account receivable for $2,200 as uncollectible.

     b. August 17, 2008—Collected the $2,200 from Jones Corp. in full.

     c. August 31, 2008—Recorded uncollectible accounts expense of $16,500.

Date	Accounts	Debit	Credit

Date	Accounts	Debit	Credit

Date	Accounts	Debit	Credit

Date	Accounts	Debit	Credit

9-4. On December 31, 2008, Rainbow Appliances has $275,000 in accounts receivable and an Allowance account with a credit balance of $240. Current period net credit sales are $771,000, and cash sales are $68,000.

Rainbow Appliances performs an aging schedule; the results follow, along with the appropriate percentages that Rainbow applies to the categories shown.

Age	Gross Accounts Receivable	Estimated Uncollectible
Not yet due	$150,000	1%
31–60 days past due	50,000	5%
61–90 days past due	40,000	10%
91–120 days past due	25,000	25%
Over 120 days past due	10,000	50%
Total	$275,000	

a. Assuming Rainbow uses the aging approach of accounting for uncollectible accounts, prepare the adjusting entry required at the end of the accounting period.

Date	Accounts	Debit	Credit

b. Assume now Rainbow uses the percentage-of-sales method of accounting for uncollectible accounts. If historical data indicate that approximately 3% of net credit sales are uncollectible, what is the amount of uncollectible accounts expense that should be recorded?

What is the balance in the Allowance for Uncollectible Accounts after adjustment?

9-5. Peterson Company, which has a December 31 year-end, completed the following transactions during 2008 and 2009:

2008	
Oct. 14	Sold merchandise to Bruce Company, receiving a 60-day, 9% note for $10,000.
Nov. 16	Sold merchandise to Marine Company, receiving a 72-day, 8% note for $9100.
Dec. 13	Received amount due from Bruce Company.
Dec. 31	Accrued interest on the Marine Company note.

2009	
Jan. 27	Collected in full from Marine Company.

Requirement

1. Prepare the necessary journal entries to record the preceding transactions.

	Date	Accounts	Debit	Credit

	Date	Accounts	Debit	Credit

	Date	Accounts	Debit	Credit

	Date	Accounts	Debit	Credit

	Date	Accounts	Debit	Credit

Do It Yourself! Question 1

Uncollectible Accounts Receivable

Now Company's December 31, 2007, balance sheet reported:

Accounts Receivable	$1,000
Allowance for Uncollectible Accounts	(85)
Accounts Receivable (net)	$915

Requirements

1. How much of the December 31, 2007, balance of accounts receivable did Now expect to collect?

2. During 2008, Now wrote off accounts receivable totaling $110. Journalize these write-offs as one transaction.

Date	Accounts and Explanation	Debit	Credit

3. During 2008, Now earned $13,000 of service revenues, all on account. Journalize these revenues as one transaction.

Date	Accounts and Explanation	Debit	Credit

4. During 2008, Now collected $12,840 cash from customers. Journalize this transaction and calculate the gross accounts receivable balance at December 31, 2008.

Date	Accounts and Explanation	Debit	Credit

_____|_____
_____|_____

5. Assume that Now estimates that 10% of accounts receivable will turn out to be uncollectible. Gross accounts receivable at December 31, 2008, were $1,050. Journalize the entry to adjust the allowance at December 31, 2008. What is the December 31, 2008, balance in the allowance?

Date	Accounts and Explanation	Debit	Credit

_____|_____
_____|_____

6. Ignoring Requirement 5, assume that Now estimates uncollectible account expense to be 0.75% of revenues. Journalize the entry to adjust the allowance at December 31, 2008. What is the December 31, 2008, balance in the allowance?

Date	Accounts and Explanation	Debit	Credit

_____|_____
_____|_____

7. Ignoring Requirements 5 and 6, assume that Now has the following information at December 31, 2008:

Age	Gross Accounts Receivable	Percentage Estimated Uncollectible
< 30 days	$ 500	1%
30–60 days	450	10%
> 60 days	100	15%
Total	$1,050	

Journalize the entry to adjust the allowance at December 31, 2008. What is the December 31, 2008, balance in the allowance? Show how accounts receivable would be reported on the balance sheet at December 31, 2008.

Date	Accounts and Explanation	Debit	Credit

8. In 2009, Now wrote off $90 of accounts receivable. On September 30, 2009, Now estimated uncollectible accounts expense was $55 for the first nine months of the year, based on the percentage-of-sales method. Journalize these transactions.

Date	Accounts and Explanation	Debit	Credit

Date	Accounts and Explanation	Debit	Credit

9. At December 31, 2009, based on the percentage-of-receivables method, Now estimated the allowance balance to be $78. Journalize Now's entry to adjust the allowance for the year-end financial statements. (Assume the December 31, 2008, balance in the allowance was $65.) What is total uncollectible accounts expense for 2009?

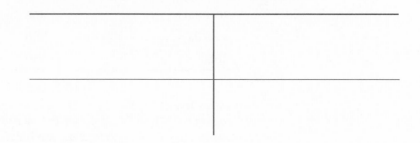

Date	Accounts and Explanation	Debit	Credit

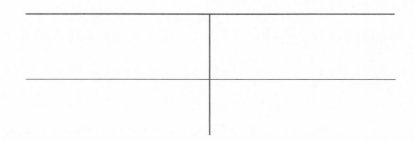

Do it Yourself! Question 2

Notes Receivable

On June 1 2008, Anderson Corp. borrowed $6,000 cash from Neo Enterprises. Anderson signed a 10-month, 5% note. Anderson paid the note plus interest in full on the due date. Both Anderson and Neo have December 31 year-ends.

Requirements

1. When is the note due? What is the total interest incurred over the life of the note? What is the maturity value of the note?

2. Prepare all journal entries for this note for _both_ companies from June 1, 2008 through the due date. Explanations are not required.

NEO Enterprises:

Date	Accounts and Explanation	Debit	Credit

Anderson Corp.:

Date	Accounts and Explanation	Debit	Credit

Neo Enterprises:

Date	Accounts and Explanation	Debit	Credit

Anderson Corp.:

Date	Accounts and Explanation	Debit	Credit

Neo Enterprises:

Date	Accounts and Explanation	Debit	Credit

Anderson Corp.:

Date	Accounts and Explanation	Debit	Credit

Quick Practice Solutions

True/False

T   1. The Allowance for Uncollectible Accounts is a contra account to Accounts Receivable. (p. 460)

T   2. Under the allowance method, the recovery of an account previously written off has no effect on net income. (p. 465)

F   3. Under the allowance method, the entry to write off an account that is determined to be uncollectible includes a credit to the Allowance for Uncollectible Accounts.

      False—The entry to write off an account that is determined to be uncollectible includes a *debit* to the Allowance for Uncollectible Accounts. (p. 464)

T   4. Under the allowance method, the entry to write off an account that has been deemed uncollectible has no effect on the total assets of the firm. (p. 460)

F   5. The direct write-off method is the preferred way to apply the accrual basis for measuring uncollectible accounts expense because it matches revenues and expenses on the income statement.

      False—The *allowance method* is the preferred way to apply the accrual basis for measuring uncollectible accounts expense because it matches revenues and expenses on the income statement. (p. 465)

F   6. Under the direct write-off method, the entry to write off an account that has been deemed uncollectible has no effect on total assets of the firm.

      False—The write-off of an account under the direct write-off method results in a credit to Accounts Receivable, which *reduces* total assets. (p. 465)

T   7. A written promise to pay a specified amount of money at a particular future date is referred to as a promissory note. (p. 465)

T   8. If the maker of a note does not pay at maturity, the maker is said to dishonor the note. (p. 473)

F   9. The acid-test ratio includes cash, inventory, and net accounts receivable in the numerator.

      False—The acid-test ratio includes cash, *short-term* investments, and net accounts receivable in the numerator. (p. 475)

F   10. Nonbank credit-card sales are recorded as a debit to Accounts Receivable and a credit to Sales Revenue in the same amount.

      False—The debit to Accounts Receivable is for an amount *less than* the credit to Sales Revenue due to the Credit-Card Discount Expense. (p. 466)

Multiple Choice

1. Chuck Battle's account of $5,000 must be written off. Which of the following would be journalized assuming that the allowance method is used? (p. 464)
   a. A debit to Battle's Accounts Receivable and a credit to Allowance for Uncollectible Accounts
   b. A debit to Allowance for Uncollectible Accounts and a credit to Battle's Accounts Receivable
   c. A debit to Cash and a credit to Uncollectible Account Expense
   d. A debit to Cash and a credit to Battle's Accounts Receivable

2. The current credit balance in Allowance for Uncollectible Accounts before adjustment is $658. An aging schedule reveals $3,700 of uncollectible accounts. What is the ending balance in the Allowance for Uncollectible Accounts? (p. 462)
   a. $3,042
   b. $3,700
   c. $4,029
   d. $4,358

3. The current debit balance in Allowance for Uncollectible Accounts before adjustment is $742. An aging schedule reveals $3,500 of uncollectible accounts. What is the amount of the journal entry for Estimated Uncollectible Accounts? (p. 462)
   a. $742
   b. $2,758
   c. $3,500
   d. $4,242

4. What is the type of account and normal balance of Allowance for Uncollectible Accounts? (p. 460)
   a. Asset, debit
   b. Contra asset, credit
   c. Liability, credit
   d. Contra liability, debit

5. If the direct write-off method is used for uncollectible receivables, what account is debited when writing off a customer's account? (p. 465)
   a. Accounts Receivable
   b. Allowance for Uncollectible Accounts
   c. Uncollectible Account Expense
   d. Sales Returns and Allowances

6. What is the effect on the financial statements of writing off an uncollectible account under the direct write-off method? (p. 465)
   a. Increases expenses and decreases liabilities
   b. Decreases net income and decreases assets
   c. Decreases assets and increases owner's equity
   d. Increases expenses and increases assets

7. Which of the following is *not* avoided when a company uses national credit cards? (p. 466)
   a. Checking a customer's credit rating
   b. Keeping an accounts receivable subsidiary ledger for each customer
   c. Having to collect cash from customers
   d. Paying a credit-card discount expense

8. A 90-day, 12% note for $20,000, dated July 10, is received from a customer. What is the maturity value of the note? (p. 470)
   a. $20,000
   b. $20,600
   c. $21,200
   d. $22,400

9. Carolina Supply accepted an 8-month, $16,000 note receivable, with 8% interest, from Reading Corporation on August 1, 2008. Carolina Supply's year-end is December 31. What is the amount of interest to be accrued on December 31, 2008? (p. 471)
   a. $320
   b. $853
   c. $533
   d. $1,280

10. Which of the following is recorded on the payee's books when a debtor dishonors a note receivable? (p. 473)
    a. Debit Uncollectible Accounts Expense
    b. Debit Accounts Receivable
    c. No entry required
    d. Debit Notes Receivable

Quick Exercises

9-1. Prepare the adjusting journal entry on December 31, 2008 for the following independent situations: (p. 464)

   a. The Allowance for Uncollectible Accounts has a $700 credit balance prior to adjustment. Net credit sales during the year are $216,000 and 4% are estimated to be uncollectible.
   b. The Allowance for Uncollectible Accounts has a $500 credit balance prior to adjustment. An aging schedule prepared on December 31 reveals an estimated uncollectible accounts amount of $7,300.
   c. The Allowance for Uncollectible Accounts has a $525 debit balance prior to adjustment. An aging schedule prepared on December 31 reveals an estimated uncollectible accounts amount of $5,100.
   d. The Allowance for Uncollectible Accounts has an $800 credit balance prior to adjustment. Net credit sales during the year are $229,000 and 3.5% are estimated to be uncollectible.

Journal				Page 1
	Date	Accounts	Debit	Credit
a.	12/31/08	Uncollectible Accounts Expense	8,640	
		Allowance for Uncollectible Accounts		8,640
		($216,000 × .04) = $8,640		

Journal				Page 1
	Date	Accounts	Debit	Credit
b.	12/31/08	Uncollectible Accounts Expense	6,800	
		Allowance for Uncollectible Accounts		6,800
		($7,300 − $500 = $6,800)		

Journal   **Page 1**

	Date	Accounts	Debit	Credit
c.	12/31/08	Uncollectible Accounts Expense	5,625	
		Allowance for Uncollectible Accounts		5,625
		($5,100 + $525 = $5,625)		

Journal   **Page 1**

	Date	Accounts	Debit	Credit
d.	12/31/08	Uncollectible Accounts Expense	8,015	
		Allowance for Uncollectible Accounts		8,015
		($229,000 × 0.35) = $8,015		

9-2. Compute the ending balance in the Allowance for Uncollectible Accounts after the adjusting entries in 9-1 have been prepared for the four independent situations, a–d. (p. 464)

    a. $9,340 ($700 + $8,640)
    b. $7,300 ($500 + $6,800)
    c. $5,100 ($5,625 − $525)
    d. $8,815 ($800 + $8,015)

9-3. Record the following independent transactions assuming the allowance method is used. (pp. 464–465)

    a. August 5, 2008—Wrote off Jones Corp. account receivable for $2,200 as uncollectible.
    b. August 17, 2008—Collected the $2,200 from Jones Corp. in full.
    c. August 31, 2008—Recorded uncollectible accounts expense of $16,500.

	Date	Accounts	Debit	Credit
a.	8/5/08	Allowance for Uncollectible Accounts	2,200	
		Accounts Receivable—Jones Corp.		2,200
		To write off Jones Corp. account receivable.		

	Date	Accounts	Debit	Credit
b.	8/17/08	Accounts Receivable—Jones Corp.	2,200	
		Allowance for Uncollectible Accounts		2,200
		To reinstate Jones Corp. account receivable.		

	Date	Accounts	Debit	Credit
c.	8/17/08	Cash	2,200	
		Accounts Receivable—Jones Corp.		2,200
		To record cash collected from Jones Corp.		

	Date	Accounts	Debit	Credit
d.	8/31/08	Uncollectible Accounts Expense	16,500	
		Allowance for Uncollectible Accounts.		16,500
		To record estimated uncollectible accounts.		

9-4.   On December 31, 2008, Rainbow Appliances has $275,000 in accounts receivable and an Allowance account with a credit balance of $240. Current period net credit sales are $771,000, and cash sales are $68,000. Rainbow Appliances performs an aging schedule; the results follow along with the appropriate percentages that Rainbow applies to the categories shown. (p. 462)

Age	Gross Accounts Receivable	Percentage Estimated Uncollectible
Not yet due	$150,000	1%
31–60 days past due	50,000	5%
61–90 days past due	40,000	10%
91–120 days past due	25,000	25%
Over 120 days past due	10,000	50%
Total	$275,000	

a.   Assuming Rainbow uses the aging approach of accounting for uncollectible accounts, prepare the adjusting entry required at the end of the accounting period.

Date	Accounts	Debit	Credit
12/31/08	Uncollectible Accounts Expense	19,010	
	Allowance for Doubtful Accounts		19,010
	($150,000 × 0.01) + ($50,000 × 0.05) + ($40,000 × 0.10) +		
	($25,000 × 0.25) + ($10,000 × 0.5) = $19,250 – $240		

b.   Assume now Rainbow uses the percentage-of-sales method of accounting for uncollectible accounts. If historical data indicate that approximately 3% of net credit sales are uncollectible, what is the amount of uncollectible accounts expense that should be recorded? $23,130

What is the balance in the Allowance for Uncollectible Accounts after adjustment? $23,370 ($240 + $23,130)

9-5.   Peterson Company, which has a December 31 year-end, completed the following transactions during 2008 and 2009:

2008

Oct. 14	Sold merchandise to Bruce Company, receiving a 60-day, 9% note for $10,000.
Nov. 16	Sold merchandise to Marine Company, receiving a 72-day, 8% note for $9,100.
Dec. 13	Received amount due from Bruce Company.
Dec. 31	Accrued interest on the Marine Company note.

2009

Jan. 27	Collected in full from Marine Company.

Requirement

Prepare the necessary journal entries to record the preceding transactions. (p. 472)

Date	Accounts	Debit	Credit
10/14/08	Notes Receivable	10,000	
	Sales		10,000

Date	Accounts	Debit	Credit
11/16/08	Notes Receivable	9,100	
	Sales		9,100

Date	Accounts	Debit	Credit
12/13/08	Cash	10,150	
	Notes Receivable		10,000
	Interest Revenue		150

Date	Accounts	Debit	Credit
12/31/08	Interest Receivable	91	
	Interest Revenue		91

Date	Accounts	Debit	Credit
1/27/09	Cash	9,246	
	Notes Receivable		9,100
	Interest Revenue		55
	Interest Receivable		91

Do It Yourself! Question 1 Solutions

Requirements

5 Report receivables on the balance sheet

1. How much of the December 31, 2007, balance of accounts receivable did Now expect to collect?

Now expects to collect $915 of the accounts receivable balance.

2 Use the allowance method to account for uncollectibles

2. During 2008, Now wrote off accounts receivable totaling $110. Journalize these write-offs as one transaction.

Allowance for Uncollectible Accounts	110	
Accounts Receivable		110

3. During 2008, Now earned $13,000 of service revenues, all on account. Journalize these revenues as one transaction.

Accounts Receivable	13,000	
Service Revenue		13,000

4. During 2008, Now collected $12,840 cash from customers. Journalize this transaction and calculate the gross accounts receivable balance at December 31, 2008.

Cash	12,840	
Accounts Receivable		12,840

Accounts Receivable			
Dec. 31, 2007 Bal.	1,000		
2008 Revenues	13,000	2008 Write-Offs	110
		2008 Cash Collections	12,840
Dec. 31, 2009 Bal.	1,050		

Use the allowance method to account for uncollectibles

5. Assume that Now estimates that 10% of accounts receivable will turn out to be uncollectible. Gross accounts receivable at December 31, 2008, were $1,050. Journalize the entry to adjust the allowance at December 31, 2008. What is the December 31, 2008, balance in the allowance?

10% × $1,050 = $105 = balance in Allowance account

Allowance for Uncollectible Accounts

2008 Write-Offs	110	Dec. 31, 2007 Bal.	85
		2008 Uncollectible Accounts Expense	X
		Dec. 31, 2008 Bal.	105

So 85 − 110 + X = 105
X = 105 + 110 − 85 = 130

Uncollectible Accounts Expense	130	
Allowance for Uncollectible Accounts		130

 Use the allowance method to account for uncollectibles

6. Ignoring Requirement 5, assume that Now estimates uncollectible account expense to be 0.75% of revenues. Journalize the entry to adjust the allowance at December 31, 2008. What is the December 31, 2008, balance in the allowance?

0.75% × $13,000 = $97.50

Uncollectible Accounts Expense	97.50	
Allowance for Uncollectible Accounts		97.50

Allowance for Uncollectible Accounts

2008 Write-Offs	110	Dec. 31, 2007 Bal.	85
		2008 Uncollectible Accounts Expense	97.50
		Dec. 31, 2008 Bal.	72.50

7. Ignoring Requirements 5 and 6, Assume that Now has the following information at December 31, 2008:

Age	Gross Accounts Receivable	Percentage Estimated Uncollectible
< 30 days	$ 500	1%
30–60 days	450	10%
> 60 days	$ 100	15%
Total	$1,050	

2 Use the allowance method to account for uncollectibles

Journalize the entry to adjust the allowance at December 31, 2008. What is the December 31, 2008 balance in the allowance? Show how accounts receivable would be reported on the balance sheet at December 31, 2008.

Age	Gross Accounts Receivable		Percentage Estimated Uncollectible		Amount Estimated Uncollectible
< 30 days	$ 500	×	1%	=	$ 5
30–60 days	450	×	10%	=	45
< 60 days	100	×	15%	=	15
Total	$1,050				$65

Allowance for Uncollectible Accounts

2008 Write-Offs	110	Dec. 31, 2007 Bal.	85
		2008 Uncollectible Accounts Expense	X
		Dec. 31, 2008 Bal.	65

5 Report receivables on the balance sheet

So 85 − 110 + X = 65

X = 65 − 85 + 110 = 90

Uncollectible Accounts Expense	90	
Allowance for Uncollectible Accounts		90

On the balance sheet:

Accounts Receivable	$1,050
Less Allowance for Uncollectible Accounts	(65)
Accounts Receivable (net)	$985

Use the allowance method to account for uncollectibles

8. In 2009, Now wrote off $90 of accounts receivable. On September 30, 2009, Now estimated uncollectible accounts expense was $55 for the first nine months of the year, based on the percentage-of-sales method. Journalize these transactions.

Allowance for Uncollectible Accounts	90	
Accounts Receivable		90

Uncollectible Accounts Expense	55	
Allowance for Uncollectible Accounts		55

 Use the allowance method to account for uncollectibles

9. At December 31, 2009, based on the percentage-of-receivables method, Now estimated the allowance balance to be $78. Journalize Now's entry to adjust the allowance for the year-end financial statements. (Assume the December 31, 2008, balance in the allowance was $65.) What is total uncollectible accounts expense for 2009?

Allowance for Uncollectible Accounts

		Dec. 31, 2008 Bal.	65
2009 Write-Offs	90		
		Sept. 2009 Expense	55
		Bal. Before Adj.	30
		Dec. 31, 2009 Adj.	X
		Dec. 31, 2009 Bal.	78

$$\text{So } 65 - 90 + 55 + X = 78$$
$$X = 78 - 65 + 90 - 55 = 48$$

Uncollectible Accounts Expense	48	
Allowance for Uncollectible Accounts		48

Total Uncollectible Accounts Expense for 2009

= Expense recorded in September 2009 + Expense recorded in December 2009

= $55 + $48 = $103

Uncollectible Accounts Expense

Jan. 1, 2009 Bal.	0	
Sept. 2009		
Expense Adjustment	58	
Dec. 2009		
Expense Adjustment	45	
Dec. 31, 2009 Bal.	103	

Do It Yourself! Question 2 Solutions

Requirements

1. When is the note due? What is the total interest incurred over the life of the note? What is the maturity value of the note?

The note is due 10 months from June 1, 2008, on April 1, 2009.

The amount of interest incurred over the entire life of the note is calculated as:

$$\text{Interest incurred} = \$6,000 \times 5\% \times \frac{10 \text{ months}}{12 \text{ months}}$$

$$\text{Interest incurred} = \$250$$

$$\text{Maturity value} = \$6,000 + \$250 = \$6,250$$

 Account for notes receivable

2. Prepare all journal entries for this note for *both* companies from June 1, 2008 through the due date. Explanations are not required.

June 1, 2008: Anderson borrowed $6,000 from Neo.

Neo Enterprises:

June 1	Notes Receivable	6,000	
	Cash		6,000

Anderson Corp.:

June 1	Cash	6,000	
	Notes Payable		6,000

December 31, 2008: accrue 5% interest on note.

 Account for notes receivable

Neo Enterprises:

Dec. 31	Interest Receivable	175	
	Interest Revenue ($6,000 × 5% × 7/12)		175

Anderson Corp.:

Dec. 31	Interest Expense		175	
	Interest Payable			175

 Account for notes receivable

March 31, 2009: Note and interest are paid in full.

Neo Enterprises:

April 1	Cash (maturity value)		6,250	
	Notes Receivable			6,000
	Interest Receivable			175
	Interest Revenue ($6,000 × 5% × 3/12)			75

Anderson Corp.:

April 1	Notes Payable		6,000	
	Interest Payable		175	
	Interest Expense		75	
	Cash			6,250

The Power of Practice

For more practice using the skills learned in this chapter, visit MyAccountingLab. There you will find algorithmically generated questions that are based on these Demo Docs and your main textbook's Review and Assess Your Progress sections.

Go to MyAccountingLab and follow these steps:

1. Direct your URL to www.myaccountinglab.com.
2. Log in using your name and password.
3. Click the MyAccountingLab link.
4. Click Study Plan in the left navigation bar.
5. From the table of contents, select Chapter 9, Receivables.
6. Click a link to work tutorial exercises.

10 Plant Assets and Intangibles

WHAT YOU PROBABLY ALREADY KNOW

You probably already know that when you decide to get a car, you must decide if you want to purchase or lease it. If you lease a car, you pay a monthly amount for the use of that vehicle, which is a benefit or expense to you. If you purchase a car for cash instead, there is still a monthly benefit to you, although there are no future payments. The benefit or cost incurred is called depreciation expense. The more a car is used, the less remaining future value to be derived from that asset. In business, the asset is reduced for the loss in usefulness or future benefit as the vehicle is used.

Learning Objectives

1 Measure the cost of a plant asset.

The **cost of a plant asset** should include all of the necessary costs to acquire the asset and get it ready for use. In addition to the purchase price of the plant asset, other items that may be necessary and would increase the cost of the asset include:

- Taxes, commissions, shipping costs, and insurance on the asset while in transit
- Installation and testing costs
- Architectural fees, building permits, and costs to repair and renovate the asset for use
- Interest on money borrowed to construct the plant asset
- Brokerage fees, survey, title and legal fees, payment of back property taxes, and the cost of clearing land and razing unneeded structures

If discounts are available and taken advantage of, those amounts would reduce the cost of the plant asset. *Review Exhibit 10-2 (p. 507) for examples of items that are considered in the cost of land. Review the section "A Lump-Sum (Basket) Purchase of Assets" in the main text to see how the cost of individual plant assets is determined when a single price is charged for the group.*

2 Account for depreciation.

Depreciation is the allocation of cost over a plant asset's useful life. The expense of depreciation is matched against the revenue generated, as shown in Exhibit 10-4 (p. 510). The three most popular methods of depreciation are the straight-line, units-of-production, and double-declining-balance methods. The adjusting entry to depreciate any plant asset is to debit Depreciation Expense and credit Accumulated Depreciation.

Three elements necessary to calculate depreciation are:

a. Asset cost—known amount on the books
b. Estimated useful life—period of asset usefulness
c. Estimated residual value—expected value at the end of the useful life

Review "Depreciation Methods" in the main text for examples of the various depreciation methods.

3 Select the best depreciation method for tax purposes.

A *modified accelerated cost recovery system (MACRS)* was established by the IRS in 1986 to provide guidance in calculating depreciation for tax purposes. It established the useful lives for various property classes. MACRS allows depreciation to be computed by the double-declining-balance method, 150%-declining-balance method, or the straight-line method. The accelerated-declining-balance methods permit more depreciation to be deducted in the early years, which conserves cash flow. *See Exhibit 10-11 (p. 519) for MACRS classifications.*

4 Account for the disposal of a plant asset.

When a plant asset is sold, it should be depreciated until the date of disposal. Then the following should be accounted for:

• Debit the cash or other proceeds received
• Debit the accumulated depreciation
• Credit the plant asset cost

The difference between the asset cost and accumulated depreciation is book value. If the book value is greater than the proceeds, a debit must also be recorded as a loss on disposal. If the book value is less than the proceeds, a credit must also be recorded as a gain on disposal.

A plant asset may also be exchanged for a new asset. The book value of the old asset is removed as described earlier. The cash paid on exchange is credited and the market value of the new asset is debited. Any difference between the market value of the new asset and the book value of the old plus cash paid is the gain or loss. *Review the related examples in "Disposing of a Plant Asset" in the main text.*

5 Account for natural resources.

Natural resources are long-term assets that include iron ore, natural gas, and timber. As the inventory of the iron, gas, or other natural resource is used up, it is considered to be depleted. The depletion entry is similar to depreciation (debit Depletion Expense and credit Accumulated Depletion). The depletion amount is determined using the units-of-production formula.

Accumulated Depletion is a contra asset account like Accumulated Depreciation. *Review "Accounting for Natural Resources" in the main text.*

6 Account for intangible assets.

Intangible assets are rights that provide future value or benefit to the organization. Patents, copyrights, franchises, and trademarks are examples of these assets. Those intangible assets with a defined useful life are amortized by the straight-line method. The entry to amortize the intangible asset is to debit Amortization Expense and to credit the intangible asset.

Goodwill represents the excess of the amount paid to purchase a company over the equity of the company. Goodwill is not amortized but may need to be written down due to a loss of value. *Review the description of the types of intangible assets and especially the treatment of goodwill included under the "Specific Intangibles" section of the main text.*

Demo Doc 1

Depreciation

Learning Objectives 1–4

Peters Corp. purchased a truck for $13,800 cash on January 1, 2008. Peters also had to pay taxes of $1,200 cash. The truck had a residual value of $1,000 and a useful life of 7 years or 100,000 miles driven. Peters has a December 31 year-end.

The truck was driven for 15,000 miles in 2008, 12,000 miles in 2009, and 17,000 miles in 2010.

Requirements

1. Calculate the total cost of the truck.

2. Calculate the depreciation expense and accumulated depreciation balance at December 31 for 2008, 2009, and 2010 using the straight-line, units-of-production, and double-declining-balance methods.

3. Using the double-declining-balance method only, show how the Truck account would look on the December 31 balance sheets for 2008, 2009, and 2010.

4. Which of the three methods maximizes income for 2008? Which method minimizes income taxes for 2008?

5. Peters sold the truck on September 1, 2011, for $7,000 cash. Journalize the sale transaction using each method. (The truck was driven for 8,000 miles in 2011.)

Demo Doc 1 Solutions

Requirement 1

Measure the cost of a plant asset

Calculate the total cost of the truck.

Part 1	Part 2	Part 3	Part 4	Part 5	Part 6	Part 7	Part 8	Part 9	Demo Doc Complete

The total cost of the truck is the total cost to make it ready for use. Any expenditure that *must be paid in order to use the asset* is part of the asset's total cost.

In this case, the truck cannot be used until the taxes are paid on the truck. Therefore, the taxes are added to the total cost of the truck.

Purchase Price	$13,800
Taxes	1,200
Total Cost of Truck	$15,000

Requirement 2

Account for depreciation

Calculate the depreciation expense and accumulated depreciation balance at December 31 for 2008, 2009, and 2010 using the straight-line, units-of-production, and double-declining-balance methods.

Straight-Line Method

Part 1	Part 2	Part 3	Part 4	Part 5	Part 6	Part 7	Part 8	Part 9	Demo Doc Complete

The straight-line method allocates an equal amount of depreciation over the useful life.

Straight-line depreciation is calculated as:

$$\frac{\text{Cost} - \text{Residual value}}{\text{Years of useful life}} = \text{Annual depreciation expense}$$

Or, in this particular question:

$$\frac{\$15,000 - \$1,000}{7 \text{ years}} = \$2,000 \text{ Depreciation expense per year}$$

Remember that cost minus residual value is sometimes called <u>depreciable cost</u> because this is the total depreciation that will be recorded over the asset's life. At the end of the asset's life, the book value equals the residual value.

Remember that the depreciation expense will be the same for *each* year. Depreciation expense does not change (unless there is a partial year as demonstrated in Requirement 5 of this question). This is why the method is called "straight-line:"

because if the annual depreciation expense is charted on a graph, it is a straight line (see Exhibit 10-9, p. 515, in the main textbook).

So depreciation expense in 2008
$$= \text{depreciation expense in 2009}$$
$$= \text{depreciation expense in 2010}$$
$$= \$2,000.$$

Accumulated depreciation is the total of *all* the depreciation expense that the company has accumulated up to a certain time. In other words, it is the sum of the depreciation expense in *every* year that has passed.

You can use a T-account to calculate accumulated depreciation each year:

Accumulated Depreciation—Truck

	12/31/08 2,000
	2008 Bal. 2,000
	12/31/09 2,000
	2009 Bal. 4,000
	12/31/10 2,000
	2010 Bal. 6,000

So in 2008, accumulated depreciation is the 2008 depreciation expense (because this is the only year of depreciation so far) = $2,000. In 2009, accumulated depreciation is the sum of the 2008 and 2009 depreciation expense = $2,000 + $2,000 = $4,000. In 2010, accumulated depreciation is the sum of the 2008, 2009, and 2010 depreciation expense = $2,000 + $2,000 + $2,000 = $6,000.

If you want to make things a little easier on yourself, instead of adding up all of the accumulated depreciation from scratch, you can instead add the current year's depreciation expense to the prior balance. In other words:

Accumulated depreciation this year
$$= \text{Accumulated depreciation last year}$$
$$+ \text{This year's depreciation expense}$$

2009 accumulated depreciation of $4,000 + $2,000 depreciation expense for 2010 = $6,000 accumulated depreciation for 2010.

The truck's book value is its cost minus its accumulated depreciation. This is the net value shown for the truck on the balance sheet.

Straight-Line Method

Year	Annual Depreciation Expense	Accumulated Depreciation	Book Value
2008	$2,000	$2,000	$13,000
2009	2,000	4,000	11,000
2010	2,000	6,000	9,000

Account for
depreciation

Units-of-Production Method

| Part 1 | Part 2 | **Part 3** | Part 4 | Part 5 | Part 6 | Part 7 | Part 8 | Part 9 | Demo Doc Complete |

The unit method is similar to the straight-line method, but instead of calculating depreciation expense per *year,* we calculate it per *unit.* It allocates an equal amount of depreciation for each unit of production. Notice how the formula is similar to the straight-line method:

$$\frac{\text{Cost} - \text{Residual value}}{\text{Units of production in useful life}} = \text{Depreciation expense per unit}$$

Or, in this particular question:

$$\frac{\$15,000 - \$1,000}{100,000 \text{ miles}} = \$0.14 \text{ Depreciation expense per actual mile driven}$$

Because a different number of miles is driven every year, the *annual* depreciation expense will be different from year to year; however, the depreciation rate per *unit/mile* remains constant.

Units of production is another way of measuring an asset's life or productivity. For example, we could say that a machine will last for 5 years, or we might say that it will have 50,000 hours of operation. Both statements are reasonable ways to express how long the machine will last. The straight-line method focuses on the *years* (for example, 5 years of life) and the unit method focuses on the *production* (such as the 50,000 hours). It is obvious from reading the question whether there are any ways to measure an asset's life other than by years. In this question, the miles driven are highlighted and are the only other measure of asset life we can use.

Under the unit method, we calculate depreciation as:

Depreciation expense this year = Units used this year × Depreciation expense per unit

So, in this question, we can calculate depreciation expense on the truck each year as:

	Actual		Rate		Annual Expense
2008	15,000 miles	×	$0.14 per mile	=	$2,100
2009	12,000 miles	×	$0.14 per mile	=	$1,680
2010	17,000 miles	×	$0.14 per mile	=	$2,380

We calculate accumulated depreciation the same way we did for the straight-line method (only the depreciation *expense* is calculated differently from method to method).

We can use a T-account to calculate accumulated depreciation each year:

Accumulated Depreciation

	12/31/08 2,100
	2008 Bal. 2,100
	12/31/09 1,680
	2009 Bal. 3,780
	12/31/10 2,380
	2010 Bal. 6,160

We can also calculate accumulated depreciation directly:

Accumulated depreciation this year
= Accumulated depreciation last year
+ This year's depreciation expense

So, in this question, we can calculate accumulated depreciation each year as:

2008	$0 + $2,100 = $2,100
2009	$2,100 + $1,680 = $3,780
2010	$3,780 + $2,380 = $6,160

Units-of-Production Method

Year	Depreciation Expense	Accumulated Depreciation	Book Value (Cost−Acc. Depn.)
2008	$2,100	$2,100	$12,900
2009	1,680	3,780	11,220
2010	2,380	6,160	8,840

 Account for depreciation

Double-Declining-Balance Method

Part 1	Part 2	Part 3	**Part 4**	Part 5	Part 6	Part 7	Part 8	Part 9	Demo Doc Complete

This method is somewhat more complicated than straight-line or unit depreciation. It allocates more depreciation in the early years than in the later years.

Instead of a set depreciation amount, we use a depreciation *rate:*

Double-declining-balance (DDB) depreciation rate
= 2/years of useful life

Or, in this particular question:

DDB rate = 2/7

You may notice that the years of useful life is the *same* denominator as we used in the straight-line method. This is why the method is called *double*-declining-balance: it is two times the amount used for straight-line (that is, 2×1/years of useful life).

To get the depreciation expense each year, we need to use the following formula:

This year's depreciation expense

= Book value (= cost − last year's accumulated depreciation)

× Depreciation rate

Sometimes the cost − last year's accumulated depreciation is called the *net* value of the asset. You will see why in Requirement 3 of this question.

Because the accumulated depreciation is used in the depreciation expense formula, we need to calculate both together every year; however, the methods we can use to calculate accumulated depreciation are the same as before.

2008 depn expense = ($15,000 − $0) × 2/7 = $4,286
Accumulated depn = $0 + $4,286 = $4,286

2009 depn expense = ($15,000 − $4,286) × 2/7 = $3,061
Accumulated depn = $4,286 + $3,061 = $7,347

2010 depn expense = ($15,000 − $7,347) × 2/7 = $2,187
Accumulated depn = $7,347 + $2,187 = $9,534

We can also use a T-account to calculate accumulated depreciation each year:

Accumulated Depreciation—Truck

	12/31/08 4,286
	2008 Bal. 4,286
	12/31/09 3,061
	2009 Bal. 7,347
	12/31/10 2,187
	2010 Bal. 9,534

It is important to keep an eye on accumulated depreciation with the double-declining-balance method. Remember, we did *not* use the residual value to calculate depreciation expense.

However, we need to ensure that the *book value* of the asset does not go below the residual value. When the book value of the asset reaches the residual value, we *stop* taking depreciation expense (even if the asset is still being used).

Double-Declining-Balance Method

Year	Depreciation Expense	Accumulated Depreciation	Book Value (Cost − Acc Depn)
2008	$4,286	$4,286	$10,714
2009	3,061	7,347	7,653
2010	2,187	9,534	5,466

Requirement 3

 Account for depreciation

Using the double-declining-balance method only, show how the Truck account would look on the December 31 balance sheets for 2008, 2009, and 2010.

Part 1	Part 2	Part 3	Part 4	**Part 5**	Part 6	Part 7	Part 8	Part 9	Demo Doc Complete

Although the question only requires this to be done for the double-declining-balance method, keep in mind that the balance sheet presentation is the *same* for *all* depreciation methods:

Cost
− Accumulated depreciation
Net value of asset

This *net* value of the asset is the *same* amount that is used in the double-declining-balance calculation for depreciation expense in the *following* year.

So on the balance sheet for each year (under the double-declining-balance method), you would see:

	2008	2009	2010
Truck	$15,000	$15,000	$15,000
− Accumulated Depreciation	(4,286)	(7,347)	(9,534)
Truck (net)	$10,714	$7,653	$5,466

Requirement 4

 Select the best depreciation method for tax purposes

Which of the three methods maximizes income for 2008? Which method minimizes income taxes for 2008?

Part 1	Part 2	Part 3	Part 4	Part 5	**Part 6**	Part 7	Part 8	Part 9	Demo Doc Complete

The depreciation expense for each method in 2008 is:

Straight-Line	$2,000
Units of Production	2,100
Double-Declining-Balance	4,286

Revenues − Expenses = Net income, so higher expense (holding revenue constant) gives a lower net income.

In this example, the straight-line method has the lowest depreciation expense, which means that it has the highest net income.

The double-declining-balance method has the highest depreciation expense, which means that it has the lowest net income and, therefore, the lowest income taxes.

Requirement 5

Peters sold the truck on September 1, 2011, for $7,000 cash. Journalize the sale transaction using each method. (The truck was driven for 8,000 miles in 2011.)

 Account for depreciation

 Account for the disposal of a plant asset

Straight-Line Method

Part 1	Part 2	Part 3	Part 4	Part 5	Part 6	**Part 7**	Part 8	Part 9	Demo Doc Complete

When an asset is sold, we must journalize that sale. However, before we can do this, we must *update the depreciation* on the asset.

Depreciation represents the portion (the *benefit*) of the asset that has been used. The truck was sold on September 1, which means that Peters got to use it for eight months of 2011 before it was sold. We must represent that use as depreciation expense.

The depreciation expense that we record for eight months is *not* the same as the amount we would record for an entire year, because it is a shorter period of time (and, therefore, the asset was used less). Therefore, we must calculate a partial year's depreciation.

Under straight-line depreciation, the *annual* depreciation expense is $2,000 (that is, for 12 months). So for eight months:

$$\text{2011 depn expense} = \$2,000 \times \frac{\text{8 months}}{\text{12 months}} = \$1,333$$

This depreciation would then be recorded as:

Sept. 1	Depreciation Expense	1,333	
	Accumulated Depreciation—Truck		1,333

This brings the total accumulated depreciation to $6,000 + $1,333 = $7,333. Now we can record the sale of the truck.

Cash was received, so it increases (a debit) by $7,000.

The truck has been sold, so that account decreases to a zero balance (a credit) by $15,000. The Accumulated Depreciation goes along with it (contra accounts *always* go with their associated account), so that account decreases to a zero balance (a debit) as well by $7,333.

Putting these amounts into the journal entry:

Sept. 1	Cash	7,000	
	Accumulated Depreciation—Truck	7,333	
	???		
	Truck		15,000

Obviously, the entry is not complete because it *does not balance*. In order to get it to balance, we need equal debits and credits, which means that we need a $15,000 − $7,000 − $7,333 = $667 debit for the entry to work.

This $667 is the balancing amount. It is either a gain on sale or a loss on sale. *Because the balancing amount is a debit,* it is a loss (an increase in expenses is a debit, which is like a loss).

So the completed entry is:

Sept. 1	Cash	7,000	
	Accumulated Depreciation—Truck	7,333	
	Loss on Sale of Truck (to balance)	667	
	Truck		15,000

2 Account for depreciation

4 Account for the disposal of a plant asset

Units-of-Production Method

Part 1	Part 2	Part 3	Part 4	Part 5	Part 6	Part 7	**Part 8**	Part 9	Demo Doc Complete

We must record the depreciation expense for the first eight months of the year.

$$\frac{\text{2011 depn}}{\text{expense}} = \frac{8,000}{\text{miles}} \times \$0.14 = \$1,120$$

Notice that we did *not* need to multiply by 8/12 like we did in the straight-line method. This is because the short period of use is *already incorporated* into the 8,000 miles. If the truck had been used for a full year, the number of miles would have been bigger, and so depreciation expense would have been higher. With the unit method, all that matters is the *actual* number of miles the truck was driven.

Depreciation is recorded as:

Sept. 1	Depreciation Expense	1,120	
	Accumulated Depreciation—Truck		1,120

Accumulated depreciation is now $6,160 + $1,120 = $7,280.

Cash was received, so it increases (a debit) by $7,000.

The truck has been sold, so that account decreases to a zero balance (a credit) by $15,000. Accumulated Depreciation decreases to a zero balance (a debit) as well by $7,280.

Putting these amounts into the journal entry:

Sept. 1	Cash	7,000	
	Accumulated Depreciation—Truck	7,280	
	???		
	Truck		15,000

In order to get it to balance, we need a $15,000 − $7,000 − $7,280 = $720 debit.

Because the balancing amount is a debit, it is a loss (an increase in expenses is a debit, which is like a loss).

So the completed entry is:

Sept. 1	Cash	7,000	
	Accumulated Depreciation—Truck	7,280	
	Loss on Sale of Truck (to balance)	720	
	Truck		15,000

2 Account for depreciation

4 Account for the disposal of a plant asset

Double-Declining-Balance Method

Part 1	Part 2	Part 3	Part 4	Part 5	Part 6	Part 7	Part 8	**Part 9**	Demo Doc Complete

2011 depreciation expense

$$= (\$15,000 - \$9,534) \times 2/7 = \$1,561.71 = 12 \text{ months of depreciation}$$

$$\$1,561.71 \quad \times \quad \frac{8 \text{ months}}{12 \text{ months}} \quad = \quad \$1,041 \quad = \quad \frac{8 \text{ months of}}{\text{depreciation}}$$

Sept. 1	Depreciation Expense	1,041	
	Accumulated Depreciation—Truck		1,041

This brings the accumulated depreciation to:

$$\$9,534 + \$1,041 = \$10,575$$

Cash was received, so it increases (a debit) by $7,000.

The truck has been sold, so that account decreases to a zero balance (a credit) by $15,000. Accumulated Depreciation decreases to a zero balance (a debit) by $10,575.

Putting these amounts into the journal entry:

Sept. 1	Cash		7,000	
	Accumulated Depreciation—Truck		10,575	
	???			
	Truck			15,000

We need a $7,000 + $10,575 − $15,000 = $2,575 credit for the entry to work.

Because the balancing amount is a credit, it is a gain (an increase in revenues is a credit, which is like a gain).

So the completed entry is:

Sept. 1	Cash		7,000	
	Accumulated Depreciation—Truck		10,575	
	Gain on Sale of Truck (to balance)			2,575
	Truck			15,000

Part 1	Part 2	Part 3	Part 4	Part 5	Part 6	Part 7	Part 8	Part 9	**Demo Doc Complete**

Demo Doc 2

Natural Resource Assets

Learning Objective 5

Xander Inc. purchased a coal mine for $900 million cash on January 1, 2008. After the purchase, an independent analyst determined that the value of the land was $200 million and that the value of the coal was $800 million (based on an estimate that there were 20 million tons of coal below the ground).

In 2008, Xander mined and sold 1 million tons of coal.

Requirements

1. Give Xander's journal entry to record the purchase of the mine.

2. Give Xander's journal entry to record depletion expense for 2008.

Demo Doc 2 Solutions

Requirement 1

Give Xander's journal entry to record the purchase of the mine.

Part 1	Part 2	Demo Doc Complete

Xander purchased two assets at one time *for one price*. This is called a <u>lump-sum purchase</u>. We need to determine how much of the purchase price to allocate to each asset.

This is important because it impacts depreciation and depletion calculations in the future (because the cost of the asset is an important number in these calculations).

We use the independent valuations to determine a *proportional* value for the assets. According to the analyst, the total value of the assets purchased = $200 million + $800 million = $1 billion.

This means that the land has a proportion of 200,000,000/1,000,000,000 = 20%.

The coal has a proportion of 800,000,000/1,000,000,000 = 80%.

The cost of each asset is assigned as this proportion of the total cost.

So the cost of the land = 20% × $900 million total cost = $180 million.

The cost of the coal = 80% × $900 million total cost = $720 million.

In the journal entry, Land and Coal Reserves are increased (debit) by these amounts and cash is decreased (credit).

Land (20% × $900,000,000)		180,000,000	
Coal Reserves (80% × $900,000,000)		720,000,000	
Cash			900,000,000

Requirement 2

Give Xander's journal entry to record depletion expense for 2008.

Part 1	Part 2	Demo Doc Complete

Depletion expense is *the same* as depreciation expense, except that this term is *only* used for natural resource assets. Depletion is always calculated using the *unit* method (never the straight-line or declining-balance methods).

The units are the amount of natural resources purchased. In this case, the units are tons of coal.

$$\frac{\text{Cost}}{\substack{\text{Units of production} \\ \text{in useful life}}} = \substack{\text{Depletion expense} \\ \text{per unit}}$$

$$\frac{\$720,000,000}{20,000,000 \text{ tons}} = \mathbf{\$36 \text{ per ton}}$$

Under the unit method, we calculate depletion as:

Depletion expense this year
= Actual units used this year $\times$ Depletion expense per unit

Depletion expense for 2008
= 1,000,000 tons $\times$ $36 per ton = $36,000,000

When we record depreciation, we increase (debit) Depreciation Expense and increase (credit) Accumulated Depreciation. The entry for depletion is *the same* except that we use Depletion Expense (debit) and Accumulated Depletion (credit).

Depletion Expense ($36 $\times$ 1,000,000)		36,000,000	
Accumulated Depletion—Coal Reserves			36,000,000

Part 1	Part 2	Demo Doc Complete

Demo Doc 3

Intangible Assets

Learning Objective 6

On July 1, 2008, Franco Co. acquired a patent from Juarez Inc. for $5,000 cash and by signing a $10,000, 6% note payable. Franco believes that the patent will have a life of 10 years.

On the same date, Franco purchased all outstanding shares of Germano Inc. for $50,000. The book value of Germano's net assets at this time was $35,000 and the market value was $40,000.

Requirements

1. Journalize Franco's purchase of the patent. What kind of asset is the patent? Why do you think so?

2. Journalize Franco's amortization expense for the patent in 2008.

3. Franco did not make any interest payments on the note in 2008. Journalize Franco's interest expense for the year.

4. Calculate the amount of goodwill that will be recorded for Franco as a result of the Germano purchase.

5. Give any necessary entry to adjust the value of Franco's goodwill if it is determined to be worth $2,500 at the end of the year.

Demo Doc 3 Solutions

Requirement 1

6 Account for intangible assets

Journalize Franco's purchase of the patent. What kind of asset is the patent? Why do you think so?

Part 1	Part 2	Part 3	Part 4	Part 5	Demo Doc Complete

Cash decreases (a credit) by $5,000 and Notes Payable increases (a credit) by $10,000.

There is also an increase to Patent (a debit) of $5,000 + $10,000 = $15,000.

July 1	Patent		15,000	
	Cash			5,000
	Note Payable			10,000

The patent is an <u>intangible asset</u>. This is because the patent is a *right* to produce a certain product or use a certain technology. A right is not a physical asset: It cannot be touched. This means that it is *intangible*.

Requirement 2

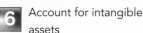

6 Account for intangible assets

Journalize Franco's amortization expense for the patent in 2008.

Part 1	Part 2	Part 3	Part 4	Part 5	Demo Doc Complete

Intangible assets are amortized. This is essentially the same as depreciation for tangible assets (outside of the name). The only difference is that for intangible assets, we usually do not record an "accumulated amortization" account, but instead *directly* reduce the asset account.

Amortization expense is usually calculated using the straight-line method.

$$\frac{\text{Amortization expense}}{\text{(annual)}} = \frac{\text{Cost of intangible asset}}{\text{Years of useful life}}$$

$$\frac{\$15,000}{10 \text{ years}} = \$1,500 \text{ per year}$$

Because the patent was purchased on July 1, only six months have been used. Therefore, we must calculate a partial year's amortization:

$$\$1,500 \quad \times \quad \frac{6 \text{ months}}{12 \text{ months}} = \frac{\$750 \text{ Amortization}}{\text{Expense for 6 months}}$$

Amortization Expense increases (a debit) by $750.

Remember that for intangible assets, we do *not* have an accumulated account. This means that instead we must decrease the Patent account (a credit) *directly* for $750.

Dec. 31	Amortization Expense—Patents	750	
	Patent		750

Requirement 3

Franco did not make any interest payments on the note in 2008. Journalize Franco's interest expense for the year.

| Part 1 | Part 2 | **Part 3** | Part 4 | Part 5 | Demo Doc Complete |

Interest expense for the year is:

$$ \$10,000 \quad \times \quad 6\% \quad \times \quad \frac{6 \text{ months}}{12 \text{ months}} \quad = \quad \$300 $$

Interest Expense is increased (a debit) and Interest Payable is increased (a credit) by $300.

Dec. 31	Interest Expense	300	
	Interest Payable		300

Requirement 4

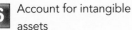

6 Account for intangible assets

Calculate the amount of goodwill that will be recorded for Franco as a result of the Germano purchase.

| Part 1 | Part 2 | Part 3 | **Part 4** | Part 5 | Demo Doc Complete |

$$ \text{Goodwill} = \frac{\text{Purchase}}{\text{price}} - \frac{\text{Market value of}}{\text{net assets}} $$
$$ = \$50,000 - \$40,000 = \$10,000 $$

This could also be calculated by preparing the journal entry for Franco to purchase Germano.

Franco increases its Net Assets (debit) by the market value of $40,000. Cash is decreased (credit) for the purchase price paid.

The remaining amount in the entry to make it balance is Goodwill:

July 1	Net Assets		40,000	
	Goodwill (to balance)		10,000	
	Cash			50,000

Requirement 5

 Account for intangible assets

Give any necessary entry to adjust the value of Franco's goodwill if it is determined to be worth $2,500 at the end of the year.

Part 1	Part 2	Part 3	Part 4	**Part 5**	Demo Doc Complete

Franco recorded the goodwill at $10,000. Because it is now worth only $2,500, it has a loss in value of $10,000 − $2,500 = $7,500. The loss is recorded (a debit) and the value of Goodwill is decreased (a credit).

Loss on Goodwill		7,500	
Goodwill			7,500

Part 1	Part 2	Part 3	Part 4	Part 5	**Demo Doc Complete**

Quick Practice Questions

True/False

_____ 1. The cost of land improvements includes fencing, paving, sprinkler systems, and lighting.

_____ 2. Land improvements are not subject to annual depreciation.

_____ 3. Book value is equal to the cost of the asset less the expected residual value.

_____ 4. The modified accelerated cost recovery system of depreciation is used for income tax purposes and segments assets into classes by asset life.

_____ 5. A loss on sale of an asset occurs when the book value is less than the cash received.

_____ 6. The depreciable cost of a plant asset is the original cost less the expected residual value.

_____ 7. Depletion expense is computed in the same manner as units-of-production.

_____ 8. Goodwill is recorded only by a company when it purchases another company and is not subject to amortization.

_____ 9. A characteristic of a plant asset is that it is used in the production of income for a business.

_____ 10. Routine repairs and maintenance are capital expenditures.

Multiple Choice

1. Which of the following is *not* a plant asset?
   a. Land
   b. Building
   c. Copyright
   d. Equipment

2. The cost of a building would include all of the following *except:*
   a. Architectural fees
   b. Clearing and grading the land prior to construction of the building
   c. Cost of repairs made to an old building to get it ready for occupancy
   d. Costs of construction

3. Five hundred acres of land are purchased for $130,000. Additional costs include $5,000 brokerage commission, $10,000 for removal of an old building, $6,000 for paving, and an $800 survey fee. What is the cost of the land?
   a. $135,800
   b. $145,800
   c. $155,000
   d. $155,800

4. Westchester Company recently sold some used furniture for $3,800 cash. The furniture cost $19,600 and had accumulated depreciation through the date of sale totaling $17,300. What is the journal entry to record the sale of the furniture?

a.

Cash	3,800	
Accumulated Depreciation—Furniture	15,800	
Furniture		19,600

b.

| Cash | 3,800 | |
| Furniture | | 3,800 |

c.

| Cash | 3,800 | |
| Gain on Sale of Furniture | | 3,800 |

d.

Cash	3,800	
Accumulated Depreciation—Furniture	17,300	
Furniture		19,600
Gain on Sale of Furniture		1,500

5. New equipment with a list price of $100,000, credit terms of 3/10 n/30, and transportation cost of $7,000 is acquired by a company. Insurance while in transit amounts to $200. Insurance on the equipment during its first year of use amounts to $800. Assuming the equipment is paid for within the discount period, what is the amount debited to Equipment?
   a. $97,000
   b. $104,200
   c. $105,000
   d. $107,200

6. Which of the following expenditures would be debited to an expense account?
   a. Cost to replace the company car's engine
   b. Addition of elevator to a building
   c. Replacement of tires
   d. All of the above

7. What is the effect of treating revenue expenditure as a capital expenditure?
   a. Understates expenses and understates owner's equity
   b. Overstates assets and overstates owner's equity
   c. Overstates expenses and understates net income
   d. Understates expenses and understates assets

8. Which of the following is true of Accumulated Depreciation?
   a. It is a contra liability account
   b. It is an expense account
   c. It is a contra asset account
   d. It is a contra equity account

9. When the amount of use of a plant asset varies from year to year, which method of determining depreciation best matches revenues and expenses?
   a. Straight-line method
   b. Double-declining-balance method
   c. Units-of-production method
   d. Either the straight-line method or the double-declining-balance method

10. Which depreciation method generally results in the greatest depreciation expense in the first full year of an asset's life?
    a. Double-declining-balance method
    b. Units-of-production method
    c. Straight-line method
    d. Either the straight-line or the double-declining-balance method

Quick Exercises

10-1. Morgan Construction bought land, a building, and equipment for a lump sum of $740,000. Following are the appraised fair market values of the newly acquired assets:

Land, $450,000
Building, $400,000
Equipment, $150,000

Determine the cost of each asset.

   a. Land _____

   _____

   b. Building _____

   _____

   c. Equipment _____

   _____

10-2. Sue Glover purchased a tract of land and contracted with a builder to build an office building on the property. She also engaged other contractors for lighting, fencing, paving, and so forth.

Based on the following transactions, determine the total costs allocated to the Land, Building, and Land Improvements accounts.

   a. Purchased land for $135,000.
   b. Paid a contractor $333,000 to design and build the office building.

c. Paid a demolition company $40,000 to remove an old structure on the property.
d. Paid $14,000 in delinquent taxes on the property.
e. Paid $34,700 for fencing.
f. Paid $39,500 for paving.
g. Paid an electrical contractor $14,900 for outdoor lighting.

Cost of land _____

Cost of building _____

Cost of land improvements _____

10-3. Venus Company acquired equipment on January 1, 2008, for $470,000. The equipment has an estimated useful life of 5 years and an estimated residual value of $30,000. Calculate depreciation expense for 2008 and 2009 under each of the following methods. The equipment is estimated to produce 150,000 units. During 2008 and 2009, the equipment produced 24,000 and 60,000 units, respectively. Round the answer to the nearest dollar where necessary.

	2008	2009
a. Straight-line method	_____	_____
b. Double-declining-balance method	_____	_____
c. Units-of-production method	_____	_____

10-4. On April 1, 2008, Carter Craft & Company purchased a mineral deposit by paying $50,000 in cash and signing a $440,000 promissory note. A geological report estimated the mineral deposit contained 140,000 tons of ore. Carter Craft & Company expects the asset to have a zero residual value when fully depleted. During 2008, 40,000 tons of ore were mined.

Prepare the journal entry for December 31, 2008, to record the depletion of the mineral deposit.

Date	Accounts	Debit	Credit

10-5.   On July 31, 2007, Austin Manufacturing acquired an existing patent for $340,000. The remaining legal life of the patent is 13 years; however, management thinks the patent will hold economic benefit for the company for only 7 more years.

Prepare journal entries for July 31, 2007, to acquire the patent and December 31, 2007, to amortize the patent.

Date	Accounts	Debit	Credit

Date	Accounts	Debit	Credit

Do It Yourself! Question 1

Depreciation

Winters Co. purchased equipment for $8,000 cash on January 1, 2008. The equipment had a residual value of $500 and a useful life of 6 years or 2,000 hours of operation. Winters has a December 31 year-end.

The equipment was used for 400 hours in 2008, 200 hours in 2009, and 300 hours in 2010.

Requirements

Account for
depreciation

1. Calculate the depreciation expense and accumulated depreciation balance at December 31 for 2008, 2009, and 2010 using the straight-line method.

Year	Depreciation Expense	Accumulated Depreciation	Book Value (Cost − Acc Depn)
2008			
2009			
2010			

Account for
depreciation

2. Calculate the depreciation expense and accumulated depreciation balance at December 31 for 2008, 2009, and 2010 using the units-of-production method.

Year	Depreciation Expense	Accumulated Depreciation	Book Value (Cost − Acc Depn)
2008			
2009			
2010			

Account for
depreciation

3. Calculate the depreciation expense and accumulated depreciation balance at December 31 for 2008, 2009, and 2010 using the double-declining-balance method.

Year	Depreciation Expense	Accumulated Depreciation	Book Value (Cost − Acc Depn)
2008			
2009			
2010			

Account for
depreciation

4. Using the units-of-production method only, show how the equipment would look on the December 31 balance sheets for 2008, 2009, and 2010.

 Account for
depreciation

 Account for the
disposal of a plant
asset

5. Winters sold the machine on March 1, 2011, for $4,000 cash. Show both journal entries to record depreciation and to record the sale transaction using each method. (The equipment was used for 100 hours in 2011.)

Straight-Line Method

Date	Accounts	Debit	Credit

Date	Accounts	Debit	Credit

Units-of-Production Method

Date	Accounts	Debit	Credit

Date	Accounts	Debit	Credit

Double-Declining-Balance Method

Date	Accounts	Debit	Credit

Date	Accounts	Debit	Credit

Do It Yourself! Question 2

Natural Resource Assets

Woody Inc. purchased logging rights in a county forest for $800,000 cash. Woody estimates that there are 40,000 tons of lumber that can be harvested from the forest. Because Woody only purchased the right to log, it does not own the land.

Requirement

5 Account for natural resources

1. Show the journal entry to record Woody's depletion expense for the first year, assuming that 15,000 tons of lumber were cut and sold.

Date	Accounts	Debit	Credit

Do It Yourself! Question 3

Intangible Assets

On October 1, 2008, Kevin Inc. acquired a trademark from Daniel Co. for $10,000 cash. Kevin believes that the trademark will have a life of 20 years.

Requirements

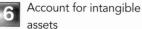 Account for intangible assets

1. Journalize Kevin's purchase of the trademark.

Date	Accounts	Debit	Credit

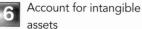 Account for intangible assets

2. Journalize Kevin's amortization expense for the trademark in 2008.

Date	Accounts	Debit	Credit

Quick Practice Solutions

True/False

  T   1. The cost of land improvements includes fencing, paving, sprinkler systems, and lighting. (p. 507)

  F   2. Land improvements are not subject to annual depreciation.
        False—Land improvements *are* subject to depreciation. (p. 507)

  F   3. Book value is equal to the cost of the asset less the expected residual value.
        False—Book value is equal to the cost of the asset less the *accumulated depreciation*. (p. 512)

  T   4. The modified accelerated cost recovery system of depreciation is used for income tax purposes and segments assets into classes by asset life. (p. 519)

  F   5. A loss on sale of an asset occurs when the book value is less than the cash received.
        False—A *gain* on sale of an asset occurs when the book value is less than the cash received. (p. 522)

  T   6. The depreciable cost of a plant asset is the original cost less the expected residual value. (p. 511)

  T   7. Depletion expense is computed in the same manner as units-of-production. (p. 524)

  T   8. Goodwill is recorded only by a company when it purchases another company and is not subject to amortization. (p. 526)

  T   9. A characteristic of a plant asset is that it is used in the production of income for a business. (p. 505)

  F   10. Routine repairs and maintenance are capital expenditures.
        False—Routine repairs and maintenance are *revenue* expenditures. (p. 509)

Multiple Choice

1. Which of the following is *not* a plant asset? (p. 525)
   a. Land
   b. Building
   c. Copyright
   d. Equipment

2. The cost of a building would include all of the following *except:* (p. 507)
   a. Architectural fees
   b. Clearing and grading the land prior to construction of the building
   c. Cost of repairs made to an old building to get it ready for occupancy
   d. Costs of construction

3. Five hundred acres of land are purchased for $130,000. Additional costs include $5,000 brokerage commission, $10,000 for removal of an old building, $6,000 for paving, and an $800 survey fee. What is the cost of the land? (p. 507)
   a. $135,800
   b. $145,800 (130,000 + 5,000 + 10,000 + 800)
   c. $155,000
   d. $155,800

4. Westchester Company recently sold some used furniture for $3,800 cash. The furniture cost $19,600 and had accumulated depreciation through the date of sale totaling $17,300. What is the journal entry to record the sale of the furniture? (p. 522)
   a.

Cash	3,800	
Accumulated Depreciation—Furniture	15,800	
Furniture		19,600

   b.

Cash	3,800	
Furniture		3,800

   c.

Cash	3,800	
Gain on Sale of Furniture		3,800

   d.

Cash	3,800	
Accumulated Depreciation—Furniture	17,300	
Furniture		19,600
Gain on Sale of Furniture		1,500

5. New equipment with a list price of $100,000, credit terms of 3/10 n/30, and transportation cost of $7,000 is acquired by a company. Insurance while in transit amounts to $200. Insurance on the equipment during its first year of use amounts to $800. Assuming the equipment is paid for within the discount period, what is the amount debited to Equipment? (p. 508)
   a. $97,000
   b. $104,200 (100,000 − 3,000 + 7,000 + 200)
   c. $105,000
   d. $107,200

6. Which of the following expenditures would be debited to an expense account? (p. 509)
   a. Cost to replace the company car's engine
   b. Addition of elevator to a building
   c. Replacement of tires
   d. All of the above

7. What is the effect of treating revenue expenditure as a capital expenditure? (p. 509)
   a. Understates expenses and understates owner's equity
   b. Overstates assets and overstates owner's equity
   c. Overstates expenses and understates net income
   d. Understates expenses and understates assets

8. What type of account is Accumulated Depreciation? (p. 525)
   a. A contra liability account
   b. An expense account
   c. A contra asset account
   d. A contra equity account

9. When the amount of use of a plant asset varies from year to year, which method of determining depreciation best matches revenues and expenses? (p. 513)
   a. Straight-line method
   b. Double-declining-balance method
   c. Units-of-production method
   d. Either the straight-line method or the double-declining-balance method

10. Which depreciation method generally results in the greatest depreciation expense in the first full year of an asset's life? (p. 513)
    a. Double-declining-balance method
    b. Units-of-production method
    c. Straight-line method
    d. Either the straight-line or the double-declining-balance method

Quick Exercises

10-1. Morgan Construction bought land, a building, and equipment for a lump sum of $740,000. Following are the appraised fair market values of the newly acquired assets:

Land, $450,000
Building, $400,000
Equipment, $150,000

Determine the cost of each asset. (pp. 507–508)

a. Land = ($450,000/$1,000,000) 3 $740,000 = $333,000
b. Building = ($400,000/$1,000,000) 3 $740,000 = $296,000
c. Equipment = ($150,000/$1,000,000) 3 $740,000 = $111,000

10-2. Sue Glover purchased a tract of land and contracted with a builder to build an office building on the property. She also engaged other contractors for lighting, fencing, paving, and so forth.

Based on the following transactions, determine the total costs allocated to the Land, Building, and Land Improvements accounts. (pp. 507–508)

a. Purchased land for $135,000.
b. Paid a contractor $333,000 to design and build the office building.

c. Paid a demolition company $40,000 to remove an old structure on the property.
d. Paid $14,000 in delinquent taxes on the property.
e. Paid $34,700 for fencing.
f. Paid $39,500 for paving.
g. Paid an electrical contractor $14,900 for outdoor lighting.

Solution:

Cost of land 189,000 ($135,000 + $40,000 + $14,000 = $189,000; transactions a, c & d)

Cost of building 333,000 (transaction b)

Cost of land improvements 89,100 ($34,700 + $39,500 + $14,900 = $89,100; transactions e–g)

10-3. **Venus Company acquired equipment on January 1, 2008, for $470,000. The equipment has an estimated useful life of 5 years and an estimated residual value of $30,000. Calculate depreciation expense for 2008 and 2009 under each of the following methods. The equipment is estimated to produce 150,000 units. During 2008 and 2009, the equipment produced 24,000 and 60,000 units, respectively. Round the answer to the nearest dollar where necessary.** (pp. 512–514)

		2008	2009
a.	Straight-line method	88,000	88,000
b.	Double-declining balance method	188,000	112,800
c.	Units-of-production method	70,400	176,000

a. $\dfrac{\$470,000 - 30,000}{5 \text{ years}} = \$88,000/\text{year}$

b. DDB rate = 1/5 years $\times$ 2 = 40% (.40)
$470,000 $\times$ .40 = $188,000
(470,000 − 188,000) $\times$ .40 = 112,800

c. $\dfrac{\$470,000 - 30,000}{150,000} \times 24,000 \text{ units} = \$70,400$

$\dfrac{\$470,000 - 30,000}{150,000} \times 60,000 \text{ units} = \$176,000$

10-4. On April 1, 2008, Carter Craft & Company purchased a mineral deposit by paying $50,000 in cash and signing a $440,000 promissory note. A geological report estimated the mineral deposit contained 140,000 tons of ore. Carter Craft & Company expects the asset to have a zero residual value when fully depleted. During 2008, 40,000 tons of ore were mined.

Prepare the journal entry for December 31, 2008, to record the depletion of the mineral deposit. (p. 524)

Date	Accounts	Debit	Credit
12/31/08	Depletion Expense	140,000	
	Accumulated Depletion—Ore		140,000
	To record depletion of mineral deposits		
	($50,000 + $440,000)/140,000 tons = $3.50/ton × 40,000 tons = $140,000		

10-5. On July 31, 2007, Austin Manufacturing acquired an existing patent for $340,000. The remaining legal life of the patent is 13 years; however, management thinks the patent will hold economic benefit for the company for only 7 more years.

Prepare journal entries for July 31, 2007, to acquire the patent and December 31, 2007, to amortize the patent. (p. 526)

Date	Accounts	Debit	Credit
7/31/07	Patents	340,000	
	Cash		340,000
	To record purchase of patent		

Date	Accounts	Debit	Credit
12/31/07	Amortization Expense—Patents	20,238	
	Patents		20,238
	To amortize patents ($340,000 × 5/84 months = $20,238)		

Do It Yourself! Question 1 Solutions

Requirements

1. Calculate the depreciation expense and accumulated depreciation balance at December 31 for 2008, 2009, and 2010 using the straight-line method.

$$\frac{\$8,000 - \$500}{6 \text{ years}} = \begin{array}{c} \$1,250 \text{ depreciation} \\ \text{expense per year} \end{array}$$

2008 accumulated depreciation = $1,250
2009 accumulated depreciation = $2,500
2010 accumulated depreciation = $3,750

Year	Depreciation Expense	Accumulated Depreciation	Book Value (Cost − Acc Depn)
2008	$1,250	$1,250	$6,750
2009	1,250	2,500	5,500
2010	1,250	3,750	4,250

2. Calculate the depreciation expense and accumulated depreciation balance at December 31 for 2008, 2009, and 2010 using the units-of-production method.

$$\frac{\$8,000 - \$500}{\begin{array}{c} 2,000 \text{ hours of} \\ \text{lifetime operation} \end{array}} = \begin{array}{c} \$3.75 \text{ depreciation} \\ \text{expense per hour of} \\ \text{actual operation} \end{array}$$

Depreciation expense each year is:

	Actual		Rate	Expense
2008	400 hours	×	$3.75 per hour =	$1,500
2009	200 hours	×	$3.75 per hour =	$ 750
2010	300 hours	×	$3.75 per hour =	$1,125

Accumulated depreciation each year is:

	Accum		Expense		
2008	$ 0	+	$1,500	=	$1,500
2009	$1,500	+	$ 750	=	$2,250
2010	$2,250	+	$1,125	=	$3,375

Year	Depreciation Expense	Accumulated Depreciation	Book Value (Cost − Acc Depn)
2008	$1,500	$1,500	$6,500
2009	750	2,250	5,750
2010	1,125	3,375	4,625

3. Calculate the depreciation expense and accumulated depreciation balance at December 31 for 2008, 2009, and 2010 using the double-declining-balance method.

DDB Rate = 2/6 = 1/3

2008   depn expense = ($8,000 − $0) × 1/3 = $2,667
        Accumulated depn = $0 + $2,667 = $2,667

2009   depn expense = ($8,000 − $2,667) × 1/3 = $1,778
        Accumulated depn = $2,667 + $1,778 = $4,445

2010   depn expense = ($8,000 − $4,445) × 1/3 = $1,185
        Accumulated depn = $4,445 + $1,185 = $5,630

Year	Depreciation Expense	Accumulated Depreciation	Book Value (Cost − Acc Depn)
2008	$2,667	$2,667	$5,333
2009	1,778	4,445	3,555
2010	1,185	5,630	2,370

4. Using the units-of-production method only, show how the equipment would look on the December 31 balance sheets for 2008, 2009, and 2010.

	2008	2009	2010
Equipment	$8,000	$8,000	$8,000
− Accumulated Depreciation	(1,500)	(2,250)	(3,375)
Equipment (net)	$6,500	$5,750	$4,6255.

5. Winters sold the machine on March 1, 2011, for $4,000 cash. Show both journal entries to record depreciation and to record the sale transaction using each method. (The equipment was used for 100 hours in 2011.)

Straight-Line Method

$$\text{2011 depn expense} = \$1,250 \times \frac{2 \text{ months}}{12 \text{ months}} = \$208$$

March 1	Depreciation Expense	208	
	Accumulated Depreciation—Equipment		208

Total accumulated depreciation = $3,750 + $208 = $3,958.

March 1	Cash	4,000	
	Accumulated Depreciation—Equipment	3,958	
	Loss on Sale of Equipment (to balance)	42	
	Equipment		8,000

Units-of-Production Method

$$\text{2011 depn expense} = 100 \text{ hours} \times \$3.75 = \$375$$

March 1	Depreciation Expense	375	
	Accumulated Depreciation—Equipment		375

Total accumulated depreciation = $3,375 + $375 = $3,750.

March 1	Cash	4,000	
	Accumulated Depreciation—Equipment	3,750	
	Loss on Sale of Equipment (to balance)	250	
	Equipment		8,000

Double-Declining-Balance Method

2011 depreciation expense

$$= (\$8,000 - \$5,630) \times 1/3 = \$790 \text{ for 12 months}$$

$$\$790 \quad \times \quad \frac{2 \text{ months}}{12 \text{ months}} \quad = \quad \$132 \text{ for 2 months}$$

March 1	Depreciation Expense	132	
	Accumulated Depreciation—Equipment		132

Total accumulated depreciation = $5,630 + $132 = $5,762.

March 1	Cash	4,000	
	Accumulated Depreciation—Equipment	5,762	
	Gain on Sale of Equipment (to balance)		1,762
	Equipment		8,000

Do it Yourself! Question 2 Solutions

Requirement

1. Show the journal entry to record Woody's depletion expense for the first year, assuming that 15,000 tons of lumber were cut and sold.

$$\frac{\text{Depletion}}{\text{per ton}} = \frac{\$800,000}{40,000 \text{ tons}} = \$20 \text{ per ton}$$

$$15,000 \text{ tons} \times \$20 \text{ per ton} = \$300,000$$

	Depletion Expense		300,000	
	Accumulated Depletion—Lumber			300,000

Do It Yourself! Question 3 Solutions

Requirements

1. Journalize Kevin's purchase of the trademark.

Jan. 1	Trademark	10,000	
	Cash		10,000

2. Journalize Kevin's amortization expense for the trademark in 2008.

$$\text{Amortization expense} = \frac{\$10,000}{20 \text{ years}} = \$500 \text{ per year}$$

$$\$500 \times \frac{3 \text{ months}}{12 \text{ months}} = \$125 \text{ for 3 months}$$

Dec. 31	Amortization Expense—Trademarks	125	
	Trademark		125

The Power of Practice

For more practice using the skills learned in this chapter, visit MyAccountingLab. There you will find algorithmically generated questions that are based on these Demo Docs and your main textbook's Review and Assess Your Progress sections.

Go to MyAccountingLab and follow these steps:

1. Direct your URL to www.myaccountinglab.com.
2. Log in using your name and password.
3. Click the MyAccountingLab link.
4. Click Study Plan in the left navigation bar.
5. From the table of contents, select Chapter 10, Plant Assets and Intangibles.
6. Click a link to work tutorial exercises.

11 Current Liabilities and Payroll

WHAT YOU PROBABLY ALREADY KNOW

You probably already know that, as an employee, you do not receive in your paycheck an amount equal to the number of hours worked times your hourly rate. The total that you have earned is called *gross pay*, which is the amount before withholdings are deducted. You may have noticed that money is withheld for federal income tax, Social Security tax, Medicare tax, and state income tax, if applicable in your state. You did not request that these amounts be deducted; they are required withholdings that your employer must make. Your employer does not keep this money; it must be remitted to the appropriate taxing agencies. When you receive your W-2 form by January 31 of the succeeding year, you can see that you are given credit for the amount of these taxes that your employer withheld on your behalf. In this chapter, we will see how your employer accounts for your paycheck.

Learning Objectives

1 Account for current liabilities of known amount.

Some current liabilities that are recorded at known amounts include accounts payable, short-term notes payable, sales tax payable, current portion of long-term notes payable, accrued expenses or liabilities, and unearned or deferred revenues. *Review the "Current Liabilities of Known Amount" section of the textbook, and be sure to take note of the presentation of current liabilities in the balance sheet in Exhibit 11-1 (p. 550).*

2 Account for current liabilities that must be estimated.

Sometimes a liability has been incurred but the amount is uncertain. Examples of this may include estimated warranty payable and contingent liabilities. *Review Exhibit 11-3 (p. 560) for contingent liability classifications and treatments.*

3 Compute payroll amounts.

The **gross pay** is the total amount earned by the employee and includes such items as the salary amount, hourly pay rate multiplied by the hours worked, commissions, bonuses, and overtime. **Net pay** is the amount the employee receives, which is equal to the gross pay less withholdings. Payroll deductions may include income taxes withheld, Social Security (FICA) tax, insurance premiums, retirement savings, and charitable contributions. *Review "Accounting for Payroll" in the main text.*

4 Record basic payroll transactions.

To record the periodic payroll, gross pay is debited to Salary Expense. All of the amounts withheld and the net pay due to the employees are credited to current liability accounts. Employers are also liable for payroll taxes. FICA and state and federal unemployment payroll tax expenses are incurred by employers and must be paid.

Most employers offer their employees some benefits such as health insurance or retirement benefits. Similar to the gross payroll and payroll taxes, the benefits are additional expenses to the employer. *Review the payroll costs and payroll accounting in Exhibits 11-4 and 11-5 (p. 562).*

5 Use a payroll system.

There are a number of documents that are involved in a payroll system. A **payroll record** contains all of the payroll information for each employee on each pay date. *Review the payroll record in Exhibit 11-6 (p. 563).*

The employer files a **payroll tax form** with the state and federal governments. It includes information such as gross wages, income taxes withheld, and Social Security and Medicare taxes. *Review the federal payroll tax form, Exhibit 11-8 (p. 565).*

An **employee earnings record** contains all of the payroll information from gross pay to net pay by employee. This is used by the employer to prepare the **W-2 forms, Employee Wage and Tax Statements**. Both the employee and IRS receive copies of this form for income tax filing. *Review Exhibits 11-9 and 11-10 (p. 566) for examples of these documents.*

6 Report current liabilities on the balance sheet.

Review the current liabilities section of the balance sheet at Exhibit 11-11 (p. 568).

Demo Doc 1

General Current Liabilities

Learning Objectives 1, 2, 6

Freddie Enterprises sells products with warranties included in the selling price. During August 2008, Freddie sold goods for $250,000 cash. These goods cost $180,000 to manufacture. Freddie is required by law to collect 7% sales tax on all sales.

Freddie estimates warranty costs to be 1.5% of the selling price. During August 2008, Freddie made $3,000 of repairs under warranty (paid in cash to a repair service).

On August 31, 2008, Freddie remitted all sales tax collected in August to the state government.

Requirements

1. Journalize all of Freddie's transactions in the month of August 2008.

2. Is sales tax payable a contingent liability? Why or why not?

3. Is warranty payable a contingent liability? Why or why not?

Demo Doc 1 Solutions

Requirement 1

Journalize all of Freddie's transactions in the month of August 2008.

Part 1	Part 2	Part 3	Demo Doc Complete

1 Account for current liabilities of known amount

During August 2008, Freddie sold goods for $250,000 cash. These goods cost $180,000 to manufacture. Freddie is required by law to collect 7% sales tax on all sales.

Freddie sold $250,000 worth of products. This means that Sales Revenue increases (a credit) by $250,000.

However, the cash that Freddie collected was *more* than $250,000 because it included the sales tax.

Freddie collected $250,000 × (1 + 7%) = $267,500 cash from the customer.

The $250,000 × 7% = $17,500 Freddie collected in sales tax is *not* revenue because it was *not earned* by Freddie and *does not belong* to Freddie. These taxes belong to the government and are owed/payable by Freddie to the government. Therefore, we must increase (a credit) the Sales Taxes Payable account by $17,500.

Cash ($250,000 × [1 + 7%])	267,500	
Sales Revenue		250,000
Sales Taxes Payable ($250,000 × 7%)		17,500

Freddie has sold these goods and so an adjustment to Inventory is necessary as well. COGS increases (a debit) and Inventory decreases (a credit) by $180,000, Freddie's cost of the products.

COGS	180,000	
Inventory		180,000

2 Account for current liabilities that must be estimated

Freddie estimates warranty costs to be 1.5% of the selling price.

We must also account for the warranties included in the selling price of the goods. Once the products are sold, the warranty is in effect. This means that Freddie has an *obligation* (that is, a *liability*) to fix the products if they break down. We must record an estimated Warranty Payable liability (a credit) of:

$$1.5\% \times \$250,000 = \$3,750$$

As the liability is recorded, so is the estimated Warranty Expense (a debit) of $3,750. There will be additional expense/cost to Freddie to make the repairs. This is good matching (as required by the matching principle under GAAP) because the expense is recorded *at the same time as the sales revenue, not when the actual cost is incurred (or warranty claim is made).*

| Warranty Expense ($250,000 × 1.5%) | 3,750 | |
| Warranty Payable | | 3,750 |

During August 2008, Freddie made $3,000 of repairs under warranty (paid in cash to a repair service).

When Freddie Enterprises makes warranty repairs, it is *meeting its warranty obligation* (that is, it is reducing its warranty liability). This causes a decrease (a debit) to Warranty Payable of $3,000.

Because the repairs were paid for in cash, the Cash account also decreases (a credit) by $3,000.

Notice that the Warranty Expense account is *not* impacted by the repairs! The expense was *already recorded* at the time of sale. To debit it again now would be double-counting the expense.

| Warranty Payable | 3,000 | |
| Cash | | 3,000 |

Note that there is $3,750 − $3,000 = $750 left in the Warranty Payable account. This remains to cover any future repairs that might be made under the warranty.

On August 31, 2008, Freddie remitted all sales tax collected in August to the state government.

The first transaction stated that during August, Freddie sold goods for $250,000 cash and collected 7% sales tax on all sales. At that time, Cash was increased by $267,500, Sales Revenue was increased by $250,000, and Sales Taxes Payable was increased by $250,000 × 7% = $17,500.

On August 31, Freddie remitted the sales taxes to the government. This means that the sales tax liability was paid in cash.

Cash is decreased (a credit) by $17,500 and Sales Taxes Payable is decreased (a debit) by $17,500.

| Sales Taxes Payable | 17,500 | |
| Cash | | 17,500 |

Requirement 2

 Report current liabilities on the balance sheet

Is sales tax payable a contingent liability? Why or why not?

Part 1	**Part 2**	Part 3	Demo Doc Complete

Sales taxes *must* be collected and remitted to the government *by law*. Ethical companies have no choice but to meet the sales taxes payable obligation. Therefore, this amount *will* be paid and it is *not* a contingent liability, as it is *not* dependent upon any outside event.

Requirement 3

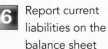 Report current liabilities on the balance sheet

Is warranty payable a contingent liability? Why or why not?

Part 1	Part 2	**Part 3**	Demo Doc Complete

Warranty payable is an *estimate*. It is not known *for sure* whether or not the products will break down or how much it might cost to repair them if they do. For this reason, warranty payable is a contingent liability because it depends upon the performance of the products after they leave Freddie's control.

Because payment for warranty repairs is probable and estimable, warranty expense and warranty payable are recorded in a journal entry, even though they are contingent upon outside events.

Part 1	Part 2	Part 3	**Demo Doc Complete**

Demo Doc 2

Current Portion of Long-Term Debt

Learning Objectives 1, 6

On August 1, 2008, Squirrel Co. signed a $400,000 note payable. Squirrel agreed to pay back $25,000 per month, beginning on January 1, 2009, and ending on April 1, 2010. Interest of 12% is paid monthly beginning January 1, 2009.

Requirement

1. Show the presentation of this note on Squirrel's December 31, 2008, balance sheet.

Demo Doc 2 Solutions

Requirement 1

 1 Account for current liabilities of known amount

6 Report current liabilities on the balance sheet

Show the presentation of this note on Squirrel's December 31, 2008, balance sheet.

Part 1	Demo Doc Complete

Of the $400,000 debt, payments totaling $25,000 × 12 = $300,000 will be repaid within the next year.

This $300,000 is the *current* portion of the debt because it will be repaid within the next year.

The remaining $400,000 − $300,000 = $100,000 will be repaid in more than one year, so it is the *long-term* portion of the debt.

Interest has been incurred on the entire $400,000 liability balance that has been outstanding over the five months since August 1, 2008.

$$\begin{array}{lcccccc} \text{Interest} \\ \text{incurred} & = & \text{Total} & \times & \text{Interest} & \times & \text{Fraction} \\ & & \text{debt} & & \text{rate} & & \text{of year} \\[2mm] & = & \$400{,}000 & \times & 12\% & \times & \dfrac{5}{12} \\[2mm] & = & \mathbf{\$20{,}000} \end{array}$$

The amount of $20,000 is recorded as Interest Payable. This interest payable is *current* because it is due in less than one year.

Note that this is *not* the total interest due on the note. It is *only* the amount that has *already* been incurred at December 31, 2008.

Current Liabilities	
Current portion of long-term debt	$300,000
Interest payable	$ 20,000
Long-Term Liabilities	
Notes payable/long-term debt (net of current portion)	$100,000

Part 1	**Demo Doc Complete**

Demo Doc 3

Payroll Liabilities

Learning Objectives 3, 4, 5

Gannon Corp. employees earn a total of $500,000 gross pay per week. All employees have the following items withheld from their pay:

    15%   Income Taxes

      8%   FICA Taxes

      4%   Pension Contributions

      2%   Union Dues

Gannon pays the following payroll taxes:

      8%   FICA Taxes

      6%   Unemployment Taxes

Requirements

1. For a normal week, journalize the following transactions:

a. Cash payment of employee salaries.

b. Accrue Gannon's payroll taxes.

c. Gannon's payment of all payroll taxes.

d. Gannon's payment of union dues.

e. Gannon's payment of pension contributions.

2. What is the employees' net pay in a normal week?

3. What is Gannon's total payroll expense in a normal week?

4. The employee at Gannon who hires new employees is also the person who processes the payroll. Is this a good internal control?

Demo Doc 3 Solutions

Requirement 1

For a normal week, journalize the following transactions:

| Part 1 | Part 2 | Part 3 | Part 4 | Demo Doc Complete |

3 Compute payroll amounts

4 Record basic payroll transactions

a. Cash payment of employee salaries.

The entire gross pay of $500,000 is all recorded as Salary Expense (a debit). However, this entire amount is not all paid to the employee in cash.

Employee Income Tax Payable increases (a credit) by:

$$\$500,000 \times 15\% = \$75,000$$

FICA Tax Payable increases (a credit) by:

$$\$500,000 \times 8\% = \$40,000$$

Pension Contributions Payable increases (a credit) by:

$$\$500,000 \times 4\% = \$20,000$$

Union Dues Payable increases (a credit) by:

$$\$500,000 \times 2\% = \$10,000$$

Cash decreases (a credit) by the pay that is *not withheld*:

$$\$500,000 - \$75,000 - \$40,000 - \$20,000 - \$10,000 = \$355,000$$

To summarize:

Employee Income Tax Payable	$500,000 × 15%	= $75,000
FICA Tax Payable	$500,000 × 8%	= $40,000
Pension Contributions Payable	$500,000 × 4%	= $20,000
Union Dues Payable	$500,000 × 2%	= $10,000

Salary Expense (gross pay)	500,000	
Employee Income Tax Payable ($500,000 × 15%)		75,000
FICA Tax Payable ($500,000 × 8%)		40,000
Pension Contributions Payable ($500,000 × 4%)		20,000
Union Dues Payable ($500,000 × 2%)		10,000
Cash (net/take home pay)		355,000

The $355,000 Cash amount is often referred to as "take-home pay" because it is the amount the employees actually receive (that is, take home) on their paychecks. Note that Gannon is *not* paying these taxes out of its own pocket. It is using money that has been held back from *employee paychecks* to make these payments.

The taxes withheld by Gannon are similar to the treatment of sales taxes payable. Gannon has the cash for them (because Gannon never paid this cash to the employees but withheld it instead) and will pass it on to the appropriate agencies in the near future just as sales taxes collected are recorded as a payable and passed on to the state government.

 3 Compute payroll amounts

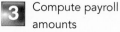 **4** Record basic payroll transactions

b. Accrue Gannon's payroll taxes.

Gannon must record Payroll Tax Expense (a debit) for all taxes the company must pay.

FICA Tax Payable increases (a credit) by Gannon's portion of the taxes:

$$\$500,000 \times 8\% = \$40,000$$

Unemployment Tax Payable increases (a credit) by:

$$\$500,000 \times 6\% = \$30,000$$

Payroll Tax Expense (to balance)		70,000	
FICA Tax Payable ($500,000 × 8%) (matching)			40,000
Unemployment Tax Payable ($500,000 × 6%)			30,000

Unlike the liabilities recorded in transaction **a** (that are paid by the employees by being taken out of their paychecks), these amounts are being paid directly by Gannon out of its own pocket.

3 Compute payroll amounts

4 Record basic payroll transactions

c. Gannon's payment of all payroll taxes.

Cash decreases (a credit) by the total of all taxes paid.
Employee Income Tax Payable decreases (a debit) by its balance of $75,000.
FICA Tax Payable decreases (a debit) by its balance of:

$$\$40,000 + \$40,000 = \$80,000$$

Unemployment Tax Payable decreases (a debit) by its balance of $30,000.

Employee Income Tax Payable		75,000	
FICA Tax Payable ($40,000 + $40,000) (matching amounts)		80,000	
Unemployment Tax Payable		30,000	
Cash (to balance)			185,000

d. Gannon's payment of union dues.

 4 Record basic payroll transactions

Union Dues Payable decreases (a debit) by its balance of $10,000. Cash also decreases (a credit) by $10,000.

Union Dues Payable		10,000	
Cash			10,000

4 Record basic payroll transactions

e. Gannon's payment of pension contributions.

Pension Contributions Payable decreases (a debit) by its balance of $20,000. Cash also decreases (a credit) by $20,000.

Pension Contributions Payable	20,000	
Cash		20,000

Requirement 2

3 Compute payroll amounts

What is the employees' net pay in a normal week?

Part 1	**Part 2**	Part 3	Part 4	Demo Doc Complete

Employees' net pay is the amount of cash they receive each week. This is the $355,000 calculated in Requirement 1a.

Requirement 3

3 Compute payroll amounts

What is Gannon's total payroll expense in a normal week?

Part 1	Part 2	**Part 3**	Part 4	Demo Doc Complete

Payroll expense is the *total* cost of having an employee. This includes the employee's salary as well as any additional taxes that do not come out of that salary (that is, that are paid out of the employer's pocket).

So payroll expense includes salary expense of $500,000 *and* payroll taxes expense of $70,000.

Total payroll expense = $500,000 + $70,000 = $570,000

Requirement 4

5 Use a payroll system

The employee at Gannon who hires new employees is also the person who processes the payroll. Is this a good internal control?

Part 1	Part 2	Part 3	**Part 4**	Demo Doc Complete

This is an internal control weakness. It is possible for this person to create fictitious employees and then issue payroll checks to them.

This creates an opportunity for fraud. The person who is responsible for hiring employees should *not* be the person who processes payroll.

Part 1	Part 2	Part 3	Part 4	**Demo Doc Complete**

Quick Practice Questions

True/False

_____ 1. Sales tax payable is shown as a long-term liability on the balance sheet.

_____ 2. An accrued expense is an expense that has not yet been paid.

_____ 3. A contingent liability is not an actual liability.

_____ 4. Optional deductions would include employee income tax, Social Security tax, union dues, and insurance premiums.

_____ 5. State and federal unemployment taxes are two required payroll deductions for employees.

_____ 6. The FICA Social Security tax is withheld from employees and is also paid by the employer in the same amount.

_____ 7. The document that includes every employee's gross pay, deductions, and net pay for the payroll period is called the Wage and Tax Statement.

_____ 8. Two employees who have the same gross pay may have different amounts withheld for income taxes depending on the number of allowances claimed on the W-4 Form.

_____ 9. An example of a contingent liability would be when you cosign a note payable for a friend.

_____10. If a company has a note payable at December 31 for $300,000, which will be paid in three equal installments every five months, $100,000 should be classified as a current liability.

Multiple Choice

1. **Which of the following is true about current liabilities?**
   a. Are due within one year or one operating cycle, whichever is longer
   b. Must be of a known amount
   c. Must be of an estimated amount
   d. Are subtracted from long-term liabilities on the balance sheet

2. **Which of the following best describes unearned revenue?**
   a. Revenue that has been earned and collected
   b. Revenue that has been earned but not yet collected
   c. Revenue that has been collected but not yet earned
   d. Revenue that has not been collected nor earned

3. **When is Warranty Expense debited?**
   a. In the period the product under warranty is repaired or replaced
   b. In the period after the product is sold
   c. In the period after the product is repaired or replaced
   d. In the period the revenue from selling the product was earned

4. When a product is repaired under warranty, the entry includes which of the following?
   a. A debit to Warranty Expense
   b. A credit to Warranty Expense
   c. A debit to Estimated Warranty Payable
   d. A credit to Estimated Warranty Payable

5. What is meant by a cafeteria plan?
   a. A free lunch program offered by the employer
   b. A choice of insurance coverage
   c. A retirement plan
   d. Employee discounts on company products and services

6. For which of the following taxes is there a ceiling on the amount of annual employee earnings subject to the tax?
   a. Only the FICA tax
   b. Only the FICA tax and the federal unemployment tax
   c. Only the state and federal unemployment taxes
   d. The FICA tax and the state and federal unemployment taxes

7. Sumiko Greer is paid $26 per hour with time and a half her regular hourly pay rate for all hours exceeding 40 per week. During the week ended January 12, Sumiko worked 45 hours. What is the gross payroll?
   a. $1,105
   b. $1,170
   c. $1,235
   d. $1,365

8. Travel America has 24 employees who are paid on a monthly basis. For the most recent month, gross earnings were $78,000, of which $27,000 is subject to unemployment taxes (federal at 0.8% and state at 5.4%). Federal income tax withholdings are 20% of total earnings. All employees have $15 per month withheld for charitable contributions. All earnings are subject to 8% FICA tax.

   What is the total employer's payroll tax expense?
   a. $4,216
   b. $7,114
   c. $7,914
   d. $9,656

9. Referring to the information in the preceding question, what is the amount of salaries payable?
   a. $51,309
   b. $54,471
   c. $55,800
   d. $56,160

10. Under what condition is a contingent liability recorded as an expense and a liability?
    a. Under no condition
    b. When the likelihood of an actual loss is remote
    c. When the likelihood of an actual loss is reasonably possible
    d. When the likelihood of an actual loss is probable and the amount can be estimated

Quick Exercises

11-1. Federal United purchased equipment costing $88,000 on October 2, 2008, by paying a 30% cash down payment and signing a 9%, 120-day note payable for the balance. Federal United's year-end is December 31.

Requirement

1. Journalize the following:

   a. The purchase of the equipment on October 2, 2008
   b. The accrual of interest on December 31, 2008
   c. Payment of the note on January 30, 2009

	General Journal			
Date	Accounts		Debit	Credit

	General Journal			
Date	Accounts		Debit	Credit

	General Journal			
Date	Accounts		Debit	Credit

11-2. Ideal Food Services had cash sales of $787,000 during the month of August 2008 and collected the 7% sales tax on these sales required by the state in which Ideal Food Services operates.

Requirements

1. Journalize the cash sale and the sales tax on August 31.

	General Journal			
Date	Accounts		Debit	Credit

2. Journalize the September 15 transaction when the sales tax is remitted to the proper agency.

	General Journal		
Date	Accounts	Debit	Credit

11-3.   Freedom Vacuums warrants all of its products for one full year against any defect in manufacturing. Sales for 2007 and 2008 were $731,000 and $854,000, respectively. Freedom Vacuums expects warranty claims to run 4.5% of annual sales. Freedom paid $30,150 and $38,290, respectively, in 2007 and 2008 in warranty claims.

   a.   Compute Freedom's Warranty Expense for 2007 and 2008.

   b.   Compute the balance in Estimated Warranty Payable on December 31, 2008, assuming the January 1, 2007, balance in the account was $2,980.

11-4.   Curtis Building Services has one employee, George North, who earns $36 per hour for a 40-hour workweek. He earns time and a half for all over-time hours. George has earned $89,200 in wages prior to the current week. From George's pay, Curtis Building Services deducts 20% for federal income tax and 8% for FICA taxes (up to $90,000 per annum). The company also withholds $100 per week for his health insurance. The federal unemployment tax rate is 0.8% up to $7,000 of employee earnings per annum. The state unemployment tax rate is 5.4% up to $7,000 of employee earnings per annum. Curtis pays $100/week for medical insurance premiums for each employee.

Requirements

1. Compute the gross pay and the net pay for George North for the current week ending December 18, 2008. George worked 48 hours. Round all amounts to the nearest dollar.

Gross Pay:

Net Pay:

2. Journalize the payroll expense.

	General Journal			
Date	Accounts		Debit	Credit

3. Journalize the payroll taxes imposed on Curtis Building Services.

	General Journal			
Date	Accounts		Debit	Credit

11-5. Use the data in Quick Exercise 11-4 to record the following:

    a. Journalize the payment of payroll to the employee on December 18, 2008.
    b. Journalize the payment of the income tax withheld and FICA for the employee and employer on December 18, 2008.
    c. Journalize the payment of the health insurance premiums withheld.

	General Journal			
Date	Accounts		Debit	Credit

	General Journal			
Date	Accounts		Debit	Credit

	General Journal			
Date	Accounts		Debit	Credit

Do it Yourself! Question 1

General Current Liabilities

Nitro Brothers sells products with warranties included in the selling price. During October 2008, Nitro sold goods for $10,000 cash. These goods cost $8,000 to manufacture. Nitro is required by law to collect 8% sales tax on all sales.

Nitro estimates warranty costs to be 1% of selling price. During October 2008, Nitro made $60 of repairs under warranty (paid in cash to a repair service).

On October 31, 2008, Nitro remitted all sales tax collected in October to the state government.

Requirement

1 Account for current liabilities of known amount

2 Account for current liabilities that must be estimated

1. Journalize all of Nitro's transactions in the month of October, 2008.

Date	Accounts	Debit	Credit

Date	Accounts	Debit	Credit

Date	Accounts	Debit	Credit

Date	Accounts	Debit	Credit

Date	Accounts	Debit	Credit

Do It Yourself! Question 2

Current Portion of Long-Term Debt

On October 1, 2008, Pulter Industries signed a $2,000 note payable. Pulter agreed to pay back $100 per month, beginning on November 1, 2008, and ending on June 1, 2010.

Pulter is also required to pay 10% interest on the note each month.

Requirement

6 Report current liabilities on the balance sheet

1. Show the presentation of this note on Pulter's December 31, 2008, balance sheet.

Do It Yourself! Question 3

Payroll Liabilities

Oxygen Co. employees earn $200,000 gross pay per week. All employees have the following items withheld from their pay:

20%	Income Taxes
8%	FICA Taxes
3%	401K Plan Contributions
1%	Union Dues

Oxygen pays the following payroll taxes:

8%	FICA Taxes
6%	Unemployment Taxes

Requirements

1. For a normal week, journalize the following transactions:

Compute payroll amounts

Record basic payroll transactions

a. Cash payment of employee salaries.

Date	Accounts	Debit	Credit

Compute payroll amounts

Record basic payroll transactions

b. Oxygen's payroll taxes.

Date	Accounts	Debit	Credit

Record basic payroll
transactions

c. Oxygen's payment of all payroll taxes.

Date	Accounts	Debit	Credit

 Record basic payroll
transactions

d. Oxygen's payment of union dues.

Date	Accounts	Debit	Credit

 Record basic payroll
transactions

e. Oxygen's payment of 401K plan contributions.

Date	Accounts	Debit	Credit

Quick Practice Solutions

True/False

<u> F </u> 1. Sales tax payable is shown as a long-term liability on the balance sheet.
False—Sales tax payable is shown as a current liability on the balance sheet. (p. 552)

<u> T </u> 2. An accrued expense is an expense that has not yet been paid. (p. 553)

<u> T </u> 3. A contingent liability is not an actual liability. (p. 555)

<u> F </u> 4. Optional deductions would include employee income tax, Social Security tax, union dues, and insurance premiums.
False—Employee income tax and Social Security tax are required deductions. (p. 559)

<u> F </u> 5. State and federal unemployment taxes are two required payroll deductions for employees.
False—State and federal unemployment taxes are paid by the employer. (p. 561)

<u> T </u> 6. The FICA Social Security tax is withheld from employees and is also paid by the employer in the same amount. (p. 561)

<u> F </u> 7. The document that includes every employee's gross pay, deductions, and net pay for the payroll period is called the Wage and Tax Statement.
False—The document that includes every employee's gross pay, deductions, and net pay for the payroll period is called the payroll record. A Wage and Tax Statement is a W-2 Form, which is sent to employees and the IRS for tax filing purposes. (p. 563)

<u> T </u> 8. Two employees who have the same gross pay may have different amounts withheld for income taxes depending on the number of allowances claimed on the W-4 Form. (p. 559)

<u> T </u> 9. An example of a contingent liability would be when you cosign a note payable for a friend. (p. 555)

<u> F </u> 10. If a company has a note payable at December 31 for $300,000, which will be paid in three equal installments every five months, $100,000 should be classified as a current liability.
False—$200,000 should be classified as a current liability because that amount will be paid within 10 months, less than one year. (p. 552)

Multiple Choice

1. **Which of the following is true about current liabilities?** (p. 550)
   a. Are due within one year or one operating cycle, whichever is longer
   b. Must be of a known amount
   c. Must be of an estimated amount
   d. Are subtracted from long-term liabilities on the balance sheet

2. **Which of the following best describes unearned revenue?** (p. 553)
   a. Revenue that has been earned and collected
   b. Revenue that has been earned but not yet collected
   c. Revenue that has been collected but not yet earned
   d. Revenue that has not been collected nor earned

3. **When is Warranty Expense debited?** (p. 554)
   a. In the period the product under warranty is repaired or replaced
   b. In the period after the product is sold
   c. In the period after the product is repaired or replaced
   d. In the period the revenue from selling the product was earned

4. **When a product is repaired under warranty, the entry includes which of the following?** (p. 554)
   a. A debit to Warranty Expense
   b. A credit to Warranty Expense
   c. A debit to Estimated Warranty Payable
   d. A credit to Estimated Warranty Payable

5. **What is meant by a cafeteria plan?** (p. 560)
   a. A free lunch program offered by the employer
   b. A choice of insurance coverage
   c. A retirement plan
   d. Employee discounts on company products and services

6. **For which of the following taxes is there a ceiling on the amount of annual employee earnings subject to the tax?** (pp. 560–562)
   a. Only the FICA tax
   b. Only the FICA tax and the federal unemployment tax
   c. Only the state and federal unemployment taxes
   d. The FICA tax and the state and federal unemployment taxes

7. **Sumiko Greer is paid $26 per hour with time and a half her regular hourly pay rate for all hours exceeding 40 per week. During the week ended January 12, Sumiko worked 45 hours. What is the gross payroll?** (p. 558)
   a. $1,105
   b. $1,170
   c. $1,235
   d. $1,365

8. **Travel America has 24 employees who are paid on a monthly basis. For the most recent month, gross earnings were $78,000, of which $27,000 is subject to unemployment taxes (federal at 0.8% and state at 5.4%). Federal income tax withholdings are 20% of total earnings. All employees have $15 per month withheld for charitable contributions. All earnings are subject to 8% FICA tax.**

   What is the total employer's payroll tax expense? (p. 558)
   a. $4,216
   b. $7,114
   c. $7,914
   d. $9,656

9. Referring to the information in the preceding question, what is the amount of salaries payable? (p. 558)
   a. $51,309
   b. $54,471
   c. $55,800
   d. $56,160

10. Under what condition is a contingent liability recorded as an expense and a liability? (p. 555)
    a. Under no condition
    b. When the likelihood of an actual loss is remote
    c. When the likelihood of an actual loss is reasonably possible
    d. When the likelihood of an actual loss is probable and the amount can be estimated

Quick Exercises

11-1. Federal United purchased equipment costing $88,000 on October 2, 2008, by paying a 30% cash down payment and signing a 9%, 120-day note payable for the balance. Federal United's year-end is December 31. (p. 551)

Requirement

1. Journalize the following:

   a. The purchase of the equipment on October 2, 2008
   b. The accrual of interest on December 31, 2008
   c. Payment of the note on January 30, 2009

General Journal				
	Date	Accounts	Debit	Credit
a	Oct. 2	Equipment	88,000	
		Cash		26,400
		Notes Payable		61,600
		To record purchase of equipment.		

General Journal				
	Date	Accounts	Debit	Credit
b.	Dec. 31	Interest Expense	1,386	
		Interest Payable		1,386
		To accrue interest expense 10/2/08–12/31/08		
		($61,600 × 9% × 90/360 = 1,386).		

General Journal				
	Date	Accounts	Debit	Credit
c.	Jan. 30	Notes Payable	61,600	
		Interest Payable	1,386	
		Interest Expense	462	
		Cash		63,448
		To pay off the note payable plus interest		
		($61,600 × 9% × 30/360 = 462).		

11-2. Ideal Food Services had cash sales of $787,000 during the month of August 2008 and collected the 7% sales tax on these sales required by the state in which Ideal Food Services operates. (p. 552)

Requirements

1. Journalize the cash sale and the sales tax on August 31.

General Journal			
Date	Accounts	Debit	Credit
Aug. 31	Cash	842,090	
	Sales		787,000
	Sales Taxes Payable		55,090
	To record cash sales including 7% sales tax.		

2. Journalize the September 15 transaction when the sales tax is remitted to the proper agency.

General Journal			
Date	Accounts	Debit	Credit
Sept. 15	Sales Tax Payable	55,090	
	Cash		55,090
	To record sales tax remittance.		

11-3. Freedom Vacuums warrants all of its products for one full year against any defect in manufacturing. Sales for 2007 and 2008 were $731,000 and $854,000, respectively. Freedom Vacuums expects warranty claims to run 4.5% of annual sales. Freedom paid $30,150 and $38,290, respectively, in 2007 and 2008 in warranty claims. (p. 554)

    a.   Compute Freedom's warranty expense for:

        2007: $32,895 ($731,000 × .045)

        2008: $38,430 ($854,000 × .045)

    b.   Compute the balance in Estimated Warranty Payable on December 31, 2008, assuming the January 1, 2007, balance in the account was $2,980.

        $5,865 ($2,980 + $32,895 + $38,430 − $30,150 − $38,290)

11-4. Curtis Building Services has one employee, George North, who earns $36 per hour for a 40-hour workweek. He earns time and a half for all overtime hours. George has earned $89,200 in wages prior to the current week. From George's pay, Curtis Building Services deducts 20% for federal income tax, and 8% for FICA taxes (up to $90,000 per annum). The company also withholds $100 per week for his health insurance. The federal unemployment tax rate is 0.8% up to $7,000 of employee earnings per annum. The state unemployment tax rate is 5.4% up to $7,000 of employee earnings per annum. Curtis pays $100/week for medical insurance premiums for each employee. (p. 558)

Requirements

1. Compute the gross pay and the net pay for George North for the current week ending December 18, 2008. George worked 48 hours. Round all amounts to the nearest dollar.

Gross Pay: $1,872 = (40 \times \$36) + (8 \times \$36 \times 1.5) = \$1,440 + \$432 = \$1,872$
Net Pay: FICA tax withheld = $\$64 = (\$800 \times 0.08)$
Federal tax withheld = $\$374 = (\$1,872 \times .20)$
Health insurance withheld = $100
Total deductions = $64 + $374 + $100 = $538
Net pay = $1,872 − $538 = $1,334

2. Journalize the payroll expense.

General Journal			
Date	Accounts	Debit	Credit
Dec. 18	Salary Expense	1,872	
	FICA Tax Payable		64
	Employee Income Tax Payable		374
	Health Insurance Payable		100
	Salary Payable to Employees		1,334
	To record payroll expenses.		

3. Journalize the payroll taxes imposed on Curtis Building Services.

General Journal			
Date	Accounts	Debit	Credit
Dec. 18	Payroll Tax Expense	64	
	FICA Tax Payable		64
	*To record payroll tax expense.**		
	($90,000 − $89,200) × 0.08 = $64		

*Note: Maximum unemployment taxes have been incurred.

11-5. Use the data in Quick Exercise 11-4 to record the following: (p. 558)

   a. Journalize the payment of payroll to the employee on December 18, 2008.
   b. Journalize the payment of the income tax withheld and FICA for the employee and employer on December 18, 2008.
   c. Journalize the payment of the health insurance premiums withheld.

		General Journal			
	Date	Accounts	Debit	Credit
a.	Dec. 18	Salary Payable to Employees	1,334	
		Cash		1,334
		To record payroll paid to employees.		

		General Journal			
	Date	Accounts	Debit	Credit
b.	Dec. 18	Employee Income Tax Payable	374	
		FICA Tax Payable	128	
		Cash		502
		To record remittance of Income Tax and FICA taxes.		

		General Journal			
	Date	Accounts	Debit	Credit
c.	Dec. 18	Health Insurance Payable	100	
		Cash		100
		To record payment of health insurance premium.		

Do It Yourself! Question 1 Solutions

Requirement

1. Journalize all of Nitro's transactions in the month of October 2008.

During October 2008, Nitro sold goods for $10,000 cash. These goods cost $8,000 to manufacture. Nitro is required by law to collect 8% sales tax on all sales.

Cash ($10,000 × [1 + 8%])		10,800	
Sales Revenue			10,000
Sales Tax Payable ($10,000 × 8%)			800
COGS		8,000	
Inventory			8,000

Nitro estimates warranty costs to be 1% of the selling price.

Warranty Expense ($10,000 × 1%)		100	
Warranty Payable			100

During October 2008, Nitro made $60 of repairs under warranty (paid in cash to a repair service).

Warranty Payable		60	
Cash			60

On October 31, 2008, Nitro remitted all sales tax collected in October to the state government.

Sales Tax Payable ($10,000 × 8%)		800	
Cash			800

Do It Yourself! Question 2 Solutions

Requirement

1. Show the presentation of this note on Pulter's December 31, 2008, balance sheet.

$$\text{Payments already made} = \$100 \times 2 = \$200.$$
$$\$2{,}000 - \$200 = \$1{,}800 \text{ to be repaid.}$$
$$12 \times \$100 = \$1{,}200 = \text{current portion.}$$
$$\$1{,}800 - \$1{,}200 = \$600 = \text{long-term portion.}$$

Interest payable only relates to the month of December (because November's interest expense was paid on December 1).

$$\text{Interest payable} = \$1{,}800 \times 10\% \times 1/12 = \$15.$$

Current Liabilities	
Current portion of long-term debt	$1,200
Interest payable	$ 15
Long-Term Liabilities	
Notes payable/long-term debt (net of current portion)	$ 600

Do It Yourself! Question 3 Solutions

Requirement

1. For a normal week, journalize the following transactions:

a. Cash payment of employee salaries.

Salary Expense (gross pay)		200,000	
Employee Income Tax Payable ($200,000 × 20%)			40,000
FICA Tax Payable ($200,000 × 8%)			16,000
401K Plan Contributions Payable ($200,000 × 3%)			6,000
Union Dues Payable ($200,000 × 1%)			2,0000
Cash (net/take home pay)			136,000

b. Oxygen's payroll taxes.

Payroll Tax Expense (to balance)		28,000	
FICA Tax Payable ($200,000 × 8%) (matching)			16,000
Unemployment Tax Payable ($200,000 × 6%)			12,000

c. Oxygen's payment of all payroll taxes.

Employee Income Tax Payable		40,000	
FICA Tax Payable ($16,000 + $16,000) (matching)		32,000	
Unemployment Tax Payable		12,000	
Cash (to balance)			84,000

d. Oxygen's payment of union dues.

Union Dues Payable		2,000	
Cash			2,000

e. Oxygen's payment of 401K plan contributions.

Pension Contributions Payable		6,000	
Cash			6,000

The Power of Practice

For more practice using the skills learned in this chapter, visit MyAccountingLab. There you will find algorithmically generated questions that are based on these Demo Docs and your main textbook's Review and Assess Your Progress sections.

Go to MyAccountingLab and follow these steps:

1. Direct your URL to www.myaccountinglab.com.
2. Log in using your name and password.
3. Click the MyAccountingLab link.
4. Click Study Plan in the left navigation bar.
5. From the table of contents, select Chapter 11, Current Liabilities and Payroll.
6. Click a link to work tutorial exercises.

12 Partnerships

WHAT YOU PROBABLY ALREADY KNOW

You probably already know that some couples sign a prenuptial agreement before getting married. A prenuptial agreement usually provides guidance as to the distribution of assets held before marriage and those acquired during marriage. The disposition of individual debt acquired before marriage may be addressed, as well as nonfinancial or lifestyle topics. The purpose of this agreement is to confirm in writing what the future marriage partners believe is fair and appropriate. Preparing written documentation avoids misunderstandings and poor communication.

This is exactly the reason why it is strongly recommended that a written partnership agreement be prepared. Important issues should be included in the partnership agreement, such as the share of profits (or losses) each partner will take, the responsibilities of each partner, voluntary withdrawal or death of a partner, provisions for the termination of the partnership, and other important guidelines.

Learning Objectives

1 Identify the characteristics of a partnership.

Some of the characteristics of a partnership include limited life, mutual agency, unlimited liability, co-ownership of property, and no partnership tax. It is advisable to create a written partnership agreement containing important components of the partnership business in case the partnership dissolves. *Review these characteristics in the "Characteristics of a Partnership" section of your textbook. Be sure to also review the advantages and disadvantages of a partnership in Exhibit 12-2 (p. 598) and the different types of partnerships in Exhibit 12-3 (p. 599).*

2 Account for partner investments.

When the partners invest personal assets in the partnership, they are recorded at market value. If liabilities are assumed by the partnership, they are also recorded and the partners' Capital accounts are credited for the net assets. *Review the "Start-up of a Partnership" in the main text.*

3 Allocate profits and losses to the partners.

Profits and losses are shared by the partners in accordance with the terms of the partnership agreement. Typical arrangements may indicate that profits and losses are split based on each partner's investment, service, or some other percentage of fractional bases. If there is no provision for allocating profits and losses in the agreement, they are split evenly. The net income or loss that is closed out into Income Summary is then closed out to the partners' Capital accounts in accordance with the indicated allocation. *Review the examples included under the "Sharing Profits and Losses, and Partner Drawings" in the main text.*

 Account for the admission of a new partner.

When a new partner is admitted, the old partnership is dissolved and a new partnership agreement should be created. This may occur in one of the following ways:

- One partner selling directly to an outside individual who is agreeable to the partners. The outgoing partner's Capital is debited and the new partner's Capital is credited for the same amount.

- A partner can join a partnership by contributing assets into the business. The new partner's Capital account may be given credit for the market value of the assets at (a) an amount exactly equal to the market value of the assets recorded on the books, (b) an amount less than the market value of the assets recorded on the books, which provides a bonus to the existing partners, or (c) an amount more than the market value of the assets recorded on the books, which provides a bonus to the new partner.

Review "Admission by Investing in the Partnership" in the main text for specific examples of partners contributing assets to the business.

5 **Account for a partner's withdrawal from the firm.**

A partner may die or decide to withdraw from the partnership. The withdrawal of a partner results in the dissolution of the partnership agreement. A withdrawal may occur in one of the following ways:

- A partner's interest may be satisfied upon death by paying the appropriate Capital amount as indicated in the partnership agreement.

- A remaining partner may purchase the deceased partner's interest. The continuing partner's Capital is increased for the same amount as the Capital account eliminated for the withdrawing partner.

- A partner can withdraw by receiving cash equal to (a) the book value of the Capital account, (b) an amount less than the book value of the Capital account, providing a bonus to the remaining partners, or (c) an amount more than the book value of the Capital account, providing a bonus to the withdrawing partner.

Review "Withdrawal of a Partner" in the main text for specific examples of the withdrawal of net assets from the business.

6 **Account for the liquidation of a partnership.**

A liquidation means that the business is going to cease operations. When this happens, the business will (a) sell the assets and allocate the gain or loss to the partners' Capital accounts based on the partnership agreement, (b) pay all of the partnership liabilities, and (c) distribute the remaining cash to the partners based on their Capital balances.

Review Exhibit 12-5 (p. 613) to see the impact of a liquidation on the related account balances.

7 **Prepare partnership financial statements.**

Partnership financial statements are similar to those of a sole proprietorship, except there is more than one owner. *Review Exhibit 12-6, Financial Statements of a Partnership (p. 614).*

Demo Doc 1

Partnerships

Learning Objectives 1–7

The Goode Partnership wants to admit Hanna Storm as a new partner on January 1, 2008. On this date, Goode had the following information:

Cash	$25,000	Liabilities	$35,000
Other assets	60,000	Ned Frist, capital	35,000
		Janice Wright, capital	15,000
Total assets	$85,000	Total liabilities and capital	$85,000

Janice has a 30% share of the profits, whereas Ned has a 70% share.

Requirements

1. Suppose Janice Wright sold her entire interest to Hanna for $40,000. Journalize the transfer of ownership. What are the Capital balances for each partner after the transfer is made?

2. (Ignoring Requirement 1) Suppose instead that the Goode Partnership were to admit Hanna as a third partner by selling her a 40% interest for $40,000 cash. Compute Hanna's Capital balance and journalize her investment. What are the Capital balances for each partner after the investment is made?

3. (Ignoring Requirement 1) Prepare the balance sheet of the Goode Partnership after Hanna is admitted to the partnership.

4. Assume that Hanna was not admitted to the partnership. During 2008, Goode earned $20,000 of net income (in cash). How much profit is allocated to each partner (Janice and Ned)? Does the partnership pay income taxes on this profit?

5. (Continuing on from Requirement 4) On January 1, 2009, the Goode Partnership was liquidated. All noncash assets were sold for $90,000, after which all liabilities were paid. How much does each partner receive upon liquidation?

Demo Doc 1 Solutions

Requirement 1

2 Account for partner investments

4 Account for the admission of a new partner

5 Account for a partner's withdrawal from the firm

Suppose Janice Wright sold her entire interest to Hanna for $40,000. Journalize the transfer of ownership. What are the Capital balances for each partner after the transfer is made?

Part 1	Part 2	Part 3	Part 4	Part 5	Demo Doc Complete

If Hanna purchases Janice's interest in the partnership, it is an outside transaction of ownership. The only portion recorded in the accounting records is the name change on the Capital account. Janice's Capital account decreases (a debit) and Hanna's Capital account increases (a credit) by $15,000.

	Janice Wright, Capital		15,000	
	Hanna Storm, Capital			15,000

The Capital balances are as they were before the transaction, with the exception of the name change:

Before Transaction		After Transaction	
Janice Wright, capital	$15,000	Hanna Storm, capital	$15,000
Ned Frist, capital	35,000	Ned Frist, capital	35,000
Total capital	$50,000	Total capital	$50,000

Once Janice withdraws from the business, the old partnership (between Janice and Ned) is dissolved. A new partnership is formed between Hanna and Ned. The new partnership can even bear the same name as the old one (and will in this example).

Requirement 2

2 Account for partner investments

4 Account for the admission of a new partner

(Ignoring Requirement 1) Suppose instead that the Goode Partnership were to admit Hanna as a third partner by selling her a 40% interest for $40,000 cash. Compute Hanna's Capital balance and journalize her investment. What are the Capital balances for each partner after the investment is made?

Part 1	Part 2	Part 3	Part 4	Part 5	Demo Doc Complete

Hanna has purchased a 40% interest in the total partnership's capital. *Regardless* of how much she pays for her share, her capital will be 40% of the *total capital after the purchase.*

Capital before purchase ($15,000 + $35,000)	$50,000
Hanna's investment in capital	40,000
Total capital after purchase	$90,000

So Hanna's share of the capital after her investment is:

$$40\% \times \$90,000 = \$36,000$$

Because Hanna has purchased an interest, the Capital balances of Janice and Ned are adjusted.

Janice and Ned now have $90,000 − $36,000 = $54,000 capital between them. This new capital amount will be split between them using their *original* partnership percentages.

Janice's Capital account is now:

$$\$54,000 \times 30\% = \$16,200$$

This is an increase of:

$$\$16,200 - \$15,000 = \$1,200$$

Ned's Capital account is now:

$$\$54,000 \times 70\% = \$37,800$$

This is an increase of:

$$\$37,800 - \$35,000 = \$2,800$$

Before Transaction		After Transaction	
Janice Wright, capital	$15,000	Janice Wright, capital	$16,200
Ned Frist, capital	35,000	Ned Frist, capital	37,800
		Hanna Storm, capital	36,000
Total capital	$50,000	Total capital	$90,000

Because Hanna paid $4,000 more for her share than the Capital amount that is being recorded ($36,000), the difference is split *proportionately* by the preexisting partners by the preexisting percentages.

For the partnership as a whole, assets increase (a debit) by Hanna's cash investment of $40,000.

Hanna's Capital account increases (a credit) by $36,000, Janice's Capital increases (a credit) by its adjustment of $4,000 × 30% = $1,200, and Ned's Capital increases (a credit) by its adjustment of $4,000 × 70% = $2,800.

Cash		40,000	
Janice Wright, Capital			1,200
Ned Frist, Capital			2,800
Hanna Storm, Capital			36,000

Requirement 3

7 Prepare partnership financial statements

(Ignoring Requirement 1) Prepare the balance sheet of the Goode Partnership after Hanna is admitted to the partnership.

Part 1	Part 2	**Part 3**	Part 4	Part 5	Demo Doc Complete

The Cash balance increases to:

$$\$25,000 + \$40,000 = \$65,000$$

Hanna Storm, Capital has a balance of $36,000.
    Ned Frist, Capital increases to:

$$\$35,000 + \$2,800 = \$37,800$$

Janice Wright, Capital increases to:

$$\$15,000 + \$1,200 = \$16,200$$

Liabilities and other assets have not changed.

<table>
<tr><td colspan="4" align="center">THE GOODE PARTNERSHIP
Balance Sheet
January 1, 2008</td></tr>
<tr><td>Cash</td><td>$ 65,000</td><td>Liabilities</td><td>$ 35,000</td></tr>
<tr><td>Other assets</td><td>60,000</td><td>Ned Frist, capital</td><td>37,800</td></tr>
<tr><td></td><td></td><td>Hanna Storm, capital</td><td>36,000</td></tr>
<tr><td></td><td></td><td>Janice Wright, capital</td><td>16,200</td></tr>
<tr><td></td><td></td><td></td><td></td></tr>
<tr><td>Total assets</td><td>$125,000</td><td>Total liabilities and capital</td><td>$125,000</td></tr>
</table>

Requirement 4

 Identify the characteristics of a partnership

3 Allocate profits and losses to the partners

Assume that Hanna was not admitted to the partnership. During 2008, Goode earned $20,000 of net income (in cash). How much profit is allocated to each partner (Janice and Ned)? Does the partnership pay income taxes on this profit?

Part 1	Part 2	Part 3	**Part 4**	Part 5	Demo Doc Complete

Profits are allocated in this partnership based on stated percentages.

Janice receives 30% of the profits, so she is allocated 30% × $20,000 = $6,000 of profit.

Ned receives 70% of the profits, so he is allocated 70% × $20,000 = $14,000 of profit.

After this allocation, Goode has the following balance sheet:

Cash	$ 45,000	Liabilities	$ 35,000
Other assets	60,000	Ned Frist, capital	49,000
		Janice Wright, capital	21,000
Total assets	$105,000	Total liabilities and capital	$105,000

Cash has increased from earning net income of $20,000 and the Capital balances for Janice and Ned have been increased for their profit allocation.

Adjusted Cash balance:

$25,000 + $20,000 = $45,000

Adjusted Janice Wright, Capital balance:

$15,000 + $6,000 = $21,000

Adjusted Ned Frist, Capital balance:

$35,000 + $14,000 = $49,000

Note that *allocation* of profit *does not necessarily mean distribution* of profit. Just as shareholders do not receive all profits a company earns as dividends, partners do not receive all income allocations as a cash distribution.

The partnership does *not* pay taxes on this profit. Instead, Janice and Ned are taxed on their individual tax returns for their allocation of profits.

Requirement 5

Account for the liquidation of a partnership

(Continuing on from Requirement 4) On January 1, 2009, the Goode Partnership was liquidated. All noncash assets were sold for $90,000, after which all liabilities were paid. How much does each partner receive upon liquidation?

Part 1	Part 2	Part 3	Part 4	**Part 5**	Demo Doc Complete

The sale of the other assets increases Cash (a debit) by $90,000 and decreases Other Assets (a credit) by $60,000, their book value.

The remaining "gain" of $90,000 − $60,000 = $30,000 is split among Janice and Ned according to their profit-sharing proportions. This "gain" is shown as an increase to Janice's and Ned's Capital accounts.

Janice receives 30% × $30,000 = $9,000 of the "gain."

Ned receives 70% × $30,000 = $21,000 of the "gain."

Jan. 1	Cash	90,000	
	Other Assets		60,000
	Janice Wright, Capital (30% × $30,000)		9,000
	Ned Frist, Capital (70% × $30,000)		21,000

The liabilities were paid after the noncash assets were sold. This is a decrease (a debit) to Liabilities of $35,000 and a decrease to Cash (a credit) of $35,000.

Jan. 1	Liabilities	35,000	
	Cash		35,000

After these transactions, Janice has a Capital balance of $21,000 + $9,000 = $30,000 and Ned has a Capital balance of $49,000 + $21,000 = $70,000.

The cash payment received on liquidation is *the amount of the Capital balances.* So Janice receives $30,000 cash and Ned receives $70,000 cash on liquidation.

Part 1	Part 2	Part 3	Part 4	Part 5	**Demo Doc Complete**

Quick Practice Questions

True/False

_____ 1. A single partner can commit the entire firm to a legal liability.

_____ 2. A partnership has an unlimited life.

_____ 3. If the partnership agreement specifies a method for allocating profits but not losses, then losses are shared in a different proportion from profits.

_____ 4. Partnership profits and losses may be allocated based on capital contributions but not on service.

_____ 5. The journal entry to close a partner's Drawing account involves a debit to the partner's Drawing account.

_____ 6. A new partner may be admitted to a partnership by purchasing some of an existing partner's interest.

_____ 7. A bonus paid to the existing partners by a new partner decreases the old partners' Capital accounts.

_____ 8. The resignation of a partner dissolves the partnership.

_____ 9. When a partner withdraws from the partnership, the withdrawing partner's Capital account is always debited for its balance.

_____ 10. Cash is distributed to partners in accordance with the net income agreement in the partnership liquidation process.

Multiple Choice

1. Which of the following is *not* an advantage of a partnership?
   a. Limited liability
   b. Ease of formation
   c. Combined resources
   d. Combined experience and talent

2. Which of the following is true for a limited partnership?
   a. Must have at least two general partners
   b. Is illegal in most states
   c. Must have at least one general partner
   d. None of the above

3. Which of the following applies to the partnership characteristic of co-ownership of property?
   a. Any asset a partner invests in the partnership becomes the joint property of all the partners.
   b. General partners co-own all assets, but limited partners do not.
   c. General partners own a larger percentage of the assets of a partnership than do limited partners.
   d. All partnership assets are co-owned by any banks making loans to the partnership.

4. Equipment with a cost of $100,000 and accumulated depreciation of $30,000 is contributed to a new partnership by Jay Bergen. The current market value of the equipment is $105,000. The replacement value of the equipment is $135,000. At what amount is the equipment recorded on the partnership books?
   a. $70,000
   b. $100,000
   c. $105,000
   d. $135,000

5. Mac and Molly formed a partnership with capital contributions of $80,000 and $120,000, respectively. Their partnership agreement called for (1) Mac to receive a $20,000 salary, (2) each partner to receive 10% based on initial capital contributions, and (3) the remaining income or loss to be divided equally. If net income for the current year is $80,000, what amount is credited to Mac's Capital account?
   a. $27,000
   b. $35,000
   c. $43,000
   d. $48,000

6. Which of the following would be recorded in the closing entry if partner A's share of net income is $35,000 and partner B's share of net income is $45,000?
   a. Credit to A's Capital account for $40,000
   b. Credit to B's Capital account for $40,000
   c. Debit to A's Capital account for $35,000
   d. Debit to Income Summary for $80,000

7. Elliott, Barry, Ben, and Jerry formed a partnership agreeing to divide profits and losses in a 2:3:4:1 relationship, respectively. Assuming that the business earned a profit of $165,000, what are Elliott and Jerry's shares, respectively?
   a. $33,000; $49,500
   b. $49,500; $16,500
   c. $60,000; $33,000
   d. $33,000; $16,500

8. Which of the following is included on a partnership balance sheet?
   a. A category for assets contributed by each partner
   b. A category for liabilities incurred by each partner
   c. An ending Drawing account balance for each partner
   d. An ending Capital account balance for each partner

9. Black and Blue formed a partnership, agreeing to share profits equally. After closing entries, the balances in their Capital accounts are $36,000 and $45,000, respectively. Blue sells her interest in the partnership to White for $52,000. Which of the following would be recorded on the books of the partnership?
a. Credit White, Capital for $45,000
b. Debit Cash for $52,000
c. Credit White, Capital for $52,000
d. Debit Blue, Capital for $52,000

10. The net income agreement for Forsyth and Guilford states net income and net loss shall be divided in a ratio of beginning Capital balances. The net loss for the current year is $50,000. On January 1 of the current year, the Capital balances were as follows: Forsyth, $55,000; Guilford, $65,000. During the current year, Forsyth withdrew $40,000 and Guilford withdrew $25,000. What are the Capital balances for Forsyth and Guilford, respectively, as of December 31 of the current year?
a. Debit $7,917; Credit $12,917
b. Credit $7,917; Credit $12,917
c. Debit $7,917; Debit $12,917
d. Debit $12,917; Credit $7,917

Quick Exercises

12-1. Wallingford, Albright, and Rowe have recently formed a partnership by investing $45,000, $60,000, and $35,000, respectively. They are considering several methods of allocating income and losses.

Requirement

1. Compute the partners' shares of profits and losses under each of the following plans:

    a. Net income is $31,800 and the partners could not agree on a plan for net income/loss division.
    b. The net loss is $18,000 and the partners agreed to share in the profits based on a 2:2:1 ratio. The agreement did not address losses.
    c. Net income is $31,800 and the partners agreed to share profits based on the relationship of their initial Capital balances.
    d. The net loss is $38,000 and the partners agreed to share profits and losses based on 15% to Wallingford, 50% to Albright, and 35% to Rowe.

Round all answers to the nearest whole dollar.

Item	Wallingford	Albright	Rowe	Total
a.				
b.				
c.				
d.				

12-2. Browning and Douglas are partners who agree to admit Taylor to their partnership. Browning has a Capital balance of $51,000 and Douglas has a Capital balance of $70,000. Browning and Douglas share net income in the ratio of 2:8. Prepare journal entries to admit Taylor to the partnership based on the following independent agreements. Round all amounts to the nearest dollar.

a. Taylor invests $66,000 cash into the partnership for a 20% interest.
b. Taylor invests $66,000 cash into the partnership for a 30% interest.
c. Taylor purchases one-third of Browning's Capital for $25,000.
d. Taylor purchases one-half of Douglas's Capital for $32,000.

General Journal			
Date	Accounts	Debit	Credit

General Journal			
Date	Accounts	Debit	Credit

General Journal			
Date	Accounts	Debit	Credit

General Journal			
Date	Accounts	Debit	Credit

12-3. Peter, Paul, and Mary are partners in the Sing Song Company and share profits and losses in a ratio of 4:4:2, respectively. Mary has been contemplating retirement. The partners' current Capital account balances, after closing entries, are $49,000, $98,000, and $147,000, respectively. The new net income agreement for Peter and Paul will be 4:2.

Requirement

1. Journalize the following transactions involving the retirement of Mary. Round to the nearest dollar if necessary:

a. The partners agree to revalue the assets. Land with a cost of $90,000 has a current market value of $127,000.

b. Inventory with a cost of $50,000 has a current market value of $35,000.

c. After the assets are revalued, the partnership agrees to give Mary $75,000 cash and a note payable for $65,000.

General Journal				
Date	Accounts		Debit	Credit

General Journal				
Date	Accounts		Debit	Credit

General Journal				
Date	Accounts		Debit	Credit

12-4. Chandler, Cherry, and Cline are partners in the CCC Company. They share profits and losses in a 3:5:2 ratio and have just closed their books for the period. The current balances in their Capital accounts are $63,000, $49,000, and $94,000, respectively. Chandler has decided to withdraw from the partnership. Prior to the withdrawal of Chandler, the partners agreed that the assets needed to be revalued. Land with a cost of $55,000 has a current market value of $88,000. Inventory with a cost of $75,000 has a current market value of $60,000. Cherry and Cline have agreed to share net income in a 2:3 ratio.

Requirements

1. Prepare the journal entries required to revalue the assets.

General Journal				
Date	Accounts		Debit	Credit

General Journal				
Date	Accounts		Debit	Credit

2. Journalize the withdrawal of Chandler under each of the following independent assumptions:

    a. The partnership gives cash to Chandler equal to his Capital balance.
    b. The paFrtnership gives $76,000 cash to Chandler.
    c. The partnership gives $56,000 cash to Chandler.

General Journal				
Date	Accounts		Debit	Credit

General Journal				
Date	Accounts		Debit	Credit

General Journal				
Date	Accounts		Debit	Credit

12-5. On August 1, 2008, Wheat, Bran, and Oats agree to liquidate their partnership. Wheat has a Capital balance of $90,000, Bran has a Capital balance of $37,500, and Oats has a Capital balance of $30,000. The partners share net income/net loss in a ratio of 4:3:3. Accounts payable amount to $60,000. Assets are shown on the balance sheet at $40,000 of cash and $177,500 of noncash assets. All the noncash assets are sold for $188,000.

Requirement

1. Journalize the following:

   a. Sell the noncash assets.
   b. Pay the liabilities.
   c. Distribute the remaining cash to the partners.

General Journal				
Date	Accounts		Debit	Credit

General Journal				
Date	Accounts		Debit	Credit

General Journal				
Date	Accounts		Debit	Credit

Do It Yourself! Question 1

Waters Partners wants to admit River Kline as a new partner on January 1, 2008. On this date, Waters had the following information:

Cash	$100,000	Liabilities	$ 80,000
Other assets	100,000	Brooke Daniels, capital	30,000
		Rainer Linfoot, capital	90,000
Total assets	$200,000	Total liabilities and capital	$200,000

Brooke Daniels has a 25% share of the profits, whereas Rainer Linfoot has a 75% share.

Requirements

2 Account for partner investments

4 Account for the admission of a new partner

1. Suppose Waters were to admit River as a partner by selling him a 30% interest for $70,000 cash. Compute River's Capital balance and journalize his investment. What are the Capital balances for each partner after the investment is made?

General Journal				
Date	Accounts		Debit	Credit

Before Transaction		After Transaction	

Account for partner investments

Account for the admission of a new partner

Account for a partner's withdrawal from the firm

2. (Ignoring Requirement 1) Suppose instead Brooke Daniels sold her entire interest to River for $50,000. Journalize the transfer of ownership. What are the Capital balances for each partner after the transfer is made?

General Journal				
Date	Accounts		Debit	Credit

Before Transaction		After Transaction	

Identify the characteristics of a partnership

Allocate profits and losses to the partners

3. Assume that River was not admitted to the partnership. During 2008, Waters earned $80,000 of net income (in cash). How much profit is allocated to each partner (Brooke and Rainer)?

Account for the liquidation of a partnership

4. (Continuing on from Requirement 3) On January 1, 2009, Waters Partners was liquidated. All noncash assets were sold for $150,000, after which all liabilities were paid. How much does each partner receive upon liquidation?

General Journal				
Date	Accounts		Debit	Credit

General Journal				
Date	Accounts		Debit	Credit

Quick Practice Solutions

True/False

  T   1. A single partner can commit the entire firm to a legal liability. (p. 597)

  F   2. A partnership has an unlimited life.

       False—A partnership has a *limited* life. (p. 597)

  F   3. If the partnership agreement specifies a method for allocating profits but not losses, then losses are shared in a different proportion from profits.

       False—If only a method of sharing profits is stated in the partnership agreement, then losses are shared the same way. (p. 601)

  F   4. Partnership profits and losses may be allocated based on capital contributions but not on service.

       False—Partnership profits and losses may be allocated based on service. (p. 601)

  F   5. The journal entry to close a partner's Drawing account involves a debit to the partner's Drawing account.

       False—The journal entry to close a partner's Drawing account involves a *credit* to the partner's Drawing account. (p. 603)

  T   6. A new partner may be admitted to a partnership by purchasing some of an existing partner's interest. (p. 604)

  F   7. A bonus paid to the existing partners by a new partner decreases the old partners' Capital accounts.

       False—A bonus paid to the existing partners by a new partner *increases* the old partners' Capital accounts. (p. 606)

  T   8. The resignation of a partner dissolves the partnership. (p. 608)

  T   9. When a partner withdraws from the partnership, the withdrawing partner's Capital account is always debited for its balance. (p. 609)

  F 10. Cash is distributed to partners in accordance with the net income agreement in the partnership liquidation process.

       False—Cash is distributed to partners based on their Capital balances. (pp. 611–613)

Multiple Choice

1. Which of the following is *not* an advantage of a partnership? (p. 597)
   a. Limited liability
   b. Ease of formation
   c. Combined resources
   d. Combined experience and talent

2. Which of the following is true for a limited partnership? (p. 598)
   a. Must have at least two general partners
   b. Is illegal in most states
   c. Must have at least one general partner
   d. None of the above

3. Which of the following applies to the partnership characteristic of co-ownership of property? (p. 597)
   a. Any asset a partner invests in the partnership becomes the joint property of all the partners.
   b. General partners co-own all assets, but limited partners do not.
   c. General partners own a larger percentage of the assets of a partnership than do limited partners.
   d. All partnership assets are co-owned by any banks making loans to the partnership.

4. Equipment with a cost of $100,000 and accumulated depreciation of $30,000 is contributed to a new partnership by Jay Bergen. The current market value of the equipment is $105,000. The replacement value of the equipment is $135,000. At what amount is the equipment recorded on the partnership books? (pp. 600–601)
   a. $70,000
   b. $100,000
   c. $105,000
   d. $135,000

5. Mac and Molly formed a partnership with capital contributions of $80,000 and $120,000, respectively. Their partnership agreement called for (1) Mac to receive a $20,000 salary, (2) each partner to receive 10% based on initial capital contributions, and (3) the remaining income or loss to be divided equally. If net income for the current year is $80,000, what amount is credited to Mac's Capital account? (pp. 601–603)
   a. $27,000
   b. $35,000
   c. $43,000
   d. $48,000

6. Which of the following would be recorded in the closing entry if partner A's share of net income is $35,000 and partner B's share of net income is $45,000? (pp. 601–603)
   a. Credit to A's Capital account for $40,000
   b. Credit to B's Capital account for $40,000
   c. Debit to A's Capital account for $35,000
   d. Debit to Income Summary for $80,000

7. Elliott, Barry, Ben, and Jerry formed a partnership agreeing to divide profits and losses in a 2:3:4:1 relationship, respectively. Assuming that the business earned a profit of $165,000, what are Elliott and Jerry's shares, respectively? (pp. 601–603)
   a. $33,000; $49,500
   b. $49,500; $16,500
   c. $60,000; $33,000
   d. $33,000; $16,500

8. Which of the following is included on a partnership balance sheet? (p. 601)
   a. A category for assets contributed by each partner
   b. A category for liabilities incurred by each partner
   c. An ending Drawing account balance for each partner
   d. An ending Capital account balance for each partner

9. Black and Blue formed a partnership, agreeing to share profits equally. After closing entries, the balances in their Capital accounts are $36,000 and $45,000, respectively. Blue sells her interest in the partnership to White for $52,000. Which of the following would be recorded on the books of the partnership? (pp. 604–605)
a. Credit White, Capital for $45,000
b. Debit Cash for $52,000
c. Credit White, Capital for $52,000
d. Debit Blue, Capital for $52,000

10. The net income agreement for Forsyth and Guilford states net income and net loss shall be divided in a ratio of beginning Capital balances. The net loss for the current year is $50,000. On January 1 of the current year, the Capital balances were as follows: Forsyth, $55,000; Guilford, $65,000. During the current year, Forsyth withdrew $40,000 and Guilford withdrew $25,000. What are the Capital balances for Forsyth and Guilford, respectively, as of December 31 of the current year? (pp. 601–603)
a. Debit $7,917; Credit $12,917
b. Credit $7,917; Credit $12,917
c. Debit $7,917; Debit $12,917
d. Debit $12,917; Credit $7,917

Quick Exercises

12-1. Wallingford, Albright, and Rowe have recently formed a partnership by investing $45,000, $60,000, and $35,000, respectively. They are considering several methods of allocating income and losses. (p. 601)

Requirement

1. Compute the partners' shares of profits and losses under each of the following plans:

a. Net income is $31,800 and the partners could not agree on a plan for net income/loss division.
b. The net loss is $18,000 and the partners agreed to share in the profits based on a 2:2:1 ratio. The agreement did not address losses.
c. Net income is $31,800 and the partners agreed to share profits based on the relationship of their initial Capital balances.
d. The net loss is $38,000 and the partners agreed to share profits and losses based on 15% to Wallingford, 50% to Albright, and 35% to Rowe.

Round all answers to the nearest whole dollar.

Item	Wallingford	Albright	Rowe	Total
a.	$ 10,600	$ 10,600	$ 10,600	$ 31,800
b.	$ (7,200)	$ (7,200)	$ (3,600)	$ (18,000)
c.	$ 10,221	$ 13,629	$ 7,950	$ 31,800
d.	$ (5,700)	$ (19,000)	$ (13,300)	$ (38,000)

12-2. Browning and Douglas are partners who agree to admit Taylor to their partnership. Browning has a Capital balance of $51,000 and Douglas has a Capital balance of $70,000. Browning and Douglas share net income in the ratio of 2:8. Prepare journal entries to admit Taylor to the partnership based on the following independent agreements. Round all amounts to the nearest dollar. (p. 604)

a. Taylor invests $66,000 cash into the partnership for a 20% interest.
b. Taylor invests $66,000 cash into the partnership for a 30% interest.
c. Taylor purchases one-third of Browning's Capital for $25,000.
d. Taylor purchases one-half of Douglas's Capital for $32,000.

General Journal

Date	Accounts	Debit	Credit
a.	Cash	66,000	
	Browning, Capital		5,720
	Douglas, Capital		22,880
	Taylor, Capital		37,400

General Journal

Date	Accounts	Debit	Credit
b.	Cash	66,000	
	Browning, Capital		1,980
	Douglas, Capital		7,920
	Taylor, Capital		56,100

General Journal

Date	Accounts	Debit	Credit
c.	Browning, Capital	17,000	
	Taylor, Capital		17,000

General Journal

Date	Accounts	Debit	Credit
d.	Douglas, Capital	35,000	
	Taylor, Capital		35,000

Calculations:

a. $66,000 + $51,000 + $70,000 = $187,000 Total Capital
$187,000 \times 0.20 = $37,400 Taylor, Capital
$66,000 - $37,400 = $28,600 bonus to existing partners
$28,600 \times 0.20 = $5,720, Browning, Capital
$28,600 \times 0.80 = $22,880, Douglas, Capital

b. $187,000 (Total Capital) $\times$ 0.30 = $56,100, Taylor, Capital
$66,000 - $56,100 = $9,900, bonus to existing partners
$9,900 \times 0.20 = $1,980, Browning, Capital
$9,900 \times 0.80 = $7,920, Douglas, Capital

12-3. Peter, Paul, and Mary are partners in the Sing Song Company and share profits and losses in a ratio of 4:4:2, respectively. Mary has been contemplating retirement. The partners' current Capital account balances, after closing entries, are $49,000, $98,000, and $147,000, respectively. The new net income agreement for Peter and Paul will be 4:2. (p. 609)

Requirement

1. Journalize the following transactions involving the retirement of Mary. Round to the nearest dollar if necessary.

a. The partners agree to revalue the assets. Land with a cost of $90,000 has a current market value of $127,000.

b. Inventory with a cost of $50,000 has a current market value of $35,000.

c. After the assets are revalued, the partnership agrees to give Mary $75,000 cash and a note payable for $65,000.

	Date	Accounts	Debit	Credit
		General Journal		
a.		Land	37,000	
		Peter, Capital		14,800
		Paul, Capital		14,800
		Mary, Capital		7,400

	Date	Accounts	Debit	Credit
		General Journal		
b.		Peter, Capital	6,000	
		Paul, Capital	6,000	
		Mary, Capital	3,000	
		Inventory		15,000

	Date	Accounts	Debit	Credit
		General Journal		
c.		Mary, Capital	151,400	
		Peter, Capital		7,600
		Paul, Capital		3,800
		Cash		75,000
		Note Payable		65,000

Calculations:

a. $127,000 − $90,000 = $37,000
$37,000 × 0.40 = $14,800 allocated to Peter and Paul, Capital
$37,000 × 0.20 = $7,400 allocated to Mary, Capital

b. $50,000 − $35,000 = $15,000
$15,000 × 0.40 = $6,000 allocated to Peter and Paul, Capital
$15,000 × 0.20 = $3,000 allocated to Mary, Capital

c. $147,000 + $7,400 − $3,000 = $151,400 Mary, Capital
$151,400 − $75,000 − $65,000 = $11,400 bonus to Peter and Paul
$11,400 × (4/6) = $7,600 allocated to Peter, Capital
$11,400 × (2/6) = $3,800 allocated to Paul, Capital

12-4.   Chandler, Cherry, and Cline are partners in the CCC Company. They share profits and losses in a 3:5:2 ratio and have just closed their books for the period. The current balances in their Capital accounts are $63,000, $49,000, and $94,000, respectively. Chandler has decided to withdraw from the partnership. Prior to the withdrawal of Chandler, the partners agreed that the assets need to be revalued. Land with a cost of $55,000 has a current market value of $88,000. Inventory with a cost of $75,000 has a current market value of $60,000. Cherry and Cline have agreed to share net income in a 2:3 ratio. (pp. 608–611)

Requirements

1. Prepare the journal entries required to revalue the assets.

General Journal				
Date	Accounts		Debit	Credit
1a.	Land		33,000	
	Chandler, Capital			9,900
	Cherry, Capital			16,500
	Cline, Capital			6,600

General Journal				
Date	Accounts		Debit	Credit
1b.	Chandler, Capital		4,500	
	Cherry, Capital		7,500	
	Cline, Capital		3,000	
	Inventory			15,000

2. Journalize the withdrawal of Chandler under each of the following independent assumptions:

    a. The partnership gives cash to Chandler equal to his Capital balance.
    b. The partnership gives $76,000 cash to Chandler.
    c. The partnership gives $56,000 cash to Chandler.

General Journal				
Date	Accounts		Debit	Credit
2a.	Chandler, Capital		68,400	
	Cash			68,400

General Journal				
Date	Accounts		Debit	Credit
2b.	Chandler, Capital		68,400	
	Cherry, Capital		3,040	
	Cline, Capital		4,560	
	Cash			76,000

General Journal				
Date	Accounts		Debit	Credit
2c.	Chandler, Capital		68,400	
	Cherry, Capital			4,960
	Cline, Capital			7,440
	Cash			56,000

Calculations:

    1a. $88,000 − $55,000 = $33,000
         $33,000 × 3/10 = $9,900
         $33,000 × 5/10 = $16,500
         $33,000 × 2/10 = $6,600

1b. $75,000 - 60,000 = 15,000$
$15,000 \times 3/10 = 4,500$
$15,000 \times 5/10 = 7,500$
$15,000 \times 2/10 = 3,000$
2a. $(63,000 + 9,900 - 4,500) = 68,400$
2b. $(76,000 - 68,400) \times 2/5 = 3,040$
$(76,000 - 68,400) \times 3/5 = 4,560$
2c. $68,400 - 56,000 = 12,400$
$12,400 \times 2/5 = 4,960$
$12,400 \times 3/5 = 7,440$

12-5. On August 1, 2008, Wheat, Bran, and Oats agree to liquidate their partnership. Wheat has a Capital balance of $90,000, Bran has a Capital balance of $37,500, and Oats has a Capital balance of $30,000. The partners share net income/net loss in a ratio of 4:3:3. Accounts payable amount to $60,000. Assets are shown on the balance sheet at $40,000 of cash and $177,500 of noncash assets. All the noncash assets are sold for $188,000. (pp. 611–613)

Requirement

1. Journalize the following:

   a. Sell the noncash assets.
   b. Pay the liabilities.
   c. Distribute the remaining cash to the partners.

		General Journal	Debit	Credit
	Date	Accounts		
a.		Cash	188,000	
		Wheat, Capital		4,200
		Bran, Capital		3,150
		Oats, Capital		3,150
		Noncash Assets		177,500

		General Journal	Debit	Credit
	Date	Accounts		
b.		Liabilities	60,000	
		Cash		60,000

		General Journal	Debit	Credit
	Date	Accounts		
c.		Wheat, Capital	94,200	
		Bran, Capital	40,650	
		Oats, Capital	33,150	
		Cash		168,000

Calculations:

   a. $188,000 - 177,500 = 10,500$
   $10,500 \times 4/10 = 4,200$
   $10,500 \times 3/10 = 3,150$
   c. $90,000 + 4,200 = 94,200$
   $37,500 + 3,150 = 40,650$
   $30,000 + 3,150 = 33,150$

Do It Yourself! Question 1 Solutions

Requirement

1. Suppose Waters were to admit River as a partner by selling him a 30% interest for $70,000 cash. Compute River's Capital balance and journalize his investment. What are the Capital balances for each partner after the investment is made?

Capital before purchase ($30,000 + $90,000)	$120,000
River's investment in capital	70,000
Total capital after purchase	$190,000

River Kline, Capital after investment:

$$30\% \times \$190,000 = \$57,000$$

Capital shared by original partners Brooke and Rainer:

$$\$190,000 - \$57,000 = \$133,000$$

Brooke Daniels, Capital balance:

$$\$133,000 \times 25\% = \$33,250$$

Rainer Linfoot, Capital balance:

$$\$133,000 \times 75\% = \$99,750$$

Cash		70,000	
	River Kline, Capital		57,000
	Brooke Daniels, Capital ($33,250 − $30,000)		3,250
	Ranier Linfoot, Capital ($99,750 − $90,000)		9,750

Before Transaction		After Transaction	
Brooke Daniels, capital	$ 30,000	Brooke Daniels, capital	$ 33,250
Rainer Linfoot, capital	90,000	Rainer Linfoot, capital	99,750
		River Kline, capital	57,000
Total capital	$120,000	Total capital	$190,000

2. (Ignoring Requirement 1) Suppose instead Brooke Daniels sold her entire interest to River for $50,000. Journalize the transfer of ownership. What are the Capital balances for each partner after the transfer is made?

River Kline, Capital		30,000	
Brooke Daniels, Capital			30,000

Before Transaction		After Transaction	
Brooke Daniels, capital	$ 30,000	River Kline, capital	$ 30,000
Rainer Linfoot, capital	90,000	Rainer Linfoot, capital	90,000
Total capital	$120,000	Total capital	$120,000

3. Assume that River was not admitted to the partnership. During 2008, Waters earned $80,000 of net income (in cash). How much profit is allocated to each partner (Brooke and Rainer)?

$$\text{Brooke is allocated } 25\% \times \$80,000 = \$20,000 \text{ of profit.}$$
$$\text{Rainer is allocated } 75\% \times \$80,000 = \$60,000 \text{ of profit.}$$

After this allocation, Waters has the following balance sheet:

Cash	$180,000	Liabilities	$ 80,000
Other assets	100,000	Brooke Daniels, capital	50,000
		Rainer Linfoot, capital	150,000
Total assets	$280,000	Total liabilities and capital	$280,000

Adjusted Cash balance:

$$\$100,000 + \$80,000 = \$180,000$$

Adjusted Brooke Daniels, Capital balance:

$$\$30,000 + \$20,000 = \$50,000$$

Adjusted Ranier Linfoot, Capital balance:

$$\$90,000 + \$60,000 = \$150,000$$

4. (Continuing on from Requirement 3) On January 1, 2009, Waters Partners was liquidated. All noncash assets were sold for $150,000, after which all liabilities were paid. How much does each partner receive upon liquidation?

$$\text{``Gain''} = \$150,000 - \$100,000 = \$50,000$$

Jan. 1	Cash	150,000	
	Other Assets		100,000
	Brooke Daniels, Capital (25% × $50,000)		12,500
	Ranier Linfoot, Capital (75% × $50,000)		37,500

Jan. 1	Liabilities	80,000	
	Cash		80,000

After these transactions, Brooke has a Capital balance of:

$$\$50,000 + \$12,500 = \$62,500$$

Rainer has a Capital balance of:

$$\$150,000 + \$37,500 = \$187,500$$

Brooke receives $62,500 cash and Rainer receives $187,500 cash on liquidation.

The Power of Practice

For more practice using the skills learned in this chapter, visit MyAccountingLab. There you will find algorithmically generated questions that are based on these Demo Docs and your main textbook's Review and Assess Your Progress sections.

Go to MyAccountingLab and follow these steps:

1. Direct your URL to www.myaccountinglab.com.
2. Log in using your name and password.
3. Click the MyAccountingLab link.
4. Click Study Plan in the left navigation bar.
5. From the table of contents, select Chapter 12, Partnerships.
6. Click a link to work tutorial exercises.

13 Corporations: Paid-In Capital and the Balance Sheet

You probably already know that you can purchase shares of a company's stock as an investment. CNBC shows the trading price of various stocks as they take place and the daily prices are reported in your financial newspapers. Much of the trading taking place is between investors rather than from the issuing corporation.

One way that a corporation issues its shares of stock is in an initial public offering (IPO). A recent popular IPO is Google. Google was doing business for six years before its founders took the company public in August 2004. The IPO provided investors an opportunity to purchase Google stock at a stated offer price of $85 a share. The market price of the stock rose quickly in trading and a year and a half after the IPO, the stock traded at over $300 per share. The cash received from the sale of the Google stock and the shareholders' equity interest were recorded on the books of Google Corporation. In this chapter, we will see how to account for the equity transactions of a corporation.

Learning Objectives

1 Identify the characteristics of a corporation.

As a **separate legal entity**, a corporation can enter into contracts, own assets in its own name, and be sued. The owners of the corporation are the stockholders. Shares of stock can be transferred to others without affecting the operation of the business. *No mutual agency* means that the owners of a corporation (stockholders) cannot commit or obligate the corporation. Stockholders are not personally liable for the obligations of the corporation. The most that a stockholder can lose is the amount invested. This is known as *limited liability*. These are some of the characteristics of a corporation. *Review these and other characteristics in your textbook, and take note of Exhibit 13-1 (p. 639) for a list of advantages and disadvantages of the corporate form of business.*

2 Record the issuance of stock.

When a company incorporates, the **par** or **stated value**, if any, will be indicated in the articles of incorporation. It is usually a nominal amount assigned to a share of stock that represents the minimum legal stated capital and does not indicate the value or worth of the stock. When the stock is sold by the corporation, the Common Stock account is credited for the par or stated value. Usually, the stock is sold above par, which is considered a premium. The excess of the stock sales price over the par or stated value is the amount credited to the **Paid-In Capital in Excess of Par** account. *Review the accounting for stock issuances under "Issuing Common Stock" in the main text.*

 Prepare the stockholders' equity section of a corporation's balance sheet.

The equity accounts are shown in the Stockholders' Equity section in the following order:

• Preferred Stock

• Common Stock

• Paid-In Capital in Excess of Par

• Retained Earnings

Review the Stockholders' Equity section of the balance sheet in Exhibit 13-7 (p. 650).

4 **Account for cash dividends.**

If the board of directors declares dividends, Retained Earnings is debited and Dividends Payable is credited. On the date of payment, the Liability is debited (reduced); Cash is also credited (reduced). *Read "Account for Cash Dividends" in the main text to review the dividend dates and learn the difference between cumulative and noncumulative preferred stock.*

5 **Use different stock values in decision making.**

Market value is the current price at which the stock is being offered for sale in the market. This value is of prime importance to investors. **Book value** indicates the amount of net assets that each common shareholder would receive if the assets were sold for the amount reported on the balance sheet. *Review the calculations of book value under "Different Values of Stock" in the main text.*

6 **Evaluate return on assets and return on stockholders' equity.**

Ratios to assess profitability include the rate of return on total assets and return on stockholders' equity. The rate of return on total assets indicates the amount of profitability per dollar of assets invested (net income + interest expense/average total assets). The rate of return on common stockholders' equity indicates the amount of profitability per dollar of common equity (net income − preferred dividends/average common stockholders' equity). Higher returns for both ratios are more favorable.

7 **Account for the income tax of a corporation.**

There may be differences between pretax income on the income statement and taxable income on the income tax return for a corporation. The income tax expense on the income statement is based on the pretax income on the income statement. However, the income tax payable liability on the balance sheet is based on the taxable income on the tax return. The difference between these two amounts results in a *deferred tax asset* or *deferred tax liability.*

Demo Doc 1

Common Stock

Learning Objectives 2, 3, 5, 6

Jack Inc. had the following information at December 31, 2008:

Stockholder's Equity	
Common Stock, 1,600,000 authorized, 350,000 issued and outstanding shares	$ 437,500
Additional Paid-In Capital	787,500
Retained Earnings	4,200,000
Total Stockholder's Equity	$5,425,000

Requirements

1. What are Jack's two main sources of corporate capital?

2. What is the par value per share of the common stock?

3. On average, what was the original issue price per share of common stock?

4. On February 12, 2009, Jack issued another 20,000 common shares for $5 cash per share. Journalize this transaction.

5. Jack earned net income of $150,000 and paid no dividends in 2009. There were no other equity transactions in 2009. Prepare the stockholder's equity section of Jack's balance sheet on December 31, 2009.

6. Calculate Jack's return on equity and book value per share for 2009.

Demo Doc 1 Solutions

Requirement 1

 Identify the characteristics of a corporation

What are Jack's two main sources of corporate capital?

Part 1	Part 2	Part 3	Part 4	Part 5	Part 6	Demo Doc Complete

Corporate capital is another term for shareholder's equity.

Jack has paid-in capital. This is money that has been received from the stockholders. Jack also has retained earnings. This represents profits earned on the stockholders' behalf (that have not yet been distributed as dividends).

Every corporation has these two sources of capital.

Requirement 2

Use different stock values in decision making

What is the par value per share of the common stock?

Part 1	**Part 2**	Part 3	Part 4	Part 5	Part 6	Demo Doc Complete

Common Stock and Preferred Stock accounts hold *only* the par value of the *issued* shares. So the $437,500 in the Common Stock account represents the par value of *all* the issued shares.

$$\frac{\text{Par value}}{\text{per share}} = \frac{\text{Common stock balance}}{\text{Number of issued common shares}}$$

$$\frac{\text{Par value}}{\text{per share}} = \frac{\$437,500}{350,000 \text{ shares}}$$

$$= \mathbf{\$1.25} \text{ per share}$$

Requirement 3

Use different stock values in decision making

On average, what was the original issue price per share of common stock?

Part 1	Part 2	**Part 3**	Part 4	Part 5	Part 6	Demo Doc Complete

When stock is issued for cash, the Cash account increases (a debit) for cash received. The Common Stock account increases (a credit) for the par value and the excess is Additional Paid-In Capital. Because the selling price per share is almost always more than the par value, this excess balancing amount to Additional Paid-In Capital is usually an increase (a credit).

We know that total debits must equal total credits for any transaction. In this case, the debit is the cash received and the credits are the increases to Common Stock and Additional Paid-In Capital. This means that:

$$\text{Cash received from share issuance} = \text{Common Stock} + \text{Additional Paid-In Capital}$$

So the total cash received from issuance of the common shares is:

$$\$1.25 \text{ par} \times 350,000 \text{ shares} = \$437,500$$
$$\$437,500 + \$787,500 = \$1,225,000$$

This amount represents all 350,000 issued shares.

$$\$1,225,000/350,000 \text{ shares} = \textbf{\$3.50} \text{ cash received per share}$$

The balancing credit to Additional Paid-In Capital is ($3.50 received − $1.25 par) $2.25 × 350,000 shares = $787,500 additional cash paid.

Requirement 4

2 Record the issuance of stock

On February 12, 2009, Jack issued another 20,000 common shares for $5 cash per share. Journalize this transaction.

Part 1	Part 2	Part 3	**Part 4**	Part 5	Part 6	Demo Doc Complete

Cash increases (a debit) by $5 × 20,000 = $100,000.

Common Stock increases (a credit) by the par value of the new shares:

$$\$1.25 \times 20,000 = \$25,000$$

Additional Paid-In Capital is the excess cash paid:

$$(\$5 - \$1.25) \times \$3.75$$
$$\$3.75 \times 20,000 \text{ shares} = \$75,000$$

This is the balancing amount in the journal entry.

		Cash ($5 × 20,000)	100,000	
		Common Stock ($1.25 × 20,000)		25,000
		Additional Paid-In Capital (to balance)		75,000

Requirement 5

3 Prepare the
stockholders' equity
section of a
corporation balance
sheet

Jack earned net income of $150,000 and paid no dividends in 2009. There were no other equity transactions in 2009. Prepare the stockholder's equity section of Jack's balance sheet on December 31, 2009.

Part 1	Part 2	Part 3	Part 4	**Part 5**	Part 6	Demo Doc Complete

Because of the stock issuance in Requirement 4, the number of outstanding common shares has increased to:

$$350,000 \text{ shares} + 20,000 \text{ shares} = 370,000 \text{ shares}$$

This must be shown for Common Stock as part of its descriptive line on the balance sheet.

The dollar amount in the Common Stock account has increased to:

$$\$437,500 + \$25,000 = \$462,500$$

The other impact of this transaction on stockholder's equity was to increase Additional Paid-In Capital to:

$$\$787,500 + \$75,000 = \$862,500$$

The net income earned by Jack will increase Retained Earnings to:

$$\$4,200,000 + \$150,000 = \$4,350,000$$

These new amounts create a new total stockholder's equity of $5,675,000.

Stockholder's Equity	
Common Stock, 1,600,000 authorized, 370,000 issued and outstanding shares	$ 462,500
Additional Paid-In Capital	862,500
Retained Earnings	4,350,000
Total Stockholder's Equity	$5,675,000

Requirement 6

6 Evaluate return on assets and return on stockholders' equity

Calculate Jack's return on equity and book value per share for 2009.

Part 1	Part 2	Part 3	Part 4	Part 5	**Part 6**	Demo Doc Complete

$$\text{Return on stockholder's equity} = \frac{\text{Net income} - \text{Preferred dividends}}{\text{Average common stockholder's equity}}$$

Common stockholder's equity means the total stockholder's equity less the preferred equity (that is, less any preferred stock or any additional paid-in capital relating to preferred stock).

Average common stockholder's equity is the *mathematical average* of the beginning and ending balances in Common Stockholder's Equity (that is, [beginning balance + ending balance]/2).

So using the data from this question:

$$\text{Return on stockholder's equity} = \frac{\$150,000 - \$0}{(\$5,425,000 + \$5,675,000)/2}$$

$$\text{Return on stockholders' equity} = 0.027 = 2.7\%$$

$$\text{Book value per share} = \frac{\text{Common stockholders' equity}}{\text{Number of common shares outstanding}}$$

Using the data from this question:

$$\text{Book value per share} = \frac{\$5,675,000}{370,000 \text{ shares}}$$

$$= \mathbf{\$15.34} \text{ per share}$$

Part 1	Part 2	Part 3	Part 4	Part 5	Part 6	**Demo Doc Complete**

Demo Doc 2

Preferred Stock

Learning Objectives 2, 4

Jill Co. issued 25,000, 6%, $100 par cumulative preferred shares on January 1, 2008, for $120 cash per share. Jill had never issued preferred shares before this date. Jill paid the following cash dividends (in total, to *all* shares):

2008	$120,000
2009	$160,000
2010	$200,000

Requirements

1. Journalize the issuance of the preferred shares on January 1, 2008, and the payment of the preferred share dividends in 2008 (assuming the dividends were declared and paid on the same day).

2. How much in dividends is Jill supposed to pay to the preferred shareholders each year?

3. Did Jill pay all of the required dividends in each year? If not, what happens to the amount not paid? How much in dividends did the preferred and common shareholders receive each year?

Demo Doc 2 Solutions

 Record the issuance of stock

 Account for cash dividends

Requirement 1

Journalize the issuance of the preferred shares on January 1, 2008, and the payment of the preferred share dividends in 2008 (assuming the dividends were declared and paid on the same day).

Part 1	Part 2	Part 3	Demo Doc Complete

The issuance of preferred shares is the same as the issuance of common shares, except for the account title.

Cash is increased (a debit) by:

$$\$120 \times 25{,}000 = \$3{,}000{,}000$$

Preferred Stock is increased (a credit) by the par value of the new shares:

$$\$100 \times 25{,}000 = \$2{,}500{,}000$$

Additional Paid-In Capital is the excess cash paid:

$$(\$120 - \$100 \text{ par}) = \$20 \times 25{,}000 \text{ shares} = \$500{,}000$$

This is the balancing amount in the journal entry.

Cash ($120 × 25,000)	3,000,000	
Additional Paid-In Capital (to balance)		500,000
Preferred Stock ($100 × 25,000)		2,500,000

When dividends are paid, Retained Earnings is decreased because the shareholders are removing some of their capital from the company. So Retained Earnings is decreased (a debit) by $120,000.

Cash is also decreased (a credit) by $120,000.

Retained Earnings	120,000	
Cash		120,000

Account for cash dividends

Requirement 2

How much in dividends is Jill supposed to pay to the preferred shareholders each year?

Part 1	Part 2	Part 3	Demo Doc Complete

Each year, every preferred share is *supposed* to receive:

$$\text{``Required'' preferred share dividends} = \text{Par value per share} \times \text{Dividend percentage}$$

First, we should calculate the "required" annual dividends per share. In this case, it is:

$$\$100 \times 6\% = \$6 \text{ per share}$$

Because there are 25,000 outstanding preferred shares, this works out to $6 × 25,000 = **$150,000** in dividends per year for all preferred shares.

Requirement 3

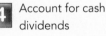

Account for cash dividends

Did Jill pay all of the required dividends in each year? If not, what happens to the amount not paid? How much in dividends did the preferred and common shareholders receive each year?

Part 1	Part 2	Part 3	Demo Doc Complete

2008

Because $120,000 is less than the "required" $150,000, we know that Jill did *not* pay all of the required dividends in 2008.

The preferred shares only received:

$$\$120{,}000/25{,}000 \text{ shares} = \$4.80 \text{ per share}$$

The difference of $150,000 − $120,000 = $30,000 is <u>dividends in arrears</u>. This amount is *not* recorded in a transaction because it has not yet been declared and, therefore, is not a liability. Dividends in arrears do *not* appear on the balance sheet. However, they are disclosed in a *note* to the financial statements.

Because the full $150,000 was not paid, the entire $120,000 goes to the preferred shareholders as dividends. The common shareholders get no dividends in 2008.

2009

For 2009, Jill must not only pay the $150,000 annual "requirement" but first must also "catch up" on the dividends in arrears of $30,000 from 2008.

So in order to completely fulfill her obligation to the preferred shareholders, Jill must pay $30,000 + $150,000 = $180,000 in dividends to the preferred shareholders.

Because $160,000 is less than $180,000, we know that Jill did *not* pay all of the required dividends in 2009.

The difference of $180,000 − $160,000 = $20,000 is <u>dividends in arrears</u>.

Because the full $180,000 was not paid, the entire $160,000 goes to the preferred shareholders as dividends. The common shareholders get no dividends in 2009.

2010

In 2010, Jill is *supposed* to pay the annual $150,000 of dividends *plus* the $20,000 dividends in arrears from 2009 for a total of $170,000.

Because $200,000 is greater than $170,000, we know that Jill did pay all of the required dividends in 2010.

The $170,000 shown above goes to the preferred shareholders, while the rest ($200,000 − $170,000 = $30,000) goes to the common shareholders.

Part 1	Part 2	Part 3	**Demo Doc Complete**

Demo Doc 3

Joe Danson owns all outstanding common shares of Joseph Corp. The corporation earned net income before tax of $80,000 in 2008 and has an income tax rate of 40%.

Requirements

1. Is Joe Danson personally liable for the income taxes owed by Joseph Corp.?

2. Calculate the amount of income tax expense that will appear on Joseph Corp.'s 2008 income statement.

Demo Doc 3 Solutions

Identify the characteristics of a corporation

Requirement 1

Is Joe Danson personally liable for the income taxes owed by Joseph Corp.?

Part 1	Part 2	Demo Doc Complete

Corporations are liable for *their own* taxes. Even as the sole owner, Joe is not liable for the taxes of the corporation.

Requirement 2

Account for the income tax of a corporation

Calculate the amount of income tax expense that will appear on Joseph Corp.'s 2008 income statement.

Part 1	Part 2	Demo Doc Complete

$$\text{Income tax expense}$$
$$= \text{Net income before tax} \times \text{Tax rate}$$
$$= \$80,000 \times 40\% = \$32,000$$

Part 1	Part 2	**Demo Doc Complete**

Quick Practice Questions

True/False

_____ 1. Stockholders in a corporation are personally liable for the debts of the corporation.

_____ 2. Most corporations have continuous lives regardless of changes in the ownership of their stock.

_____ 3. Par value is an arbitrary amount assigned by a company to a share of its stock.

_____ 4. A credit balance in Retained Earnings is referred to as a deficit.

_____ 5. When a corporation sells par value stock at an amount greater than par value, other income is reported on the income statement.

_____ 6. Dividends become a liability of the corporation on the payment date.

_____ 7. The owners of cumulative preferred stock must receive all dividends in arrears plus the current year's dividends before the common stockholders get a dividend.

_____ 8. A stock's market price is the price for which a person could buy or sell a share of the stock.

_____ 9. The book value of a stock is the amount of owners' equity on the company's books for each share of its stock.

_____10. The rate of return on total assets measures a company's success in using assets to earn income for those financing the business.

Multiple Choice

1. **What is the document called that is used by a state to grant permission to form a corporation?**
   a. Charter
   b. Proxy
   c. Stock certificate
   d. Bylaw agreement

2. **Which of the following statements describing a corporation is true?**
   a. Stockholders are the creditors of a corporation.
   b. A corporation is subject to greater governmental regulation than a proprietorship or a partnership.
   c. When ownership of a corporation changes, the corporation terminates.
   d. Stockholders own the business and manage its day-to-day operations.

3. **Which of the following best describes paid-in capital?**
   a. Investments by the stockholders of a corporation
   b. Investments by the creditors of a corporation
   c. Capital that the corporation has earned through profitable operations
   d. All of the above

4. **Which of the following best describes retained earnings?**
   a. It is classified as a liability on the corporate balance sheet.
   b. It does not appear on any financial statement.

c. It represents capital that the corporation has earned through profitable operations.

d. It represents investments by the stockholders of a corporation.

5. **What individual(s) has the authority to obligate the corporation to pay dividends?**
   a. Total stockholders
   b. The board of directors
   c. The president of the company
   d. The chief executive officer

6. **A corporation issues 1,800 shares of $10 par value common stock in exchange for land with a current market value of $23,000. How would this be recorded in the Land account?**
   a. Debited for $23,000
   b. Credited for $18,000
   c. Credited for $20,000
   d. Debited for $18,000

7. **Which of the following would be recorded for the issuance of 55,000 shares of no-par common stock at $13.50 per share?**
   a. Credit to Paid-In Capital in Excess of No-Par Value—Common for $742,500
   b. Credit to Common Stock for $742,500
   c. Credit to Cash for $742,500
   d. Debit to Paid-In Capital in Excess of No-Par Value—Common for $742,500

8. **Which of the following is true for dividends?**
   a. Dividends are a distribution of cash to the stockholders.
   b. Dividends decrease both the assets and the total stockholders' equity of the corporation.
   c. Dividends increase retained earnings.
   d. Both (a) and (b) are correct.

9. **Dividends on cumulative preferred stock of $2,500 are in arrears for 2008. During 2009, the total dividends declared amount to $10,000. There are 6,000 shares of $10 par, 10% cumulative preferred stock outstanding and 10,000 shares of $5 par common stock outstanding. What is the total amount of dividends payable to each class of stock in 2009?**
   a. $5,000 to preferred, $5,000 to common
   b. $6,000 to preferred, $4,000 to common
   c. $8,500 to preferred, $1,500 to common
   d. $10,000 to preferred, $0 to common

10. **Which of the following is true about dividends in arrears?**
    a. They are a liability on the balance sheet.
    b. They are dividends passed on cumulative preferred stock.
    c. They are dividends passed on noncumulative preferred stock.
    d. They are dividends passed on common stock.

Quick Exercises

13-1. Journalize the following transactions:

a. **Firm Body Corporation sells 12,000 shares of $10 par common stock for $13.00 per share.**

b. **Firm Body Corporation sells 5,000 shares of $50 par, 10% cumulative preferred stock for $59 per share.**

c. Received a building with a market value of $115,000 and issued 6,400 shares of $10 par common stock in exchange.

d. Firm Body Corporation reports net income of $66,000 at the end of its first year of operations.

General Journal				
Date	Accounts		Debit	Credit

General Journal				
Date	Accounts		Debit	Credit

General Journal				
Date	Accounts		Debit	Credit

General Journal				
Date	Accounts		Debit	Credit

13-2. The following is a list of stockholders' equity accounts appearing on the balance sheet for O'Neil Corporation on December 31, 2008:

Common stock, $10 par value	$300,000
Paid-in capital in excess of par—common	200,000
Retained earnings	225,000
Preferred stock, $50 par value	125,000
Paid-in capital in excess of par—preferred	30,000

Determine the following:

a. How many shares of preferred stock have been issued?

b. What was the average issuance price of the preferred stock per share?

c. How many shares of common stock have been issued?

d. What is total paid-in capital?

e. What is total stockholders' equity?

13-3. Bowen Corporation organized on January 1, 2008. Bowen Corporation has authorization for 90,000 shares of $10 par value common stock. As of December 31, 2008, Bowen has issued 50,000 shares of its common stock at an average issuance price of $15. Bowen also has authorization for 50,000 shares of 5%, $50 par value, noncumulative preferred stock. As of December 31, 2008, Bowen has issued 12,000 shares of preferred stock at an average issuance price of $68 per share. Bowen reports net income of $47,000 for its first year of operations ended December 31, 2008.

Requirement

1. Prepare the stockholders' equity section of the balance sheet for Bowen Corporation dated December 31, 2008.

13-4. Following is the stockholders' equity section of the balance sheet for Watson Corporation as of December 1, 2009:

Preferred stock, $100 par, 6% cumulative, 10,000 shares authorized, 7,500 shares issued	$ 750,000
Common stock, $10 par, 200,000 shares authorized, 130,000 shares issued	1,300,000
Paid-in capital in excess of par—common	520,000
Total paid-in capital	$2,570,000
Retained earnings	450,000
Total stockholders' equity	$3,020,000

Watson Corporation reports the following transactions for December 2009:

Dec. 5 **Declared the required cash dividend on the preferred stock and a $0.40 dividend on the common stock.**

  20 **Paid the dividends declared on December 5.**

Requirements

1. Journalize the transactions.

General Journal			
Date	Accounts	Debit	Credit

General Journal			
Date	Accounts	Debit	Credit

2. What is the total stockholders' equity after posting the entries?

13-5. Sparks Corporation has gathered the following data for the current year:

Net Income	$40,000
Interest Expense	6,000
Income Tax Expense	12,500
Preferred Dividends	3,600

Balance Sheet Data	Beginning of Year	End of Year
Current assets	$ 68,000	$ 81,000
Current liabilities	41,000	39,000
Plant assets	340,000	365,000
Long-term liabilities	100,000	90,000
Common stockholders' equity	217,000	267,000
Preferred stockholders' equity	50,000	50,000

Requirements

1. Calculate return on assets.

2. Calculate return on equity.

3. Comment on how these measures are used.

Do It Yourself! Question 1

Common Stock

Dinner Co. had the following information at December 31, 2008:

Stockholder's Equity	
Common Stock, 500,000 authorized, 50,000 issued and outstanding shares	$100,000
Additional Paid-In Capital	50,000
Retained Earnings	400,000
Total Stockholder's Equity	$550,000

Requirements

 Use different stock values in decision making

1. What is the par value per share of the common stock?

 Use different stock values in decision making

2. On average, what was the original issue price per share of the common stock?

2 Record the issuance of stock

3. On January 9, 2009, Dinner issued another 10,000 common shares for $4 cash per share. Journalize this transaction.

General Journal				
Date	Accounts		Debit	Credit

Do It Yourself! Question 2

Preferred Stock

Lunch Corp. issued 5,000, 8%, $20 par cumulative preferred shares on January 1, 2008, for $25 cash per share. Lunch had never had preferred shares before this date. On December 31, 2008, Lunch paid $5,000 in cash dividends to its shareholders. On December 31, 2009, Lunch paid $15,000 in cash dividends to its shareholders.

Requirements

1. Journalize the issuance of the preferred shares on January 1, 2008.

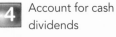 Record the issuance of stock

General Journal				
Date	Accounts		Debit	Credit

Account for cash dividends

2. How much in dividends is Lunch supposed to pay to the preferred shareholders each year?

Account for cash dividends

3. How much of the $5,000 paid as dividends in 2008 went to the preferred and common shareholders?

Account for cash dividends

4. How much of the $15,000 paid as dividends in 2009 went to the preferred and common shareholders?

Quick Practice Solutions

True/False

   F   1. Stockholders in a corporation are personally liable for the debts of the corporation.

           False—Stockholders are *not* personally liable for the debts of the corporation. (p. 638)

   T   2. Most corporations have continuous lives regardless of changes in the ownership of their stock. (p. 638)

   T   3. Par value is an arbitrary amount assigned by a company to a share of its stock. (p. 645)

   F   4. A credit balance in Retained Earnings is referred to as a deficit.

           False—A *debit* balance in Retained Earnings is referred to as a deficit. (p. 643)

   F   5. When a corporation sells par value stock at an amount greater than par value, other income is reported on the income statement.

           False—When a corporation sells par value stock at an amount greater than par value, paid-in capital in excess of par value is recorded. There is no effect on the income statement from a company's stock transactions. (p. 647)

   F   6. Dividends become a liability of the corporation on the payment date.

           False—Dividends become a liability of the corporation on the *declaration* date. (p. 654)

   T   7. The owners of cumulative preferred stock must receive all dividends in arrears plus the current year's dividends before the common stockholders get a dividend. (p. 656)

   T   8. A stock's market price is the price for which a person could buy or sell a share of the stock. (p. 657)

   T   9. The book value of a stock is the amount of owners' equity on the company's books for each share of its stock. (p. 657)

   T 10. The rate of return on total assets measures a company's success in using assets to earn income for those financing the business. (p. 659)

Multiple Choice

1. **What is the document called that is used by a state to grant permission to form a corporation?** (p. 638)
   a. Charter
   b. Proxy
   c. Stock certificate
   d. Bylaw agreement

2. **Which of the following statements describing a corporation is true?** (p. 639)
   a. Stockholders are the creditors of a corporation.
   b. A corporation is subject to greater governmental regulation than a proprietorship or a partnership.

c. When ownership of a corporation changes, the corporation terminates.

d. Stockholders own the business and manage its day-to-day operations.

3. **Which of the following best describes paid-in capital?** (p. 641)

    a. Investments by the stockholders of a corporation

    b. Investments by the creditors of a corporation

    c. Capital that the corporation has earned through profitable operations

    d. All of the above

4. **Which of the following best describes retained earnings?** (p. 641)

    a. It is classified as a liability on the corporate balance sheet.

    b. It does not appear on any financial statement.

    c. It represents capital that the corporation has earned through profitable operations.

    d. It represents investments by the stockholders of a corporation.

5. **What individual(s) has the authority to obligate the corporation to pay dividends?** (p. 654)

    a. Total stockholders

    b. The board of directors

    c. The president of the company

    d. The chief executive officer

6. **A corporation issues 1,800 shares of $10 par value common stock in exchange for land with a current market value of $23,000. How would this be recorded in the Land account?** (p. 648)

    a. Debited for $23,000

    b. Credited for $18,000

    c. Credited for $20,000

    d. Debited for $18,000

7. **Which of the following would be recorded for the issuance of 55,000 shares of no-par common stock at $13.50 per share?** (p. 648)

    a. Credit to Paid-In Capital in Excess of No-Par Value—Common for $742,500

    b. Credit to Common Stock for $742,500

    c. Credit to Cash for $742,500

    d. Debit Paid-In Capital in Excess of No-Par Value—Common for $742,500

8. **Which of the following is true for dividends?** (p. 654)

    a. Dividends are a distribution of cash to the stockholders.

    b. Dividends decrease both the assets and the total stockholders' equity of the corporation.

    c. Dividends increase retained earnings.

    d. Both (a) and (b) are correct.

9. **Dividends on cumulative preferred stock of $2,500 are in arrears for 2008. During 2009, the total dividends declared amount to $10,000. There are 6,000 shares of $10 par, 10% cumulative preferred stock outstanding and 10,000 shares of $5 par common stock outstanding. What is the total amount of dividends payable to each class of stock in 2009?** (pp. 654–657)

    a. $5,000 to preferred, $5,000 to common

    b. $6,000 to preferred, $4,000 to common

    c. $8,500 to preferred, $1,500 to common

    d. $10,000 to preferred, $0 to common

10. **Which of the following is true about dividends in arrears?** (p. 656)

    a. They are a liability on the balance sheet.

    b. They are dividends passed on cumulative preferred stock.

    c. They are dividends passed on noncumulative preferred stock.

    d. They are dividends passed on common stock.

Quick Exercise Solutions

13-1.   Journalize the following transactions. (pp. 645–650)

a. Firm Body Corporation sells 12,000 shares of $10 par common stock for $13.00 per share.

b. Firm Body Corporation sells 5,000 shares of $50 par, 10% cumulative preferred stock for $59 per share.

c. Received a building with a market value of $115,000 and issued 6,400 shares of $10 par common stock in exchange.

d. Firm Body Corporation reports net income of $66,000 at the end of its first year of operations.

	Date	Accounts	Debit	Credit
		General Journal		
a.		Cash	156,000	
		Common Stock		120,000
		Paid-In Capital in Excess of Par—Common		36,000

	Date	Accounts	Debit	Credit
		General Journal		
b.		Cash	295,000	
		Preferred Stock		250,000
		Paid-In Capital in Excess of Par—Preferred		45,000

	Date	Accounts	Debit	Credit
		General Journal		
c.		Building	115,000	
		Common Stock		64,000
		Paid-In Capital in Excess of Par—Common		51,000

	Date	Accounts	Debit	Credit
		General Journal		
d.		Income Summary	66,000	
		Retained Earnings		66,000

13-2.   The following is a list of stockholders' equity accounts appearing on the balance sheet for O'Neil Corporation on December 31, 2008:

Common stock, $10 par value	$300,000
Paid-in capital in excess of par—common	200,000
Retained earnings	225,000
Preferred stock, $50 par value	125,000
Paid-in capital in excess of par—preferred	30,000

Determine the following: (pp. 645–650)

a. How many shares of preferred stock have been issued?

$$\$125,000/\$50 = 2,500$$

b. What was the average issuance price of the preferred stock per share?

$$(\$125,000 + \$30,000)/2,500 = \$62$$

c. How many shares of common stock have been issued?

$$\$300,000/\$10 = 30,000$$

d. What is total paid-in capital?

$$\$300,000 + \$200,000 + \$125,000 + \$30,000 = \$655,000$$

e. What is total stockholders' equity?

$$\$655,000 + \$225,000 = \$880,000$$

13-3.   Bowen Corporation organized on January 1, 2008. Bowen Corporation has authorization for 90,000 shares of $10 par value common stock. As of December 31, 2008, Bowen has issued 50,000 shares of its common stock at an average issuance price of $15. Bowen also has authorization for 50,000 shares of 5%, $50 par value, noncumulative preferred stock. As of December 31, 2008, Bowen has issued 12,000 shares of preferred stock at an average issuance price of $68 per share. Bowen reports net income of $47,000 for its first year of operations ended December 31, 2008.

Prepare the stockholders' equity section of the balance sheet for Bowen Corporation dated December 31, 2008. (pp. 645–650)

Bowen Corporation Stockholders' Equity December 31, 2008	
Paid-in capital:	
Preferred stock, 5%, $50 par, 512,000 shares issued	$ 600,000
Paid-in capital in excess of par—preferred	216,000
Common stock, $10 par, 90,000 shares authorized, 50,000 shares issued	500,000
Paid-in capital in excess of par—common	250,000
Total paid-in capital	$1,566,000
Retained earnings	47,000
Total stockholders' equity	$1,613,000

13-4. Following is the stockholders' equity section of the balance sheet for Watson Corporation as of December 1, 2009:

Preferred stock, $100 par, 6% cumulative, 10,000 shares authorized, 7,500 shares issued	$ 750,000
Common stock, $10 par, 200,000 shares authorized, 130,000 shares issued	1,300,000
Paid-in capital in excess of par—common	520,000
Total paid-in capital	$2,570,000
Retained earnings	450,000
Total stockholders' equity	$3,020,000

Watson Corporation reports the following transactions for December 2009: (pp. 654–657)

Dec. 5 Declared the required cash dividend on the preferred stock and a $0.40 dividend on the common stock.

20 Paid the dividends declared on December 5.

Requirements

1. Journalize the transactions.

General Journal			
Date	Accounts	Debit	Credit
12/5/09	Retained Earnings	97,000	
	Dividends Payable		97,000

General Journal			
Date	Accounts	Debit	Credit
12/20/09	Dividends Payable	97,000	
	Cash		97,000

2. What is the total stockholders' equity after posting the entries?

$2,923,000 ($3,020,000 − $97,000)

13-5. Sparks Corporation has gathered the following data for the current year: (p. 659)

Net Income	$40,000
Interest Expense	6,000
Income Tax Expense	12,500
Preferred Dividends	3,600

Balance Sheet Data	Beginning of Year	End of Year
Current assets	$ 68,000	$ 81,000
Current liabilities	41,000	39,000
Plant assets	340,000	365,000
Long-term liabilities	100,000	90,000
Common stockholders' equity	217,000	267,000
Preferred stockholders' equity	50,000	50,000

Requirements

1. Calculate return on assets.

$40,000 + $6,000 = $46,000
$46,000/$427,000* = 10.8%

*$68,000 + $3,40,000 = $408,000
$81,000 + $365,000 = $446,000
$408,000 + $446,000 = $854,000
$854,000/2 = $427,000

2. Calculate return on equity.

$40,000 − $3,600 = $36,400
$36,400/$242,000* = 15.0%

*$217,000 + $267,000 = $484,000
$484,000/2 = $427,000

3. Comment on how these measures are used.

The return on assets is used as a standard profitability measure that shows the company's success in using its assets to generate income. It helps investors compare one company to another, especially within the same industry.

The return on equity is used as a standard profitability measure that shows the relationship between net income and average common stockholders' equity. The higher the rate of return, the more successful the company.

Do It Yourself! Question 1 Solutions

Requirements

1. What is the par value per share of the common stock?

$$\begin{array}{r} \text{Par value} \\ \text{per share} \end{array} = \frac{\$100{,}000}{50{,}000 \text{ shares}}$$

$$= \ \$2 \text{ per share}$$

2. On average, what was the original issue price per share of the common stock?

Total cash received from issuance of the common shares (par + additional paid-in capital):

$$\$100{,}000 + \$50{,}000 = \$150{,}000$$

$$\frac{\$150{,}000}{50{,}000 \text{ shares}} = \ \$3 \text{ cash received per share}$$

3. On January 9, 2009, Dinner issued another 10,000 common shares for $4 cash per share. Journalize this transaction.

Cash ($4 × 10,000)		40,000	
Additional Paid-In Capital (to balance)			20,000
Common Stock ($2 × 10,000)			20,000

$$\$4 \text{ paid} - \$2 \text{ par} \ = \ \$2 \text{ excess cash}$$

$$\$2 \text{ excess cash} \times 10{,}000 \text{ shares} \ = \ \text{Additional Paid-In Capital } \$20{,}000 \text{ balancing amount}$$

Do It Yourself! Question 2 Solutions

Requirements

1. Journalize the issuance of the preferred shares on January 1, 2008.

Cash ($25 × 5,000)	125,000	
Additional Paid-In Capital (to balance)		25,000
Common Stock ($20 × 5,000)		100,000

2. How much in dividends is Lunch supposed to pay to the preferred shareholders each year?

Preferred shareholders are *supposed* to receive:

$$\$20 \text{ par} \times 8\% = \$1.60 \text{ per share annually}$$

$$\$1.60 \times 5,000 = \textbf{\$8,000} \text{ dividends per year for all outstanding preferred shares}$$

3. How much of the $5,000 paid as dividends in 2008 went to the preferred and common shareholders?

The full $8,000 was not paid; therefore, the entire $5,000 goes to the preferred shareholders. Common shareholders get nothing.

$$\$8,000 - \$5,000 = \$3,000 \text{ of dividends in arrears}$$

4. How much of the $15,000 paid as dividends in 2009 went to the preferred and common shareholders?

Preferred shareholders received:

$$\$8,000 + \$3,000 = \$11,000$$

Common shareholders received:

$$\$15,000 - \$11,000 = \$4,000$$

The Power of Practice

For more practice using the skills learned in this chapter, visit MyAccountingLab. There you will find algorithmically generated questions that are based on these Demo Docs and your main textbook's Review and Assess Your Progress sections.

Go to MyAccountingLab and follow these steps:

1. Direct your URL to www.myaccountinglab.com.
2. Log in using your name and password.
3. Click the MyAccountingLab link.
4. Click Study Plan in the left navigation bar.
5. From the table of contents, select Chapter 13, Corporations: Paid-In Capital and the Balance Sheet.
6. Click a link to work tutorial exercises.

B Investments and International Operations

Demo Doc 1

Long-Term Investments

On January 1, 2008, Unity Corp. purchased the following investments for cash:

20,000 shares Lake Corp. stock	$60,000
4,000 shares Drop Corp. stock	$10,000

Both Lake and Drop have 50,000 common shares outstanding. During 2008, Lake and Drop had the following information:

	Net Income	Cash Dividends per Share	Market Price per Share at 12/31/08
Lake Corp.	$120,000	$0.70	$2.50
Drop Corp.	$ 60,000	$0.60	$3.00

Requirements

1. What kind of investments are these?

2. For each investment, journalize the following transactions for Unity Corp.:

a. Purchase of investment on January 1, 2008

b. Dividends received from the investments during 2008

c. Any adjustment for net income earned by the investment

d. Any adjustment for the investment's year-end market price

Demo Doc 1 Solutions

Requirement 1

What kind of investments are these?

Part 1	Part 2	Demo Doc Complete

In order to determine the investment type, we need to know what percentage of the company Unity holds.

$$\% \text{ Ownership} = \frac{\text{\# of shares held by investor company}}{\text{Total \# of outstanding common shares of investee company}}$$

$$\begin{array}{cc} \% \text{ Ownership of} \\ \text{Lake Corp.} \end{array} = \frac{20{,}000 \text{ shares}}{50{,}000 \text{ shares}}$$

$$= 40\%$$

An investment between 25% and 50% ownership is an **equity method** investment. The Lake Corp. shares are an equity method investment.

$$\begin{array}{cc} \% \text{ Ownership of} \\ \text{Drop Corp.} \end{array} = \frac{4{,}000 \text{ shares}}{50{,}000 \text{ shares}}$$

$$= 8\%$$

An investment less than 25% ownership is an **available-for-sale** investment. The Drop Corp. shares are an available-for-sale investment.

Requirement 2

For each investment, journalize the following transactions for Unity Corp.:

a. Purchase of investment on January 1, 2008

Part 1	Part 2	Demo Doc Complete

Lake Corp.

Cash is decreased (a credit) by $60,000.
Equity Method Investment—Lake Corp. is increased (a debit) by $60,000.

Equity Method Investment—Lake Corp.		60,000	
Cash			60,000

Drop Corp.

Cash is decreased (a credit) by $10,000.

Long-Term Available-for-Sale Investment—Drop Corp. is increased (a debit) by $10,000.

Long-Term Available-for-Sale Investment—Drop Corp.		10,000	
Cash			10,000

b. Dividends received from the investments during 2008

Lake Corp.

Cash is received, so it is increased (a debit) by:

$$\$0.70 \text{ per share} \times 20,000 \text{ shares} = \$14,000$$

Under the equity method, we are trying to capture changes in Lake Corp.'s *equity,* or more accurately, its *retained earnings.* It is as if Unity has purchased a piece of Lake's retained earnings. As Lake's retained earnings change in value, so does Unity's investment in Lake Corp.

When Lake Corp. pays a dividend, its retained earnings decrease. This means that the value of Unity's Lake Corp. Investment has also decreased (a debit) by $14,000.

Cash ($0.70 × 20,000)		14,000	
Equity Method Investment—Lake Corp.			14,000

Lake Corp. Investment

Jan. 1	60,000		
		14,000 dividends received	
Bal.	46,000		

Drop Corp.

Cash is received, so it is increased (a debit) by:

$$\$0.60 \text{ per share} \times 4,000 \text{ shares} = \$2,400$$

For available-for-sale investments, *Dividend Revenue* is also increased (a credit) by $2,400.

Cash ($0.60 × 4,000)		2,400	
Dividend Revenue			2,400

Notice that the Drop Corp. Investment (available-for-sale) recorded the dividends received as *Dividend Revenue,* while the value of the Lake Corp. Investment was decreased.

c. Any adjustment for net income earned by the investment

Lake Corp.

When Lake Corp. earns net income, its retained earnings increases. This means that under the equity method, the value of Unity's investment in Lake Corp. *also* increases.

Equity Method Investment—Lake Corp. is increased (a debit) by Unity's share of Lake's net income:

$$40\% \times \$120,000 = \$48,000$$

Unity's share of Lake's net income also impacts Unity's net income. The $48,000 is also recorded as Equity Method Investment Revenue (a credit) on Unity's income statement.

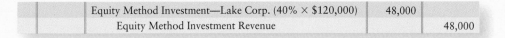

	Equity Method Investment—Lake Corp. (40% × $120,000)	48,000	
	Equity Method Investment Revenue		48,000

Lake Corp. Investment

Jan. 1	60,000		
	48,000 net income	14,000 dividends received	
Bal.	94,000		

Drop Corp.

Available-for-sale investments do *not* adjust for net income. *Instead,* they adjust for year-end market price (see transaction **d**). There is no entry for Drop Corp.

d. Any adjustment for the investment's year-end market price

Lake Corp.

Equity method investments do *not* adjust for year-end market price. *Instead,* they adjust for net income (see transaction **c**). There is no entry for Lake Corp.

Drop Corp.

We are required to adjust the value of available-for-sale investments to market price at year-end (for presentation on the balance sheet).

This means that we must adjust the Drop Corp. Investment from its original balance of $10,000 to its new market value:

$$\$3 \text{ market price per share} \times 4,000 \text{ shares} = \$12,000$$

The Drop Corp. Investment has increased in value by:

$$\$12,000 - \$10,000 = \$2,000$$

However, instead of adjusting the Investment account directly, we adjust an *Allowance* account. In this way, we are able to keep a record of the original cost of the investment in the Drop Corp. Investment account, yet report the investment at market price on the balance sheet (by combining it with the Allowance account).

So the allowance to adjust investments to market is increased (a debit) by $2,000.

This increase is an *unrealized* gain (a credit) of $2,000. We know that the gain is unrealized because there is no cash involved in the transaction to ensure that the gain is "real." In the case of available-for-sale investments, we are uncertain because the stock was not actually sold. Market prices change constantly and today's gain could be tomorrow's loss. We emphasize this uncertainty on the income statement by highlighting this gain as an *unrealized* (paper) gain.

Allowance to Adjust Investment to Market	2,000	
Unrealized Gain [($3 × 4,000) − $10,000]		2,000

Part 1	Part 2	**Demo Doc Complete**

Demo Doc 2

Foreign Currency Transactions

Global Industries had the following transactions during 2008:

a. Performed services on account for a Jordanian company for 40,000 dinar. $1 U.S. = 2.00 dinar.

b. Purchased equipment from an Egyptian company on account for 300,000 Egyptian pounds. 1 pound = $0.17 U.S.

c. Adjusted for a change in the value of the dinar. $1 U.S. now = 1.60 dinar.

d. Paid for the equipment when 1 pound = $0.16 U.S.

e. Received cash from the Jordanian company when $1 U.S. = 2.50 dinar.

Requirements

1. Journalize these transactions for Global Industries.

2. Based on these 2008 transactions, identify whether the dinar, the pound, and the U.S. dollar are strong or weak.

Demo Doc 2 Solutions

Requirement 1

Journalize these transactions for Global Industries.

Part 1	Part 2	Demo Doc Complete

a. Performed services on account for a Jordanian company for 40,000 dinar. $1 U.S. = 2.00 dinar.

For this *initial* transaction (that is, *before* there has been any fluctuation in exchange rates), we can simply journalize the entry as usual with the calculated U.S. dollar amount.

$$\$1 \text{ U.S.} = 2.00 \text{ dinar}$$
$$\text{therefore 1 dinar} = \$1/2.00 = \$0.50 \text{ U.S.}$$

When Global performs services, they are earning service revenue. This increases (a credit) Service Revenue by:

$$40,000 \times \$0.50 = \$20,000$$

Accounts Receivable is also increased (a debit) by $20,000.

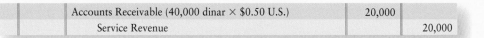

Accounts Receivable (40,000 dinar × $0.50 U.S.)	20,000	
Service Revenue		20,000

b. Purchased equipment from an Egyptian company on account for 300,000 Egyptian pounds. 1 pound = $0.17 U.S.

Again, with this *initial* transaction, we can analyze the entry as usual.
Equipment is increased (a debit) by:

$$300,000 \times \$0.17 = \$51,000$$

Accounts Payable is also increased (a credit) by $51,000.

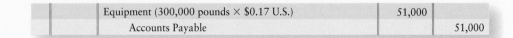

Equipment (300,000 pounds × $0.17 U.S.)	51,000	
Accounts Payable		51,000

c. Adjusted for a change in the value of the dinar. $1 US now = 1.60 dinar.

An adjustment will obviously change the value of the account receivable; however, it will *not* change the value of the service revenue. No new revenue has been earned (or unearned); instead, this adjustment is due to foreign currency fluctuations beyond Global's control. Therefore, the balance to the Accounts Receivable adjustment will be foreign currency gain or loss.

$$1 \text{ U.S. now} = 1.60 \text{ dinar}$$
$$\text{therefore } 1 \text{ dinar} = \$1/1.60 = \$0.625 \text{ U.S.}$$

The account receivable from the Jordanian company is now worth:

$$40,000 \times \$0.625 = \$25,000$$

Because the receivable is recorded at $20,000, we must increase Accounts Receivable (a debit) by:

$$\$25,000 - \$20,000 = \$5,000$$

The corresponding credit (a balancing amount) goes to Foreign-Currency Gain (gain because it is a *credit*).

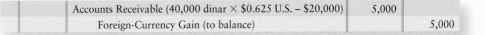

Accounts Receivable (40,000 dinar × $0.625 U.S. – $20,000)	5,000	
Foreign-Currency Gain (to balance)		5,000

d. Paid for the equipment when 1 pound = $0.16 U.S.

The equipment was sold for 300,000 pounds and they expect to receive 300,000 pounds.

If 1 pound now = $0.16 U.S. the account payable is now:

$$300,000 \times \$0.16 = \$48,000$$

Therefore, Cash is decreased (a credit) by $48,000.

The liability is completely satisfied, so Accounts Payable *must* be decreased (a debit) by the full $51,000 (because there is no longer any liability to pay).

The difference is a balancing amount to Foreign-Currency Gain of:

$$\$51,000 - \$48,000 = \$3,000$$

In this case, the balancing amount is a credit, which is a gain.

Accounts Payable	51,000	
Cash (300,000 pounds × $0.16 U.S.)		48,000
Foreign-Currency Gain (to balance)		3,000

Notice it is *not* that the contract has changed, it is the value of the *U.S. dollar* that has changed.

e. Received cash from the Jordanian company when $1 U.S. = 2.50 dinar.

$$\$1 \text{ U.S. now} = 2.50 \text{ dinar}$$
$$\text{therefore } 1 \text{ dinar} = \$1/2.50 = \$0.40 \text{ U.S.}$$

If 1 dinar now = $0.40 U.S., the account receivable is now:

$$40,000 \times \$0.40 = \$16,000$$

Therefore, Cash is increased (a debit) by $16,000.

The receivable is completely collected, so Accounts Receivable *must* be decreased (a credit) by the full $25,000 (because there is no longer any further amount to collect).

The difference is a balancing amount to Foreign-Currency Loss of:

$$\$16,000 - \$25,000 = -\$9,000$$

In this case, the balancing amount is a debit, which is a loss.

Cash (40,000 dinar × $0.40 U.S.)	16,000	
Foreign-Currency Loss (to balance)	9,000	
Accounts Receivable		25,000

Requirement 2

Based on these 2008 transactions, identify whether the dinar, the pound, and the U.S. dollar are strong or weak.

Part 1	Part 2	Demo Doc Complete

The dinar went from $0.50 U.S. to $0.625 U.S. to $0.40 U.S. This means that over time, the dinar became less valuable as compared to the U.S. dollar. Therefore, the dinar is **weakening** when compared to the U.S. dollar.

The pound went from $0.17 U.S. to $0.16 U.S. This means that over time, the pound became less valuable as compared to the U.S. dollar. Therefore, the pound is **weakening** when compared to the U.S. dollar.

The U.S. dollar became more valuable relative to the pound, and more valuable as compared to the dinar. So the U.S. dollar is strong.

Part 1	Part 2	Demo Doc Complete

Quick Practice Questions

True/False

_____ 1. If a trading investment has decreased in value, the year-end adjustment requires a debit to Loss on Trading Investment.

_____ 2. Available-for-sale investments may be classified as current assets or as long-term assets.

_____ 3. The Allowance to Adjust Investment to Market account is a companion account that is used with the Short-Term Investment account to bring the investment's carrying amount to current market value.

_____ 4. An investor with a stock holding between 20% and 50% of the investee's voting stock may significantly influence decisions on dividends, product lines, and other important matters.

_____ 5. Companies owning less than 50% of the outstanding stock in a subsidiary prepare consolidated financial statements.

_____ 6. Minority interest is that portion of a subsidiary's stock that is owned by stockholders other than the parent company.

_____ 7. Goodwill is the excess of the cost to acquire another company over the sum of the market value of its net assets.

_____ 8. Held-to-maturity investments are reported on the balance sheet at amortized cost.

_____ 9. A foreign-currency transaction gain or loss occurs when the exchange rate changes between the date an order is placed and the date the merchandise is received.

_____ 10. If the U.S. dollar value of a Russian ruble is $0.035 on January 1 and increases to $0.037 on February 1, the U.S. dollar has weakened.

Multiple Choice

1. **How are trading securities reported on the balance sheet?**
   a. At market value as either current assets or long-term investments on the balance sheet
   b. At market value as current assets on the balance sheet
   c. At cost as current assets on the balance sheet
   d. At lower of cost or market as current assets on the balance sheet

2. **Where would a loss on the sale of a trading investment appear on the financial statements?**
   a. On the income statement as part of other gains and losses
   b. On the balance sheet as a current liability
   c. On the income statement as an operating expense
   d. On the balance sheet as a contra equity account

3. The entry to record dividends received from a trading investment includes which of the following?
   a. A debit to Short-Term Investment
   b. A credit to Dividend Revenue
   c. A credit to Short-Term Investment
   d. A credit to Gain from Short-Term Investment

4. A short-term investment has been properly classified by the investor as a trading investment. If the stock was bought on June 17, 2007, for $10,000, and it is now worth $13,500 on December 31, 2007, which of the following will occur?
   a. A direct increase of $3,500 to Retained Earnings that is not reported on the income statement.
   b. Dividend Revenue of $3,500 is reported on the income statement.
   c. A $3,500 gain would appear on the income statement, even though the gain is unrealized.
   d. The short-term investment will appear on the balance sheet at $10,000 on December 31.

5. Which of the following accounting treatments for available-for-sale investments is in accordance with GAAP?
   a. Available-for-sale investments are reported on the balance sheet at historical cost.
   b. Available-for-sale investments are reported at historical cost and an Allowance to Adjust the Investment to Market account is established.
   c. Available-for-sale investments are reported on the balance sheet at market value.
   d. The Available-for-Sale Investment account should be adjusted to its market value on the balance sheet date and the unrealized gain or loss of adjusting from cost to market should be shown on the income statement.

6. McGovern Corp. owns 45% of the stock of Mather Corp. Mather Corp. declares and pays cash dividends of $45,000 to McGovern Corp. Which of the following will occur on the books of McGovern Corp.?
   a. The investment in Mather Corp. on the balance sheet will increase by $45,000.
   b. Dividend revenue of $45,000 will be reported on the income statement.
   c. The investment in Mather Corp. on the balance sheet will decrease by $45,000.
   d. A gain of $45,000 will be reported on the income statement.

7. Which of the following is true for available-for-sale investments?
   a. Available-for-sale investments include all stock investments other than trading securities.
   b. Available-for-sale investments are always classified as short-term.
   c. Available-for-sale investments are intended to be sold in the very near future.
   d. Available-for-sale investments include all bond investments other than trading securities.

8. On January 1, 2009, Investor Company acquires 25% of the 20,000 shares of common stock of Investee Company and has significant influence over the Investee Company. On December 31, 2009, Investee Company reports net income of $100,000. What account should Investor Company debit?
   a. Long-Term Equity-Method Investment for $25,000
   b. Cash for $25,000
   c. Long-Term Equity-Method Investment for $100,000
   d. Cash for $100,000

9. White Corp. purchased $20,000 of 8% bonds on March 1, 2008, for a purchase price of 90. White expects to hold the bonds until their maturity date, March 1, 2013. Interest on the bonds will be paid every March 1 and September 1 until maturity. Assuming the premium or discount is amortized every interest payment using straight-line amortization, how much interest revenue will be recorded by White on September 1, 2008?
   a. $1,200
   b. $1,000
   c. $800
   d. $600

10. A U.S. company sells merchandise to a British firm for 100,000 British pounds. Assume the exchange rates for the British pound were as follows:

   Date of sale: $1.54

   Date of collection: $1.53

   Date merchandise resold by British Firm: $1.52

   What is the foreign-currency gain or loss for the U.S. company on this transaction?
   a. $2,000 gain
   b. $1,000 loss
   c. $3,000 gain
   d. $3,000 loss

Quick Exercises

B-1.   In early 2008, Rocket Corporation invested some idle cash in the stock of another business. Journalize the following events that took place in 2008 and 2009:

2008:

Feb. 1   **Rocket Corporation purchased 1,500 shares of stock in Missile Company for $15.50 per share. This investment was classified as a trading investment.**

Nov. 15   **A dividend of $1.00 per share was received on the Missile Company stock.**

Dec. 31   **Rocket Corporation prepares financial statements for the year ended December 31, 2008. On this date, the Missile Company stock is worth $16.25 per share.**

2009:

Jan. 27   **Rocket Corporation sold 750 shares of Missile Company stock for $16.50 per share.**

General Journal				
Date	Accounts		Debit	Credit

General Journal				
Date	Accounts		Debit	Credit

General Journal				
Date	Accounts		Debit	Credit

General Journal				
Date	Accounts		Debit	Credit

B-2. Zipper Corporation engaged in the following transactions involving long-term available-for-sale investments in 2007:

June 14 Purchased 3,500 shares of Button Corporation common stock for $13 per share.

Sep. 15 Button Corporation pays a $0.65 per share dividend to all common stockholders.

Dec. 31 The market price of Button Corporation stock is $13.75 per share.

Journalize these transactions.

General Journal				
Date	Accounts		Debit	Credit

General Journal				
Date	Accounts		Debit	Credit

General Journal				
Date	Accounts		Debit	Credit

B-3. John Corporation purchased 250,000 shares of Deere Corporation common stock on January 2, 2008, for $550,000. Deere Corporation has 625,000 shares outstanding. Deere Corporation earned net income of $330,000 and paid dividends of $100,000 during 2008.

   a. What method should be used to account for the Deere Corporation investment?

   b. How much revenue will be recorded by John Corporation in 2008 from its investment in Deere Corporation?

   c. What is the balance in John Corporation's investment account at the end of 2008?

   d. Assume all of the above facts except that on January 2, 2008, John Corporation purchased 75,000 shares of Deere Corporation. How much revenue will be recorded by John Corporation in 2008 from its investment in Deere Corporation?

B-4. On October 1, 2007, Ace company paid $52,400 to purchase $50,000 of bonds that carry an 8% interest rate and will mature 5 years from the date of purchase. Interest on the bonds is paid September 30 and March 31 of each year. The company plans to hold the bonds until maturity and amortizes the premium or discount on bonds using the straight-line method each interest payment date. As of December 31, 2007, the bonds had a market value of $53,500.

Requirements

1. Prepare all necessary journal entries for 2007 dealing with the investment in bonds.

	General Journal			
Date	Accounts		Debit	Credit

	General Journal			
Date	Accounts		Debit	Credit

	General Journal			
Date	Accounts		Debit	Credit

2. Show how the bonds would be presented on the balance sheet at December 31, 2007.

B-5.   The Helms Company engaged in the following transactions during 2008:

Apr. 1 Purchased merchandise from a Mexican supplier at a cost of 100,000 pesos. The exchange rate on this date was $0.32 per peso.

May 5 Paid for the merchandise purchased on April 1. The exchange rate on this date was $0.31 per peso.

June 10 Sold goods to a Canadian buyer at a selling price of $83,000 Canadian dollars. The exchange rate on this date was $0.67 U.S. dollars for each Canadian dollar.

July 30 Received payment from the Canadian buyer for the goods sold on June 10. The exchange rate on this date was $0.65 U.S. dollars for each Canadian dollar.

Requirements

1. Prepare the journal entries necessary to record each of the above transactions.

General Journal				
Date	Accounts		Debit	Credit

General Journal				
Date	Accounts		Debit	Credit

General Journal				
Date	Accounts		Debit	Credit

General Journal				
Date	Accounts		Debit	Credit

2. During the periods of time covered by the transactions, was the U.S. dollar getting stronger or weaker relative to the Mexican peso and the Canadian dollar?

Do It Yourself! Question 1

Long-Term Investments

On January 1, 2008, Giant Co. purchased the following investments for cash:

10,000 shares Rock Co. stock	$ 15,000
40,000 shares Boulder Co. stock	$240,000

Both Rock and Boulder have 100,000 common shares outstanding.

During 2008, Rock and Boulder had the following information:

	Net Income	Cash Dividends per Share	Market Price per Share at 12/31/08
Rock Co.	$100,000	$0.20	$1.40
Boulder Co.	$350,000	$0.50	$6.50

Requirements

1. What kind of investments are these?

2. For *each* investment, journalize the following transactions for Giant Co.:

a. Purchase of investments on January 1, 2008

General Journal				
Date	Accounts		Debit	Credit

General Journal				
Date	Accounts		Debit	Credit

b. Dividends received from the investments during 2008

General Journal				
Date	Accounts		Debit	Credit

General Journal				
Date	Accounts		Debit	Credit

c. Any adjustment for net income earned by the investment

General Journal				
Date	Accounts		Debit	Credit

General Journal				
Date	Accounts		Debit	Credit

d. Any adjustment for the investment's year-end market price

General Journal				
Date	Accounts		Debit	Credit

General Journal				
Date	Accounts		Debit	Credit

Do It Yourself! Question 2

Foreign-Currency Transactions

Requirement

1. Journalize the following transactions for Omni Inc.:

a. Performed services on account for a French company for 2,000 euro. 1 euro = $1.11 U.S.

General Journal				
Date	Accounts		Debit	Credit

b. Purchased machinery from a Japanese company on account for 800,000 yen. 1 yen = $0.009 U.S.

General Journal				
Date	Accounts		Debit	Credit

c. Adjusted for a change in the value of the euro. 1 euro now = $1.18 U.S.

General Journal				
Date	Accounts		Debit	Credit

d. Paid for the machinery when 1 yen = $0.0089 U.S.

General Journal				
Date	Accounts		Debit	Credit

e. Received cash from the French company when 1 euro = $1.22 U.S.

General Journal				
Date	Accounts		Debit	Credit

Quick Practice Solutions

True/False

T 1. If a trading investment has decreased in value, the year-end adjustment requires a debit to Loss on Trading Investment. (p. 1311)

T 2. Available-for-sale investments may be classified as current assets or as long-term assets. (p. 1309)

F 3. The Allowance to Adjust Investment to Market account is a companion account that is used with the Short-Term Investment account to bring the investment's carrying amount to current market value.

False—The Allowance to Adjust Investment to Market account is a companion account that is used with the *Available-for-Sale account* to bring the investment's carrying amount to market value. (p. 1312)

T 4. An investor with a stock holding between 20% and 50% of the investee's voting stock may significantly influence decisions on dividends, product lines, and other important matters. (p. 1313)

F 5. Companies owning less than 50% of the outstanding stock in a subsidiary prepare consolidated financial statements.

False—Companies owning *more* than 50% of the outstanding stock in a subsidiary prepare consolidated financial statements. (p. 1316)

T 6. Minority interest is that portion of a subsidiary's stock that is owned by stockholders other than the parent company. (p. 1317)

T 7. Goodwill is the excess of the cost to acquire another company over the sum of the market value of its net assets. (p. 1316)

T 8. Held-to-maturity investments are reported on the balance sheet at amortized cost. (p. 1317)

F 9. A foreign-currency transaction gain or loss occurs when the exchange rate changes between the date an order is placed and the date the merchandise is received.

False—A foreign-currency transaction gain or loss occurs when the exchange rate changes between the date of purchase and date of *payment*. (p. 1323)

F 10. If the U.S. dollar value of a Russian ruble is $0.035 on January 1 and increases to $0.037 on February 1, the U.S. dollar has weakened.

False—If the U.S. dollar value of a Russian ruble is $0.035 on January 1 and increases to $0.037 on February 1, the U.S. dollar has *strengthened*. (p. 1323)

Multiple Choice

1. How are trading securities reported on the balance sheet? (p. 1311)
    a. At market value as either current assets or long-term investments on the balance sheet
    b. At market value as current assets on the balance sheet
    c. At cost as current assets on the balance sheet
    d. At lower of cost or market as current assets on the balance sheet

2. Where would a loss on the sale of a trading investment appear on the financial statements? (p. 1311)
    a. On the income statement as part of other gains and losses
    b. On the balance sheet as a current liability
    c. On the income statement as an operating expense
    d. On the balance sheet as a contra equity account

3. The entry to record dividends received from a trading investment includes which of the following? (p. 1312)
    a. A debit to Short-Term Investment
    b. A credit to Dividend Revenue
    c. A credit to Short-Term Investment
    d. A credit to Gain from Short-Term Investment

4. A short-term investment has been properly classified by the investor as a trading investment. If the stock was bought on June 17, 2007, for $10,000, and it is now worth $13,500 on December 31, 2007, which of the following will occur? (p. 1311)
    a. A direct increase of $3,500 to Retained Earnings that is not reported on the income statement.
    b. Dividend Revenue of $3,500 is reported on the income statement.
    c. A $3,500 gain would appear on the income statement, even though the gain is unrealized.
    d. The short-term investment will appear on the balance sheet at $10,000 on December 31.

5. Which of the following accounting treatments for available-for-sale investments is in accordance with GAAP? (p. 1312)
    a. Available-for-sale investments are reported on the balance sheet at historical cost.
    b. Available-for-sale investments are reported at historical cost and an Allowance to Adjust the Investment to Market account is established.
    c. Available-for-sale investments are reported on the balance sheet at market value.
    d. The Available-for-Sale Investment account should be adjusted to its market value on the balance sheet date and the unrealized gain or loss of adjusting from cost to market should be shown on the income statement.

6. McGovern Corp. owns 45% of the stock of Mather Corp. Mather Corp. declares and pays cash dividends of $45,000 to McGovern Corp. Which of the following will occur on the books of McGovern Corp.? (p. 1314)
    a. The investment in Mather Corp. on the balance sheet will increase by $45,000.
    b. Dividend revenue of $45,000 will be reported on the income statement.
    c. The investment in Mather Corp. on the balance sheet will decrease by $45,000.
    d. A gain of $45,000 will be reported on the income statement.

7. Which of the following is true for available-for-sale investments? (p. 1309)
   a. Available-for-sale investments include all stock investments other than trading securities.
   b. Available-for-sale investments are always classified as short-term.
   c. Available-for-sale investments are intended to be sold in the very near future.
   d. Available-for-sale investments include all bond investments other than trading securities.

8. On January 1, 2009, Investor Company acquires 25% of the 20,000 shares of common stock of Investee Company and has significant influence over the Investee Company. On December 31, 2009, Investee Company reports net income of $100,000. What account should Investor Company debit? (p. 1314)
   a. Long-Term Equity-Method Investment for $25,000
   b. Cash for $25,000
   c. Long-Term Equity-Method Investment for $100,000
   d. Cash for $100,000

9. White Corp. purchased $20,000 of 8% bonds on March 1, 2008, for a purchase price of 90. White expects to hold the bonds until their maturity date, March 1, 2013. Interest on the bonds will be paid every March 1 and September 1 until maturity. Assuming the premium or discount is amortized every interest payment using straight-line amortization, how much interest revenue will be recorded by White on September 1, 2008? (p. 1317)
   a. $1,200
   b. $1,000
   c. $800
   d. $600

10. A U.S. company sells merchandise to a British firm for 100,000 British pounds. Assume the exchange rates for the British pound were as follows:

   Date of sale: $1.54

   Date of collection: $1.53

   Date merchandise resold by British Firm: $1.52

   What is the foreign-currency gain or loss for the U.S. company on this transaction? (p. 1323)
   a. $2,000 gain
   b. $1,000 loss
   c. $3,000 gain
   d. $3,000 loss

Quick Exercises

B-1. In early 2008, Rocket Corporation invested some idle cash in the stock of another business. Journalize the following events that took place in 2008 and 2009: (p. 1310)

2008:

Feb. 1 Rocket Corporation purchased 1,500 shares of stock in Missile Company for $15.50 per share. This investment was classified as a trading investment.

Nov. 15 A dividend of $1.00 per share was received on the Missile Company stock.

Dec. 31 Rocket Corporation prepares financial statements for the year ended December 31, 2008. On this date the Missile Company stock is worth $16.25 per share.

2009:

Jan. 27 Rocket Corporation sold 750 shares of Missile Company stock for $16.50 per share.

General Journal			
Date	Accounts	Debit	Credit
Feb. 1	Short-Term Investment	23,250	
	Cash		23,250

General Journal			
Date	Accounts	Debit	Credit
Nov. 15	Cash	1,500	
	Dividend Revenue		1,500

General Journal			
Date	Accounts	Debit	Credit
Dec. 31	Short-Term Investment	1,125	
	Gain on Trading Investment		1,125

General Journal			
Date	Accounts	Debit	Credit
Jan. 27	Cash	12,375	
	Short-Term Investment		12,188
	Gain on Sale of Investment		187

B-2. Zipper Corporation engaged in the following transactions involving long-term available-for-sale investments in 2007: (p. 1312)

June 14 Purchased 3,500 shares of Button Corporation common stock for $13 per share.

Sept. 15 Button Corporation pays a $0.65 per share dividend to all common stockholders.

Dec. 31 The market price of Button Corporation stock is $13.75 per share.

Journalize these transactions.

General Journal			
Date	Accounts	Debit	Credit
June 14	Long-Term Available-for-Sale Investment	45,500	
	Cash		45,500

General Journal			
Date	Accounts	Debit	Credit
Sept. 15	Cash	2,275	
	Dividend Revenue		2,275

General Journal			
Date	Accounts	Debit	Credit
Dec. 31	Allowance to Adjust Investment to Market	2,625	
	Unrealized Gain on Available-for-Sale Investment		2,625

B-3.   John Corporation purchased 250,000 shares of Deere Corporation common stock on January 2, 2008, for $550,000. Deere Corporation has 625,000 shares outstanding. Deere Corporation earned net income of $330,000 and paid dividends of $100,000 during 2008. (pp. 1313–1315)

a.   What method should be used to account for the Deere Corporation investment?
Equity method

b.   How much revenue will be recorded by John Corporation in 2008 from its investment in Deere Corporation?
$330,000 × (250,000/625,000) = $132,000

c.   What is the balance in John Corporation's investment account at the end of 2008?
$550,000 + $132,000 − ($100,000 × 250,000/625,000) =
$682,000 − $40,000 = $642,000

d.   Assume all of the above facts except that on January 2, 2008, John Corporation purchased 75,000 shares of Deere Corporation. How much revenue will be recorded by John Corporation in 2008 from its investment in Deere Corporation?
$100,000 × (75,000/625,000) = $12,000

B-4.   On October 1, 2007, Ace company paid $52,400 to purchase $50,000 of bonds that carry an 8% interest rate and will mature 5 years from the date of purchase. Interest on the bonds is paid September 30 and March 31 of each year. The company plans to hold the bonds until maturity and amortizes the premium or discount on bonds using the straight-line method each interest payment date. As of December 31, 2007, the bonds had a market value of $53,500. (p. 1317)

Requirements

1. Prepare all necessary journal entries for 2007 dealing with the investment in bonds.

General Journal			
Date	**Accounts**	**Debit**	**Credit**
Oct. 1	Long-Term Investment in Bonds	52,400	
	Cash		52,400

General Journal			
Date	**Accounts**	**Debit**	**Credit**
Dec. 31	Interest Receivable	1,000	
	Interest Revenue ($50,000 \times .08 \times 3/12$)		1,000

General Journal			
Date	**Accounts**	**Debit**	**Credit**
Dec. 31	Interest Revenue	120	
	Long-Term Investment in Bonds ($2,400 \times 3/60$)		120

2. Show how the bonds would be presented on the balance sheet at December 31, 2007.

The investment in bonds would be classified as a long-term investment on the balance sheet.

Long-term investments:	
Long-term investment in bonds	$52,280

B-5.   The Helms Company engaged in the following transactions during 2008: (pp. 1323–1324)

Apr. 1   Purchased merchandise from a Mexican supplier at a cost of 100,000 pesos. The exchange rate on this date was $0.32 per peso.

May 5   Paid for the merchandise purchased on April 1. The exchange rate on this date was $0.31 per peso.

June 10   Sold goods to a Canadian buyer at a selling price of $83,000 Canadian dollars. The exchange rate on this date was $0.67 U.S. dollars for each Canadian dollar.

July 30   Received payment from the Canadian buyer for the goods sold on June 10. The exchange rate on this date was $0.65 U.S. dollars for each Canadian dollar.

Requirements

1. Prepare the journal entries necessary to record each of the above transactions.

General Journal

Date	Accounts	Debit	Credit
April 1	Inventory	32,000	
	Accounts Payable		32,000

General Journal

Date	Accounts	Debit	Credit
May 5	Accounts Payable	32,000	
	Foreign-Currency Gain		1,000
	Cash		31,000

General Journal

Date	Accounts	Debit	Credit
June 10	Accounts Receivable	55,610	
	Sales Revenue		55,610

General Journal

Date	Accounts	Debit	Credit
July 30	Cash	53,950	
	Foreign-Currency Loss	1,660	
	Accounts Receivable		55,610

2. During the periods of time covered by the transactions, was the U.S. dollar getting stronger or weaker relative to the Mexican peso and the Canadian dollar?

During the periods of time covered by the transactions, the U.S. dollar strengthened relative to the Mexican peso and the Canadian dollar.

Do It Yourself! Question 1 Solutions

Requirements

1. What kind of investments are these?

$$\text{\% Ownership of Rock Co.} = \frac{10{,}000 \text{ shares}}{100{,}0000 \text{ shares}}$$
$$= 10\%$$

The Rock Co. shares are an **available-for-sale investment.**

$$\text{\% Ownership of Boulder Co.} = \frac{40{,}000 \text{ shares}}{100{,}0000 \text{ shares}}$$
$$= 40\%$$

The Boulder Co. shares are an **equity method investment.**

2. For *each* investment, journalize the following transactions for Giant Co.:

a. Purchase of investments on January 1, 2008
Rock Co.

Long-Term Available-for-Sale Investment—Rock Co.	15,000	
Cash		15,000

Boulder Co.

Equity Method Investment—Boulder Co.	240,000	
Cash		240,000

b. Dividends received by the investments during 2008
Rock Co.

Cash ($0.20 × 10,000)	2,000	
Dividend Revenue		2,000

Boulder Co.

Cash ($0.50 × 40,000)	20,000	
Equity Method Investment—Boulder Co.		20,000

c. Any adjustment for net income earned by the investment
Rock Co.

No entry.

Boulder Co.

Equity Method Investment—Boulder Co. (40% × $350,000)	140,000	
Equity Method Investment Revenue		140,000

d. Any adjustment for the investment's year-end market price
Rock Co.

Unrealized Loss [$15,000 – ($1.40 × 10,000)]	1,000	
Allowance to Adjust Investment to Market		1,000

Boulder Co.

No entry.

Do It Yourself! Question 2 Solutions

Requirements

1. Journalize the following transactions for Omni Inc.:

a. Performed services on account for a French company for 2,000 euro. 1 euro = $1.11 U.S.

Accounts Receivable (2,000 euro × $1.11 U.S.)	2,220	
Service Revenue		2,220

b. Purchased machinery from a Japanese company on account for 800,000 yen. 1 yen = $0.009 U.S.

Machinery (800,000 yen × $0.009 U.S.)	7,200	
Accounts Payable		7,200

c. Adjusted for a change in the value of the euro. 1 euro now = $1.18 U.S.

Accounts Receivable (2,000 euro × $1.18 U.S. – $2,220)	140	
Foreign-Currency Gain (to balance)		140

d. Paid for the machinery when 1 yen = $0.0089 U.S.

If 1 yen now = $0.0089 U.S. the account payable:

$$= 800{,}000 \times \$0.0089 = \$7{,}120$$

Accounts Payable	7,200	
Cash (800,000 yen × $0.0089 U.S.)		7,120
Foreign-Currency Gain (to balance)		80

e. Received cash from the French company when 1 euro = $1.22 U.S. euro.

If 1 euro now = $1.22 U.S., the account receivable:

$$= 2{,}000 \times \$1.22 = \$2{,}440$$

Cash (2,000 euro × $1.22 U.S.)	2,440	
Foreign-Currency Gain (to balance)		80
Accounts Receivable (2,220 + 140)		2,360

The Power of Practice

For more practice using the skills learned in this chapter, visit MyAccountingLab. There you will find algorithmically generated questions that are based on these Demo Docs and your main textbook's Review and Assess Your Progress sections.

Go to MyAccountingLab and follow these steps:

1. Direct your URL to www.myaccountinglab.com.
2. Log in using your name and password.
3. Click the MyAccountingLab link.
4. Click Study Plan in the left navigation bar.
5. From the table of contents, select Appendix B, Investments and International Operations.
6. Click a link to work tutorial exercises.

Glindex   A Combined Glossary/Subject Index

Aging-of-accounts methods. *A way to esti-mate bad debts by analyzing individual accounts receivable according to the length of time they have been receivable from the customer. Also called the balance-sheet approach,* 253, 261

Allowance for Doubtful Accounts. *A contra account, related to accounts receivable, that holds the estimated amount of collec-tion losses. Also called Allowance for Uncollectible Accounts,* 254

Allowance method. *A method of recording collection losses on the basis of estimates instead of waiting to see which customers the company will not collect from,* 253

Amortization. *Systematic reduction of the asset's carrying value on the books. Expense that applies to intangibles in the same way depreciation applies to plant assets and depletion to natural resources,* 314
　discount (bonds), 476
　effective-interest method, 474–480, 488–489
　straight-line method, 467–478, 486–487
　see also Liabilities, long-term

Appraisal costs. *Costs incurred to detect poor-quality goods or services,* 776

Asset. *An economic resource that is expected to be of benefit in the future,* 4

Average-cost method. *Inventory costing method based on the average cost of inventory during the period. Average cost is determined by dividing the cost of goods available for sale by the number of units available,* 153, 154, 161–163

B

Balance sheet. *An entity's assets, liabilities, and owner's equity as of a specific date. Also called the statement of financial posi-tion,* 7
　see also Corporations paid in capital, and the balance sheet; Current liabili-ties and payroll; Receivables

Bank reconciliation. *Document explaining the reasons for the difference between a depositor's cash records and the deposi-tor's cash balance in its bank account,* 220, 222–226, 238–240

Batch processing. *Computerized accounting for similar transactions in a group or batch,* 187

Bond carrying value, 477

Bonds payable. *Groups of notes payable issued to multiple lenders called bond-holders,* 467
　carrying amount, 468
　see also Liabilities, long-term

Book value. *Amount of owners' equity on the company's books for each share of its stock,* 402

Breakeven point. *The sales level at which operating income is zero: Total revenues equal total expenses,* 668

　see also Cost-volume-profit (CVP) analysis
Business decisions, special. *See* Special business decisions and capital budgeting

C

Callable bonds. *Bonds that the issuer may call or pay off at a specified price when-ever the issuer wants,* 468

Capital budgeting. *See* Special business decisions and capital budgeting
Cash. *See* Internal control and cash
Cash-basis accounting. *Accounting that records transitions only when cash is re-ceived or paid,* 61, 71

Cash budget. *Details how the business expects to go from the beginning cash balance to the desired ending balance. Also called the state-ment of budgeted cash receipts and pay-ments,* 700

Cash flows. *See* Statement of cash flows
Cash payments journal. *Special journal used to record cash payments by check. Also called the check register or cash disburse-ments journal,* 188

Cash receipts journal. *Special journal used to record cash receipts,* 188

Chart of accounts. *A list of all of the busi-ness's account titles and account numbers assigned to those titles,* 30

Closing entries. *Entries that transfer the rev-enue, expense, and owner withdrawal bal-ances to the capital account*
　preparing, 101–105

Common-size analysis. *See* Vertical analysis
Common-size financial statement, 540, 545–547, 555

Common-size treatment. *A financial state-ment that reports only percentages (no dollar amounts),* 540

Common stock. *The class of stock that rep-resents the basic ownership of the corpora-tion,* 402, 403–407, 419

Confidentiality standard, 579

Constraint. *Restrict production or sale of a product vary from company to company,* 801–802

Continuing operations, 432, 441–445

Contra account. *An account that always has a companion account and whose normal balance is opposite that of the companion account,* 133

Contribution margin. *Sales revenue minus variable expenses,* 668, 670

Contribution margin ratio. *Ratio of contri-bution margin to sales revenue,* 668, 670–671

Control account. *An account whose balance equals the sum of the balances in a group of related accounts in a subsidiary ledger,* 192

Convertible bonds. *Bonds that may be con-verted into the common stock of the issuing company at the option of the investor,* 468

Corporate capital (or shareholder's equity), 404

Corporations, retained earnings and the income statement
　income statement presentation and earnings per share (demo doc), 441–445
　　corporate income statement, analyzing, 441–445
　learning objectives, 431–432
　　corporate income statement, analyzing, 432
　　distinguishing stock splits from stock dividends, 432
　　retained earnings, reporting restrictions on, 432
　　stock dividends, accounting for, 431–432
　　treasury stock, accounting for, 432
　practice questions, 446–465
　　income statement presentation and earnings per share, 454
　　solutions to, 455–465
　　stock splits and dividends, 452
　　treasury stock, 453
　stock splits and dividends (demo doc)
　　distinguishing stock splits from stock dividends, 434, 435–436
　　stock dividends, accounting for, 435, 436
　treasury stock (demo doc), 437–440
　　accounting for, 437–439
　　retained earnings, reporting restrictions on, 440

Corporations paid in capital and the bal-ance sheet
　common stock (demo doc), 403–407
　　characteristics of a corporation, identifying, 404
　　issuance of stock, recording, 405
　　return on assets and return on stock-holders' equity, evaluating, 407
　　stockholders' equity section of a corporation's balance sheet, preparing, 406
　　stock values in decision making, using different, 404–405
　demonstration document 3, 412–413
　　characteristics of a corporation, identifying, 413
　　income tax of a corporation, account-ing for, 413
　learning objectives, 401–402
　　cash dividends, accounting for, 402
　　characteristics of a corporation, identi-fying, 401
　　income tax for a corporation, account-ing for, 402
　　return on assets and return on stockholders' equity, evalu-ating, 402
　　stockholders' equity section of a corporation's balance sheet, preparing, 402
　　stock issuance, recording, 401–402
　　stock values in decision making, using different, 402

Internal failure costs. *Costs incurred when the company detects and corrects poor-quality goods or services before delivery to customers,* 776

Internal rate of return (IRR). *The rate of return (based on discounted cash flows) that a company can expect to earn by investing in the project. The discount rate that makes the net present value of the project's cash flows equal to zero,* 802, 812–813

International operations. *See* Investments and international operations

Inventoriable product costs. *All costs of a product that GAAP requires companies to treat as an asset for external financial reporting. These costs are not expensed until the product is sold,* 568

Inventory
  ending, estimating by gross profit method, 154
  errors, measuring effects of, 154
  in manufacturing company, stages and accounts for, 568

Inventory turnover. *Ratio of cost of goods sold to average inventory. Measures the number of times a company sells its average level of inventory during a year,* 126

Investing activities. *Activities that increase or decrease long-term assets; a section of the statement of cash flows,* 502

Investment center, 700

Investments and international operations
  foreign-currency transactions (demo doc), 843–846
    strengths and weaknesses in, identifying, 846
    transactions, journalizing, 844
  long-term investments (demo doc), 838–842
    investment type, deterring, 839
    transactions, journalizing, 839–840
  practice questions, 847–867
    foreign-currency transactions, 856–857
    long-term investments, 853–855
    solutions to, 858–867

J

Job cost record. *Document that accumulates the direct materials, direct labor, and manufacturing overhead costs assigned to each individual job,* 601

Job order costing. *A system that accumulates costs for each batch, or job. Law firms, music studios, healthcare providers, mail-order catalog companies, building contractors, and custom furniture manufacturers are examples of companies that use job order costing systems,* 601
  learning objectives, 601–602
    job order and job process costing, distinguishing between, 601
    manufacturer's job order costing system, recording manufacturing overhead transactions in, 602

  manufacturer's job order costing system, recording materials and labor transactions in, 601
  service companies, calculating unit costs for, 602
  under- or overallocated manufacturing overhead, recording transactions for completion and sales of finished goods and adjustments for, 602
  manufacturers, job order costing for (demo doc), 603–606
    job order and job process costing, distinguishing between, 604
    recording materials and labor transactions in, 604–606
  manufacturing overhead, allocating (demo doc), 607–610
    recording, in a job order costing system, 608–609
    under- or overallocated, recording transactions for completion and sales of finished goods and adjustments for, 609–610
  practice questions, 611–629
    solutions to, 620–629

Journal. *The chronological accounting record of an entity's transactions,* 31
  see also Transactions, recording

Just-in-time (JIT). *A system in which a company produces just in time to satisfy needs. Suppliers deliver materials just in time to begin production and finished units are completed just in time for delivery to customer,* 594, 776, 783

L

Labor time record. *Identifies the employee, the amount of time spent on a particular job, and the labor cost charged to the job; a record used to assign direct labor cost to specific jobs,* 606

Last-in, first-out (LIFO) inventory costing method. *Inventory costing method: The last costs into inventory are the first costs out to cost of goods sold. Leaves the oldest costs—those of beginning inventory and the earliest purchases of the period—in ending inventory,* 153, 154, 158–159, 164

Ledger. *The record holding all the accounts,* 34
  see also Transactions, recording

Leverage. *Earning more income on borrowed money than the related interest expense, thereby increasing the earnings for the owners of the business,* 468

Liabilities, long-term, 106
  bonds payable (effective-interest amortization) (demo doc), 474–480
    bonds payable, accounting for, 475, 478, 479, 480
    bonds payable, retirement and conversion of, accounting for, 479, 480
    borrowing, showing advantages and disadvantages of, 480
    interest expense, measuring by the straight-line amortization method, 475–477, 478

  bonds payable (straight-line amortization) (demo doc), 469–473
    bonds payable, accounting for, 469–472, 473
    bonds payable, retirement and conversion of, accounting for, 472, 473
  learning objectives, 467–468
    bonds payable, accounting for, 467
    bonds payable, retirement and conversion of, accounting for, 468
    borrowing, showing advantages and disadvantages of, 468
    interest expense, measuring by the straight-line amortization method, 467–468
    liabilities, reporting on balance sheet, 468
  practice questions, 481–499
    bonds payable (effective-interest amortization), 488–489
    bonds payable (straight-line amortization), 486–487
    solutions to, 490–499
  see also Current liabilities and payroll

Liability. *An economic obligation (a debt) payable to an individual or an organization outside the business,* 4

LIFO. *See* Last-in, first-out

Limited liability. *No personal obligation of a stockholder for corporation debts. A stockholder can lose no more on an investment in a corporation's stock than the cost of the investment,* 401

Long-term asset. *A liability other than a current liability,* 105–106

Long-term liabilities. *See* Liabilities, long-term

Lower-of-cost-or-market (LCM) Rule. *Rule that an asset should be reported in the financial statements at whichever is lower—its historical cost or its market value,* 154

Lump-sum purchase, 311

M

MACRS. *See* Modified accelerated cost recovery system

Management accounting. *The branch of accounting that focuses on information for internal decision makers of a business,* 567

Management accounting, introduction to
  demonstration document for, 569–574
    management and financial accounting, distinguishing between, 570
    merchandising company, classifying costs and preparing statements for, 572–574
    service company, classifying costs and preparing statements for, 571–572
    trends, identifying, 570
  learning objectives, 567–568
    ethical judgments, making, 568
    management and financial accounting, distinguishing between, 567
    manufacturing company, classifying costs and preparing statements for, 568

SINGLE PC LICENSE AGREEMENT AND LIMITED WARRANTY

READ THIS LICENSE CAREFULLY BEFORE OPENING THIS PACKAGE. BY OPENING THIS PACKAGE, YOU ARE AGREEING TO THE TERMS AND CONDITIONS OF THIS LICENSE. IF YOU DO NOT AGREE, DO NOT OPEN THE PACKAGE. PROMPTLY RETURN THE UNOPENED PACKAGE AND ALL ACCOMPANYING ITEMS TO THE PLACE YOU OBTAINED THEM FOR A FULL REFUND OF ANY SUMS YOU HAVE PAID FOR THE SOFTWARE. *THESE TERMS APPLY TO ALL LICENSED SOFTWARE ON THE DISK EXCEPT THAT THE TERMS FOR USE OF ANY SHAREWARE OR FREEWARE ON THE DISKETTES ARE AS SET FORTH IN THE ELECTRONIC LICENSE LOCATED ON THE DISK:*

1.   **GRANT OF LICENSE and OWNERSHIP:**   The enclosed computer programs and data ("Software") are licensed, not sold, to you by Pearson Education, Inc. publishing as Prentice Hall ("We" or the "Company") and in consideration of your payment of the license fee, which is part of the price you paid and your agreement to these terms. We reserve any rights not granted to you. You own only the disk(s) but we and/or our licensors own the Software itself.   This license allows you to use and display your copy of the Software on a single computer (i.e., with a single CPU) at a single location for <u>academic</u> use only, so long as you comply with the terms of this Agreement. You may make one copy for backup, or transfer your copy to another CPU, provided that the Software is usable on only one computer.

2.   **RESTRICTIONS:**   You may <u>not</u> transfer or distribute the Software or documentation to anyone else. Except for backup, you may <u>not</u> copy the documentation or the Software. You may <u>not</u> network the Software or otherwise use it on more than one computer or computer terminal at the same time. You may <u>not</u> reverse engineer, disassemble, decompile, modify, adapt, translate, or create derivative works based on the Software or the Documentation. You may be held legally responsible for any copying or copyright infringement that is caused by your failure to abide by the terms of these restrictions.

3.   **TERMINATION:**   This license is effective until terminated. This license will terminate automatically without notice from the Company if you fail to comply with any provisions or limitations of this license. Upon termination, you shall destroy the Documentation and all copies of the Software. All provisions of this Agreement as to limitation and disclaimer of warranties, limitation of liability, remedies or damages, and our ownership rights shall survive termination.

4.   **LIMITED WARRANTY AND DISCLAIMER OF WARRANTY:**   Company warrants that for a period of 60 days from the date you purchase this SOFTWARE (or purchase or adopt the accompanying textbook), the Software, when properly installed and used in accordance with the Documentation, will operate in substantial conformity with the description of the Software set forth in the Documentation, and that for a period of 30 days the disk(s) on which the Software is delivered shall be free from defects in materials and workmanship under normal use. The Company does <u>not</u> warrant that the Software will meet your requirements or that the operation of the Software will be uninterrupted or error-free. Your only remedy and the Company's only obligation under these limited warranties is, at the Company's option, return of the disk for a refund of any amounts paid for it by you or replacement of the disk. THIS LIMITED WARRANTY IS THE ONLY WARRANTY PROVIDED BY THE COMPANY AND ITS LICENSORS, AND THE COMPANY AND ITS LICENSORS DISCLAIM ALL OTHER WARRANTIES, EXPRESS OR IMPLIED, INCLUDING WITHOUT LIMITATION, THE IMPLIED WARRANTIES OF MERCHANTABILITY AND FITNESS FOR A PARTICULAR PURPOSE. THE COMPANY DOES NOT WARRANT, GUARANTEE OR MAKE ANY REPRESENTATION REGARDING THE ACCURACY, RELIABILITY, CURRENTNESS, USE, OR RESULTS OF USE, OF THE SOFTWARE.

5.   **LIMITATION OF REMEDIES AND DAMAGES:**   IN NO EVENT, SHALL THE COMPANY OR ITS EMPLOYEES, AGENTS, LICENSORS, OR CONTRACTORS BE LIABLE FOR ANY INCIDENTAL, INDIRECT, SPECIAL, OR CONSEQUENTIAL DAMAGES ARISING OUT OF OR IN CONNECTION WITH THIS LICENSE OR THE SOFTWARE, INCLUDING FOR LOSS OF USE, LOSS OF DATA, LOSS OF INCOME OR PROFIT, OR OTHER LOSSES, SUSTAINED AS A RESULT OF INJURY TO ANY PERSON, OR LOSS OF OR DAMAGE TO PROPERTY, OR CLAIMS OF THIRD PARTIES, EVEN IF THE COMPANY OR AN AUTHORIZED REPRESENTATIVE OF THE COMPANY HAS BEEN ADVISED OF THE POSSIBILITY OF SUCH DAMAGES. IN NO EVENT SHALL THE LIABILITY OF THE COMPANY FOR DAMAGES WITH RESPECT TO THE SOFTWARE EXCEED THE AMOUNTS ACTUALLY PAID BY YOU, IF ANY, FOR THE SOFTWARE OR THE ACCOMPANYING TEXTBOOK. BECAUSE SOME JURISDICTIONS DO NOT ALLOW THE LIMITATION OF LIABILITY IN CERTAIN CIRCUMSTANCES, THE ABOVE LIMITATIONS MAY NOT ALWAYS APPLY TO YOU.

6.   **GENERAL:**   THIS AGREEMENT SHALL BE CONSTRUED IN ACCORDANCE WITH THE LAWS OF THE UNITED STATES OF AMERICA AND THE STATE OF NEW YORK, APPLICABLE TO CONTRACTS MADE IN NEW YORK, AND SHALL BENEFIT THE COMPANY, ITS AFFILIATES AND ASSIGNEES. HIS AGREEMENT IS THE COMPLETE AND EXCLUSIVE STATEMENT OF THE AGREEMENT BETWEEN YOU AND THE COMPANY AND SUPERSEDES ALL PROPOSALS OR PRIOR AGREEMENTS, ORAL, OR WRITTEN, AND ANY OTHER COMMUNICATIONS BETWEEN YOU AND THE COMPANY OR ANY REPRESENTATIVE OF THE COMPANY RELATING TO THE SUBJECT MATTER OF THIS AGREEMENT. If you are a U.S. Government user, this Software is licensed with "restricted rights" as set forth in subparagraphs (a)-(d) of the Commercial Computer-Restricted Rights clause at FAR 52.227-19 or in subparagraphs (c)(1)(ii) of the Rights in Technical Data and Computer Software clause at DFARS 252.227-7013, and similar clauses, as applicable.

Should you have any questions concerning this agreement or if you wish to contact the Company for any reason, please contact in writing at the following address or online at http//247.prenhall.com:
Pearson Education
Director, Media Production
1 Lake Street
Upper Saddle River, New Jersey 07458